ETHICS AND LANGUAGE

Ethics and Language

BY

Charles L. Stevenson

New Haven and London: Yale University Press

Printed in the United States of America by
The Carl Purington Rollins Printing-Office of the
Yale University Press, New Haven, Connecticut.

Distributed in Great Britain, Europe, and Africa by
Yale University Press, Ltd., London; in Canada by
McGill-Queen's University Press, Montreal; in Latin
America by Kaiman & Polon, Inc., New York City; in India by
UBS Publishers' Distributors Pvt., Ltd., Delhi; in
Japan by John Weatherhill, Inc., Tokyo.

To

L. D. S.

"Good" is alleged to stand for a unique, unanalyzable concept . . . [which] is the subject matter of ethics. This peculiar ethical use of "good" is, we suggest, a purely emotive use. When so used the word stands for nothing whatever, and has no symbolic function. Thus, when we so use it in the sentence, "*This* is good," we merely refer to *this*, and the addition of "is good" makes no difference whatever to our reference. When on the other hand, we say "*This* is red," the addition of "is red" to "this" does symbolize an extension of our reference, namely, to some other red thing. But "is good" has no comparable *symbolic* function; it serves only as an emotive sign expressing our attitude to *this*, and perhaps evoking similar attitudes in other persons, or inciting them to actions of one kind or another . . . Of course, if we define "the good" as "that of which we approve of approving," or give any such definition when we say "This is good," we shall be making an assertion. It is only the indefinable "good" which we suggest to be a purely emotive sign. The "something more" or "something else" which, it is alleged, is not covered by any definition of "good" is the emotional aura of the word.

Ogden and Richards

It is not pretended that a moral theory based upon realities of human nature and a study of the specific connections of these realities with those of physical science would do away with moral struggle and defeat . . . [But it] would at least locate the points of effective endeavor and would focus available resources upon them. It would put an end to the impossible attempt to live in two unrelated worlds . . . It would find the nature and activities of one person coterminous with those of other human beings, and therefore link ethics with the study of history, sociology, law and economics . . . It would enable us to state problems in such forms that action could be courageously and intelligently directed to their solution. It would not assure us against failure, but it would render failure a source of instruction. It would not protect us against the future emergence of equally serious moral difficulties, but it would enable us to approach the always recurring troubles with a fund of growing knowledge . . . Until the integrity of morals with human nature and of both with the environment is recognized, we shall be deprived of the aid of past experience to cope with the most acute and deep problems of life.

John Dewey

Preface

THE problems of ethics are older than Socrates and the Sophists, and have persisted throughout all subsequent philosophy. If time has not left them wholly unchanged, that is because each generation has seen them in a fresh perspective. I have examined them anew, and in keeping with current trends of thought, have sought to gain a perspective from a study of language and meaning. But I have often taken language as a point of departure, extending my analysis in whatever direction it has led. In particular, I have given attention to the methods, both rational and nonrational, that are used in ethical discussions.

Apart from my emphasis on language, my approach is not dissimilar to that of Hume. We must "glean up our experiments in this science from a cautious observation of human life, and take them as they appear in the common course of the world, by men's behavior in company, in affairs, and in their pleasures." Perhaps this is not the only possible approach; but I hope I have been successful in showing that empiricism, so often criticized as distorting ethics, or discrediting it, can in fact give it a place whose importance is beyond question.

There is a marked distinction between the conclusions that are drawn *about* normative ethics and those that are drawn *within* it. In characterizing the latter my empiricism bears a qualification, but one which will establish it more firmly, I hope, by moderating its claims. I have sought to show, always in scientifically intelligible terms, that normative ethics is more than a science— that it encounters its own difficulties, and has its own characteristic functions. Such a view does not require a faith in some higher type of knowledge, beyond that to which the sciences can attain. It requires only the realization that ethical issues involve personal and social decisions about what is to be approved, and that these decisions, though they vitally depend upon knowledge, do not themselves constitute knowledge.

I wish to express grateful indebtedness to my colleagues—particularly to Professor C. W. Hendel and Professor F. S. C. Northrop, who have read the whole of my manuscript and offered many helpful suggestions. Professor Ernst Cassirer (now at Columbia) has helped me on several bibliographical points; and Professor F. B. Fitch and Professor M. C. Beardsley (now at Holyoke) have joined me in many profitable discussions. The Yale University Press has given me its constant assistance.

I have received helpful criticisms from the members of the Committee on Manuscripts, of the American Philosophical Association, and wish to thank them for their considerate attention.

The editor of *Mind* has generously permitted me to incorporate parts of my earlier articles on ethics, as indicated specifically in the text. The following publishers and editors have kindly allowed me to quote from the works mentioned: Harcourt, Brace and Co., *The Principles of Literary Criticism,* by I. A. Richards, *The Meaning of Meaning,* by C. K. Ogden and I. A. Richards, and *The Mind and Society,* by V. Pareto; Henry Holt and Co., *Human Nature and Conduct,* by John Dewey; The Macmillan Co., *Principles of Economics,* by F. W. Taussig, *The History of Economic Thought,* by L. H. Haney, and *Methods of Ethics,* by H. Sidgwick; Oxford University Press, *Religion and Science,* by Bertrand Russell; Putnam's Sons, *The Quest for Certainty,* by John Dewey; the editor of *The Philosophical Review,* "Knowledge as Aptness of the Body," by D. W. Prall; the editor of *Philosophy of Science,* "The Biological Basis for Ethics," by R. W. Gerard.

C. L. S.

Berkeley College, Yale University,
  September 20, 1944.

Contents

ETHICS AND LANGUAGE

I

Kinds of Agreement and Disagreement

1

THIS book deals not with the whole of ethics, but with a narrowly specialized part of it. Its first object is to clarify the meaning of the ethical terms—such terms as "good," "right," "just," "ought," and so on. Its second object is to characterize the general methods by which ethical judgments can be proved or supported.

Such a study is related to normative (or "evaluative") ethics in much the same way that conceptual analysis and scientific method are related to the sciences. One would not expect a book on scientific method to do the work of science itself; and one must not expect to find here any conclusions about what conduct is right or wrong. The purpose of an analytic or methodological study, whether of science or of ethics, is always indirect. It hopes to send others to their tasks with clearer heads and less wasteful habits of investigation. This necessitates a continual scrutiny of what these others are doing, or else analysis of meanings and methods will proceed in a vacuum; but it does not require the analyst, as such, to participate in the inquiry that he analyzes. In ethics any direct participation of this sort might have its dangers. It might deprive the analysis of its detachment and distort a relatively neutral study into a plea for some special code of morals. So although normative questions constitute by far the most important branch of ethics, pervading all of common-sense life, and occupying most of the professional attention of legislators, editorialists, didactic novelists, clergymen, and moral philosophers, these questions must here be left unanswered. The present volume has the limited task of sharpening the tools which others employ.

2

OUR first question, though seemingly peripheral, will prove to be of central importance:

What is the nature of ethical *agreement* and *disagreement?* Is it parallel to that found in the natural sciences, differing only with regard to the relevant subject matter; or is it of some broadly different sort?

If we can answer the question, we shall obtain a general understanding of what constitutes a normative *problem;* and our study of terms and methods, which must explain how this kind of problem becomes articulate and how it is open to argument or inquiry, will be properly oriented. There are certain normative problems, of course, to which the question is not directly relevant—those which arise in personal deliberation, rather than in interpersonal discourse, and which involve not disagreement or agreement but simply uncertainty or growing conviction. But we shall later find that the question is indirectly relevant even to them; and meanwhile there is a convenience in looking chiefly to the interpersonal problems, where the use of terms and methods is most clearly evidenced.

For simplicity let us limit our explicit attention to "disagreement," treating the positive term by implication. And let us begin by distinguishing two broad kinds of disagreement. We can do this in a wholly general way, temporarily suspending any decision about which kind is most typical of normative ethics, and drawing our examples from other fields.

The disagreements that occur in science, history, biography, and their counterparts in everyday life, will require only brief attention. Questions about the nature of light-transmission, the voyages of Leif Ericsson, and the date on which Jones was last in to tea, are all similar in that they may involve an opposition that is primarily of beliefs. (The term "beliefs" must not, at least for the moment, include reference to ethical convictions; for whether or not the latter are "beliefs" in the present sense is largely the point that is to be discussed.) In such cases one man believes that p is the answer, and another that not-p, or some proposition incompatible with p, is the answer; and in the course of discussion each tries to give some manner of proof for his view, or revise it in the light of further information. Let us call this "disagreement in belief."

There are other cases, differing sharply from these, which may yet be called "disagreements" with equal propriety. They involve an opposition, sometimes tentative and gentle, sometimes strong, which is not of beliefs, but rather of attitudes—that is to say, an opposition of purposes, aspirations, wants, preferences, desires, and so on.[1] Since it is tempting to overintellectualize these situations, giving too much attention to beliefs, it will be helpful to examine them with care.

Suppose that two people have decided to dine together. One suggests a restaurant where there is music; another expresses his disinclination to hear music, and suggests some other restaurant. It may then happen, as we commonly put it, that they "cannot easily agree on which restaurant to choose." The disagreement springs more from divergent preferences than from divergent beliefs, and will end when they both *wish* to go to the same place. It will be a mild, temporary disagreement for this simple case—a disagreement in miniature; yet it will be a "disagreement" in a wholly familiar sense.

Further examples are easily found. Mrs. A has social aspirations, and wants to move with the elite. Mr. A is easy-going, and loyal to his old friends. They accordingly disagree about what guests they will invite to their party. The curator of the museum wants to buy pictures by contemporary artists; some of his advisers prefer the purchase of old masters. They disagree. John's mother is concerned about the dangers of playing football, and doesn't want him to play. John, even though he agrees (in belief) about the dangers, wants to play anyhow. Again, they disagree. These examples, like the previous one, involve an opposition of attitudes, and differ only in that the attitudes in question are a little stronger, and are likely to be defended more seriously. Let us refer to disagreement of this sort as "disagreement in attitude." [2] Two men will be said to disagree in attitude when they have opposed attitudes to the same object—one approving of it, for instance, and the other disapproving of it—and when at least one of them has a motive for altering or calling into question the attitude of the other. Let us be careful to observe, however, that

1. The term "attitude" is here used in much the same broad sense that R. B. Perry gives to "interest." See his *General Theory of Value* (Longmans, Green, 1926), particularly p. 115.
2. In all of the examples given there may be a *latent* disagreement in belief, in addition to the disagreement in attitude. This is likely to be true of any example that is not painfully artificial; but the present examples are serviceable enough for their introductory purpose.

when one man is seeking to alter another's attitudes, he may at the same time be preparing to alter his own attitudes in the light of what the other may say. Disagreement in attitude, like disagreement in belief, need not be an occasion for forensic rivalry; it may be an occasion for an interchange of aims, with a reciprocal influence that both parties find to be beneficial.

The two kinds of disagreement differ mainly in this respect: the former is concerned with how matters are truthfully to be described and explained; the latter is concerned with how they are to be favored or disfavored, and hence with how they are to be shaped by human efforts.

Let us apply the distinction to a case that will sharpen it. Suppose Mr. Nearthewind maintains that most voters favor a certain bill, and Mr. Closerstill maintains that most of them are against it. It is clear that the two men disagree, and that their disagreement concerns *attitudes*—namely, the attitudes they believe the voters to have. But are Nearthewind and Closerstill disagreeing in attitude? Clearly not. So far as their above contentions show, they are disagreeing in *belief about* attitudes, and need not be disagreeing *in* attitude at all. Disagreement in belief about attitudes is simply a special sort of disagreement in belief, differing from disagreement in belief about head colds only with regard to subject matter. It implies not an opposition of the attitudes of the speakers, but only an opposition of certain of their beliefs that refer to attitudes. Disagreement *in* attitude, however, implies an opposition of the very attitudes of the speakers. Nearthewind and Closerstill may have opposing beliefs about attitudes without having opposing attitudes, just as they may have opposing beliefs about head colds without having opposing head colds. In so far as they are seeking detached descriptions of the state of human attitudes, they are disagreeing in belief; for attitudes enter only as a topic for cognitive study.

A parallel distinction holds for the positive term, "agreement," which may designate either convergent beliefs or convergent attitudes. And agreement in belief must still be distinguished from agreement in attitude, even when the beliefs are about attitudes. It will be convenient to use "agreement," whether in belief or in attitude, as the logical contrary of "disagreement," rather than as its full contradictory. People may neither agree nor disagree—as will happen when they are in a state of mutual indecision or irresolution, or when they simply "differ," having divergent beliefs or attitudes without a sufficient motive for making them alike.

Let us continue to preserve expository economy by giving explicit attention to "disagreement," treating "agreement" mainly by implication. The opposite procedure, which perhaps would seem more natural, has not been adopted for this simple reason: Our distinctions will subsequently be carried over to ethical *methodology*. For this special purpose disagreement requires closer scrutiny than agreement; for although the norms which are generally accepted, and embodied in the mores of any given society, are undoubtedly more numerous than the controversial ones, the latter present instances where methods of reasoning are more overtly employed, and more readily available for illustration and study.

We must now see how the two sorts of disagreement are related, still illustrating our conclusions by examples that are not (or at least not obviously) ethical.

It is by no means the case that every argument represents one sort of disagreement to the exclusion of the other. There is often disagreement of both sorts. This is to say little more than that our beliefs and attitudes must not be compartmentalized. Our attitudes, as many have pointed out, often affect our beliefs, not only by causing us to indulge in wishful thinking, but also by leading us to develop and check such beliefs as point out the means of getting what we want. And conversely, our beliefs often affect our attitudes; for we may alter our form of approval of something when we change our beliefs about its nature. The causal connection between beliefs and attitudes is usually not only intimate but reciprocal. To ask whether beliefs in general direct attitudes in general, or whether the causal connection goes rather in the opposite direction, is simply a misleading question. It is like asking, "Do popular writers influence public taste, or does public taste influence them?" Any implication that the alternatives are mutually exclusive can only be rejected. The influence goes both ways, although at times only one direction of influence may predominate.

There is accordingly a close relationship between the sorts of disagreement that have been distinguished. Indeed, in some cases the existence of one may wholly depend on the existence of the other. Suppose that A and B have convergent attitudes toward the *kind* of thing that X *actually* is, but indicate divergent attitudes to X itself simply because A has erroneous beliefs about it, whereas B has not. Discussion or inquiry, correcting A's errors, may resolve the disagreement in belief; and this in turn may be sufficient to resolve the disagreement in attitude. X was an occasion for the latter sort of disagreement *only* because it was an occasion for the former.

In cases of this sort one might be inclined to reject the expression, "Both kinds of disagreement were initially present, the one depending on the other," and say instead, "Only disagreement in belief was initially present, the disagreement in attitude with regard to X being simply apparent." If X was designated without ambiguity, however, so that the same X could be *recognized* by both parties regardless of their divergent beliefs about it, then the latter idiom would be seriously misleading. One man was definitely striving for X, and the other definitely striving to oppose it; and if this involved ignorance, where one of the men was acting to defeat his broader aims, it remains altogether appropriate to say that the initial divergence in attitude, so far as X was concerned, was genuine. It is convenient to restrict the term "apparent" disagreement to cases which involve ambiguity —to cases where the term that seems to designate X for both parties actually designates Y for one of them.

The relationship between the two sorts of disagreement, whenever it occurs, is always factual, never logical. So far as the logical possibilities are concerned, there may be disagreement in belief without disagreement in attitude; for even if an argument must always be motivated, and to that extent involve attitudes, it does not follow that the attitudes which attend opposed beliefs must themselves be opposed. People may share the ideals and aims which guide their scientific theorizing, for instance, and still reach divergent beliefs. Similarly, there may be disagreement in attitude without disagreement in belief. Perhaps every attitude must be accompanied by some belief about its object; but the beliefs which attend opposed attitudes need not be incompatible. A and B may both believe that X has Q, for instance, and have divergent attitudes to X *on that very account,* A approving of objects that have Q and B disapproving of them. Since it may also happen that both sorts of disagreement occur conjointly, or that neither should occur, the logical possibilities are all open. Hence one must appeal to experience to determine which of the possibilities, in any given case or class of cases, is in fact realized. But experience clearly shows, as we shall later see in detail, that the cases which involve *both* sorts of disagreement (or agreement) are extremely numerous.

We have now seen how the sorts of disagreement can be distinguished, and how (in a very broad way) they are related. There is only one further point, among these preliminary considerations, that deserves mention. Our distinction between the sorts of disagreement has presupposed a more general one—that between beliefs and attitudes. Like so many psychological distinctions, the latter is not easily made clear. Would further analysis serve to undermine it? Does any sharp separation reflect an antiquated school of thought, in which beliefs are so many mental photographs, the product of a special cognitive faculty, whereas attitudes stand apart as the drives or forces of a totally different faculty?

A moment's consideration will show that the distinction can be preserved in a much more legitimate manner. It is possible, for instance, to accept the pragmatic contention that beliefs and attitudes must both be analyzed, partly at least, with reference to dispositions to action. Such a view in no way suggests that beliefs and attitudes are "identical," so long as it is soberly understood. It shows that they are more alike than the older psychologists suspected, but it does not make them alike in every respect. The common genus does not obliterate all differentiae.

If it is difficult to specify just *how* beliefs and attitudes differ, it remains the case that for practical purposes we do and must make such a distinction every day. A chess expert, playing with a novice, uses an opening that appears very weak. An onlooker wonders, "Does he make the move because he *believes* that it is a strong one, or because, out of charity to his opponent, he doesn't *want* to make a strong one?" The distinction here between a belief and a want (attitude) is certainly beyond any practical objection. One can imagine the expert, with constant beliefs about the opening, using it or not in accordance with his changing desires to win; or one can imagine him, with constant desires to win, using it or not in accordance with his changing beliefs. If in imagining this independent variation of the "causal factors" involved one is tempted to hypostatize either "belief" or "attitude," the fault must be corrected not by dispensing with the terms in favor of purely *generic* talk about action, but rather by coming to understand the full complexity of reference that lies behind the convenient simplicity of language. To say that beliefs and attitudes are distinguishable factors, and that an action which they determine will vary with a variation in either one, is to use a familiar English idiom, which makes good sense so long as it is not pressed into some artificially simple mold. It is parallel to the statement that the selectivity and sensitivity of a radio are distinguishable factors, and that the quality of reception which they determine will vary with a variation in either one. Such a statement need not make "selectivity" and "sensitivity" designate hypostatic "parts" of the radio; nor does the parallel statement about beliefs and attitudes require a hypostatic psychology.

In the example of the chess player, it may be added, there is no lack of empirical criteria by which the onlooker may determine *which* attitudes and *which* beliefs determine the expert's play. No matter where the onlooker's inferences may lead him, he must *begin* by observing the expert's behavior, and can find there all the evidence that a practical decision requires. The behavior that enables him to decide this is endlessly more complicated than the simple move of the pawn.

3

WE may now return to our central question, and ask how people agree or disagree in cases that are typical of normative ethics.

If we seek help in answering the question by turning to the writings of others, we shall find the inquiry somewhat unrewarding. The question was never clearly asked. It would seem, however, that writers have tended implicitly to emphasize agreement and disagreement in belief, leaving agreement and disagreement in attitude unmentioned. This is obvious in the case of theories which permit ethics to have nothing to do with attitudes. It holds equally true, though this may not be so obvious, for many theories that have given attitudes a pre-eminent place. The latter point must receive special attention, since it throws into relief the conclusions that will later be presented here.

Let us consider the theory that has been defended by I. A. Richards.[8] Although Richards was primarily concerned with

3. *Principles of Literary Criticism* (Harcourt, Brace, 1924), chap. vii. See Chap. XII, Sec. 3 of the present volume for remarks on the somewhat similar theory advanced by R. B. Perry.

aesthetics, his theory of value is quite general, and relevant to evaluation in ethics. He writes: "We can now extend our definition. Anything is valuable which will satisfy an appetency [i.e., desire, which may be unconscious] without involving the frustration of some equal or more important appetency." And again, "The importance of an impulse [i.e., appetency or aversion] can be defined . . . as the extent of the disturbance of other impulses in the individual's activities which the thwarting of the impulse involves." [4] Roughly speaking, then, "X is valuable" is taken to have the same meaning as "X will satisfy more appetencies than it frustrates."

This definition, which is accompanied by remarks about the *psychological* nature of normative inquiry,[5] helps us to discern Richards' tacit conception of ethical disagreement. He takes it to be a kind of disagreement in *belief*. Arguments about the value of X are, by definition, arguments about whether X will satisfy more appetencies than it frustrates. Whether X will or will not do this is a matter of empirical fact, open to scientific inquiry. If disagreement in science, including psychology, is essentially in belief, disagreement about value must be of the same sort. When psychologists have conflicting theories about people's attitudes (or appetencies, for the latter are atomic attitudes, as it were), does this involve an opposition of the psychologists' attitudes or only of their beliefs? To say the former would be a pleasantly satirical exaggeration, but scarcely a literal truth.

4. Richards, *op. cit.*, pp. 48, 51. Italics have been omitted.
5. Richards' stress on psychology is evident from this quotation: "Critical remarks are about the values of experiences, and the reasons for regarding them as valuable, or not valuable. We shall endeavour in what follows to show that critical remarks are merely a branch of psychological remarks." *Idem*, p. 23. If he had made no comments of this sort, but had simply presented his definition of "valuable," there would be room for doubt about his conception of ethical agreement and disagreement; for as we shall see in Chapters IX and XII, particularly p. 268 ff., the definition may serve a more complicated purpose than its apparent one. But when such remarks accompany the definition, the interpretation that is to follow becomes justifiable. It should be noted, however, that there are divergent elements in Richards' theory of value, not always brought together in a consistent fashion. He writes, for instance: "Keats, by universal qualified opinion, is a more efficient poet than Wilcox, and that is the same thing as saying that his works are more valuable." *Idem*, p. 206. One is puzzled to know just how much importance to attach, here, to the terms "universal" and "qualified." And there is a passage from Richards' earlier work, *The Meaning of Meaning* (Harcourt, Brace, 1923, written in collaboration with C. K. Ogden), which suggests a quite different theory of value than that of *Principles of Literary Criticism*. This passage has been quoted at the beginning of the present volume.

In brief, Richards emphasizes disagreement in *belief about* attitudes, but not disagreement *in* attitude. Between these two, as we have previously seen,[6] there is a world of difference.

Let us illustrate the distinction in a way that shows its full bearing on the present case. Both A and B believe that X will satisfy more of *A's* appetencies than it frustrates, and both believe that it will *not* satisfy more of *B's* appetencies than it frustrates. To that extent they agree in belief about attitudes; but we clearly must not infer that they will agree *in* attitude. In much the same way, both may believe that X will satisfy more appetencies than it frustrates for both of them, taken together (A's preponderantly satisfied appetencies outnumbering B's preponderantly frustrated ones), or that it will do so for every member of some broad group of people (A being a member of this group, and B not), or that it will do so for the majority of all people (A being among the majority and B not), and so on. Here there will be agreement in belief about attitudes, in varying degrees of comprehensiveness; but again we cannot infer that A and B will agree *in* attitude. And suppose, even, that they both believe X will satisfy more appetencies than it frustrates, in the long run, for each and every individual, with no exceptions. Will their agreement in belief about attitudes on this point imply their agreement in attitude? There will be no strict implication. Although B believes that his attitudes, like those of all others, will eventually be satisfied by X, he may not subordinate his *immediate* attitudes to those which must be reckoned with in the long run; hence he will be opposed to X. And this may not be the case for A. One can have much agreement in belief about attitudes— all that Richards can hope for—and find, *conceivably* at least, that agreement in attitude is still to be obtained.

Richards' analysis is only one of many which, though emphasizing attitudes, virtually ignore agreement and disagreement in attitude. Emphasis on agreement and disagreement in belief is characteristic of any theory that makes normative ethics a branch of psychology. It is characteristic of any theory tha⁺ makes normative ethics exclusively a branch of *any* science, whether biology, sociology, or the others.[7] If agreement or disagreement on scientific issues is always in belief—and this has no exceptions[8] that need now concern us—and if ethics is a branch of science, then it must follow that agreement or disagreement in ethics is always in belief.

It must not be thought that *all* theorists have ignored disagreement in attitude. Richards has not done so uniformly.[9] Perhaps Hume half-utilized the conception,[10] perhaps Hobbes did so, and perhaps many many others have done so by implication. Yet even those who are closest to the conception do not write in a way that permits of a consistent interpretation. As their exposition proceeds, disagreement in attitude becomes confusedly identified with something else—and usually with disagreement in belief about attitudes.

4

THE present views can now be stated, though at first only in synoptic form.

When ethical issues become controversial, they involve disagreement that is of a *dual* nature. There is almost inevitably disagreement in belief, which requires detailed, sensitive attention; but there is also disagreement in attitude. An analysis which seeks a full picture of ethics, in touch with practice, must be careful to recognize both factors, neither emphasizing the former to the exclusion of the latter, nor the latter to the exclusion of the former. Only by this means can it reveal the varied functions of the ethical terms, and make clear how the methods of ethics compare with those of the natural sciences. Only by this means, indeed, can it envisage its proper task; for the central problem of ethical analysis—one might almost say "the" problem—is one of showing in detail how beliefs and attitudes are related.

If we examine the concrete ethical problems that arise in daily life, we shall easily see that they have much to do with beliefs.

quiry into whether X satisfies more appetencies than it frustrates must, inevitably, include an inquiry into the causal relations between X and Y, Z, W, etc., where the latter are objects of appetencies. This set of relations cannot be studied within psychology alone, but may involve problems of economics, sociology, geography, and so on. Psychology will simply be the most *conspicuous* of the sciences involved.

8. For a discussion of one of the exceptions, see Chap. XIII, Sec. 2.
9. Cf. the concluding sentences of p. 9, n. 5, in the present volume.
10. Hume and some others are discussed in Chap. XII.

Unless an object is to be evaluated in ignorance, it must be viewed in its living, factual context. Disagreement in belief about this context, which may in turn occasion divergent evaluations of the object, must accordingly be recognized as an important source of ethical controversy.

The beliefs that are relevant to determining the value of an object may be extremely complicated—no less so than the network of causes and effects in which the object lies. There can be no thought of marking off certain beliefs as ethically relevant, and certain others as ethically irrelevant. Potentially, *any* belief has a bearing on ethics. This is a point which many theorists have been careful to recognize; but they have too often recognized it only for certain aspects of ethics—and aspects which are commonly thought to be of little philosophical interest. When an issue is concerned with the value of something as a means to further ends, then (so the familiar contention runs) a great many beliefs, dealing with means-ends relationships, quite obviously become relevant. But when issues concern ultimate ends—and these issues are taken to be of central philosophical importance —then the relevant beliefs become much less diversified. The beliefs that are then involved are thought to be limited, perhaps, to special divisions of psychology or biology; or perhaps to some peculiarly ethical field that lies beyond the scope of scientific investigation. Such views are not the only ones that can be found in the philosophical tradition, but they are sufficiently prevalent to deserve attention.

Now the present work, diverging from these views, will endeavor to show that the full range of men's beliefs, in all their variety, are no less relevant in establishing ends than they are in establishing means. This conclusion will be based upon a logical and psychological analysis of how means and ends are related— an analysis that is not dissimilar, in its broad outlines, to that found in the ethical writings of John Dewey. The details of such an analysis become somewhat technical, and cannot profitably be developed at present, even in cursory form. They will be treated at length in Chapter VIII. But it has been necessary to anticipate their general purport, even at this early stage; for they will show that beliefs may be relevant throughout the whole structure of ethics, and that any effort to minimize their variety can only result in grievous oversimplifications.

Yet if the controversial aspects of ethics may involve disagreement in belief, and in ways that may become very complicated, it must not be thought that they involve this kind of disagreement exclusively. In normative ethics any description of what is the case is attended by considerations of what is to be felt and done about it; the beliefs that are in question are preparatory to guiding or redirecting attitudes. Moral judgments are concerned with *recommending* something for approval or disapproval; and this involves something more than a disinterested description, or a cold debate about whether it is already approved, or when it spontaneously will be. That a moralist is so often a reformer is scarcely an accident. His judgments plead and advise, and open the way to counteradvice. In this way moral judgments go beyond cognition, speaking to the conative-affective natures of men.

When moral judgments are mutually accepted, they testify to convergent forms of influence, which must be present in any society where there are established standards. But often the standards are still in a formative stage, or in a process of transition or readjustment. There is then a divergence of men's aims, some wanting to go in new ways and others to continue in the old ones. The issue that arises is marked by disagreement in attitude; and if this kind of disagreement is often directed, in its growth and resolution, by a great variety of beliefs, there yet remains every necessity of separating it off for special attention, and of examining the characteristic problems which it introduces.

It is disagreement in attitude, which imposes a characteristic type or organization on the beliefs that may serve indirectly to resolve it, that chiefly distinguishes ethical issues from those of pure science.

These conclusions are based upon observations of ethical discussions in daily life, and can be clarified and tested only by turning to that source:

The trustees for the estate of a philanthropist have been instructed to forward any charitable cause that seems to them worthy. One suggests that they provide hospital facilities for the poor, the other that they endow universities. They accordingly raise the ethical question as to which cause, under the existing circumstances, is the more worthy. In this case we may naturally assume that the men are unselfish and farsighted, having attitudes that are usually referred to, with praise, as "moral ideals" or "altruistic aims." And we may assume that each man respects the other's aims, being no less interested in reconsidering his own suggestion than in leading the other to accept it. There need be no hint of disputatiousness or acrimony; but obviously, there will be a tentative disagreement in attitude. Since the one man begins by favoring the hospitals, and the other the universities, their discussion must continue until one shares the initial attitude of the other, or until both come to favor some intermediate or alternative policy.

In addition to this disagreement in attitude, the discussion is almost certain to involve disagreement in belief. Perhaps the men will disagree (with partial uncertainty, no doubt, and a mutual effort to acquire further knowledge) about the present state of the poor, and the extent to which hospital facilities are already provided for them. Perhaps they will disagree about the financial state of the universities, or the effects of education on private and social life. Beliefs about these matters may be important in determining the direction of their attitudes. We have previously observed that beliefs and attitudes stand in close causal dependence, and here we have only another instance of this general truth.

If we examine the discussion further, we shall find that the discrepancies and uncertainties in belief may become very complicated, requiring elaborate inquiries for their resolution. Yet it manifestly will not do, on this account, to insist that attitudes are comparatively inessential. Disagreement in attitude is the factor which gives the argument its fundamental unity and motivation. In the first place, it determines what beliefs will relevantly be discussed or tested; for only those beliefs which are likely to have a bearing on either party's attitudes will be à propos. Any others, however interesting they may be in themselves, will be foreign to the ethical point in question. In the second place, it determines when the argument will terminate. If the men come to agree in belief about all the factual matters they have considered, and if they continue to have divergent aims in spite of this—one still favoring the hospitals and the other the universities—they will still have an ethical issue that is unresolved. But if they come to agree, for instance, in favoring the universities, they will have brought their ethical issue to an end; and this will be so even though various beliefs, such as those about certain social effects of education, still remain debatable. Both men may conclude that these remaining beliefs, no matter how they are later settled, will have no decisive effect on their attitudes. In these two respects, then, concerned with the scope of the argument and the conditions which terminate it, disagreement in attitude demands attention. Beliefs still retain their ethical significance, but attitudes must also be given their proper place.

A further example will show that *beliefs about* attitudes have no exceptional status in normative ethics, but take an equal place beside beliefs of other sorts. When a union leader and a representative of a company are disputing whether the employees ought, in justice, to have higher pay, they are certainly not bent on "comparing introspective notes" (as Frank Ramsey once put it[11]) about the state of their attitudes. It is not usual, in such cases, for either party to have any doubt about how the other feels. Nor are they primarily discussing what the general attitude of the public may be; for although that is a relevant point, the dispute may continue long after it has been established. Are they giving exclusive attention to whether a higher wage scale will satisfy more desires than it frustrates? We have implicitly seen, in connection with the views of I. A. Richards, that this consideration may not seem wholly final to those whose desires are in the minority. We shall see subsequently[12] that it presupposes from the start a modified democratic ideal which, however defensible it may be, must yet be defended, and which cannot be defended without opening anew the very same questions about ethical disagreement, and the manner of resolving it, that we have been analyzing.

Obviously, the argument has some additional motivating force than that of establishing agreement in *belief about* attitudes. It may partly be concerned with beliefs of this sort, beyond doubt, and partly with beliefs of other sorts, such as those about the company's financial state, the precedent that an increased wage scale would establish, the high cost of living, and so on; but these many beliefs are attended by another factor: The union's attitudes are marshaled in favor of higher wages; the company's attitudes are marshaled against them. The attitudes of both cannot be satisfied. Hence a disagreement in attitude pervades the whole argument; and the beliefs that enter, whether or not they are about attitudes, become relevant because they are likely to *alter* the attitudes of the parties who are arguing. If the union,

---

11. *Foundations of Mathematics* (Harcourt, Brace, 1931), p. 289.
12. See Chap. XII, Sec. 3.

for instance, has reason to believe that the weight of public sentiment is opposed to it, it may on that account moderate its claims about what the workers deserve; but such a belief is far from a final consideration; for the union may insist, alternatively, that it has been dealt with unjustly both by the company and by the public.

This example differs from the previous one in that the attitudes are likely to be more selfish; and perhaps on that account the opponents may argue forensically, each uncompromisingly bent on vanquishing his opponent, without any thought of subjecting his own aims to self-criticism. It may suggest ordinary bargaining and competition, rather than the more typically "moral" considerations of duty or guilt. Shall such an argument be said to fall within normative ethics? The answer will be negative if "ethics" is restricted to a narrow sense. But let us here use the term more broadly, letting it include all issues in which there is a serious questioning of aims or conduct. This broader sense is not unconventional, and will be convenient for marking off a field of study which, for the purposes of the present analysis, is homogeneous. We shall subsequently have to distinguish between the ethical issues that are "peculiarly moral" and those which are not; but for an inquiry into meanings and methods this distinction will prove to be of secondary importance.

Let us now consider some examples that will emphasize disagreement in attitude. Although this is only one of the factors that give rise to ethical controversy, it is the factor which has been most seriously neglected in ethical analysis; hence it must receive our attentive consideration, both here and throughout the volume.

Suppose that we are trying to convince a man that something he did was wrong. He replies: "I fully agree that it was, and for that very reason I am all the more in favor of doing it over again." Temporarily puzzled to understand him, we shall be likely to conclude, "This is his paradoxical way of abusing what he considers our outworn moral conventions. He means to say that it is really all right to do it, and that one ought to do it flagrantly in order to discredit the many people who *consider* it wrong." But whatever we may make of his meaning (and there are several other interpretations possible) we shall scarcely take seriously his protestations of agreement. Were we not trying all along to make him disapprove of his action? Would not his ethical agreement with us require that he share our disfavor —that he agree with us in *attitude?*

Agreement and disagreement in attitude are so characteristic of ethics that their presence is felt even when judgments are relatively isolated, and do not lead to any overt discussion. When a man dwells continually on his own merits, tells what a very good man he is, and insists that he always does his duty, we often suspect him of defending a secret feeling of inferiority. If he were sure of himself, we say to ourselves, he would not look for our approval with so much concern; he would not have to try, by his ethical judgments, to direct our approval in a way that strengthens his self-esteem. Note how quickly and naturally we assume, in this common-sense diagnosis, that his judgments are trying to cope with a suspected disagreement in attitude. He thinks that our attitudes may be psychologically incompatible with his own attitude of self-esteem, and he is lamely trying to *change* our attitudes to some more respectful form.

Or again, consider how frequently, in daily life, people direct their judgments to the several points of effective control. A teacher has urged a delinquent boy that he oughtn't to steal. Finding her efforts unavailing, she then sees the boy's parents, urging them that they ought to change their way of training him. What she wishes to do, obviously, is to make the boy so adverse to stealing that he will stop it. Her second judgment forwards this purpose by reinforcing the first; it supplements her direct influence upon the boy by an indirect one, mediated by a change in the attitudes of the parents. Does not this use of ethical judgments, consciously directed to the points of effective control, testify to a motive of altering rather than describing—to a motive of redirecting attitudes?

Consider, with the same point of emphasis, J. S. Mill's well-known pun on the word "desirable," in *Utilitarianism.*[13] He there treats the statement, "If something is desired it is desirable," as though it were axiomatic, the antecedent being the "sole evidence it is possible to produce" for the consequent. If "desirable" meant *capable of being desired*, the statement would indeed be innocent. But Mill intends the word to carry all the import of "good." Thus understood, the statement so far from being axiomatic becomes highly controversial. And it becomes so for a reason that is easily understood. "That which is desired is desirable" is a statement

13. Chap. iv, par. 3.

characteristic of the easy-going man who wishes to encourage people to leave their present desires unchanged; and conversely, the statement, "That which is desired is *not* desirable," is characteristic of the stern reformer, who seeks to alter or inhibit existing desires. Statements about what is desir*able*, unlike those about what is desir*ed*, serve not to describe attitudes, merely, but to intensify or alter them. The alleged axiom is controversial, then, because it leads to disagreement in attitude. Although it seems innocuous to those content with a ready *status quo*, it is intolerable to those who are striving to make fundamental changes in men's aims; and it is particularly insidious because its concealed pun makes it seem to give the former people alone an axiomatic support. In defense of Mill it must be mentioned that he was assuredly not seeking this effect; for the chapter referred to, with its well-known logical fallacies, shows every sign of having been written in a moment of confusion. But as an example of the hazards of neglecting disagreement in attitude, the confusion is illuminating.

The same point can be made in a more general way by a variant of the "relativity argument." People with different racial or temperamental characteristics, or from different generations, or from widely separated communities, are likely to disagree more sharply on ethical matters than on factual ones. This is easily accounted for if ethics involves disagreement in attitude; for different temperaments, social needs, and group pressures would more directly and urgently lead these people to have opposed attitudes than it would lead them to have opposed factual beliefs. The contention that ethics involves disagreement in attitude thereby gains in probability. It finds confirmation from what it explains, like any other hypothesis. Used alone, the relativity argument cannot pretend to be final; but used in conjunction with other observations, it has an important and legitimate place.

These illustrations could be continued at length; but for the moment only this need be added, to preserve proper emphasis. Although the controversial aspects of ethics spring from disagreement in attitude—a factor which, having been too little heeded in traditional theory, will here require constant attention—they rarely if ever spring from this kind of disagreement alone. Beliefs are the guides to attitudes; hence the issues that arise in establishing and testing them, or in giving them a practical organization, retain a vital place throughout all normative discourse. If we are to understand the basic nature of ethical problems, and thus to economize the energies that are directed to resolving them, we must ever be sensitive to the *dual* nature of ethical disagreement. Attitudes and beliefs both play their part, and must be studied in their intimate relationship.

II

Working Models

1

OUR conclusions about disagreement have prepared the way for a study of the ethical terms, and the characteristic features of ethical methodology. The present chapter will deal with both of these topics, but in a manner that is deliberately oversimplified. In place of a detailed analysis of ethical judgments, it will provide only "working models" for analysis—definitions which approximate to ethical meanings with sufficient accuracy to be of temporary help. Methods of proving or supporting ethical judgments will be considered only to the extent that the working models suggest them. This procedure will serve to introduce the essential features of our study, stress their interdependence, and indicate the points that will later require more careful development.

Let us begin with some remarks about meaning. This much will be directly evident from the preceding chapter: Any definition which seeks to identify the meaning of ethical terms with that of scientific ones, and which does so without further explanation or qualification, is extremely likely to be misleading. It will suggest that the questions of normative ethics, like those of science, give rise to an agreement or disagreement that is exclusively in *belief*. In this way, ignoring disagreement in attitude, it will lead to only a half-picture, at best, of the situations in which the ethical terms are actually used.

This conclusion must not be pressed insensitively, without regard to the ambiguities and flexibilities of language. It may well be that at *some* times *all* of the effective meaning of ethical terms is scientific, and that at *all* times *some* of it is; but there remain multitudes of familiar cases in which the ethical terms are used in a way that is *not exclusively* scientific, and we must recognize a meaning which suits them to their additional function.

What is the nature of this extrascientific meaning? Let us proceed by analogy, comparing ethical sentences with others that are less perplexing but have a similar use.

Interesting analogues can be found in ordinary imperatives. Is there not a ready passage from "You ought to defend your country" to "Defend your country"? Or more prosaically, is not the expression, "You oughtn't to cry," as said to children, roughly interchangeable with "Stop crying"? There are many differences, unquestionably; but there are likewise these similarities: Both imperative and ethical sentences are used more for encouraging, altering, or redirecting people's aims and conduct than for simply describing them. Both differ in this respect from the sentences of science. And in arguments that involve disagreement in attitude, it is obvious that imperatives, like ethical judgments, have an important place. The example about the restaurant, for instance, by which the conception of disagreement in attitude was first introduced,[1] might begin with the use of imperatives exclusively:

A: Meet me at the Glenwood for dinner at 7.00.
B: Don't let's go to a restaurant with music. Meet me at the Ambassador instead.
A: But do make it the Glenwood . . . etc.

So the argument might begin, disagreement in attitude being indicated either by the ordinary second person form of the imperative, or by the first person plural form that begins with "Let's."

On account of this similar function of imperative and ethical sentences, it will be useful to consider some definitions that *in part* identify them. These definitions will not be adequate to the subtleties of common usage; they will be markedly inaccurate. But they will preserve in rough form much that is essential to ethical analysis, and on that account will be instructive approximations. It is they which will constitute the "working models" that have previously been mentioned.

There are many ways in which working models can be devised, but those which follow are perhaps the most serviceable:

(1) "This is wrong" means *I disapprove of this; do so as well.*
(2) "He ought to do this" means *I disapprove of his leaving this undone; do so as well.*
(3) "This is good" means *I approve of this; do so as well.*

1. P. 3.

It will be noted that the definiens in each case has two parts: first a declarative statement, "I approve" or "I disapprove," which describes the attitudes of the speaker, and secondly an imperative statement, "do so as well," which is addressed to changing or intensifying the attitudes of the hearer. These components, acting together, readily provide for agreement or disagreement in attitude. The following examples will illustrate how this is so:

A: This is good.
B: I fully agree. It is indeed good.

Freely translated in accordance with model (3) above, this becomes,

A: I approve of this; do so as well.
B: I fully concur in approving of it; (continue to) do so as well.

Here the declarative parts of the remarks, testifying to convergent attitudes, are sufficient to imply the agreement. But if taken alone, they hint too much at a bare description of attitudes. They do not evidence the *contagion* of warmly expressed approval— the interaction of attitudes that makes each man's favorable evaluation strengthen and invigorate the other's. This latter effect is highly characteristic of an articulate ethical agreement; and the imperatives in our translated version of the example do something (though in a most imperfect way) to make it evident.

Let us consider an example of disagreement:

A: This is good.
B: No, it is bad.

Translated in accordance with the working models, this becomes,

A: I approve of this; do so as well.
B: No, I disapprove of it; do so as well.

The declarative parts of the remarks show that the men have opposed attitudes, one approving and the other disapproving. The imperative parts show that each man is suggesting that the other redirect his attitudes. Since "disagreement in attitude" has been defined with exclusive reference to an opposition of attitudes and efforts to redirect them or call them into question, it will be clear that a place for this sort of disagreement is retained (though again only in an imperfect way) by the working models that have been suggested.

But if the models are to help us more than they hinder us, they must be used with extreme caution. Although they give a needed emphasis to agreement and disagreement in attitude, they give no emphasis to agreement and disagreement in belief. Hence the *dual* source of ethical problems is not made evident. If traditional theory too often lost sight of attitudes in its concern with beliefs, we must not make the opposite error of losing sight of beliefs in our concern with attitudes. The latter error, which would give ethics the appearance of being cut off from reasoned argument and inquiry, would be even more serious than the former.

It is possible to avoid this error, however, and at the same time to retain the working models as rough approximations. Although it may at first seem that the full nature of ethical issues, and the relative importance of their component factors, should be made evident from the definitions of the ethical terms alone, this requirement is not an inviolable one. It may be dispensed with provided that the proper weight of emphasis is established elsewhere. The central requirement for a definition, then, is simply that it *prepare the way* for a complete account. Now if the models had accentuated beliefs at the expense of attitudes, the emphasis could not easily have been corrected by subsequent remarks; and for that reason it has been necessary to deviate from definitions of the traditional sort. But when the models accentuate attitudes at the expense of beliefs, the correct emphasis can easily be reëstablished. We shall later turn to a study of methodology, where in the nature of the case there must be close attention to the cognitive aspects of ethics. If we are careful, in that connection, to restore beliefs to their proper place, recognizing their great complexity and variety, we shall preserve a proper weighting of the factors involved.

Throughout the present chapter, accordingly, and in several of the chapters that follow, the analysis of meanings will emphasize agreement and disagreement in attitude, whereas the analysis of methods will emphasize agreement and disagreement in belief. The intimate relationship between the two factors will not be obscured by this procedure, but rather, as we shall see, will be made all the more evident. Yet it is important to realize that the procedure is somewhat arbitrary, and that an alternative to it will be needed to make our analysis complete. In the meanwhile, every care must be taken to prevent the discussion of meaning, whenever it proceeds in temporary isolation from the rest of analysis, from suggesting that beliefs have only an inconsequential, secondary role in ethics. Such a view is wholly foreign to the present work, and foreign to the most obvious facts of daily experience.

If we avoid this confusion, we shall find that the working models are often instructive. The imperative sentence, which is one of their constituents, has a function that is of no little interest. To understand this, let us compare (3), the working model for "good,"[2] with one that is closely parallel to it:

(4) "This is good" means *I approve of this and I want you to do so as well.*

This differs from (3) only in that the imperative sentence, "Do so as well," gives place to the declarative sentence, "I want you to do so as well." The change *seems* trivial, for it is often the case that "Do so and so," and "I want you to do so and so" have the same practical use. "I want you to open the window," for instance, has much the same imperative effect, usually, as "Open the window." The imperative function is not confined to the imperative mood. And *if* the declarative sentence which occurs in (4) is taken to have an imperative function, then to belabor the distinction between (3) and (4) is indeed trivial. It remains the case, however, that (4) is likely to be confusing. Although "I want you to do so as well" may be taken to have an imperative function, it also may not. It may be taken as a bare introspective report of the speaker's state of mind, used to describe his wants, to communicate beliefs about them for cognitive purposes, rather than to secure their satisfaction. (If such an interpretation is unlikely to occur in common life, it may easily occur amid the perplexing abstractions of philosophical theory.) In particular, (4) may suggest that "This is good" is used primarily, or even exclusively, to express *beliefs about* attitudes. It may accentuate agreement or disagreement in belief to the exclusion of agreement or disagreement in attitude. Definition (3) is preferable to (4) because it is not open to this misinterpretation. Its component imperative, being never used *merely* as an introspective report, renders unambiguously explicit the fact that "good" is used not

2. P. 21.

only in expressing beliefs about attitudes, but in strengthening, altering, and guiding the attitudes themselves.

The misleading character of definition (4) can be shown by a continuation of the second example on page 22. Translated after the manner of (4), rather than (3), this becomes:

A: I approve of this, and want you to do so as well.
B: No. I disapprove of this, and want you to do so as well.

Taken purely as introspective reports, these statements are logically compatible. Each man is describing his state of mind, and since their states of mind may be different, each may be correct. Now remembering that the statements purport to be translations, respectively, of "This is good" and "No, it is bad," one may be inclined to conclude: "Then according to definition (4) people don't really disagree about what is good or bad. They may think that they do, but only because of an elementary confusion in the use of pronouns." G. E. Moore has actually used this as a *reductio ad absurdam* of any definition which makes "good" refer wholly to the speaker's own attitudes;[3] and granted the tacit assumptions on which he works, his point is well taken. But if "I want you to do so as well" is interpreted as having an imperative function, supplementing its descriptive one—or better, if this declarative sentence is replaced by an imperative one, following definition (3)—and if ethical controversy is recognized to involve disagreement in attitude, then the preposterous consequence that "people don't really disagree in ethics" becomes a consequence, it is suggested, not of neglecting Moore's indefinable quality of goodness, but of insisting that ethical controversy centers *entirely* upon beliefs—and indeed, beliefs which are to be found by scrutinizing ethical sentences themselves, isolated from the many other sentences that form a part of their living context. It must be remarked, however, that this refusal to look beyond beliefs (which usually ends, paradoxically enough, by making too little of them rather than too much) is no more characteristic of Moore than of many of his "naturalistic" opponents, and that he is

3. *Ethics* (Henry Holt, 1911), pp. 100–102; and *Philosophical Studies* (Harcourt, Brace, 1922), p. 333. The present writer has made a detailed criticism of this argument, and some parallel ones, in "Some of Moore's Arguments against Ethical Naturalism," in *The Philosophy of G. E. Moore*, edited by P. A. Schilpp (Evanston and Chicago, Northwestern University, 1942).

usually more careful than they in pressing a mutual presupposition to its logical conclusions.

The nature of the working models has now been indicated. To the question, "What distinguishes ethical statements from scientific ones?" it has been answered: Ethical statements have a meaning that is approximately, and in part, imperative. This imperative meaning explains why ethical judgments are so intimately related to agreement and disagreement in attitude, and helps to indicate how normative ethics can be distinguished from psychology and the natural sciences.

2

WE must now turn to questions about method. When people argue about evaluative matters, by what sort of reasoning can they hope to reach agreement? The answer can as yet be presented only in a schematic form. It will presuppose that the working models can be accepted without further criticism; and since that is manifestly not the case, only rough approximations will be possible.

The model for "This is good" consists of the conjunction of (a) "I approve of this," and (b) "Do so as well." If a proof is possible for (a) and (b) taken separately, then and only then will it be possible for their conjunction. So let us see what can be done with the sentences separately.

Sentence (a) offers no trouble. It makes an assertion about the speaker's state of mind, and like any psychological statement, is open to empirical confirmation or disconfirmation, whether introspective or behavioristic.

Sentence (b), however, raises a question. Since it is an imperative, it is not open to proof at all. What is it like to prove a command? If we told a person to close the door, and received the reply, "Prove it!" should we not, to speak mildly, grow somewhat impatient?

Thus it would seem that ethical judgments are amenable only to a partial proof. So far as "This is good" includes the meaning of (a) a proof is possible, but so far as it includes the meaning of (b) the very request for a proof is nonsensical. We seem forced to a distressingly meager conclusion: If a man says "X is good," and if he can prove that he really approves of X, then he has all the proof that can be demanded of him.

So, indeed, it now *seems*. But it does so only because we have tacitly assumed that a proof in ethics must be exactly like a proof in science. The possibility that ethical judgments may have a *different sort* of proof has not been considered. Or rather, since "proof" may be a misleading term, let us put it this way: It has yet to be considered whether there is some "substitute for a proof" in ethics, some support or reasoned argument which, although different from a proof in science, will be equally serviceable in removing the hesitations that usually prompt people to ask for a proof.

If there is some such analogue to proof, it must unquestionably be considered in the present study of methodology. Otherwise the study will be open to a gross misunderstanding. It may lead people to suppose that the meagerness of proof *in the strict sense* deprives ethics of a "rational foundation" or "intersubjective validity" that is sorely needed; whereas all that is needed may in fact be provided for by the analogue mentioned.

To develop this point, let us return to imperatives, which have presented a methodological perplexity. Although imperatives cannot be "proved," are there not reasons or arguments which may at least "support" them?

The question is by no means difficult. An imperative may be met by the question "Why?" and this "Why?" asks for a *reason*. For instance: If told to close the door, one may ask "Why?" and receive some such reason as "It is too drafty," or "The noise is distracting." Or again, if a person is told to work harder, he may ask "Why?" and receive some such reply as "If you don't you will become an unhappy sort of dilettante." These reasons cannot be called "proofs" in any but a dangerously extended sense, nor are they demonstratively or inductively related to an imperative; but they manifestly do *support* an imperative. They "back it up," or "establish it," or "base it on concrete references to fact." And they are analogous to proofs in that they may remove the doubts or hesitations that prevent the imperative from being accepted.

The *way* in which the reasons support the imperative is simply this: The imperative is used to alter the hearer's attitudes or actions. In asking "Why?" the hearer indicates his hesitancy to comply. He will not do it "just because he is told to." The supporting reason then describes the situation which the imperative seeks to alter, or the new situation which the imperative seeks to bring about; and if these facts disclose that the new situation will satisfy a preponderance of the hearer's desires, he will hesitate to obey no longer. More generally, reasons support imperatives by altering such beliefs as may in turn alter an unwillingness to obey.

But do these remarks require elaboration? A moment's consideration will show that they do not; for they coincide with the remarks about agreement that have been made in Chapter I. We saw there that since attitudes tend to alter with altered beliefs, agreement in attitude may often be obtained by securing agreement in belief. Here we need only apply this general principle to a special type of case. The connection becomes apparent when the above paragraph is stated in different terminology:

An imperative is used to secure the satisfaction of the speaker's desire. The question "Why?" expressing the hearer's hesitation to comply, indicates an actual or incipient counterdesire. There is accordingly a disagreement in attitude. The reason, supporting the imperative, locates a possible source of disagreement in belief; and if the latter is settled, then, since beliefs and attitudes stand in intimate causal relationship, the disagreement in attitude may be caused to vanish in a way that makes the imperative willingly obeyed.

The "substitute proofs" or "supporting reasons" that we have been seeking can thus be recognized as familiar acquaintances under a new name: they are the expressions of belief that so often play an important, if indirect, role in situations that involve disagreement in attitude. Nor are these supporting reasons peculiar to imperatives. They may be used wherever disagreement in attitude occurs, whether it is indicated by laudatory or derogatory words, rhetorical questions, metaphors, animated inflections of voice, and so on.

With regard to the judgment that here particularly concerns us—"This is good" as schematically analyzed by definition (3), page 21—the relevance of the supporting reasons will be obvious. Although the imperative component of the definiens, "Approve as well," is inadequate to the subtleties of ethics, it is doubly marked for use in disagreement in attitude; the very fact that it is an imperative at all so marks it, and it is marked again by its direct mention of the hearer's approval. Since reasons may support any statement that leads to agreement or disagreement in attitude, they clearly may support this one.

Supporting reasons are particularly important in ethics—far more so than the narrow proof that was mentioned on page 26.

When a man says "X is good" he is seldom called upon to prove that he now approves of X. He is called upon, rather, to adduce considerations which will make his attitudes acceptable to his opponent, and to show that they are not directed to situations of whose nature he is ignorant. This more important procedure, typical of ethical issues, always requires supporting reasons. We shall find in Chapters IX and X, where the working models give place to a descriptively "richer" analysis, that these conclusions must be amended; but the essential features will remain.

The following example, with comments interspersed, will serve to show more concretely how supporting reasons may occur in an argument that is characteristically ethical:

A: *Jones is fundamentally a good man.*

This judgment (a) asserts that A approves of Jones, and (b) acts (quasi-) imperatively to make B, the hearer, have a similar attitude.

B: *Why do you say that?*

B indicates his hesitancy or unwillingness to concur in approving of Jones. Disagreement in attitude is thus apparent.

A: *His harsh manner is only a pose. Underneath, he has the kindest of hearts.*

A reason is now given, describing a characteristic of Jones that B may not know about, and which is likely to elicit B's favor.

B: *That would be interesting, if true. But does he ever express this kind heart of his in actions?*

The reason is acknowledged to be relevant, but its truth is questioned. Disagreement in belief now comes to play an important part in the argument. It is closely related to the disagreement in attitude previously noted; for if A and B can agree in belief about Jones' kindness, they are likely to agree on whether or not to approve of him.

A: *He does. His old servant told me that Jones never uttered an unkind word to her, and recently provided her with a luxurious pension. And there are many such instances. I was actually present when . . . etc.*

A here provides an empirical proof—not a direct proof of his initial judgment, but of the reason which supports it.

B: *Well, I confess I do not know him intimately. Perhaps he is a good man.*

B here complies with the (quasi-) imperative component of A's initial judgment, by indicating his approval. His reluctance has been altered by A's well-proved reason. Agreement in belief has brought about agreement in attitude.

This example shows in miniature how ethical judgments (the working models remaining essentially uncriticized) may be supported by reasons of an important kind, and just how the reasons become relevant. It shows as well how very naturally these reasons serve some of the purposes of a proof. They lead the hearer to accept the judgment willingly, without any feeling that it is "dogmatic" or "arbitrary" or "unfounded."

Before leaving this provisional, introductory account of methods, there is a further question which must receive attention. At the beginning of this section, it will be remembered, ethical proofs were found to be distressingly meager. To supplement them, "substitute proofs" were sought, which might serve the purposes of a proof, even though they were not exactly like scientific proofs. Such substitutes were readily found in the "supporting reasons" for the judgments—reasons which may bring about agreement in attitude by securing agreement in belief. But it has yet to be asked whether reasons of this sort are sufficient to provide ethics with an adequate "foundation." That is to say: Theories of ethics which stress attitudes have often been accused of "building morality on shifting sands," providing no check for the caprices and fads to which human attitudes are subject. Or they have been accused of sanctioning a vicious tolerance, tantamount to chaos, by implying that "Anything which a person feels to be good, *is* good, for him." Does the present account of methodology, once support by reasons is acknowledged, become free from such charges? Or is it rather the case that the present account is still too meager, and that some further method must be sought, even though it be sought blindly and despairingly, if ever moral codes are to have their needed authority?

The full answer cannot be developed now; but a provisional, dogmatic answer will helpfully anticipate subsequent chapters. Clearly, the present account of methodology will fail to content the great number of theorists who are embarked on "the quest for certainty." The supporting reasons here mentioned have no sort of *logical* compulsion. Persons who make opposed ethical judgments may (so far as theoretical possibility is concerned) continue to do so in the face of all manner of reasons that their argument includes, even though neither makes any logical or empirical error. Supporting reasons have only to do with beliefs; and in so far as they in turn are proved by demonstrative or empirical methods, only agreement in belief will, in the first instance, be secured. Ethical agreement, however, requires more than agreement in belief; it requires agreement in attitude. Accordingly, unless some further method can be found, a reasoned agreement in ethics is theoretically possible only to the extent that agreement in belief will cause people to agree in attitude.

How serious is this requirement? To what extent *will* agreement in belief cause people to agree in attitude? If the answer is to be grounded not on hopes but on facts, it must inescapably run thus: We usually *do not know*, before the outcome of any argument, whether the requirement holds true for it or not; and although it is often convenient to assume that it does, to prolong enlightening argument and delay purely hortatory efforts to secure ethical agreement, the assumption can be only heuristic, without a proper basis of confirmation. Those who seek an absolutely definitive method for normative ethics, and who want to rule out the possibility of rival moral codes, each equally well supported by reasons, will find that the present account gives them less than they want.

But the serious question concerns not what people now want; for in this connection people want, and have always wanted, what they cannot clearly articulate, and perhaps want an absurdity. The serious question concerns what people *would* want if they thought more clearly. If confusions about ethical methodology were swept away—confusions which are often more serious in ethical theory than in ethical practice—and if the psychological mechanisms which these confusions have fostered were accordingly readjusted, would people *then* feel that some more "objective" conception is required? To this question the present work will answer with a definite negative. But since methodological confusions are deeply rooted, and the psychological mechanisms which they have fostered are very stubborn, the reader must exercise patience in awaiting further explanation.

3

THE working models and the conceptions of method to which they have led are somewhat crude. Let us consider how they must subsequently be altered.

The first inadequacy of the models is simply this: The imperative component, included to preserve the hortatory aspects of ethical judgments, and stressed as useful in indicating agreement or disagreement in attitude, is really too blunt an instrument to perform its expected task. If a person is explicitly commanded to have a certain attitude, he becomes so self-conscious that he cannot obey. Command a man's approval and you will elicit only superficial symptoms of it. But the judgment, "This is good," has no trace of this stultifying effect; so the judgment's force in encouraging approval has been poorly approximated.

A further point, somewhat parallel to this, is more serious. Imperatives are often used to exert a unilateral influence. When a man gives direct orders, he may not take kindly to a dissenting reply. Although this is not the only way in which imperatives are used, it is a familiar one; and when imperatives enter bluntly into a context, as they do in the working models, only this usage may be brought to mind. So the models may give a distorted impression of the purposes for which moral influence is exerted. They may suggest that a moralist is obsessed by a desire to make others over into his own pattern—that he wishes only to propagate his preconceived aims, without reconsidering them.

Now if certain moralists have motives of this sort, there can be no doubt that others do not. One who exerts an influence need not thereby cut himself off from all counterinfluence; he may initiate a discussion in which the attitudes of all parties become progressively modified, and directed to objects whose nature is more fully understood. There are many men whose influence looks beyond their own immediate needs, and takes its welcome place in a coöperative moral enterprise. Proceeding with a desire to see all sides of a question, they have no desire for a debater's conquest, and are anxious to submit their moral judgments to the test of other points of view. Although moral judgments are not always advanced in this spirit, we must remember that there is manifestly such a possibility, which in many cases is actualized. There is no excuse for that hardheadedness which can see no more in human nature than the qualities which human nature is ashamed to recognize.

The working models, then, are likely to misrepresent both the manner in which moral influence is exerted and the motives which attend it. How may their inadequacies be avoided? The answer is suggested by current theories about language and meaning—

theories which promise to have marked repercussions on philosophy, and which have been emphasized by several contemporary writers on ethics.[4] The effect of ethical terms in directing attitudes, though not wholly dissimilar to that of imperatives, must be explained with reference to a characteristic and subtle kind of *emotive meaning*. The emotive meaning of a word is the power that the word acquires, on account of its history in emotional situations, to evoke or directly express attitudes, as distinct from describing or designating them. In simple forms it is typical of interjections; in more complicated forms it is a contributing factor to poetry; and it has familiar manifestations in the many terms of ordinary discourse that are laudatory or derogatory. In virtue of this kind of meaning, ethical judgments alter attitudes, not by an appeal to self-conscious efforts (as is the case with imperatives), but by the more flexible mechanism of *suggestion*. Emotive terms present the subject of which they are predicated in a bright or dim light, so to speak, and thereby *lead* people, rather than command them, to alter their attitudes. And they readily permit a mutual influence of this sort, as distinct from a unilateral one. The exact nature of emotive meaning, the way in which it functions, and the way in which it coöperates with beliefs, gestures, tones of voice, and so on, are somewhat involved considerations that must be left until later. It need only be remarked, for the present, that emotive meaning need not be taken as usurping the position that rightfully belongs to descriptive meaning. It has many legitimate functions, in ethics and elsewhere, and becomes objectionable only when it is abused.

It is not sufficient, however, to correct only the imperative component of the working models. A further inadequacy attends their declarative component, which for many contexts is much too simple. In order to accentuate agreement and disagreement in attitude, the models reduce descriptive meaning to a bare minimum, suggesting that ethical judgments express beliefs that are solely about the speaker's own attitudes. Now the most obvious objection to this procedure—that it neglects the many other beliefs that are relevant to ethics—is one which we have seen to have no foundation. If the beliefs are stressed, as in the preceding section, in connection with methodology—if they are made evident from the supporting reasons that attend ethical judgments, rather than from the meaning of the judgments them-

4. For references and further discussion, see pp. 265 ff.

selves—the full nature of ethical issues is properly recognized. But a more serious difficulty now arises, revealing an inadequacy of the models that is genuine and not easily surmounted. Ethical terms are noted for their ambiguity; yet of this ambiguity nothing has been said. So our procedure, though sensitive to the beliefs that enter into ethics, is by no means sufficiently sensitive to the various forms of language in which these beliefs are expressed. If we should suppose, as the working models may easily lead us to suppose, that important beliefs are *never* expressed by ethical judgments themselves—that they are *always* expressed by the sentences that present supporting reasons for the judgments—we should ignore the flexibility of common language, and hence obscure the very factor which, throughout the whole body of ethics, is most urgently in need of attention.

The object of the present study is not to devise, in arbitrary fashion, a sense for ethical terms that suits them to a limited, technical purpose; it is rather to free the language of everyday life from confusion. It is essential, for this purpose, to realize that everyday life presents us not with "a" usage of terms, but with many different usages. Nor is this a phenomenon which arises from trivial causes, which analysis can easily offset. Ambiguity will always persist in common discourse; hence the practical task lies not in seeking to eliminate it, but rather in seeking to make its presence evident, and by a careful study of its origins and functions, to render it no longer a source of error.[5]

The full complexity of the problem, however, has not as yet been envisaged. In mentioning the "ambiguity" of ethical terms, the above remarks may call to mind only clear-cut examples of it, like that of the term "grip," meaning now a grasp of the hand and now a small suitcase. It suggests that some definite number of senses for the ethical terms has been sharply if tacitly distinguished in ordinary usage, and that the separation of one from another requires only a conscious scrutiny of our established verbal habits. In point of fact this is far from the case. Ethical terms are more than ambiguous; they are *vague*. Although certain factors, at any one time, are definitely included among the designata of the terms, and certain others definitely excluded, there are

5. See the Bergen Lecture delivered by I. A. Richards at Yale, in 1940, and published in *Furioso* (summer issue, 1941). Richards argues, most plausibly, that we should "study . . . ambiguity, not to fear it but to welcome it as our best opportunity for growth in understanding."

many others which are neither included nor excluded. No decision
has been made about these, either by the speaker or by the dictionary. The limits of the undecided region are so subject to fluc-
tuation, with varying contexts and varying purposes, that it becomes arbitrary, so far as common usage is concerned, to specify
where one sense of the terms leaves off and another begins.

A simple example of vagueness can be found in the word "red."
There is a certain region on the spectrum to which this term definitely refers, and another broader one to which it definitely does
not refer; but between them there are near-orange hues which
(in ordinary usage, as distinct from some technical use in
science) people have neither decided to call "red" nor decided
to call "not red." We may, of course, draw an arbitrary line
through the undecided region, and say that *this* is where red
ends. But if we do so, there will always be many other places
where we might have drawn it with equal propriety. Or instead
of drawing one line we may draw many, seeking to make explicit
the broader and narrower senses of the term by letting each mark
represent the boundary of a different sense. But if we do this, the
number of lines that we draw, and the places where we draw
them, will be no less arbitrary than before. Over the undecided
region common usage permits us to do as we please.[6]

The vagueness of ethical terms is of the same sort, but extreme; the undecided referents are more numerous and diverse.
An ethical term may accordingly be adapted to a broad range of
uses, sometimes for purposes that will easily bear examination,
and sometimes not. We all know that a politician who promises
"justice" commits himself to very little, unless he defines the
term before the election. The term "good" is no less flexible. It
may be used to mean such qualities as reliable, charitable, honest, and so on, and may even have such a specific reference as that
to going faithfully to church on Sundays. These need not be
qualities that a speaker alleges to go along with goodness, con-
tingently, but can be qualities that he wishes to assign to the
logical connotation of "good." On the other hand, the term may
be denied all this variety of descriptive reference, and thinned
out to refer only to the attitudes of the speaker. We have always
a choice of making its descriptive meaning rich or poor. And it is

6. See Bertrand Russell, "Vagueness," *Australasian Journal of Psychology and Philosophy* (1923); and Max Black, "Vagueness," *Philosophy of
Science* (1937).

of great importance to realize that neither choice will violate the elastic requirement of "natural English usage."

If we now return to the working models, we shall readily see that their inadequacy, so far as descriptive meaning is concerned, is only partial. They provide a meaning which can be *assigned* to the ethical terms, and which is well suited to certain contexts. Yet if they are taken as typical of all contexts, and sufficient in themselves to clarify common usage, they will represent only another contribution to linguistic fiction. They must be supplemented, at least, by a number of alternative definitions. And ultimately, definitions of all sorts must not be conceived as exhausting the possibilities of ethical language, but only of revealing, by example, its enormous flexibility.

4

ALTHOUGH this chapter has provided only an outline of our study, barely mentioning certain topics, and developing others quite roughly, it has introduced several points that are of central importance. The ethical terms cannot be taken as fully comparable to scientific ones. They have a quasi-imperative function which, poorly preserved by the working models, must be explained with careful attention to emotive meaning; and they have a descriptive function which is attended by ambiguity and vagueness, requiring a particularly detailed study of linguistic flexibility. Both of these aspects of language are intimately related to ethical methodology; and although this relationship has as yet been studied only in a partial, imperfect way, enough has been said to suggest an interesting possibility: The reasons which are given for an ethical judgment, although open to the ordinary tests so far as their own truth or falsity is concerned, may give support *to the judgment* in a way that neither inductive nor deductive logic can exhaustively characterize, and which must therefore become the subject matter of a further type of inquiry.

III

Some Pragmatic Aspects of Meaning

1

IF we are to reach a more detailed understanding of ethics, guarding its issues from confusion, and opening them to economical types of inquiry, we must pay constant attention to ethical language, and the logical and psychological factors which permit it to have its characteristic functions. The need of this approach, and the central topics it introduces, will be evident from the preceding chapter.

Certain parts of the study could be developed immediately, with reference to ethical examples alone; but there are other parts of it which require more comprehensive treatment. A background must be sought in a general theory of signs, yielding conclusions that can subsequently be extended to the more specific problems that concern us. This is especially necessary in connection with the emotive uses of language, which in spite of many recent studies are still in need of careful examination. And care is needed, no less urgently, in showing how emotive and descriptive meanings are related, each modifying the other. These topics, lying somewhat beyond the narrower province of ethical analysis, will form the subject matter of the present chapter. There can be no hope or pretense, of course, of exhausting so large a subject, but perhaps enough can be said to serve present purposes.

2

THE emotive meaning of words can best be understood by comparing and contrasting it with the expressiveness of laughs, sighs, groans, and all similar manifestations of the emotions, whether by voice or gesture. It is obvious that these "natural" expressions are direct behavioristic symptoms of the emotions or feelings to which they testify. A laugh gives direct "vent" to the amusement which it accompanies, and does so in such an intimate, inevitable way that if the laugh is checked, some degree of amusement is likely to be checked as well. In much the same way a sigh gives immediate release to sorrow; and a shrug of the shoulders integrally expresses its nonchalant carelessness. One must not, merely on this account, insist that laughs, sighs, and so on, are literally a part of language, or that they have an emotive meaning; but there remains an important point of analogy: Interjections, which *are* a part of language, and which do have an emotive meaning, are *like* sighs, shrieks, groans, and the rest in that they can be used to "give vent" to the emotions or attitudes in much the same way. The word "hurrah," for instance, serves much the same purpose as any simple cry of enthusiasm, and releases the emotions with equal directness.

There is clearly a difference between interjections, which directly vent emotions, and words like "emotion" itself which *denote* them. The exact difference, with all its ramifications, will require patient analysis, but this much is obvious at the outset: words which denote emotions are usually poor vehicles for giving them active expression. One has only to pronounce "enthusiasm" like an interjection, trying to accompany it with the gestures and intonation characteristic of a shriek or of "hurrah," to see what a relatively impotent instrument it is for use in giving the emotions any direct outlet.

Emotive words, then, whatever else must be said of them, are suitable for "venting" the emotions, and to that extent are akin not to words which denote emotions, but rather to the laughs, groans, and sighs that "naturally" manifest them. But here the analogy ends. From the point of view of linguistic theory, interjections and "natural" manifestations of the emotions must be contrasted. The former make up a recognized grammatical part of speech, whereas the latter do not; the former are of interest to the etymologist and phonetician, whereas the latter are of scientific interest only to the psychologist or physiologist. And one speaks of the "meaning" of an interjection in a narrow sense, whereas one would hesitate to speak so narrowly of the "meaning" of a groan or laugh. There is a sense, to be sure, in which a groan "means" something, just as a reduced temperature may at times "mean" convalescence, or a tariff may "mean" restricted trade; but this sense of "meaning" is wider than any that are common in linguistic theory. Why is it that "natural" manifestations of emotions are ascribed meaning only in this broader sense, whereas interjections, so like them in function, may be ascribed meaning in a narrower sense?

An essential part of the answer is simply this: The expressiveness of interjections, unlike that of groans or laughs, depends on conventions that have grown up in the history of their usage. Had interjections been used in different living contexts, they would have been suited to the venting of somewhat different feelings. People groan in all languages, so to speak, but say "ouch" only in English. In learning French, one must learn to substitute "helas" for "alas," but one may sigh just as usual. Linguists are largely concerned with the study of verbal conventions; hence they are more interested in interjections than in expressions which are not conventionalized. And philosophers will do well to share this interest, though for a different reason. Conventionalized emotive meaning, far more than natural expressiveness, is likely to be confused with the descriptive aspects of language, and so fill the world with fictitious philosophical "entities."

In Edgar Rice Burroughs' extravaganzas, it is narrated that the Green Men of Mars always express their amusement (even a relaxed, kindly sort of amusement) by piercing shrieks, and express their anger by hearty laughter. Such practices, it is explained, are all accidental matters of convention, and seem surprising to us earth-dwellers only because we are not habituated to them. If this were so, if we laughed and groaned only because we happened to be trained to do so, rather than because of almost inevitable predispositions, then laughs and groans would be interesting subject matter for linguistic theory. They would, in all essentials, *be* interjections. But until Mr. Burroughs' psychology finds stronger confirmation, such sounds need give earthborn philologists and philosophers no concern.

To a certain extent some interjections retain, in addition to their conventionalized powers, a "phonetic suitability" that parallels the naturalness of laughs or sighs. The pure sound of a word may have a physiological fitness for venting certain emotions, which coöperates with the habits formed by past usage. (This is similar to onomatopoeia, but not wholly so. An onomatopoetic word mimics the sound of what it *designates;* hence its fitness for expressing feelings is secondary to its fitness for naming an object.) But on the whole, phonetic suitability is a minor factor. A man may learn to pronounce a foreign oath before he knows its use, and will not yet feel that it is an easy vehicle for expressing his temper. Even when he learns that it is an oath, he will find it less forceful than some corresponding word in his own language, which has behind it the accumulated energy of his linguistic habits.

Once a word has become ingrained into our habits of emotional expression, it retains its place with no little persistence. This is easily observed in daily life. In fact it is often discovered by children. When boys simulate a sweet, kindly tone of voice, and then proceed to swear at their dog—trying to see if the dog "really understands" their words—they find the experiment difficult. The habits that attend the abusive words are too strong, and stultify the agreeable intonation.

Emotive terms remain fully subject, of course, to the general forces of philological change. Slang words come and go; the profanities of yesterday may become the parlor terms of tomorrow.[1] And yet emotive change has sluggish rules of its own. One cannot easily introduce emotive terms by fiat, as one can introduce technical scientific terms. They must run their course, not easily interrupted, and some have an emotive life that outlasts their descriptive one.

So far we have seen only how emotive terms are dependent on the habits of the *speaker*. There is an equally important aspect of their use which concerns the habits of the *hearer*. This can most readily be seen where one interjection replaces another, all else remaining roughly the same. When an actress properly utters the word "alas" she heightens the sympathies of her audience. In good measure the audience is swayed by her gestures and intonation, and by the general situation presented in the play. But the audience's habitual reaction to "alas" must not be neglected. For suppose that the actress should train herself, with all the care that such a feat would require, to preserve the same tragic gestures and intonation, but to replace the word "alas" by the word "hurrah." The scene would then become crude burlesque, so forcibly and incongruously would the habitual responses to "hurrah" clash with the manner of its utterance. To evoke sympathy the actress must use a word-vehicle whose emotive meaning is appropriately ingrained into the hearers' habits, else her gestures and intonation will be unavailing.

1. See H. L. Mencken *The American Language* (Alfred A. Knopf, New York, 1919). In 4th ed. chap. vi, Secs. 5–8.

It is clear, then, so far as one may generalize from these extremely simple examples, that emotive words are fitted both to express the feelings of the speaker and to evoke the feelings of the hearer, and that they derive this fitness from the habits that have been formed throughout the course of their use in emotional situations.

A very close parallel to emotive meaning, in some ways more instructive than that of laughs and groans, can be found in the customs of etiquette. The parallel is so close that one might almost call etiquette a form of emotive sign language. There are certain aspects of "good manners," of course, which are aesthetic in nature, and others which are practical; but a great many others are conventions as arbitrary as linguistic ones, and as unintelligible to foreign eyes as words are to foreign ears. That a man should tip his hat, or walk on the curb side, that the hostess at dinner should be served first, that the fork should be conducted to the mouth with the right hand, and so on, are conventional "symbols" for expressing social deference, and some are parts of the American "dialect," unfamiliar in England. To trace the origin of these customs is to trace their "etymology," and leads one to similarly heterogeneous sources. Like interjections (and unlike laughs and sighs) good manners owe their expressiveness to force of habit, and with changing habits may become "archaic" or "obsolete." And just as interjections must be attended, to reach their full emotional effect, by a relevant situation and suitable intonation, so the conventional gestures of etiquette must be executed in their appropriate place and with suitable graciousness, if they are actually to manifest the deference which they, much more than less habitual gestures, are particularly suited to express.

3

THE above account has explained how certain emotive terms are put to use, but it has presented no clear *definition* of "emotive meaning." Although no rigorous definition of the term can here be attempted, let us work toward an approximate one, freely digressing to examine any points of interest that arise in the course of doing so.

It will be misleading to use the term at all unless "meaning" can be ascribed some conventional sense that marks off a genus, of which emotive meaning will be a species, and descriptive meaning another. Emotive meaning must be a kind of meaning, or else it had better be rebaptized. So our first task will be to single out the generic sense of "meaning" that is required.

There is one sense (among many others) which, though conventional enough, will be unsuitable for our purpose. In this sense the "meaning" of a sign is that *to which* people *refer* when they use the sign. (E.g.: "The meaning of 'cake' is edible"; "The meaning of 'hardness' is a characteristic of flint.") It will be convenient to replace "meaning," so used, by the term "referent," following Ogden and Richards.[2] The sense cannot be the generic one required, for we shall want to say that some words (such as "alas") have no referent, but do have a kind of meaning—namely, emotive meaning.

Another sense of "meaning" promises to be more serviceable. In this sense, the "meaning" of a sign must be defined in terms of the psychological reactions of those who use the sign. It may be called "meaning in the psychological sense," or in Morris'[3] terminology, "meaning in the pragmatic sense." (E.g.: "The meaning of 'cake' cannot conceivably be eaten, even though cake is edible." "The meaning of 'hardness' is not a characteristic of flint, even though hardness itself is.") If this sense of "meaning" were sufficiently clear, it could readily be taken as designating the required genus, of which emotive and descriptive meanings would be species; for the species could be distinguished by the kind of psychological processes that were involved.

But this generic, psychological sense of "meaning" is unfortunately not clear. Indeed, a proper definition of it has long been one of the most troublesome aspects of linguistic theory. The reason for this can readily be seen:

2. *Meaning of Meaning*, pp. 10 ff. Perhaps Ogden and Richards would prefer to recognize only *objects* as referents, and not *qualities* such as hardness. But note that if "hardness" is replaced in any sentence by "softness," empirical verification will be wholly changed. Hence "hardness" has an analogue of a naming function, and since this cannot be easily absorbed into the pure sign or the refer*ence* (concept), the other corners of the well-known meaning triangle, it is suggested that the term "referent" (or Morris' term, "designatum") be extended to include it. There is unquestionably something perplexing in the language that we use in talking about qualities—as any philosophical discussion of universals will testify—but until someone carefully untangles the perplexity, it will not do to dismiss qualities with a nonchalant nominalism or conceptualism. Such a procedure only goes on with the old controversies, adding nothing, and is equally non-commonsensical.

3. Charles W. Morris, "Foundations of the Theory of Signs," *International Encyclopedia of Unified Science*, Vol. I, No. 2 (University of Chicago Press, 1938).

One of the requirements for any definition of "meaning," so long as that term is to remain suitable for talking about language, is that meaning *must not vary* in a bewildering way. Some variation must of course be allowed, else we shall end with a fictitious entity, serene and thoroughly useless amid the complexities of actual practice; but "meaning" is a term wanted for marking off something relatively constant amid these complexities, not merely for paying them deference. A sense is needed where a sign may "mean" less than it "suggests"—a sense in which meanings are helpful to the understanding of *many* contexts, not some vagrant sense in which a word has a wholly different "meaning" every time it is used.

If the meaning of a sign must be relatively constant, how can "meaning" possibly be defined in terms of the psychological reactions that attend the sign? These reactions are by no means constant, but vary markedly from situation to situation. At a football game "hurrah" may express vigorous emotion, but elsewhere it may be attended by only the faintest echo of emotion. For one who assorts mail, "Connecticut" may cause only a toss of the hand, but for an old resident it may bring a train of reminiscences. How can a constant "meaning" be found amid this psychological flux?

As the latter example shows, the problem of defining a psychological sense of "meaning" is by no means confined to emotive situations; it is equally perplexing for situations which involve a referent. Between sign and referent (e.g., between the word "Connecticut" and the state of Connecticut) a rather constant relation must hold. This relation is preserved by *meaning* in the psychological sense in question; for if "Connecticut" is divorced from the psychological habits of those who use the word, it becomes devoid of any referent, no more interesting than any other complex noise. And yet the psychological responses that attend the word are observed to vary. How can a constant relation be maintained by such inconstant means? How is it possible (so one may confusedly picture the situation) to suspend a weight at a fixed distance from a frame, when the only string that can suspend it is continually varying in length?

Let us illustrate the perplexity a little further, still emphasizing the generic sense of "meaning," but taking examples from situations that we shall later want to designate more specifically as "emotive."

Just as one may not identify the meaning of "Connecticut"

with its immediate psychological repercussions, even for the psychological sense in question, so one may not identify the meaning of an interjection with the full-bodied emotion that at any time accompanies its use in a living context. The accompanying emotions vary with so many inconstant factors (such as voice, gesture, situation, mood, etc.) that the actual degree and kind of emotion which attend a word at one time are rarely the same as those which attend it at another. If we called each of these emotions a different "meaning," we should divert "meaning" to the vagrant sense that we have decided to avoid.

For the same reason we may not define the "meaning" of an interjection as the "emotional association" of a word, or as "the aura of feeling that hovers about a word." *Which* associations? *Which* aura? Do not these shadowy associations vary, just as the full-bodied emotions do? And if it is suggested that the associations must be those which accompany the word out of any living context (as when "alas" is pronounced experimentally in the comfort of one's study) then the way is opened to serious confusions: In the first place, since the immediate associations of a word out of its living context are very slight, one would naturally conclude that "emotive meaning," defined in terms of them, is very slight, and so think of it as having little importance. This would be unfortunate, for "emotive meaning" is often used, however vaguely and confusedly, in a sense that merits the attention it is beginning to receive. In the second place, the identification of emotive meaning with associations may foster a crude distortion of introspection. It may suggest that the associations continue to accompany the word in concrete, living situations, contributing to the general emotional tone of the situations in a purely additive way. As if the word "alas," in the above example of the actress, were suitable because it introduces its "associations" as "extra units" of emotion—units that are introspectively distinguishable, all at one glance, from those due to the general situation presented in the play. No one would believe this if he stopped to think about it; but misleading terminology has perpetuated fictions that are still more absurd, and it must not be allowed to confuse the present issue.

Emotive meaning, then, is not a full-bodied emotion, and not a shadowy association; nor is descriptive meaning an image or a toss of the hand. To say this is to rule out an inconvenient way of speaking, not to state a fact. We must, to reiterate, retain for the term "meaning" a sense which, although psychological, permits us to say that meaning is relatively unchanging. How shall such a sense be found?

The question is perplexing only when we look for the answer in a naïve way. It is as if we were trying to define the "purchasing power" of a dollar,[4] and, properly requiring that this be something relatively constant, were puzzled to find that dollars were always being used to buy different things. "Is the purchasing power the book I bought yesterday, or is it really the dinner I bought last night?" Or let us take a further example. Let us compare the meaning of a word with the stimulating power of coffee, and consider how we might proceed to define "stimulating power."

Is this power of the coffee simply the stimulated feeling that attends drinking it? This will clearly not do. The stimulating power must be relatively constant, varying only with different brands used, or with different ways of preparing it, and so on; but the feelings that attend drinking it are subject to a much greater variation. When a man is thoroughly exhausted, coffee may be insufficient to stimulate him at all; but when he is nervously wrought up, the same amount of coffee may stimulate him to the highest degree. How can the constant power to stimulate be identified with these inconstant states of mind?

Perhaps the stimulating power may be identified with the stimulation that coffee produces under some specified, artificially simple set of circumstances. But this too is inadvisable. It is not easy to specify simple circumstances under which the stimulation will be sufficiently constant. Even if this could be done, misconceptions might arise. In the first place, if the stimulation produced under these circumstances were unusually slight, one might think that the stimulating power of coffee was slight, and so negligible. In the second place, one might think that this same degree of stimulation attends coffee under all other circumstances, augmenting one's energy in a purely additive way . . .

And so on. It will now be clear how closely these suggestions parallel our repudiated definitions of "meaning," particularly in connection with the emotive situations. The attendant problem is precisely the same. We have a term—whether "meaning" or "stimulating power"—that must be defined with reference to

4. The example is borrowed from Max Black, who may, however, wish to reject much of the analysis of meaning that is to follow.

psychological reactions. These reactions fluctuate; but the term must designate something relatively stable. So an analysis of the one term is likely to throw light on the other.

A clue is readily given by the word "power." This term, so familiar in Locke, and a descendant of Aristotle's "potentiality," is in many cases very misleading, since it tempts one to hypostatization and anthropomorphism; but in several modern studies[5] the important aspects of its use have been subject to a very promising analysis. In these studies the term "power" usually gives place to the term "dispositional property," and from now on the latter term will be used here. Before employing the term for present purposes, however, let us become clearer about its usage. Space will permit only a cursory study, in which accuracy will often have to be sacrificed to simplicity; but such a treatment will even so be helpful. It will lead us to a better understanding of "meaning," and so in the direction of a definition of "emotive meaning."

4

THE word "disposition" (or "power," or "potentiality," or latent ability," or "causal characteristic," or "tendency," etc.) is useful in dealing with complicated *causal* situations, where some specified sort of event is a function of many variables. To illustrate, let us continue the above example. Although coffee often "causes" stimulation, it is never the *only* cause. The degree of stimulation will depend as well on many other factors—the initial state of a man's fatigue, the absorptive state of his stomach, the constitution of his nervous system, and so on. The situation may accordingly be schematized in this way:

$$\text{Variations in} \begin{cases} C \text{ (amount of} \\ \quad \text{coffee drunk)} \\ A \\ \\ B \end{cases} \begin{cases} \text{determine} \\ \text{variations} \\ \text{in} \end{cases} \Big\} \begin{cases} \text{(actual} \\ \text{stimulation).} \end{cases}$$

Here A stands for a *set* of conditions which are subject to change

5. C. D. Broad, *Mind and Its Place in Nature* (Harcourt, Brace, 1925), pp. 430–436; *Examination of McTaggart's Philosophy* (Cambridge, 1933), I, 266–272; *The Philosophy of Francis Bacon* (Cambridge, 1926), pp. 30–39. And Rudolph Carnap, "Testability and Meaning," *Philosophy of Science*, Vol. III, No. 4, and Vol. IV, No. 1.

The present account will be closer to Broad than to Carnap, since Broad's analysis lends itself more readily to a simplified presentation.

from time to time—the "attendant circumstances" under which the coffee is drunk. B stands for other conditions, less markedly subject to change, such as the chemical components of the coffee. The B factors have an important place in any discussion of dispositional properties; but for the next few pages let us be content to ignore them, to simplify exposition.

There will, of course, be no constant correlation between C and S taken alone; for the correlation will vary with variations in A. And yet the relation of C to S may be very important. With *each* constant condition of A, S may vary with C in *some* way; and with certain conditions of A, variations in C may cause S to vary greatly. To designate this relation, it is convenient to say that coffee (to which C makes conspicuous reference) has a "disposition" to produce S—which is of course only another way of saying that coffee "is a stimulant."

Let us take a further example. The "solubility" of sugar is its disposition to dissolve. And for this disposition, as for all others, we may distinguish factors corresponding to those above. Putting the sugar into water is a factor comparable to C; the temperature of the water and the degree to which it is stirred are factors comparable to A; the chemical composition of the sugar is comparable to B; and the actual dissolving of the sugar is comparable to S. The statement, "Sugar is soluble," refers to such a causal milieu, though it does not stipulate precisely what the A and B factors are.

These examples are by no means equivalent to a formal definition of "disposition," but they will permit us to proceed with freedom from the more serious confusions.

We must now consider in what sense an object may have an "unchanging" disposition to produce some effect, even though no fixed degree of that effect constantly attends it. This, of course, is simply our problem of explaining how the stimulating power of coffee may remain unchanged, even though the degree of stimulation that attends drinking it does not; and we shall soon see that much the same explanation must be given for *meaning*. With reference to the symbols previously used, the explanation is briefly this:

If for each constant state of A, there is some or another *fixed* way in which C is correlated with S, then the disposition of coffee to stimulate (and so, *mutatis mutandis,* for parallel examples) is said to remain unchanged.

More specifically: Let A retain some constant state, say A_1, and suppose that on each day of a given week it is found that the number of units of C is always double the number of units of S. Again, let A retain some other constant state, say A_2, and suppose that on each day of the same week it is found that the number of units of C is always triple the number of units of S. By a continuation of such experiments it would be possible to conclude, inductively, that for *each* constant condition of A, there is *some* correlation between C and S that remains fixed over the week; or in other words, that the disposition of coffee to stimulate has remained unchanged during that interval. (Note that this correlation need not be the same for all states of A; all that is required is that for each state of A there should be one or another fixed correlation.)

On the other hand, let A retain some constant state, say A_1; and suppose that on *one day* the number of units of C is double the number of units of S, but that on a *later day* it is triple. Here the correlation between C and S has not remained fixed, *even though A has*. The disposition of coffee to stimulate has *changed* during the interval.

Thus the disposition *need* not be said to change just because the effects do; though a change in the effects may *sometimes* indicate a change in the disposition. The unchanging disposition does not require an unchanging S, but rather a correlation between C and S that changes *only* if A changes.

It will be obvious that our imagined experimental tests have been artificially simple. The references to the "number of units" of stimulation, for instance, are more definite than practice may permit, and "more-or-less" comparisons must often take the place of numerical ones. Again, it may be practically impossible to hold the A factors constant; hence their variation must be "allowed for," or be made to cancel out, roughly, by statistical methods. But these and other points, however important they would be to a full study, are more detailed than our simplified treatment can include, and will be granted no further attention.

Let us now give somewhat closer attention to the several factors that any dispositional property involves, and provide a terminology for discussing them:

(a) There will be some relatively simple factor, like C above, which conspicuously affects the object that *has* the disposition. Let us call this a "stimulus." For dispositions assigned to living organisms, this term will have the sense that is current in psychology. For other dispositions it must be taken in an extended sense. Thus the stimulus for the disposition of water to freeze is a temperature of 32° F. or less.

In a similarly extended sense we may use "response" to designate whatever it is that an object has a disposition to do.

A disposition is said to exist at a given time even though the stimulus and response are not occurring at that time. And we may conveniently say, introducing an ambiguity that is too obvious to be misleading, that a disposition *has* a stimulus even when no concrete stimulus is occurring, and that it *has* a response even when no concrete response is occurring—meaning thereby that there is a *kind* of factor lawfully correlated with another, given the general situation, in stimulus-response fashion. A disposition will be "realized" whenever its response concretely occurs, along with a concrete stimulus, and "unrealized" when the response does not occur.

(b) There will be a more complicated set of factors, like A above, which are the "attendant circumstances" under which the disposition may be realized. A variation in these factors may alter the precise form that the response assumes, but as we have seen the disposition is not said to alter *merely* because these factors do. It is sometimes convenient to say that the disposition continues to exist when certain of these factors are totally absent, even though the response may then fail to occur with the stimulus; but unless they are usually present in some form, the disposition will be realized so infrequently that it probably will not be worth mentioning.

(c) There will be other factors, like B of page 47, that have hitherto been relatively neglected, and must now receive more attention. They are likely to be more permanent than the attendant circumstances, and differ conspicuously in that a variation in them *does* lead us to say that the disposition has varied. Whether or not a given factor is to be classified as belonging to this group, rather than to the attendant circumstances, will largely be determined by the usage of the specific names for dispositions, such as "solubility," "resiliency," "stimulating power," and so on. When a person decides that a variation in a certain factor is to be a criterion for saying that a dispositional property, so named, has itself varied (as distinct from saying that the manner of its realization has varied), he thereby decides that this factor is a B factor, relative to the specific name in question. (Many of the specific names for dispositions are vague, of course, permitting certain factors to be classified either as attendant circumstances or as B factors, at will; hence the criterion for change in a disposition is often rough.) Some of the B factors will be remote and others immediate. Thus in the example of the "stimulating powers" of coffee, a remote factor would be the way the coffee was grown, and an immediate one would be the amount of caffeine present. The most immediate set of factors, varying when and only when the disposition is said to vary, will be called the "basis" of the disposition.

The bases of a great many dispositions are unknown; and indeed, much of the usefulness of the term "disposition," and of the many common terms that designate specific dispositional properties, lies in permitting one to talk about correlations between stimulus and response, under attendant circumstances, before knowing what the basis of a disposition is. As Broad has remarked,[6] not a little was known about heat, taken as a disposition of certain objects to affect the human organism, long before the basis of the disposition was explained by the atomic theory. And there are many other dispositional properties—almost all of those mentioned in psychology, and a great many even in physics and chemistry—where the nature of the basis is still highly problematical. This is by no means a fatal difficulty; for some or another basis can often be inferred to be present, and can be presumed, even though little else is known about it, to retain rather permanently such qualities as it has. That is to say, realizing that the stimulus and attendant circumstances are not sufficient to produce the response, and finding that they in fact produce it, an experimenter can infer that some basis is present as an additional factor. And finding that the correlation between stimulus and response varies in a predictable manner with variations in the attendant circumstances, he can infer that the basis is not changing. To be sure, if he knows the precise basis, he will be in a more secure position, having richer inductive evidence from which to judge whether the correlations between stimulus and response will continue in the future; but his ignorance of the basis is simply a difficulty, not a fatal one. Nor is "basis" a name that *disguises* his ignorance; for the term marks off causal factors which he knows about indirectly, through their effect, and

6. *The Philosophy of Francis Bacon*, p. 32.

it may guide him progressively to a more adequate knowledge of them.

If the basis were always known, changes in it could be taken as definitive tests for changes in the disposition. But since it is usually unknown, there is a practical advantage in explaining changes in the disposition with reference to correlations between stimulus, response, and attendant circumstances, as was done in the preceding pages.[7]

It will be observed that neither the term "disposition" nor the terms designating the several factors in a dispositional property have been formally defined. For the most part they have been clarified by examples. Since the issue is highly controversial on points of detail, the writer will not presume to attempt any more rigorous analysis, hoping that a simplified approximation will not be without practical use.[8] There are, however, two sources of confusion that must receive passing attention:

It is tempting to hypostatize a disposition, taking it as a special "object" that exists over and above its more "tangible" components. In point of fact, one who gives the stimulus, response, attendant circumstances, and basis of a disposition, and who states in detail their correlation, has said all about the disposition that there is to say. The correlation between the several factors is of primary importance, but a correlation is not, to be sure, an extra object. In the same quest for "tangibility," it is tempting to identify a disposition with its basis; but this again will not do. One may know a great deal about certain factors that

7. There is a further reason for this procedure. It may be that certain fundamental dispositions have no basis, as Broad has in effect maintained in *Mind and Its Place in Nature*, pp. 435 f. This is a matter which the present account cannot take time to discuss, but it is well not to explain "change" in a disposition in a way that presupposes a contrary view.

8. A full analysis would introduce certain broader topics, such as (a) the meaning of "cause" and "law," and (b) the meaning of "perception" and "matter." As to (b), it will be noted that by Locke's views, the secondary qualities of an object, as predicates of that object, would be dispositional, whereas the primary ones would not. But by subsequent and more plausible theories, the primaries and secondaries are given much the same status. Are there *any* qualities of an object, then, which are *not* dispositional? If so, are they wholly unknowable qualities of a Kantian thing-in-itself? It is the writer's assumption that an adequate development of the problem would serve both to preserve certain properties of objects as nondispositional and also to avoid any wholly unknowable "substances"; but this cannot be developed here, and is mentioned only as an indication of the elementary level on which the present account is regrettably but inevitably compelled to proceed.

in fact constitute the basis of a disposition, but unless he knows how these factors are correlated with the stimulus, response, and attendant circumstances, he cannot be said to know a great deal about the disposition.[9]

A further source of confusion lies in a vacuous way of taking a disposition as the cause of its own response. Consider, for instance, the statement, "This ball bounces because it has a disposition to do so." This does not explain why the ball bounces; for although the term "disposition" implies that the response of bouncing comes with *some* stimulus, under *some* attendant circumstances, coöperating with *some* basis, its complete indeterminateness about what these factors are renders it trivial. The statement, "Man's rational faculty causes him to reason" is trivial in the same way.

It must not be thought, however, that all such idioms are equally open to criticism. The statement, "This ball bounced higher than that because of its greater resiliency" is by no means trivial, even though "resiliency" may partially be defined as a disposition to bounce. Here an empirical advance is indicated by the fact that certain other possible explanations are excluded: the ball might have bounced higher because it was dropped farther, or because it was dropped on a more resilient surface. Again, "Bees build hives because they have an instinct to do so" need not be trivial. An instinct, though a complicated disposition, is not *any* disposition, but one which, unlike a habit, is relatively free from changes with changing environments; and to know this about hive-building is not unimportant. (The "faculty psychology" was vacuous not because it used the dispositional terms, but because it misused them.) In general, any statement of the form "D caused R," where D is a disposition and R its response, will be of empirical interest to whatever extent it specifies definite tests for D that extend beyond the tests for R, and so relates R to a larger inductive setting. Our last cases, unlike the first ones, succeeded in meeting this requirement. The word "cause" may seem objectionable in such contexts, but common usage

9. If "disposition" were adequately defined, the definition would presumably have to be given "in use." Any terms so defined tempts one to hypostatize. For an account of "definitions in use" see A. N. Whitehead and Bertrand Russell, *Principia Mathematica*, Introduction to the 1st ed., chap. iii. A very lucid account is given by A. J. Ayer, in *Language, Truth and Logic* (Gollancz, 1936), chap. iii.

sanctions the idiom, and for many purposes it is quite useful, so long as the underlying considerations are understood.

When a disposition, D, is said to be the cause of E, and when E is *not* any part of the response of D, there is no special difficulty. If there is a lawful connection between the appearance of D and that of E, the connection may be called "causal" in a rough but familiar sense. Thus the *poisonous* nature of certain drugs may cause the government to restrict their sale. The causes *of* a disposition are usually the same as the *remote* B factors; and these too bring no difficulty so long as the disposition itself is not defined in terms of them. Thus the process of heating, hammering, and cooling steel in a certain way causes it to become more *elastic*. There is no objection, of course, to defining a specific name for a dispositional property with reference to some of its causes; but it must then be realized that any assertion which ascribes these causes to the disposition, so named, will not give additional information about it.

Broad has called attention to "orders" of dispositions,[10] in a way that is best clarified by example. If magnetism is taken as a disposition of the first order, then the disposition of a metal to *acquire* magnetism (which iron has, but copper has not) will be a disposition of the second order. In general, a first-order disposition may be the response of a second-order disposition, which may conceivably be the response, in turn, of a third-order one, and so on. Once we have seen, as above, that a *disposition* may be the *effect*, in an intelligible sense, of something else, we can readily see that it may itself be a response—i.e., that kind of effect whose causes are constituted by some stimulus, basis, and attendant circumstances. The possibility of orders of dispositions is thus manifest.

5

HAVING now explained (very roughly, but perhaps serviceably) the nature of dispositional properties, and the sense in which a disposition may be "unchanging," we may return to our problem about meaning. Let us at first consider meaning-situations entirely from the point of view of a hearer, neglecting any reader,

10. See his *Examination of McTaggart's Philosophy*, I, 48, where the distinction has an interesting application to the old controversies about "Innate Ideas."

speaker, or writer. So simplified, the view to be defended is essentially this:

The meaning of a sign, in the psychological sense required, is not some specific psychological process that attends the sign at any one time. It is rather a dispositional property of the sign, where the response, varying with varying attendant circumstances, consists of psychological processes in a hearer, and where the stimulus is his hearing the sign.

This implies that the relation between the hearing of a sign and the reaction to the sign is an elaborate causal one; for dispositional properties always involve a causal milieu. Although causal theories of meaning are often criticized, it is difficult to see how, for the sense of "meaning" in question, any other view can be plausible. The sign produces certain effects in the ear or eye, and in the nerves; and any further processes must be effects of a more remote sort.[11] Moreover, the hearing of the sign (stimulus) is not the only cause of the psychological processes that ensue (response); and for the remaining causal factors, it is possible to indicate attendant circumstances, and infer to the presence of a basis, in the way that any dispositional property requires.

Such a view all but eliminates the difficulty that was mentioned in Section 3—the need, and seeming impossibility of obtaining, a sense in which the "meaning" of a sign can remain constant even though its psychological effects vary. We shall find that the difficulty reappears for certain of the more controversial aspects of the analysis; but on the whole it vanishes when the problem is freed from artificial simplification and hypostatization. Variations in the response do not imply, necessarily, variations in the disposition. We have seen, for the analogous case of coffee, that whenever a variation in the response can be accounted for by a variation in the attendant circumstances, the disposition can be said to remain unchanged.[12] This holds no less obviously for the particular sort of disposition which is called the meaning of a sign. The psychological processes that attend the sign may vary, but the meaning of the sign need not be said to vary to the same extent; for the meaning is a disposition, whereas the psychological processes are simply the response. Thus a sign's meaning, for the dispositional sense of "meaning" in question, will be

11. Or "epiphenomena"; but see Chap. XIV, p. 301, n. 7.
12. Cf. pp. 48 ff.

more constant than the sign's psychological effects—and that is precisely what the considerations of Section 3 demanded.

It cannot be pretended, of course, that these remarks stipulate any precise test for determining when the meaning of a given sign has changed. Any such precision would require a sharp demarcation between the factors that are to be considered among the attendant circumstances of a meaning and those that are not, whereas the present account will provide the demarcation only by means of occasional examples. Hence the phrase "change in meaning" will itself be vague; there will be border-line cases in which it becomes arbitrary whether one says, "The meaning of this sign has changed," or, "Although the meaning of this sign has not changed, the attendant circumstances have come to be such that people's usual reaction to it has changed." The vagueness can *partially* be eliminated for the phrase "change in descriptive meaning," as we shall later see; but it cannot, within the compass of the present work, be eliminated for the phrase "change in emotive meaning"—nor is it likely that any more exhaustive account would be able, in practice, to attain full precision. It can reasonably be hoped, however, that the vagueness will not be fatal to our present purposes.[13] The phrase "change in meaning" is roughly serviceable in common usage, and becomes confusing only when, amid the artificialities of insensitive theory, it is pressed into some hypostatic sense, where unique "entities" take the place of analysis. For our subsequent problems in ethics, little more will be needed than to dispel these artificialities. Though a great deal will remain for an adequate linguistic theory, we must here be content with the initial, modest steps of pointing to its complexities, as yet little explored.

Passing attention must now be given to a point that might otherwise be misunderstood. Meaning has been taken as a dispositional property of a *sign,* not of the *persons* who *use* the sign. The latter alternative, however, would not have been impossible. In general, whenever a dispositional property has factors that involve several objects (as distinct from events) it makes little difference which object is said to *have* the disposition. Thus one may say either that sugar has a disposition to dissolve in water

---

13. In dealing with the ethical terms the present work does not seek permanently to remove vagueness, for its object there is to call attention to the flexibilities of ordinary language. In dealing with "change in meaning," however, where it would be convenient to have a term for technical use, vagueness would be removed if that were possible.

or that water has a disposition to dissolve sugar, and one may say either that coffee has a disposition to stimulate people or that people have a disposition to be stimulated by coffee. In the same way, one may say either that a sign has a disposition to produce responses in people or that people have a disposition to respond to the sign. The former way of speaking, though not mandatory, will here be adopted. We usually ascribe meaning to a sign, not a person; so if "meaning" is to designate a disposition, the disposition too had better be ascribed to the sign.

This way of speaking may at first seem odd, simply because we usually expect the basis of a disposition to be *in* the object said to have the disposition. In the case of meaning this will obviously not be so. The basis, whatever its ultimate psychological nature may be, will be in the people who use the sign, not in the sign itself. But this seems only of idiomatic interest; it can make no great difference where the basis is located, so long as its presence can be inferred. In fact we implicitly recognize this in parallel cases. If people permanently ceased to be stimulated by coffee under all the usual circumstances, we should doubtless say that coffee had *ceased* to be "a stimulant," and we should say this even if we knew that the change was not in the coffee but in the permanent constitution of human beings. In effect, we recognize aspects of human nature as parts of the basis of the "stimulant," rather than as attendant circumstances; for a change in attendant circumstances *without* a change in the basis would not bring a change in the disposition.[14] The basis, even in this example, need not be confined to the object that has the disposition; and the same holds for the basis of a sign's meaning.

In adopting the idiom, "This sign has a meaning," we must remember that the phrase is elliptical, and must often be expanded to the form "This sign has a meaning for people of sort K." This is parallel to saying that "X is a stimulant" is elliptical, and must often be expanded to the form "X is a stimulant for people of sort K." Just as an X may be a stimulant for certain people and not for others, so a sign may have a meaning for certain people and not for others.

Let us now proceed, still seeking no more than a rough analysis, to limit the *kind* of disposition that is to be called a "meaning." To all words, even nonsense syllables, may be ascribed

14. Cf. p. 49 (b) and (c).

some disposition to affect a hearer; and we shall not want to say that all of them are meaningful. The restriction can partially be obtained by specifying the causes of the disposition, as follows:

A sign's disposition to affect a hearer is to be called a "meaning" (for the not unconventional sense in question) only if it has been caused by, and would not have developed without, an elaborate process of conditioning which has attended the sign's use in communication.[15]

This proviso, though it will be subject to implicit qualification as we proceed, does much to limit "meaning" to a sense that is suitable for linguistic theory. It excludes nonsense syllables, and the ordinary "nonlinguistic" signs. A cough may, in a sense, "mean" that a person has a cold, but will not have a meaning in the present sense; for the elaborate conditioning, developed for purposes of communication, will be lacking.

Let us next drop the artificial restriction of considering only the hearer, and include the reader, speaker, and writer as well. The reader is easily included. We need only recognize that meaning is a disposition whose stimulus must be specified disjunctively, as *either* reading *or* hearing the sign. This is often done in the case of other dispositional properties. E.g., the stimulus for the disposition of powder to explode may be *either* a shock *or* a spark.

The speaker and writer introduce greater complexity into the analysis. They call attention to the need of recognizing a "passive" disposition of a sign—that is to say, a disposition *to be* used. If there is a correlation between some range of a person's psychological processes and his use of a sign, we may say, granted that the other factors can be classified as attendant circumstances and basis, that the sign has a disposition *to be* used. This disposition will be a part of the "meaning" of the sign, granted the proviso introduced just above. The psychological processes, which from the hearer's point of view were the response, become from the speaker's point of view the stimulus.

Meaning thereby becomes a conjunction of dispositions, one passive and one not. But it will be convenient to speak of it as "one" disposition, in spite of this. The criterion of unity for a disposition is rarely precise in ordinary parlance, and often need not be. Thus we may say that magnetism is "one" disposition; or we may say that it is "two," namely, a disposition of an ob-

15. Cf. pp. 39, 52 f.

ject to draw certain others to it *and* a disposition to induce electric currents in a coil of wire. The criterion of unity is often conveniently allowed to vary with one's purposes.

Having seen that the psychological correlates of a sign may be both a stimulus and a response, we must note that their relationship with signs is often reciprocal. When a man is trying to "clear up his ideas," for instance, he may "talk things over with himself," or "write them down" with many revisions. Certain crude psychological processes lead to certain words, which in turn lead to less crude processes, which in turn lead to other words, which in turn lead to still less crude processes, and so on. As Sapir has remarked, "The product grows with the instrument, and thought may be no more conceivable, in its genesis and daily practice, without speech than is mathematical reasoning practicable without the lever of an appropriate symbolism." [16] In addition to clarifying one's ideas in this way, one may give form to one's moods by use of poetic language. The causal relation between the physical and psychological aspects of language is thus not confined to one simple interplay. It is as if, to press an analogy now grown painfully forced, a man who was stimulated by coffee used his increased energy to make and drink more coffee.

It is this complicated interplay between signs and their psychological correlates which may have led certain theorists to view causal theories of meaning with suspicion. Language has so elaborate a function that any causal explanation seems too clumsy. But one need only imagine the causal situation more sensitively, with a full appreciation of its complexities. The present emphasis on dispositions, with parallels to nonpsychological examples, only hints at the complexity; it is half analysis, half analogy. But so far as it is analogy, it must be taken not as a permanent substitute for a more involved scheme, but only as a device for pointing to it, and for suggesting the further work that must be done. Advances in biology have come not from postulating vital forces, but from a sensitivity to multiple causes; and those who have come to realize, with Wittgenstein, that "colloquial language is a part of the human organism and is not less complicated than it," [17] will expect linguistic theory to take the same course.

A practical mastery of a language like our own, though it makes

16. Edward Sapir, *Language* (Harcourt, Brace, 1921), pp. 14 f.
17. *Tractatus Logico-Philosophicus* (Harcourt, Brace, 1922), 4.002.

great strides in early childhood, reaches its maturity only with the full maturity of an individual's intellect; and this development is itself possible only in a linguistic environment that has been developing over a vast period of history. It is scarcely to be expected that meaning, with so complicated a growth, should prove simple in its nature. We become insensitive to this complexity, among other reasons, because we consciously deal with only a part of it. We feel that the meaning of a term is as simple as the process of explaining its use to one who understands many other terms. But in such a process the meaning is by no means built up from the beginning. The old machinery, so to speak, need only be connected up to a new switch. The definition of a term makes use of the complicated dispositions that have already been developed for the definiens; nor would the definition be recognized for what it is, had we not some such word as "definition" with which to christen it.

6

WE must now leave meaning in the generic sense and return to emotive meaning. The latter may be taken as a more specific disposition, in the following way:

Emotive meaning is a meaning in which the response (from the hearer's point of view) or the stimulus (from the speaker's point of view) is a range of emotions.

Thus emotive meaning will be a kind of meaning, as the considerations of Section 3 demanded. And it will be so in the way that any disposition may be a kind of another. In general, when the stimulus, or response, or both, of one disposition have ranges that fall within those of another disposition, the first is commonly called a specific kind of the second. Thus a medicine's disposition to cure some limited class of illnesses is more specific than its disposition to cure a broader class of them. The dispositions may be realizable under different attendant circumstances, and a part, only, of the basis for the general one may be relevant to the more specific one; but for many purposes it is sufficient to mention only the stimulus and response. Emotive meaning can be considered a "kind" of meaning in this familiar way; for emotions fall within the broader range of psychological responses that were specified for meaning in general. In a similar way, we may classify kinds of emotive meaning with reference to kinds of emotion.

The term "emotion" is introduced temporarily, since the term "emotive" suggests it; but hereafter it will be convenient to replace "emotion" by "feeling or attitude"—both to preserve terminological uniformity throughout the book and to emphasize an important distinction. The term "feeling" is to be taken as designating an affective state that reveals its full nature to immediate introspection, without use of induction. An attitude, however, is much more complicated than that, as our previous examples will have suggested. It is, in fact, itself a complicated conjunction of dispositional properties (for dispositions are ubiquitous throughout all psychology), marked by stimuli and responses which relate to hindering or assisting whatever it is that is called the "object" of the attitude. A precise definition of "attitude" is too difficult a matter to be attempted here; hence the term, central though it is to the present work, must for the most part be understood from its current usage, and from the usage of the many terms ("desire," "wish," "disapproval," etc.) which name specific attitudes. Meanwhile it is important to see that immediate feelings are far more simple than attitudes, and that attitudes must not, amid temptations to hypostatize, be confused with them.

To whatever extent the emotive meaning of a sign is a disposition to evoke attitudes, it will be a disposition of the second order.[18] But it remains possible to include dispositions to produce feelings as well; and to that extent emotive meaning will be a first-order disposition.

We may now see, more clearly than before, that emotive meaning may remain roughly constant even though the immediately introspectable states of mind that attend it may vary. In the first place, the meaning will be less subject to variation than its responses (or stimuli); for different concrete responses, given a constant disposition, are only to be expected with different attendant circumstances. In the second place, if the responses are themselves dispositions (i.e., if the meaning is in part a second-order disposition to evoke attitudes) there will be still greater latitude for change in the immediately introspectable states of mind; for the same attitude may have a variety of introspective manifestations.

It may be presumed, in spite of this, that a meaning will remain only *roughly* constant. The continual variation of our psychological make-up leaves nothing unaltered, including the basis

18. Cf. p. 53.

of meaning. But only marked changes are of practical importance. With slight changes people say "there is no change"; and for most purposes this way of speaking is not only permissible but of great convenience.

These remarks help us to see that an attention to emotive meanings, and a careful selection of certain emotive terms rather than others, may enable a speaker to evoke attitudes that are of great strength. For example:

> A (in debate) : I favor this bill because it restricts the degree of *license* allowed to business.
> B: License? It is really a way of suppressing *liberty*—that freedom of enterprise which is the cornerstone of our democracy.

Although B's rejection of "license" in favor of "liberty" need not, of course, be a purely emotive change—for the terms lend themselves to definitions that sharply differentiate their descriptive meaning—it will be obvious that if B does not trouble to define either of them, or to clarify their usage by his subsequent examples, the change will be primarily emotive. And the effect on the audience may be no less strong on that account. Now if we thought of emotive meaning as the pale associations of a word out of context, and confusedly assumed that these associations must augment attitudes in a purely additive way, we might ask how the "mere" emotive meaning of the words could make so much difference. But the perplexity vanishes when we envisage the manifold conditions under which language operates. An emotive word makes use of an elaborate process of conditioning, of long duration, which has given it its emotive disposition. This disposition, granted suitable attendant circumstances, enables the word to act not additively but much more strongly, like a spark that ignites prepared tinder. To be sure, the suitable attendant circumstances cannot be taken for granted, but an effective orator will be careful to control them. He will first try to hold his audience's attention, win their respect, enliven them by his gestures, and so on. But when the attendant circumstances are thus prepared, he must take care to select, at strategic moments, a word which has a strong and fixed emotive disposition. Without the appropriate circumstances, the word will be unavailing; but without the appropriate word, the circumstances may amount to nothing. It is upon this latter fact that the importance of a study of emotive meaning depends. Whether we wish to employ emotive terms or to avoid them, it is imperative to understand the strong effect that they can often produce.

7

OUR study of emotive meaning must now be interrupted by a discussion of descriptive meaning. This will be of interest on its own account, and doubly so in permitting emotive and descriptive meaning to be compared and related, as will be undertaken in the next section. Two questions about descriptive meaning will require particular attention:

(a) What *kind* of psychological processes is a sign, in virtue of its descriptive meaning, disposed to produce?

(b) How do descriptive meanings attain the precision that is needed for practicable communication?

To the first of these questions it is natural enough to answer that a sign's descriptive meaning is its disposition to produce *cognitive* mental processes, where "cognitive" is to be taken as a general term designating such specific kinds of mental activity as believing, thinking, supposing, presuming, and so on. But this answer is far from a full solution; it is merely a step toward envisaging the broader problem with which meaning-theory must inevitably deal—the nature of cognition. This is an involved matter that has long been a stumbling block in psychology and epistemology, nor can the present work pretend to throw fresh light upon it. Some passing remarks, however, may not be amiss.

A "cognitive" reaction cannot plausibly be identified, if we are to preserve the intended sense of the term, with a "flat piece of experience" that reveals its full nature to introspection at the time that the reaction occurs. Those who have sought to identify it with imagery, as Hume did, have been criticized too often to require further attention here. And those who take it as a unique experience, with an indefinable "self-transcendence," are working on a hypothesis which, since indefinables put an end to further analysis, should be accepted only as a last resort. There are, perhaps, certain feelings that are peculiar to cognition, like the feeling of tension that comes from "expecting something to happen"; but these do not readily allow one to understand what "self-transcendence" could be.[19] There remains, then, the alternative

19. For a discussion of such views, see E. B. Titchener, *Lectures on the Experimental Psychology of the Thought Processes* (Macmillan, 1909),

of supplementing a purely introspective definition—though there is no occasion for abandoning introspection altogether—by making reference to dispositions to action. (Note that the term "disposition" is again making its appearance.) That there is *some* connection between cognition and action will not be denied; and perhaps it is impossible even to give an adequate definition of "cognition" when actions are left out of account.[20]

Analyses which take cognition as (in part) a disposition to actions have several points in their favor. They are much better than others in providing for the variety of introspective manifestations that attend "the same thought" or "the same belief." Thus when a man believes something for several days, we commonly take this as exemplifying cognition. But clearly, during the several days there will be no constant introspective manifestation of his belief. At most times it will be totally outside his conscious attention. And even when he is "consciously aware" of his belief, there will be no single, fixed experience by which his awareness is always marked. This latter point is perplexing to a purely introspective psychology; but to a psychology which takes the affective aspects of a belief as varying manifestations of a constant disposition to action, there is relatively little difficulty. Moreover, the dispositional view readily explains how one can "have a belief without acting on it"; for in such a case the disposition is simply unrealized.[21] And the view can give an intelligible analysis of such a phrase as, "Although his belief was false, it *referred to* something." What the belief is said to "refer to" must be related, though in a very complicated manner, to the stimulus or response factor of the belief. A false belief will then *have* a reference to something else in much the same sense that a disposition *has* a stimulus or response, even though no concrete stimulus or response exists.[22] These are respects in which a dispositional view of cognition promises to have no little fidelity to the distinctions of common sense—nor is common sense an unworthy ally.

In developing the view, however, one immediately encounters

Lecture II; and Ledger Wood, *The Analysis of Knowledge* (Princeton, 1941), chap. i.

20. See William James, "The Function of Cognition," *The Meaning of Truth*. Written in 1884, this article does not represent James's final views, nor is it wholly tenable; but it remains of great interest as an attempt to supplement an "image theory" of cognition with a more behavioristic one.

21. Cf. p. 49.

22. Cf. p. 49.

an overwhelming complexity. *What kind* of disposition to actions is to be called "cognitive"? Unless this is answered, the definition will have only its genus, without the required differentiae; yet in providing the differentiae it is impossible, in practice, to hope for more than the vaguest approximation. When a man "puts his knowledge into action" he may do any one of a great number of things. Now if his actions are the *response* of a disposition, they may vary even when the disposition does not; but we must at least limit the *range* over which they may vary, else the disposition will not be marked off as "cognitive." That is the difficulty; and it is equally difficult to specify the range for the *stimulus*.

How, for instance, will a man "act on" the belief that it is raining? Perhaps he will put on his raincoat, or reach for his umbrella; perhaps he will simply pick up a book, instead of going out; perhaps he will close the windows, and fold up the chairs on the porch; perhaps he will phone a friend to cancel a tennis game for the afternoon, and so on. Any of these actions, and the list might have been extended indefinitely, will be among the possible responses for this cognitive disposition. The stimuli will be no less complicated. It is not enough to mention the sight and sound of the rain, for these are more likely to be the causes of the belief itself than stimuli which prompt a specific action upon it; so among the stimuli must be included, say, the man's sight of his raincoat, or someone's reminding him of the open windows, or his remembering his tennis engagement, and so on. It is easy to draw up such partial lists, but quite another thing to specify the general classes into which the members of the lists must fall. If it is difficult to specify them for a particular belief, it is no less difficult to make clear what distinguishes beliefs in general, and cognitive dispositions in general, from all other dispositions to action.

If the problem lay wholly in this complexity, perhaps it would not be of great importance. We should need only to acknowledge, with Frank Ramsey, that philosophy is often less a "system of definitions" than a "system of descriptions of how definitions might be given,"[23] not forgetting that such a "system of descriptions," even when it is imperfect, may be sufficient to clear away the more troublesome confusions. But in fact the complexity seems indicative of a further problem, to which we must now attend. Suppose that a man, believing that it is raining, should in

23. *Foundations of Mathematics*, p. 263.

fact put on his raincoat. Is he acting *solely* on the belief that it is raining? Clearly not. He would not have put it on unless he *also believed* that it would serve to keep him dry when he went out, and unless he *wanted* both to go out and to keep dry. This example illustrates a principle whose application is quite general, namely: No concrete action can be related exclusively to one, simple belief; it must also be related to many *other* beliefs —usually a complicated system of them—and must be related to attitudes as well. Thus there are many dispositions involved, all of them relevant to any given action. Change *any* of these dispositions, and, with all else constant, the action will change as well.

How shall we account for this? Shall we say that the man's putting on his raincoat was in fact the response of his belief that it was raining, and classify his other beliefs and his attitudes among the *attendant circumstances* which, with a certain stimulus, made the response take just this form? Perhaps; but we must remember that the term "attendant circumstances" has been introduced largely by examples, and that the previous examples have none of them prepared us for attendant circumstances like these, which are themselves dispositions.

For a study of the present sort, where no empirical contribution to the problem is sought, but only a schema that will guard against the more gross oversimplifications, it will be sufficient to suggest an analogy—some example which is more easily understood, and which will illustrate how dispositional properties may mutually influence each other. Perhaps the following will serve, though very humbly: A small ball of iron is surrounded by electromagnets; the current is switched on, and the ball moves in a certain way. Now each of the magnets has a disposition to affect the motion of the ball, but the actual motion of it cannot be related to one of these dispositions alone; it must be related to all. Change any of the magnets, and, all else remaining constant, the motion of the ball will change as well. In spite of many differences, this case parallels the one in question. Several dispositional properties are present together, each making a difference to the way any other is realized.

There is clearly nothing mysterious about such a situation. The term "disposition" is used, as always, to refer to a complicated milieu in which a given sort of event has many causes. Here the situation is complicated enough to require the mention of several dispositions. It is convenient to distinguish them, and give separate attention to each, so long as a knowledge of how each would be realized in the absence of the others permits one to infer, with only a little more inductive evidence, how they will be realized when present conjointly. Even if the dispositions cannot be studied in isolation—as is the case for cognition but not the case for the magnets—one can observe what difference is made by a *change* in one of them, all else remaining roughly constant; and if this change is evidenced by other tests than that involving the given response to be predicted, a knowledge of it may be of practical use.

It is after this fashion, perhaps, that cognition must be conceived—as a disposition whose response is modified by that of many other dispositions. But two points must be clearly understood: In stressing dispositions to *action*, the present account is not presenting an uncompromising defense of behavioristic psychology. As has previously been remarked, there are certain immediate experiences which are involved, in various ways, in the processes to which the term "cognitive" is usually applied. An adequate study would undoubtedly have to take account of them —though it would seem that they too are only dispositionally present in cognition. The present emphasis on overt action is intended to supplement an introspective analysis, not to discredit it. And further: any mechanical analogy such as that of the magnets must serve, here as elsewhere, not to disguise the full complexity of the problem but rather to reveal it. A belief is much more complicated than any phenomenon studied in physics, and may involve, so far as anyone can now know, causal explanations that are irreducibly peculiar to biology or psychology. But if the mechanical examples serve as a starting point for the imagination, foreshadowing much more complicated conceptions, they may help to dispel those too simple "simple entities" which so often enter philosophy and psychology as fictitious substitutes for logical constructions.

These remarks do no more than suggest why it is difficult to give the differentiae for "cognition"; they do not surmount the difficulty. Nor will there be any attempt here to present an adequate definition of the term. Since a parallel difficulty arises for defining "attitude," one that again has not been surmounted, it will be observed that the key terms that are used in the present work—in the analysis both of meaning in general and of ethical meanings—have only such clarity as is afforded by instances of their usage, together with admonitions not to hypostatize and oversimplify. This is not an agreeable admission; but it is difficult to see how, at the present stage of linguistic and psychological theory, any more persistent quest for a definition would be rewarding. An inquiry cannot rest until its key terms are perfectly clear; for it is only by pressing on the inquiry, in any such way as is possible, that greater clarity can ultimately be obtained.

We must be content, then, to say that descriptive meaning is the disposition of a sign to affect cognition, though we must remember that this remark only approximates to a proper definition. To whatever extent cognition is itself dispositional in nature, descriptive meaning will be a second-order disposition. Thus the distinction between descriptive and emotive meaning depends largely on the kind of psychological disposition that a sign, in its turn, is disposed to evoke.

No attempt has been made here to deal with one of the most difficult problems that meaning-theory includes—that of explaining how separate words, each one with its own meaning, can combine to yield sentence-meanings. It is feasible, perhaps, to take each word as having a disposition to affect cognition, just as the full sentence does. The problem reduces, then, to one of explaining the interplay of the dispositions of the several words, when realized conjointly. The analogy of the magnets will still serve, used now to illustrate the relationship of *meanings* rather than of *beliefs*. We may compare the meaning of each word with the disposition of some one of the magnets, and compare the meaning of the sentence with the disposition that may be assigned to the group of magnets. Each word has an independent meaning in the sense that if it is replaced by certain others in any context, there will be a typical sort of difference in the meaning of the context; but the precise way in which the word's meaning is realized will depend on the meaning of the other words that accompany it.

Of the two questions mentioned at the beginning of this section, we may now proceed to the second, namely: How do descriptive meanings attain the precision that is needed for practicable communication? This question is best developed by example:

Compare "It is 99 miles from X to Y" with "It is 100 miles from X to Y." With suitable substitutions for "X" and "Y," each of these phrases becomes a sentence that has a descriptive meaning. We have no difficulty in distinguishing the meaning of the one from that of the other. But if descriptive meanings are dispositions of signs to produce further dispositions, how, amid this causal complexity, can such nice distinctions be preserved? By what device do we keep our reactions to the one sentence permanently different from those to the other?

To understand this, we must consider the function of *linguistic rules,* which relate symbols *to each other.* (To speak in Morris' terminology: an understanding of this part of "pragmatics" requires that we look to certain related aspects of "syntax.") Let us see this by example:

Consider how a child uses large numbers before he has learned arithmetic. "100" means *many,* "1,000" means *very, very many,* and "1,000,000" means *an enormously great many.* How do these symbols attain a more precise meaning as the child grows older? In great measure, precision is due to arithmetical *rules.* A child learns to say "100 comes next after 99," "10 times 10 is 100," "1,000 divided by 10 is 100," and so. By acquiring a *mechanical* ability to speak in this way, the child is conditioned to go from one numerical expression to another, and thereby comes to react more constantly to any one of them than he would to a sign for which no rules were provided. The meaning of each symbol is modified by that of every other symbol to which the rules of arithmetic relate it. (Note that the modification of the meaning (disposition) itself is in question, not merely the circumstances under which the disposition is realized.) A child does not first acquire a full understanding of a mathematical symbol, and then learn rules for manipulating it; rather, these rules are a part of the very conditioning process upon which a full understanding of the symbol depends. It is thus (to repeat Sapir's phrase) that "the product grows with the instrument."

In the context that was previously mentioned—"It is 100 miles from X to Y"—such rules are readily seen at work. Any variation in its descriptive meaning is counteracted by an activity with symbols ("100, that's twice fifty," or "100 miles, that's two hours at fifty miles per hour," etc.) to which recourse is made when occasion requires it. The rules which this symbolic activity follows are simply fixed procedures, established by rote memory or written tables of reference, of going from one symbol to another in a mechanical way. They are by no means sufficient to establish a meaning from the beginning, but they render more fixed any rough meanings that may have developed in other ways.[24] The precise way in which rules do this—the way in which, by mechanically relating signs, they alter the meanings of the signs —is a problem in the psychology of language that has never been investigated; but it is obvious, whatever the detailed explanation may be, that rules do have some such effect, and that they are necessary for any precise communication.

Linguistic rules are not confined to mathematics; they have a function that pervades the whole of descriptive language. Suppose, for instance, that a man is deciding whether he has any living great aunt. In a rough way he understands the term "great aunt" to begin with; but so long as the term is isolated from others his reaction will be too inconstant for practical use. He may accordingly say, "Great aunt—that would be a sister of one of my grandparents; or in other words, a sister of one of the parents of my parents." To talk in this way requires only rote memory of definitions, though this may be supplemented by other devices, such as written definitions, or a diagram of a family tree. It is by such a procedure—that of referring back to other signs— that we preserve a fixed descriptive meaning. The process of referring back is more a preliminary to knowledge than its attainment; but it is often indispensable for clearing up a sign's meaning, making it suitable for some empirical context in which it is later used.

Again, consider the sentence, "John is a remarkable athlete." This might have a disposition to make people think that John is tall, simply because so many athletes are. But we should not ordinarily say that it "meant" anything about tallness, even though it "suggested" it. The reason for this is simply that linguistic rules do not connect "athlete" with "tall." Rather, we say, "An athlete may or may not be tall"; and this very remark emphasizes a rule. It *isolates* the disposition of the word "athlete" from that of "tall," and so isolates what "athlete" *means* from what it *suggests*.

24. It is sometimes maintained that the logical constants, like "or" and "not," acquire their meaning solely from the linguistic rules that govern them. But obviously, the actual learning process is much more complicated than that. A child who is told to bring either this or that is frowned upon when he brings neither and praised when he brings one. The frowns and praises are parts of the nonlinguistic circumstances that help to give "or" its meaning; and it is not easy to see, for the psychological sense of "meaning" that is here in question, how they or their equivalent could be dispensed with.

Under linguistic rules we must include all manner of "a priori" statements, definitions,[25] and the stipulations that exclude certain combinations of words. (An instance of the last is, "A preposition must not be used without its object.") Whether such statements have any *other* function than that of rendering descriptive meanings permanent is a question that cannot here be discussed; but they obviously have at least this function.

The relation of rules to descriptive meanings is so close that it must be mentioned, qualifying the remarks that have preceded, in course of defining "descriptive meaning." Thus the full definition (rough to whatever extent "cognition" is improperly analyzed) can be given in this way:

The "descriptive meaning" of a sign is its disposition to affect cognition, provided that the disposition is caused by an elaborate process of conditioning that has attended the sign's use in communication, and provided that the disposition is rendered fixed, at least to a considerable degree, by linguistic rules. (Exception: a term without previous use in communication may be assigned a descriptive meaning if linguistic rules relate it to words that have had such a use.)

The proviso about linguistic rules is essential if we are to distinguish between what a sign means and what it suggests—as in the example of "athlete" above. When a sign persistently suggests something, this may be taken as a disposition of the sign; but being unchecked by linguistic rules, it will not be a "descriptive meaning" in the sense (not at all unconventional) which is here defined. Moreover, this proviso gives a little more precise test for determining when a sign's meaning has *changed*,[26] for among the many criteria for change in meaning we may now include a change in the linguistic rules with which the sign is made to comply.

---

25. But definitions need not always be so classified. When they describe how people actually use language, or predict how the speaker will subsequently use it, they become ordinary contingent statements about language. Only when they are used as symbolic exercises for clearing one's head, or establish a routine procedure of referring back from the definiendum to the definiens, do they serve to preserve linguistic rules. Note that it is one thing to give a psychological *description of* clarifying one's meanings, and another thing to clarify them. The latter, though it is the subject matter of an empirical (psychological) inquiry, is not itself an empirical inquiry—just as taking physical exercise, though it may be empirically studied, is not empirical study.

26. Cf. p. 55.

Note that a sign may be said to have a descriptive meaning even though its disposition to affect cognition is not *wholly* fixed by linguistic rules. It need only be fixed "to a considerable degree." This more lenient requirement permits one to say that a word may have a descriptive meaning which is *vague*. Whenever a descriptive meaning is vague, it is subject to constant changes of a slight nature, the linguistic rules being insufficient or too poorly specified to prevent this.[27] Vagueness is often removed by *stipulating* additional rules for a sign's use; but before these are stipulated, we shall want to say (so long as there were a number of rules to begin with, applied in people's habits) that the sign, for all its vagueness, was not void of all descriptive meaning. This useful way of speaking is readily preserved by the lenient requirement that has been introduced—that descriptive meaning must be fixed "to a considerable degree" by linguistic rules. When a sign becomes subject to fewer and fewer rules, and so more and more vague, there comes a point where we may say that it loses descriptive meaning altogether (even though it may still, on occasion, affect cognition) ; but the exact point at which this occurs can itself conveniently remain vague, since any sharp distinction is unnecessary for our purposes.

8

HAVING distinguished between emotive and descriptive meaning, we are now in a position to ask how the two are related.

It is evident that a sign may have both kinds of meaning. That is to say, it may at once have a disposition to affect feelings or attitudes and a disposition to affect cognition. Since most common words do in fact have a meaning of both sorts, let us begin by giving this aspect of the relationship closer attention.

The growth of emotive and descriptive dispositions in language does not represent two isolated processes. There is a continual interplay. It may happen—to take only a simple and not wholly typical instance—that a word acquires a laudatory emotive meaning partly because it refers, *via* its descriptive meaning, to some-

27. Cf. pp. 34 ff. "Vagueness" was there explained in terms of the relation between a sign and its designatum—i.e., semantically. It will be obvious, however (since a sign and its designatum are always related *via* descriptive meaning, in the present, psychological sense) that there will be a "pragmatic" counterpart to vagueness; and since descriptive meaning depends on linguistic rules, in part, there will also be a "syntactical" counterpart of vagueness.

thing which people favor. "Democracy" has a pleasing emotive meaning to most Americans because its referent pleases them. But if the two sorts of meaning often grow up together, it does not follow that they must always change together. Either may come to vary while the other remains roughly constant; and it is largely on this account that the distinction between them is important.

Suppose, for example, that a group of people should come to disapprove of certain aspects of democracy, but continue to approve of other aspects of it. They might leave the descriptive meaning of "democracy" unchanged, and gradually let it acquire, for their usage, a much less laudatory emotive meaning. On the other hand, they might keep the strong laudatory meaning unchanged, and let "democracy" acquire a descriptive sense which made reference only to those aspects of democracy (in the older sense) which they favored. It is often essential, if failures in communication are to be avoided, to determine which of these changes is taking place; and the distinction between emotive and descriptive meaning is of great use in studying the matter.

A particularly interesting phenomenon depends upon the "inertia," so to speak, of meaning. Suppose, though quite artificially, that a term's laudatory emotive meaning has arisen *solely* because its descriptive meaning refers to something which people favor. And suppose that a given speaker succeeds in changing the descriptive meaning of the term, in a way which his audience temporarily sanctions. One might expect that the emotive meaning will undergo a parallel change, automatically. But in fact it often will not. Through inertia, it will survive a change in the descriptive meaning on which it originally depended. And if we remember, dropping the artificial assumption above, that emotive meaning seldom depends on descriptive reference alone, but likewise on the gestures, intonations, and emotionally vigorous contexts with which the term has previously been associated, it is easy to see why emotive meaning can often survive quite sharp changes in descriptive meaning.

We shall find that the inertia of emotive meaning is of great interest to our subsequent study of ethics. Let us accordingly introduce the following terminology: To whatever extent emotive meaning is *not* a function of descriptive meaning, but either persists without the latter or survives changes in it, let us say that it is "independent." Thus nonmetaphorical interjections will have a wholly independent emotive meaning, but most words, including "democracy," "liberty," "magnanimity," and so on, will have an emotive meaning which is independent only in part. On the other hand, to whatever extent emotive meaning is a function of descriptive meaning, changing with it after only a brief "lag," let us say that it is "dependent."

The independence of emotive meaning can be roughly tested by comparing descriptive synonyms which are not emotive synonyms. Thus to whatever extent the laudatory strength of "democracy" exceeds that of "government where rule is by popular vote," the emotive meaning of the former will be independent. But such a test is far from exact, since it makes no allowance for the independent emotive meaning that may be common to *both* terms. Nor is it always easy to find descriptive synonyms; for whenever such synonyms differ emotively, people usually proceed (for reasons that will be given in Chapter IX) to redefine one of them in a way that brings a descriptive difference as well.

To see some further relations between emotive and descriptive meaning, let us turn briefly to the subject of metaphor. Though metaphors are not of primary concern to the present work, they will be useful in illustrating important distinctions.

People often say that although a metaphorical statement "has" a literal meaning, it is not to be "taken" literally. Let us see what that implies. A statement such as "All the world's a stage" has a verbal similarity to "All the third floor is a laboratory," "All the eastern district is an army camp," etc., and so suggests that application of the linguistic rules by which the cognitive dispositions of language are usually preserved. To say that the metaphorical statement "has a literal meaning" is a way of saying that, in accordance with these rules, including the rules that govern the individual words in other contexts, it has an ordinary descriptive meaning. To say that this meaning is "not taken literally" is to say that the attendant circumstances—the living context in which the sentence is uttered, and particularly the hearer's expectations of what the speaker would be likely to intend—are such that the descriptive disposition is not in fact realized in any usual way. This is by no means an exact analysis of the situation, but it points to a truth which is obvious once it is stated: The very distinction between a sentence's metaphorical and literal import cannot adequately be made without reference to the linguistic rules (syntax) that govern its component words throughout a linguistic system, and thereby preserve descriptive dispositions that are *usually* realized in a nonmetaphorical way.

The literal meaning of a metaphorical sentence must be sharply distinguished from what may be called its "interpretation." For example: If a person were instructed to express "All the world's a stage" in plain prose, he might give such "interpretations" as, "Real life is often like a play," or "There is a routine in real life, each man going through a prearranged course," or even "There is a great deal of trivial make-believe in each man's conduct." Now clearly, none of these interpretations has a descriptive meaning which is identical with the literal meaning (in the sense above explained) of the metaphorical sentence; for the latter is "not taken" in its literal meaning, whereas any of the interpretations is. Rather, the "interpretation" may be defined as a sentence which is to be taken literally, and which *descriptively means* what the metaphorical sentence *suggests*. We have seen elsewhere that a sentence may suggest, with regard to cognition, much more than it descriptively means.[28] Metaphorical sentences are replete with such suggestions. The function of an interpretation is to reduplicate the suggestive force of the metaphor in other terms—terms which have the same effect not as a part of their suggestiveness, but as a part of their descriptive meaning, realized in the ordinary way.

It must be remembered, however, that no sentence can ever descriptively mean *exactly* what another suggests. This is so, if for no other reason, because the descriptive meaning of a sentence is made definite by the operation of linguistic rules, which cause it systematically to be modified by the descriptive dispositions of many other terms in the language; whereas the suggestiveness of a sentence, going beyond any fixed rules, will be far more vague. There is no such thing as giving an exact translation of a metaphor into nonmetaphorical terms. One can only give interpretations, and these are always approximate. It is usually necessary to give not one interpretation but many, each of which will give, with too great a precision, a small part of what the metaphor suggests by its richly vague figure. What sometimes passes as "the" interpretation of a metaphor is in fact only a foveal one, which may too easily cause one to forget the many that are peripheral. Thus the second of the three interpretations above for "All the world's a stage" might seem "the" interpre-

28. Cf. pp. 69, 70.

tation, since it is most developed in Shakespeare's context; but
the third one, even though it is not developed, could plausibly be
taken as pointing out a partial but relevant aspect of the metaphor's full reverberations.[29]

Let us now see how these cognitive aspects of metaphor have a
bearing on its emotive aspects. It will be clear that the strongly
moving effect of certain metaphors has relatively little to do with
"independent" emotive meaning; it is closely related to the metaphor's descriptive meaning (even though this is not taken literally) and to its possible interpretations. Just *how* this relationship takes place is an endlessly complicated matter, on which
any attempt at an adequate analysis would be only rash. But
perhaps the following observations will have a modest use.

For certain simple metaphors, such as the colloquialism, "He
is a pig," the emotional effect seems in part due to the full realization of dependent emotive meaning even though the descriptive meaning is not, in the context, fully realized. Thus "he" is
given the derogation that the word "pig," simply because it literally refers to pigs, has come to acquire. To that extent a metaphor serves merely to separate off the emotive effect of a word
from its usual descriptive effects, and so to increase the number
of emotive tools that language offers.

But metaphor is obviously much more than this. It often happens that a word which has relatively little emotive effect when
used literally has a much greater one when used metaphorically.
"All the world's a stage" is much more moving than any set of
literal contexts that use the same words. No doubt this is in part
due to the dependent emotive meaning of the possible interpretations, and to the music of the line; but it is difficult to believe
that these factors are sufficient to complete, or even to suggest, a
full explanation. It would seem that the attendant circumstances,
preventing the metaphor's literal meaning from being realized in
any ordinary way, serve thereby to intensify the form in which
each term's emotive disposition is realized. The general problem
lies in explaining how the unusual realization of the one disposition affects the realization of the other. Now it is easy to suggest rough physical analogues. A match, having dispositions to
produce both flame and smoke, will produce more than the usual

---

29. See William Empson's *Seven Types of Ambiguity* (Harcourt, Brace,
1931) for a wealth of illustrative material on this and other aspects of
poetic language.

amount of smoke whenever certain attendant circumstances make it produce less than the usual amount of flame. But such parallels, as we have seen, can do no more than point to a greater complexity; and they are so inadequate for suggesting the rich complexity of poetic metaphors that their usefulness is meager. It can only be remarked, then, that an adequate explanation of the emotional effects of metaphor lies in a little-charted region of psychology—where a psychophysical explanation is barely to be hoped for, and where any purely introspective analysis is less likely to indicate the *modus operandi* than to provide a series of interesting but disorganized examples.

This much, however, may profitably be concluded: Emotive and descriptive meaning, both in their origin and practical operation, stand in extremely close relationship. They are distinguishable *aspects* of a total situation, not "parts" of it that can be studied in isolation. For varying purposes, the one or the other may require a preponderance of theoretical *attention*. And in practice it is often necessary, lest general intelligibility be sacrificed to an overwhelming body of details, to pretend that they are more neatly separable than they are. Such a compromise must often be made in the analysis of ethics that is to follow, and as a compromise it will serve its purpose. But should the procedure seem anything more than a compromise, the subject of metaphor must stand as a reminder of all that is left unmentioned.[30]

9

BEFORE concluding these remarks about meaning, it may be well to guard against the tendency, too common among popular writers, to separate meanings into the sheep and the goats—a procedure which militates against detachment, and hides the need of a more detailed classification.

In particular, the term "emotive" is sometimes used in an extremely rough way, until it labels a wastebasket for the many aspects of linguistic usage that are detrimental or irrelevant to the purposes of science. Under "emotive" utterances come to be included not only those which are disposed to alter feelings or

30. For some remarks dealing specifically with "sleeping metaphors" see p. 143. An instructive study of metaphor has been made by I. A. Richards, *The Philosophy of Rhetoric* (Oxford, 1936), chaps. v and vi, and *Interpretation in Teaching* (Harcourt, Brace, 1938), *passim*. Since the present account sometimes diverges from Richards, he must not be credited with its inadequacies; but the writer must express an indebtedness to him, both on this topic and on many others.

attitudes, but also those which are hypostatic, anthropomorphic, ambiguous, vague, misleading, incoherent, or in any way confused. Now this use of the term is natural enough, and not always inconvenient, for linguistic confusions are often attended by strong emotive effects; but the usage is not at all fortunate when it leads one to suppose, as it too readily does, that any expression classifiable as "emotive" is thereby perfectly put in its place, requiring no further attention.

It would be well to supplement the terms "emotive" and "descriptive" by subdividing meaning in a number of other ways. If meaning is taken as a disposition of a sign to produce psychological reactions, one may subdivide it by classifying the psychological reactions in any way that occasion requires. Thus for certain terms that have a marked, persistent disposition to produce images, it may be convenient to speak of "pictorial meaning."[31] If some form of pictorial meaning proved always to attend emotive or descriptive meaning, that would be a contingent matter that would in no way jeopardize the distinction. At certain times, even for purposes of science, pictorial meaning may be definitely sought, in the hope of making graphic certain complicated conceptions. James' expression, "the stream of consciousness," is useful in this respect. At other times, when the images may intervene to obscure or give a fictionalizing simplicity to complicated descriptive phrases, it may be helpful to find descriptive equivalents which are relatively free from pictorial meaning.

To take another instance: There are certain expressions which on account of inadvertent hypostatization, grammatical incoherency, and the like, are persistently disposed to evoke the state of mind that John Wisdom calls "philosophical perplexity."[32] In the broad, psychological sense here employed these expressions may be said to have a "meaning." One may deny, however, that they have a descriptive meaning, on the ground that their linguistic rules are too rough, or that the perplexed state which they are disposed to evoke is not cognitive; and one may deny that their meaning is *wholly* emotive, on the ground that the perplexed state which they evoke is so different from what is

31. See Virgil C. Aldrich, "Pictorial Meaning and Picture Thinking," *The Kenyon Review* (summer issue, 1943).
32. See the article bearing that title in *Proceedings of the Aristotelian Society* for 1936–37.

usually called a "feeling or attitude" that it is best classified in some other way. It may consequently be useful to recognize a separate kind of meaning for these cases—one that could be designated, for instance, as "confused meaning."

There will be inevitable controversies about just where to draw the line between descriptive and confused meanings, for the distinction is itself no clearer than the meaning of the term "cognitive." But such controversies exist in any case, and until they are settled, the term "confused" seems more fortunate than "emotive" as a temporary counter with which the matter can be discussed. Emotive meaning, so long as it is not attended by any confusion, has such a variety of uses in literature and daily life that no judicious person could consider it a "linguistic ill"; and if on occasion it becomes troublesome, there are recognized ways of nullifying or diminishing its effect, as by the use of a compensating tone of voice, or by the alternation of laudatory and derogatory terms. Confused meaning, however (if we judge by those instances that would certainly be so rated, and not those whose status is still a matter of controversy), is always a "linguistic ill"; and the means of correcting and controlling it are very complicated. Some confusions are eradicable only after the most careful analysis, and perhaps only after a careful diagnosis of how the confusion has originated.

In certain cases a statement which has a confused meaning (again neglecting the controversial cases) will *also* have an emotive meaning; and it may be that the latter is largely a consequence of the former. Once the confusion is dispelled, the emotive meaning greatly decreases. The emotive meaning is then related to the confused meaning just as "dependent" emotive meaning[33] is related to descriptive meaning. Let us accordingly generalize the usage of the terms "dependent" and "independent," previously introduced, giving the former a reference to any kind of meaning whose existence is conditional to that of any other kind of meaning. Thus there will be emotive meaning dependent on descriptive meaning, as before; but there will also be emotive meaning dependent on confused meaning. One may go on, of course, recognizing emotive meaning dependent on pictorial meaning; and there will be use for such a term as "quasi-dependent emotive meaning," designating that which is conditional to the cognitive *suggestiveness* of a sign—i.e., conditional

33. See pp. 72 f.

to a descriptive disposition which, though too inconstant and too little modified by linguistic rules to be called a "descriptive meaning," may yet make a great difference to the way in which any emotive disposition is usually realized. It must be remembered, of course, that any sort of dependent emotive meaning will not be identical with the sort of meaning *on which* it depends, for there will be a difference in the kind of response in question—a difference which it may be important to emphasize even though both kinds of response repeatedly occur together. It must be remembered further that the distinction between *dependent* and *independent* emotive meaning does not rest (thus differing from the distinction between laudatory and derogatory emotive meaning) on the kind of feelings or attitudes that constitute the response, but rather upon the conditions under which the disposition itself has originated and will continue to exist. If these points are kept clear, the term "dependent" is of no little service in discussing many aspects of a sign's range of effects.

Any more detailed classification of meanings, and of dependent emotive meanings, must be expected to vary with varying purposes. There is nothing mandatory about the present classification; but it is certainly mandatory that the term "emotive," whether by these distinctions or others, be kept as a tool for use in careful study, not as a device for relegating the nondescriptive aspects of language to limbo.

10

THE object of this chapter has been to outline a psychological (or "pragmatic") sense of meaning, of which emotive meaning may be considered a specific kind. By taking meaning as a dispositional property of a sign, it has defended an essentially causal view of meaning. More specifically, it has sought to explain how a sign's meaning can be constant even though its psychological effects vary, and how the effect of a sign on feelings and attitudes, in virtue of emotive meaning, can be much more powerful than any "additive" effect of its passing associations. It has sought further to show that the several aspects of language are closely interrelated.

At no time has the account sought to develop an empirical study of meaning. That would require a vast and detailed inquiry into the conditions under which meaning-dispositions originate, into the way in which their realization varies with various attendant circumstances, and into the basis of the dispositions. Such matters lie far beyond the present work, which hopes only to free the rough empirical knowledge of language that we acquire in common life from naïve confusions and oversimplifications. Indeed, the chapter sometimes does little more than show that language about language must share some of the complexities of all language. But even this has its modest use in cutting through the vacuities of much traditional theory, and will be of assistance in forwarding a workable understanding of ethics.

IV

First Pattern of Analysis

1

WE were lead to a discussion of meaning by the study of such a term as "good." According to the definition presented in Chapter II, "This is good" is synonymous with "I approve of this; do so as well." This was instructive only as a working model, or first approximation to analysis. We have seen that the phrase, "Do so as well," used to stress agreement and disagreement in attitude, is much too crude. And the phrase, "I approve of this," although it gives a *possible* descriptive meaning to the judgment, is for many contexts arbitrarily simple. Our discussion of meaning will help us to remedy these deficiencies, and secure an analysis that is sensitive to the nuances and flexibilities of ordinary discourse.

Let us see how we can dispense with the overt imperative that was used in the working models, recognizing a more appropriate emotive meaning in its place.

This is not an easy task, and every care must be taken to avoid a superficial approach to it. One may be tempted to suppose that only an improved version of the working models is required. Some other phrase, less crude than the imperative, may seem to be available—some phrase that will preserve the emotive meaning of "good" without noticeably distorting it. One may be inclined to suggest, for instance, that "This is good" has the same meaning (apart from linguistic flexibilities) as "Oh that you might approve of this as I do!" or "I approve of this, how fine it is!"

A moment's attention will show that these phrases fare no better than the working models. They have emotive meanings which fit them for strengthening or redirecting attitudes, and so *resemble* "This is good" in a rough way; but there is no situation in which they may replace the latter without changing emotive subtleties. The same is true of all other efforts to find an exact definition. Closer approximations can be obtained by defining any ethical term with reference to others; for "This is good" is emotively very close, for instance, to "This is *worthy* of being approved." But even so, slight differences remain.

The term "good" is indefinable, then, if a definition is expected to preserve its customary emotive meaning. It has *no* exact emotive equivalent. This is a simple fact which should occasion neither surprise nor perplexity. The term is indefinable for the same reasons that "hurrah" is indefinable. (One need only attempt to interchange "Hurrah" and "How exciting!" to see that the terms are only *roughly* synonymous.) Although our language affords many terms that have the same descriptive meaning, it is more economical with its emotive terms. Each term bears the characteristic stamp of its emotional history.

Yet it must not be supposed that the emotive meaning of "good" can receive no further study. One need only "characterize" its meaning, as distinct from defining it. Consider this parallel case, which typifies many others: The word "nigger" is followed in Webster's dictionary by the phrase, "Negro— now usually contemptuous." Note that the descriptive meaning is indicated by a *definition*, "nigger" and "Negro" being to that extent taken as synonyms; but the emotive meaning is dealt with in another way. No emotive synonym parallels the descriptive synonym, as would have been roughly the case had the definition read, " 'Nigger' has the same meaning as 'Negro, bah!' " The emotive meaning is simply *characterized* as being contemptuous, and thus distinguished from that of "Negro," which is by no means contemptuous. Now "good" may be treated in a parallel fashion. Its descriptive meaning may be defined, though not without the complications of ambiguity and vagueness that will later concern us; but its emotive meaning cannot accurately be preserved in this way, and must be characterized.

A definiendum and its definiens have the *same* meaning; a sign whose meaning is characterized and the characterizing sign do *not* have the same meaning. When sign Y characterizes the meaning of sign X, the meaning of X is the *referent* of Y, not the (psychological) *meaning* of Y. Thus the emotive meaning of "good" is not defined when it is characterized; but that is no obstacle to the analysis of ethics, just as it is no obstacle to lexicography.

Since the emotive meaning of a term is of a dispositional nature, its psychological effects will vary with the attendant circumstances. This is markedly the case for "good." Very often the term does no more than *indicate* agreement of disagreement in attitude, serving only to prepare the way for relevant discussion, should discussion prove necessary. At other times its effect may be strongly hortatory. There are even times when its usual emotive effect is reversed, as when it is used in irony, or when it is accompanied by the tone of voice that suggests "goody-goody." These passing observations will be sufficient to show that the emotive aspects of ethics cannot be treated in a simple fashion. At present, however, we need only understand the general type of inquiry that is needed. A characterization of the ethical terms must be developed little by little, with constant references to examples, and will be implicitly in question throughout the pages which are to follow.

A term which has an emotive meaning is not always used for purposes of exhortation. It is important that this be kept in mind, or else the present work, which must often emphasize emotive meaning, may seem to emphasize the hortatory aspects of ethics beyond measure. Let us immediately take pains, then, to guard against this possible misconception by mentioning some cases in which the ethical terms are practically devoid of any emotive *effects*.

The most familiar of these cases, too simple to be of much interest in themselves, are important for others that they typify. There are times when "good" has much the same use as "effective," as in the context, "Wearing oilskins is a good means of keeping dry in a storm." And there are times when it has much the same use as the phrase, "in accordance with the customs of the times," as might be the case (though not necessarily) in the context, "Infanticide was good in Sparta, but not in Athens." These senses illustrate a use of the term that is almost purely descriptive. The emotive meaning, if we choose to say that it still exists in such contexts, is *realized* in them to a wholly negligible degree. Just as descriptive meaning is checked in metaphor by the peculiarities of the attendant circumstances, so here, conversely, emotive meaning is checked. In consequence any disagreement that attends "good," so used, is likely to be disagreement in belief exclusively, and amenable to the ordinary empirical methods of solution.

Parallel cases are by no means rare. "Good" sometimes has the same use as "almost universally approved," or "approved by members of our community," or "usually approved by you (the hearer) and me (the speaker)," etc. Here the reference to attitudes is in effect descriptive rather than emotive, much as in the context "Infanticide was good in Sparta." When the reference is not historical, but contemporary, there is always the *possibility*, of course, that "good" may resume its emotive effects, acting to *build up* agreement in attitude or increase its intensity. But when the agreement in attitude can be taken for granted, "good" tends to be used in a tone of voice which makes emotive meaning inactive. The term is then a rough counterpart of a purely descriptive one, whose designation becomes evident from the context.

There are emotively active and emotively inactive uses of literally all the ethical terms. This is so familiar a matter that it is often the source of wordplay, as in the couplet:

> When there's wine and there's women and song,
> Then it's wrong not to do something wrong.

The first "wrong" is derogatory, and any old-school moralist who objected to its insidious influence would disagree in attitude; but the second "wrong" serves as a descriptive term whose referent, in the context, our moralist would find only too obvious.

When ethical terms are used in contexts that are not emotively active, the contexts may be called "ethical" provided that the term has a very broad sense. It would impose a greater strain on our linguistic habits, perhaps, to call them "normative." In any case, such contexts require no further attention. The occasional confusions that attend them will be evident from the remainder of our study; and the methods of proving them are the ordinary methods of science, which in practice are sufficiently well understood.

2

FOR the contexts that are most typical of normative ethics, the ethical terms have a function that is *both* emotive and descriptive. The descriptive function requires attentive consideration. If we are to treat it adequately, heeding linguistic flexibility, we cannot hope to end the matter by giving one simple definition. We must examine many "samples," as it were, of the way in which the ethical terms *can* be used, when occasion requires. The "One-And-Only-One-True-Meaning superstition," as Richards has called it,[1] can have serious consequences in any field of inquiry, and in ethics it is fatal to all further advance.

The nature of linguistic flexibility has been briefly indicated in preceding chapters;[2] but its bearing on the present work is so extremely intimate that it must now be considered in more detail. In particular, we must see how the remarks about linguistic rules, included in Chapter III, are specifically related to the terms of ethics.

There can be no doubt that the term "good," even when its emotive functions seem to be the predominating ones, can help us in one way or another to obtain information. If Mrs. Smith tells her daughter that Jones is a "good" suitor, we may, knowing Mrs. Smith of old, be reasonably well assured that Jones is wealthy. If a low-brow says that a play is "good," we may have reason to believe that our high-brow friends will dislike it. If Johnson is praised as a "good" conversationalist, we may conclude that he seldom bores people. And much the same holds for contexts that have a peculiarly "moral" ring. A respected friend tells us that Brown has "good" intentions, and we conclude that Brown habitually tries to be considerate and altruistic. A clergyman tells us "what a very good girl" Mary is, and we feel confident, on this testimony, that Mary is chaste, kind, and pious.

Now does "X is good" actually *mean,* in part and on occasion, what it thus leads us to conclude, or does it merely *suggest*[3] these conclusions? Perhaps it merely suggests them, for the inferences depend so largely upon our knowledge of the speaker's psychological habits. Our belief about Jones will depend on our knowing Mrs. Smith of old, and our belief about Mary will depend on our knowledge of what sort of person the clergyman is. But this is no answer. The question is not *whether* we use our psychological knowledge of the speaker, but *how* we use it. Do we use it to determine *what sense* of "good" the speaker was using, assuming that each speaker uses it in a somewhat different sense? And having done so, do we reach our subsequent conclusion (whether about wealth or chastity) by drawing analytic consequences of the sense of "good" in question? Or do we presume that "good" refers, so far as its descriptive meaning is concerned, only to the speaker's approval, and use our knowledge of his psy-

1. *Philosophy of Rhetoric,* p. 39.
2. Pp. 34 ff., and 70 f.
3. Cf. pp. 69 f.

chological peculiarities simply to determine what kind of thing he would be likely to approve of? Do we, in short, make use of our special knowledge of the speaker before determining the *meaning* of his words, or afterward?

The answer will depend, it may seem, on the precise sense in which "good" was actually used in each case. This is a helpful beginning, but still misleading. In point of fact, "good" had *no* precise sense; it was used vaguely. The distinction which the question presupposes, that between what "good" *means* and what it *suggests*, is often beyond the precision of ordinary language. It is a distinction between descriptive dispositions of the term, one of which is preserved by linguistic rules and the other is not. In the rigorous discourse of science or mathematics, which avails itself of interrelated sets of definitions or formal postulates, the distinction is readily made. In the rough contexts of daily life, however, a great many rules are not stipulated, being imperfectly evident from people's linguistic habits; and even those rules which are occasionally stipulated are not constantly followed. Certain rules, of course, *are* always observed; for "good," whatever else, is "not bad" and "not indifferent." But many other rules remain as mere possibilities. If such a rule is specifically called to a person's attention he may accept it—though usually only temporarily, for a given purpose. Not until a great many rules are permanently settled, though, do we get beyond the undecided region that separates descriptive meaning from suggestiveness. When rules are *in the course of becoming* generally accepted, there is a long period over which we may either accept or reject them without violence to conventional language. Our decision may settle the matter for our own usage, and determine what is *afterward* to be called the term's descriptive meaning, and what is to be called its suggestiveness; but our finished product is by no means the same as the raw material.

We may then, if we like, insist that the conclusions in the above examples were simply suggested by "X is good"; and we may also say that they were analytically implied by it. Either answer will serve to stipulate rules for the use of "good." They will be our rules, it must be noted, not those "secretly applied" in the examples, and discovered in retrospect. Though the more general rules may be "discovered," a great many must be "provided." Such is the typical situation with vague terms. When subject to definition or analysis, their meaning is seldom treated as a *fait accompli* (as might be the case when a scientific term is analyzed for the benefit of a beginner) ; rather the meaning is in the course of *becoming* what the analyst makes of it. And the analyst has a choice in deciding what it shall become, no matter how anxious he is to abide by common usage. As Wittgenstein once remarked: To remove vagueness is to outline the penumbra of a shadow. A sharp line is there after we draw it, not before.

We must be sensitive, then, to the fact that ethical terms are not predestined to abide by any one set of rules, and that analysis cannot "discover" the "real" sense. Yet vagueness is not to be dealt with capriciously. If analysis cannot disclose "the" sense, its sample definitions must be guided by the broad purposes for which any ethical term is commonly used. Otherwise it will increase the extent of vagueness and ambiguity, instead of rendering it better understood.

These remarks, though mainly concerned with the descriptive aspects of the ethical terms, indirectly throw light on their emotive aspects. We have seen that "good" can be given a descriptive sense that is quite complicated. A great part of the term's emotive meaning may then be *dependent* on the descriptive meaning,[4] eliciting the hearer's favor only as a consequence of first presenting him with beliefs about qualities that he admires. This will not happen unless the speaker and hearer are explicit in agreeing on the definition—a matter which, as we shall later see, may itself raise a problem that is essentially normative. Yet the point is of interest in showing that not all of the emotional effect of "good" is hortatory. Much of it may testify to the relationship between beliefs and attitudes, which is central to all ethics.

The situation is not greatly different when "good" is given a descriptive sense that is relatively simple. The more complicated senses, linguistically possible, need not be wholly obliterated by this process. They may remain in the form of cognitive suggestions. Much of the emotive meaning may then be *quasi-dependent*,[5] eliciting the hearer's favor not by definitely designating qualities that he admires, but simply by calling them to mind in a vague way. When this occurs every care is needed in preventing influence from being mediated by falsehoods. The judgment "X is good" may suggest to one hearer that X has certain qualities and to another that X has certain other qualities; whereas the

4. Cf. p. 73.
5. Cf. pp. 78 f.

speaker may have had in mind still another set of qualities. Hence the judgment may result in that kind of agreement in attitude which, though influenced by beliefs, has its basis not in agreement in belief but in a concealed divergence of beliefs. Each man comes to believe that X has whatever qualities *he* personally admires. If some of these beliefs are false, that may easily escape attention, both because of the excessive vagueness of the language used in expressing them and because of the effect of *independent* emotive meaning (which remains as a *part* of the full meaning of "good," even when the greater part is dependent or quasi-dependent) in temporarily diverting attention from careful inquiry. For those who wish to exploit error, a ready linguistic weapon is here available. For those who wish to minimize or eliminate error, linguistic caution will always be mandatory. This caution can be exercised by relating the judgment, "X is good," to a full body of supporting reasons—reasons which clearly designate, rather than merely suggest, the factual qualities that are ascribed to X, and so facilitate an inquiry into their presence or absence.

More could be said in a similar vein. The ethical terms are sometimes used hypostatically, as if an object were somehow "clothed" in its goodness. If this hypostatization is persistent, and increases the emotional effect of "good," it may occasion (for the usage of certain people) an emotive meaning that is dependent on confused meaning.[6] Or it may occasion emotive meaning that is dependent on pictorial meaning. These topics, although essential to a full study, are so intimately a part of larger questions of psychology and epistemology, and are so complicated in themselves, that no adequate study of them can here be attempted; and such passing treatment that they can receive must be reserved for a later chapter.[7] For the moment, then, it will suffice to emphasize that the emotive meaning of good is not wholly independent, but only partly so. It may be dependent on any other sort of meaning; and because of the flexibility of language, it is always, in part, either dependent on descriptive meaning or quasi-dependent.

6. Cf. pp. 77 ff.
7. Chap. VI, particularly pp. 145 ff.

3

IF we are to take proper account of linguistic flexibility, we must divide our study into two parts, or "patterns" of analysis. The first pattern will be simply an extension of the working models of Chapter II. The vagueness of the ethical terms will be removed, as an illustration of one of the possibilities, by limiting their descriptive reference to the speaker's own attitudes. All other information they may convey will be taken as merely suggested. The second pattern will illustrate many other possibilities, allowing the descriptive references of the ethical terms to become as complicated as any occasion or context may require. It will let descriptive suggestions, as the first pattern would classify them, acquire the more definite status of descriptive meanings. Emotive meaning will enter into both patterns, though it will vary in the extent to which it is dependent, as distinct from quasi-dependent.

Since the nature of the first pattern has been indicated by the working models, it may seem that the greater part of our attention can now be directed to the second pattern. That would be the case, no doubt, if our interests were wholly in the study of language. But we have the additional task of marking off and emphasizing the distinguishing aspects of ethical issues and methods; and for this purpose the first pattern is particularly illuminating. It lends itself to a relatively simple presentation, in which most of the central points can be made clear. And once they are clear, it is not at all difficult to understand the additional problems that the second pattern will introduce. For this reason, then, the first pattern will be studied in detail throughout the several chapters which follow, attention to the second pattern being delayed until Chapter IX. It must not be supposed, meanwhile, that the second pattern will present definitions that are linguistically less conventional than those of the first. In this respect there is nothing whatsoever that should make us prefer either pattern to the other.

The first pattern deals not with any one ethical term, but with a great many of them. Even when it is illustrated in connection with one term, such as "good," there will be several alternative senses which must be recognized. Hence it is appropriately called a "pattern" for making definitions, not a specific definition in itself. For example:

When "good" is assigned a descriptive meaning that refers, generically, to the speaker's favorable attitudes, and an emotive meaning that may serve to evoke the favor of the hearer, it does not become a peculiarly *moral* term. It is no less suitable for the context, "He is a good fellow," than for the context, "He is a (morally) good man." This broad, generic sense can readily give place, of course, to two or more specific ones, each of which will still fall within the first pattern. We may recognize a sense where "good" abbreviates "morally good," and refers not to *any* kind of favor that the speaker has, but only to the kind that is marked by a special seriousness or urgency. And we may recognize another sense, similar to that of "swell" or "nice," which refers descriptively to attitudes of the common-garden variety. (For each of these more specific senses, in appropriate contexts, there will be differences in emotive effects.) Thus "good," within the limits of the first pattern of analysis, can be given either one broad sense or several specific ones.

The peculiarly moral attitudes, associated with the moral senses of the ethical terms, are not easily described, but can roughly be marked off in this fashion: It will be recalled that an attitude is a *disposition* to act in certain ways and to experience certain feelings, rather than itself a simple action or feeling. If we wish to distinguish one sort of attitude from another, then, we can proceed by specifying the different sorts of response that attend typical stimuli. Let us apply this to the present case. Suppose that a man morally disapproves of a certain kind of conduct. If he observes this conduct in others, he may then feel indignant, mortified, or shocked; and if he finds himself given to it, he may feel guilty or conscience-stricken. But suppose that he dislikes this conduct, as distinct from morally disapproving of it. He may then be simply displeased when he observes it in others, and simply annoyed with himself when he finds that he is given to it. Similarly, if he morally approves of something, he may feel a particularly heightened sense of security when it prospers; whereas if he merely likes it, he may feel only an ordinary sort of pleasure. These differences in response, given similar stimuli, help to distinguish the attitudes which are moral from those which are not. The full distinction, should occasion require it, could be made by supplementing these remarks by others of a similar kind.

An interesting psychological problem, extending well beyond

these initial distinctions, lies in accounting for the *origin* of moral attitudes. Very little can here be ventured in this connection, but it will be useful, perhaps, to guard the question from superficiality. Those who become impatient with the sententiousness of certain moralists may be inclined to dismiss their issues with a gesture, and having insisted that the moral attitudes are "simply due to training," may feel that little more need be said. However pardonable this impatience may sometimes be, it can be of no service to careful thinking. In the first place, even if training is a necessary condition to the formation of moral attitudes, it is by no means a sufficient one. Without training, a child's impulses might be free of moral urgency; but if the training could appeal to no spontaneous inclination of the child to do what he was trained to do, it would produce very weak moral sentiments, or none at all. In the second place, the term "training" designates an extremely complicated situation, which cannot be passed over as soon as it is named.

One cannot suppose that training depends wholly on punishments and rewards that are overt and tangible. There are teachers, for instance, who can discipline children merely by smiles and frowns, whereas others cannot maintain discipline at all. The effectiveness of training obviously depends upon the *prestige* that the teacher establishes. Children recognize certain adults as occupying a position of authority, and deny this position to others. A frown from an authority is always a source of distress, but a paddling from any lesser person is a source of temporary discomfort. An authority must often be obeyed even when he is not present to enforce his commands; for the child's sense of security may require the realization that the authority *would* approve of him, *if* he knew. The full explanation of these commonplace observations would require an involved theory of human motivation. And any attempt to trace the effect of training on moral attitudes, in all their variety, and in their interplay with other attitudes and with beliefs, would require an even more involved theory, in which the conceptions of prestige and authority, inseparable from training, would have an important place.

Whatever else may be the case, it will be evident that training does not destine moral attitudes to maintain their initial direction. A man who first feels a moral compulsion to advance one cause may subsequently, after a period of disillusionment, espouse a different cause with the same fervor. Once formed, the moral attitudes may become independent of their source, and when the objects toward which training directed them give place to new objects, there may be little change in the responses of feeling which give them their distinctive character. This change in object is sometimes due to new authorities, replacing those who first influenced the moral attitudes; but at other times it may be due to a man's effort to free himself from all authorities, and to clarify his aims by his own reflections.[8]

Although much more might be said about the moral attitudes, further inquiry will not be necessary. The moral senses of the ethical terms are no more interesting, for our purposes, than the nonmoral ones; for the topics that they introduce raise no special problems of language or methodology. The particular reasons that support "he is a good man" will, of course, differ from those that support "He is a good fellow"; but a study of the general relationship between the reasons and the judgments need not be concerned with these differences. In what follows the ready words "approve" and "disapprove" will often be used, and perhaps they may suggest moral attitudes; but they may be taken to typify any kind of attitude in question.[9]

We must now consider some points of detail. It has been said that the first pattern will limit descriptive reference to the speaker's attitudes. This has a marked exception in the case of ethical *questions*. "Is X good?" is a remark that prompts an ethical judgment from the hearer, and can readily be taken to

8. Jerome Frank, in *Law and the Modern Mind* (Tudor, 1936), has argued that those who seek to repudiate all authorities are often unable to do so. There is a sense of security which an unquestioning dependence upon authority brings with it, and a heightening of certain satisfactions. So in the absence of trustworthy human authorities, fictitious authorities are invented, taking the form of abstract principles, half-anthropomorphically conceived. By this means Frank endeavors to explain the "basic legal myth" of a system of law that exists beyond the law of the statutes, which legislators are expected to "discover," rather than "create." He might have extended his theory to account for all conceptions of objective values. Although Frank's theory is of a speculative nature that must inevitably be controversial, it is of great interest, and well supported by knowledge of legal practice and legal theory.

9. Thus "ethical analysis," as here understood, includes most of what R. B. Perry would call the "theory of value," except that it makes no reference to the terms peculiar to aesthetics, and only passing reference (Chap. IX, pp. 215 ff.) to those of economics. Evaluation in aesthetics can be analyzed in very much the present way; but so many details would arise that the writer's views on the subject must be reserved for some later time.

mean, "Do *you* approve of X, and shall I?" The phrase, "Shall I?" is a request for influence, and can be roughly compared to a request to be commanded, as in the context, "Shall I take the left turn, or the right?" It will be obvious that in the ethical context, the reference extends beyond the speaker's attitudes, and includes those of the hearer. Should this stipulation seem out of accord with the ordinary usage of "good," in ethical questions, it must be remembered that the first pattern explores only one possibility of removing the vagueness of language, and that alternative interpretations will be provided by the second pattern.

In all other first-pattern contexts, the descriptive meaning of a judgment will be taken to refer to the speaker's attitudes *at the time of speaking*, even though the verb is not in the present tense. Thus "King John *was* bad" becomes, descriptively, not "I disapprov*ed* of King John," but rather, "I *now* disapprove of King John, who once exist*ed*." The tense of the verb indicates the time element of that which is judged, rather than that of the speaker's attitudes. Similarly, "The end of all war *will* be an unqualified good" descriptively becomes "I *now* approve of the end of all war, which *will* come." This stipulation is in accordance with common usage, and helps to show why the ethical terms, their emotive meaning added to this descriptive meaning, are so suitable for use in seeking agreement in attitude. The emotive meaning affects the *hearer's* attitudes "now" (i.e., at or near the time of utterance) ; hence if the descriptive meaning refers to the attitudes which the speaker has "now," the full meaning of the judgment will help to make their attitudes converge. How permanently they will converge will depend, of course, on how permanent the speaker's present attitudes are and on how permanently the hearer has been influenced. (It is often the case that a judgment, unless it is carefully supported by reasons, will exert an influence that is not permanent.)

In an extended sense, still within the first pattern, a judgment may be analyzed as asserting that the *speaker's* attitudes *are* permanent. In that case he will be maintaining a falsehood if a temporary attitude leads him to call something good. It will be evident from a later discussion,[10] however, that this point is of little consequence.

Should the first pattern seem artificially simple, it must be

10. Chap. VII, Secs. 4 and 5. See also Chap. X.

reiterated that not all the aspects of ethics need be directly evident from the definition of its terms.[11] When the descriptive meaning of "good" is taken to be exclusively about the *speaker's* attitudes, no attention is thereby called to the social conventions or "mores" that may have influenced his judgment. Yet it is quite possible to mention these independently, as a psychological fact about how this speaker's attitudes (and so his judgment) came to take their particular direction. The mores have an enormous role in determining what things any man will declare to be good; they influence the selection of grammatical subjects to which he ascribes ethical predicates. But it does not follow that the mores must be mentioned in *defining* the ethical predicates. In fact that might easily be misleading. If the mores influence a man's judgment, so, in a more humble way, do any man's judgments influence the mores. It is as a resultant of this man's judgment acting with or against that man's—multiplied to social proportions, and attended by the countless other factors that any sociological explanation must recognize—that the mores come to be what they are, and go through their slow changes. Ethical judgments, though influenced, exert an influence. So if a specification of any existent set of mores were included in the definition of an ethical term, that might too easily emphasize their effect on the judgments, neglecting that of the judgments on them. When the descriptive reference is limited to the speaker's attitudes, on the other hand, the influence of the judgments on the mores is properly emphasized. Nor is it overemphasized; for the opposite direction of influence is also suggested by the first pattern. Any speaker will at other times be a hearer, and if those who address ethical judgments to him are indicating *their* several attitudes, with attendant emotive effects, and with supporting reasons, he will be subject to their cumulative influence—an influence which becomes "social pressure" when, as a result of a previous set of reiterated, reciprocal influences of the same sort, it takes on a concerted direction.

To take a further example: The first pattern may seem artificially "thin" because it makes no reference to acting on principle —i.e., acting in accordance with an ethical *generalization,* and hence in accordance with attitudes directed to broad *classes* of objects. But clearly, one can urge that it is good to act on principle (that it is good to make and heed general judgments about

11. Cf. pp. 23 f.

what is good) without departing from the first pattern. Such a normative contention does not *follow* from the *definition* of "good" by this pattern, but anyone who approves of acting on principle, and wishes to induce others to do so, can still make *use* of "good," in a first-pattern sense, without abandoning his moral aim. If controversy should arise about *what* principle is to be acted on, one can readily use the same sense of "good" in stating the principle. "It is good to act altruistically," for instance, states a principle which the speaker is recommending; and it can be recommended without being made true by definition.

It is indubitable that principles have a conspicuous place in normative ethics. Even when a man makes a specific judgment about X, his influence on the hearer's attitudes will usually extend more widely, over some class of objects into which X falls; for the hearer, like the speaker, will instinctively avail himself of the psychological economy that comes from ordering the objects of his attitudes in some rough sort of classification. He can then react with favor or disfavor to an object, heeding only the defining characteristics of the class into which it falls; and if this sometimes breeds a gross insensitivity to the *peculiar* nature of this or that given object, it has the compensation of making use of analogies, and of permitting roughly appropriate actions on occasions when delay is impracticable. Thus a principle (which is a judgment about a class of objects) is often "latent" in a specific judgment. It is "latent," however, only in the sense that the speaker might have provided it, if asked, or that the hearer may supply it for himself—though the speaker and hearer might not be prepared to mention the *same* principle.[12] But if principles are widely current in ethics, that is something which can be made evident from the broad classes of which the ethical terms are overtly or implicitly predicated, and need not be mentioned in defining the terms themselves. Thus in the case of principles no less than in the case of the mores, the first pattern does not make ethics artificially simple. Matters that are unmentioned by the definitions reappear in another form.

The first pattern would remain roughly acceptable (though only as one type of analysis, to be supplemented by the second pattern) if descriptive meaning were eliminated entirely. "Good"

12. The Kantian term "maxim" can perhaps be interpreted to have the meaning of "latent principle"; but the status given to maxims by the categorical imperative is somewhat foreign, of course, to the point of view here defended.

would then *suggest* that the speaker approved, simply because of its laudatory emotive meaning; but it would not *descriptively mean* anything about his approval. Note, however, that that would only repudiate certain linguistic rules by which the reference of "good" to approval would otherwise be preserved. Since these rules, no less than a recognition of emotive meaning, are serviceable in pointing to agreement and disagreement in attitude, and since common usage makes them more natural than not, the first pattern will preserve them. Those who wish to recognize a *wholly* emotive sense of "good" may do so; but such an analysis will introduce no features that the present one cannot account for.[13]

The degree to which the first pattern approximates to common usage, and the way in which it gives simply one kind of sense, existing amid many alternatives, can be seen by studying almost any simple context. Consider, for instance, the statement, "I approve of this, but it is bad." This may, of course, like any other ethical statement, be assigned a number of meanings. Said by an intractable child, it might amount to, "I approve of this, but my elders abuse me for doing so." Said by a man of troubled conscience, it might indicate a conflict of attitudes: "My selfish inclinations favor this, but my altruistic ones oppose it." Or suppose that a similar statement is made by a political reformer: "I approve of the public housing project, but it is bad." Our habitual efforts to make consistent sense out of any utterance may still lead us to do so here. "Do you mean," we may ask, "that you approve only of *certain* consequences of the project, and that *others* make you disapprove of it as a whole?" Suppose that the reformer replies, "No, I mean that I wholly and unqualifiedly approve of the project, and at the same time I insist that it is wholly and unqualifiedly bad." If we are unusually patient, we may still seek for a plausible meaning. Perhaps he now uses

13. If the ethical terms were taken as wholly emotive, certain technical simplifications would result. *All* descriptive reference would then be suggested, not meant; hence the study of methods, to be presented in the following chapter, could be developed in a more uniform way, and the study of words like "I" and "now," to be presented in Chap. VII, would not be needed. But if we are to have a full understanding of the flexibilities of language, this simplicity is not desirable. We must deal with all the important possibilities; and the purely emotive senses of the ethical terms, though among these possibilities, are not complicated enough to require any attention beyond that which our general study of emotive meaning has provided.

"bad" in mockery, parodying what "those fools his opponents" always say. But if his tone of voice permits no such interpretation, we shall, no doubt, be bewildered at the man's deliberate efforts to contradict himself. And by the first pattern, of course, the statement does indeed become a contradiction. "X is bad" becomes, by this pattern, "I disapprove of X," together with emotive meaning that acts to make the hearer disapprove in the same way. Hence the reformer has affirmed both his unqualified approval and his unqualified disapproval of the same measure. It can be of no service to ethics to insist that "I approve of X and X is bad" is *always* a contradiction—as the alternative interpretations above will show; but it lends itself to that interpretation unless explanatory remarks are made. Hence the first patterr lies well within the several alternatives of analysis that common usage permits.

4

HAVING until now dealt mainly with "good" and "bad," let us go on to consider some of the other ethical terms.

Certain theorists are accustomed to make a sharp distinction between "good" and "right," as though the terms involved quite disparate problems of analysis. The present writer can find little ground for such a distinction, either in common usage or elsewhere. There are slight emotive differences, and different ranges of ambiguity for the more specific senses; but that is true of any pair of ethical terms. Only one point of difference is conspicuous, and that is not at all profound. Note that it is quite idiomatic to say, "He is a good man," or "That is a good book," but not at all idiomatic to say "He is a right man," or "That is a right book." Thus "right" is much less suited than "good" for judging *persons* or *things;* and a moment's consideration will show that it is usually reserved for judging people's *actions*. It is quite idiomatic to say, "His philanthropic action was morally right." Now it is difficult to believe that this is anything more than a linguistic nicety, together with a means of giving the adjective "right," by a limitation of the substantives it can modify, an emotive meaning that makes it influence actions more specifically and directly. In other respects "right" acts like "good" (for the first-pattern type of analysis) in indicating the speaker's favorable attitude, and influencing that of the hearer.

It is only to be expected that certain ethical terms should be specialized off for judging actions; for the speaker's *motives* in making a judgment habitually involve those of altering actions, where the alteration of attitudes is simply a mediating step. We tell A that his action is "right" partly to encourage him in such actions—and may "state the principle involved," rather than allow it to be "latent," so that the "next case" will be more adequately indicated. Or when we address a judgment about A's action not to A but to B, we hope either that B will subsequently join us in encouraging A, or others like A, or that he will take A's "right" action as a precedent for his own conduct. The word "wrong" has an opposite effect, preventing certain actions; and note that when moral judgments are insufficient to deter a man, we often take more forcible steps, which when socially organized become the penalties provided by law. We shall have occasion to see subsequently[14] that the motivation of many ethical judgments is far less "calculated" than this, and indeed, is more complicated than can now be mentioned; but obviously, the motive of altering actions must not be neglected. The word "right," specialized for dealing directly with actions, accordingly serves an important purpose.

It must be remembered, however, that this purpose is served by many other words than "right." The word "good," even when it is predicated of *things*, has the same effect, and differs only in that it operates more indirectly. Thus "This is a morally good book" has the effect (for those who have not, disillusioned by the ways of traditional moralists, built up defenses against moral judgments altogether) of influencing the hearer to read the book, or of influencing others to, or of encouraging authors to write similar books, or of leading people to take the book as providing a model for their own conduct, and so on. Like any term used in influencing attitudes, "good" may have its ultimate repercussions on actions, whether or not it is predicated of actions; and it differs from "right" largely in that it need not be used to indicate the actions so specifically.

Yet if the difference is not of great consequence, it is sufficient to prevent any simple identification of the terms. It will not do, for instance, to say that "He is a good man" has precisely the same meaning as "His actions are usually right"—thereby trying to avoid the difference by changing the grammatical subject of the sentence. This is a possible procedure for the second pattern of analysis, and we shall see there, implicitly, that it may have broader repercussions than may at first appear. But for the first pattern, if for the moment we neglect emotive meaning, it is parallel to an identification of "I approve of him" with "I approve of the way in which he usually acts." Common usage here lends itself to a distinction. The latter statement indicates the particular respect in which "he" is approved. The former, although it commonly suggests that there are *some* respects in which "he" is approved (*such as* his actions, or his motives, or his unrealized possibilities), does not indicate just what these respects are. The former is less specific than the latter. Since "good," whenever it is not predicated of an action, will always be indefinite in its reference to actions, it cannot readily be *translated* into terms of "right"; and the alternative procedure, wholly adequate for analytic purposes, is simply to point out that the latter term has a more restricted usage.

These remarks single out only one possible sense of "right," and a corresponding sense of "wrong," saying nothing about the range of ambiguity. We shall be in a better position to note the ambiguities, however, if we first look to some other terms.

The terms "duty," "obligation," and "ought," like the term "right," usually occur in judgments that are overtly about actions. It may seem that they can be *equated* with "right"; but if the latter is used in the sense above indicated, not even a rough equation is possible. Consider, for instance, the statement:

It is (morally) right for him to be exceptionally charitable, but not his duty or obligation—nothing that he positively ought to do.

This would not ordinarily be taken as a contradiction, as it would have to be if "right" were synonymous with the other terms. Evidently, "right" has a less coercive effect. It *praises* for *commission,* whereas "duty" and the others *blame* for *omission.* To reach a closer approximation, one must indicate the blame by using "wrong," rather than "right," and indicate the omission by using a negated infinitive clause—as in the following statement:

It would be (morally) wrong for him *not* to be charitable, but being charitable is not his duty or obligation—nothing that he positively ought to do.

This *would* ordinarily be taken as a contradiction, unless there were reason to suppose that the words were being used in an odd sense. It helps to show that "To do X is a duty" (and the other expressions) may roughly be equated with "It is wrong not to do X," rather than with "It is right to do X."[15] In other words, the descriptive meaning (as was anticipated in the case of "ought" by the working models (page 21) is the same as that of "I *dis*approve of *not* doing X," rather than "I approve of doing X."

The difference here emphasized is readily understood by example. We may *dis*approve of a man's *not* supporting his family, but have no positive approval of his doing so—taking the latter, as we say, "just as a matter of course." And vice versa, we may approve of a man's risking his life in the interest of advancing medical knowledge (or any such "virtue that goes beyond duty") without disapproving of its omission. It often happens, to be sure, that when we approve of X's being done we also disapprove of its not being done; and the one statement so often *suggests* the other that for certain contexts a linguistic rule could be provided that gives them the same descriptive meaning. This is a matter of vagueness, however. The statements may also be kept distinct; and the above examples will help to clarify the sense in which they are distinct.

The shade of menace that often attends "duty" and "ought" is the emotive, quasi-imperative counterpart of their use in indicating strong disapproval of omission. We usually do not bother to tell a person that he *ought* to do something unless we suspect that the free run of his impulses will otherwise lead him to neglect it. "Ought" and "duty" come as constraints, seeking to repress the hearer's free impulses by building up any counter-impulses that may be latent in him. When used without an intelligent understanding of human nature, these words become instruments for producing serious conflicts of attitude, and on occasion may lead to pathological inhibitions. Rebellious adolescents often make the moralist out as a villain for that reason. It is obvious, however, that these coercive terms *need* not be divorced from an understanding of human nature, as John Dewey has so earnestly pleaded.[16] One may laugh the "old" moralists out of court and still become a "new" moralist—as those who

15. Cf. G. E. Moore, *Ethics*, p. 36.
16. Particularly in *Human Nature and Conduct*.

"repudiate morality" actually do. And any moralist, whether old or new, may have occasion to create a conflict of attitudes in certain of his hearers, as the only practical alternative to allowing their prevalent attitudes to remain unchecked. Even those to whom the coercive terms are addressed may find them not unwelcome, helpful in preserving a fixity of purpose when spontaneous impulses lapse into vacancy. When Emerson writes, "Dark . . . the hour . . . and dull the wit, no flood of thoughts, no lovely pictures in memory or in hope, only heavy, weary duty, moving on cart-wheels along the old ruts of life . . ." [17] he finds his sense of duty—his disapproval of neglect built up by judgments of others or by his self-coercion—a poor substitute for healthy, positive interests; yet it remains to tide him through a period of dejection—an economical defense against shortsighted indifference.

This discussion can only hint at the flexibility of ethical language, and at the subtler distinctions. The words "duty," "obligatory," and "ought," here taken as roughly intertranslatable, have in fact slightly different emotive colorings, and there is a difference in the range of their descriptive ambiguities. "Ought" has many nonmoral usages, for instance, whereas "duty" and "obligation" are usually limited to moral contexts.[18] For further illustrations of ambiguity (though there can be no attempt at an exhaustive treatment of them) let us return to the word "right."

It will be obvious that "right," like "good" and "ought," has many nonmoral uses, being sometimes the equivalent of "correct," or "effective," or "usually approved." In such cases the realization of its emotive meaning, given the context, may be negligible. But in its evaluative usages there are still many ambiguities, even within the limits of the first pattern. Under certain circumstances "right" may become a coercive term, like "duty";[19] for we so frequently support disapproval of omission with approval of commission (just as we support punishments with rewards) that the two functions readily come to be associated with the same word. There is the further sense in which

17. *Journals*, May 6, 1838.
18. Throughout the present work the word "moral" is used in opposition to "nonmoral," rather than "immoral," and has reference to a special sort of attitude. Cf. pp. 90 ff
19. W. D. Ross selects such a sense, though somewhat apologetically, in *The Right and the Good* (Oxford, 1930), p. 4.

"right," used as a noun, is equivalent to "privilege"—as in the
ritual used by the president of Yale in conferring a degree: "I
remind you of its duties, and admit you to its rights." But the
identification of "rights" and "privileges" only points to further
ambiguities. One's "privilege" may be either that which one has
no duty to *refrain* from doing, or that which *others* ought to
permit one to do, or that which others *in fact* permit one to do;
and there are corresponding senses of "right." In a further sense,
a man's "right" is that which he ought *to be given.* Thus "The
employees have a right to higher wages" has the meaning of
"The employees ought to be given higher wages." For any of
these senses, it may be added, there are corresponding ones whose
reference is limited to the obligations, privileges, etc. that have
a legal sanction.[20] So one might continue, pointing out the multitude of ambiguities to which all the ethical terms are subject;
but for the moment the present illustrations will be sufficient.

5

ANY analysis of ethics which stresses attitudes is likely to in-
cur the charge of superficiality—or perhaps the charge of will-
fully discrediting "moral ideals" in favor of "mere expediency"
or "self-interest." The ethical theory of the Sophists, as Plato
presents it, was unquestionably disillusioned, and any theory
even faintly reminiscent of theirs is likely to seem equally so. We
must consider whether such a charge is applicable to the present
analysis.

There are, to be sure, *seeming* consequences of the first pattern
by which the well-intentioned critic may pardonably be disconcerted. When "good" is assigned no other descriptive reference
than that to the speaker's approval, the statement "Whatever I
approve of is good" appears to have all the certainty of an
analytic statement. But is it analytic? "It is not," the critic will
urge, "in any proper sense of 'good'; and that is why the first
pattern must be rejected. By making 'Whatever I approve of is
good' analytic, in your distorted sense, you lead people to think
that it must be accepted in the proper sense. Thus you insinuate
that whatever you approve of must always be accepted as *really*

20. An interesting (though not always logically neat) discussion of legal
terms will be found in W. N. Hohfeld's *Fundamental Legal Conceptions*
(Yale University Press, 1919).

good. However little you may intend to do so, you mask an irresponsible egotism by a crude wordplay."

The suspicion of egotism is readily dispelled by pointing out that the "I" that is used, in "I approve of this," does not refer exclusively to the present writer. It refers to *any* speaker, and so favors no one person's attitudes over those of any other. But this is likely to provoke a further criticism: "You imply, then, that whatever *anybody* approves of is good. Such a view can lead only to moral chaos. Is ethics to tolerate the caprices of men's approval, or is it to point out what is worth approval?"

Similar objections are often urged against "psychological naturalism," and they are not without their use in correcting a naturalism of the cruder sort. But they have nothing to do with the present analysis. They ignore emotive meaning, and its effect in provoking or reconciling disagreement in attitude. Let us consider this in more detail.

Under very exceptional circumstances, "Whatever I approve of is good" (the first of the alleged "implications") might serve as nothing more than an analytic statement, stipulating a rule that marks the first pattern of analysis. But under most circumstances the emotive meaning of "good" interferes with that purpose, and makes the statement have many additional repercussions. Suppose that the statement is made not with artificiality, but seriously, in a living context. The emotive effect of "good" will, as usual, direct the *hearer's* approval to that of which it is predicated; so it will here urge him always to approve of what the *speaker* approves of, no matter what that may be. Now if the speaker happens to be an absolute monarch, and the hearer a fawning courtier, the emotive effect may meet with no resistance. "Yes, sire! Whatever you approve of *is* good, for you alone are a guide to us." And so might be the more guileless reply of a thoroughly dispirited child to a tyrannical father. "Yes, father, you always know best." But if the speaker and hearer are ordinary men, used to treating each other as equals, the answer will be of another sort: "You are not serious. Are you to become my sole authority about what is good? I might agree that *some* of the things you approve of are good, but I must know first what they are, and will in any case reserve the general privilege of disagreeing with you." It will now be obvious that the speaker's statement can serve as much more than a linguistic rule. Its emotive meaning eclipses this simple function, and makes it an instrument for use in modifying the attitudes of others. The predicate does not *merely* "say over again" what has been said in the subject; it *adds* an emotive *appeal*. It urges the hearer to accept as his own *any* favorable attitude that the speaker may have, never venturing a counterinfluence. Such a sweeping effort to exert an influence is of course fantastic in any ordinary situation. Any critic who supposed it to be a consequence of the present analysis could only be expected to demur, to say the least.

The statement, "Whatever I approve of is good," is manifestly egotistical, so long as the speaker uses it as an emotively active instrument—so long as he sets himself up like an absolute monarch, expecting the hearer never to disagree with him in attitude. But so far from denying the egotism, the present account has readily explained it. It is by no means the case that the analysis requires anyone to make such a statement, or to agree with it when it is made by another. The first pattern acknowledges it *only* when its use is confined to stating a linguistic rule. When it does more than this—when it emotively acts to make the hearer accept the attitudes of the speaker—then the analysis does not accept it. Nor for that matter does it reject it. Analysis cannot serve to make men less egotistical; it has the humble function of clarifying muddled thinking. Since "Whatever I approve of is good" would not usually be taken as *just* a linguistic rule, but rather as a means of emotively propagating the speaker's attitudes, analysis will do well to avoid it in favor of a statement that will have a purely linguistic function. The required statement is readily found in, "Whenever I say that anything is good, I mean, following the first pattern, and apart from emotive meaning, only that I approve of it." In this context "good" is talked about, rather than used, and so does not become emotively active. The effect of the statement in stipulating a linguistic rule is thereby isolated. The rule will be further isolated if one adds, "If you agree with me in belief about my attitudes, you do not thereby commit yourself to agree with me *in* attitude."

The further statement, "Whatever *anyone* approves of is good," which our imagined critic found conducive to "moral chaos," is irrelevant for much the same reasons. It seems to vitiate the first pattern only when its emotive repercussions become confusingly involved with a linguistic rule. The rule can be isolated in the form, "If anyone says that he approves of something, he introduces no new *descriptive* meaning by adding that it is good." Such a rule holds for the first pattern, though it will be rejected for the second; but in any case it is innocent. Some little care is required, however, in developing the consequences of the rule. The emotive meaning of "good" may again interfere, along with a complication that will subsequently appear. One must take care, for instance, before concluding:

(a) If any person says that he approves of anything, then he *implies* that it is good, provided, of course, that "good" is used by *him*, and so refers to *his* approval only.

It may be objected: "But people often want to say that they approve of something *without* implying that it is good; they may wish to indicate their approval as a mere fact about themselves, leaving any discussion about what is good for another time." This is quite true, even for those who follow the first pattern; but it is readily explained. "Good" is emotively strong in a way that "approve" is not. A person does not proceed from "I approve of this" to "This is good," accordingly, unless he wishes (as he sometimes may not) to recommend the object in question to the approval of his hearers. Now (a) above seems to require a person to go from the one statement to the other, as a matter of mere logic; whereas it obviously does not require this so long as the latter is emotively more active. Hence (a) is very likely to be misleading, even though (for the first pattern only, and disregarding emotive meaning) it is logically correct. It is like the statement, "If anyone says that a man is a Negro, he implies that the man is a nigger." Emotive meaning causes an otherwise innocent tautology to exaggerate the extent of people's emotive efforts. Similarly, one must guard against concluding:

(b) Whenever a person says that he approves of something, and I acknowledge that he does, I thereby acknowledge that it is good.

This is not merely misleading, but actually no consequence of the first pattern at all. If "I" acknowledge that another person approves of something, "I" certainly do not acknowledge that it is good in the sense that refers to "my" approval; and by the first pattern, when "I" use "good" the word *does* refer to "my" approval. Note that (b) drops the proviso that (a) properly includes—that which restricts the implication to contexts in which "good" is used by the same person who says "I approve." [21] This being clear, we may proceed to the main point of the present discussion:

When "Whatever anyone approves of is good" is taken as a consequence of the first pattern, both of the confusions illustrated by (a) and (b) are involved. The steps in drawing such a conclusion might be as follows:

If any person, A, says that he approves of something, X, then by the first pattern his statement strictly implies that X is good, provided that "good" is used by him, and so refers to his approval only. (This is like (a) ; it exaggerates A's emotive efforts, even though it is otherwise correct.)

Hence the statement, "If A approves of X, X is good" is an analytic statement which I, who am making this inference, am required to accept. (This involves the same fallacy as (b). The proviso that "good" must be used by A, and so refer to *his* approval, is quietly dropped. Instead, "good" comes to refer to the approval of the man who is advancing the present type of critical argument.)

Since A may be *any* person, and X *any* object of his attitudes, then "Whatever any person approves of is good" is analytic, and I must accept it. (This puts the above into other words.)

That such a consequence follows from the first pattern of analysis shows how absurd that pattern is.

This argument begins by suggesting that A's statement of his approval had more emotive force than it did have; it then, by a sleight of hand with pronouns, makes it appear that the person advancing the argument is logically obliged to accept the same attitudes that A does, and exert the same alleged emotive pressure; and it ends, of course, by remonstrating against any analysis that requires this.

"Whatever anyone approves of is good" clearly does not follow then, from the first pattern of analysis. It is interesting to see in fact, what this statement amounts to when analyzed *in accord*

21. The error is a common one for all "indicator" terms, as Nelson Goodman calls them—that is, for terms like "I," "now," "here," and so on, whose different utterances have a different descriptive reference, depending upon the person who uses them, or on the time or place that they are used. For the reference to Goodman's analysis, and a further application of it, see Chap. VII, Sec. 4.

ance with the first pattern. It becomes, descriptively: "If anybody approves of anything, then so do I"; and it acts emotively to make the hearer share this remarkably obsequious state of mind. It indicates that the speaker is prepared to disagree in attitude with *nobody*. He will presumably take *both* sides in any disagreement in attitude he witnesses, approving *and* disapproving of the same thing, and urging others to do likewise. Thus by the first pattern the statement becomes just as foolish as common sense would ordinarily consider it. If the statement really followed from the first pattern with the meaning that the first pattern ascribes to it, there would indeed be ample grounds for distress. Any stable society presupposes some measure of agreement in attitude; and this is often obtained by progressively resolving disagreement by means of moral exhortation and moral argument. A statement which urges a docile (and indeed, inconsistent) omni-tolerance, instead of active participation in disagreement in attitude, with efforts to resolve it, will certainly foster some sort of "chaos." Should the first pattern be taken to imply such a statement, however, that would be a result of our present state of linguistic chaos, more than a cause of some future moral one.

As to the remark, "'Good' has to do with what is *worthy* of approval, not with what *is* approved," which is what our imaginary critic ended by implying[22]—that, of course, is essentially the case. "This is good" is more nearly approximated, in its full meaning, by "This is worthy of approval" than by "I approve of this"; for "worthy" has an emotive strength which "approve" lacks. And "worthy," like "good," lends itself to discussions that involve agreement or disagreement in attitude. It does not, as "approve" does, readily lend itself to discussions which look only to agreement in *belief about* attitudes, which our critic so understandably feels to be of a psychological character, rather than a moral one. In fact, by the first pattern, "X is worthy of approval" becomes descriptively, "I approve of X's being approved by others," or else (and vagueness permits a choice) "I approve of X"; but it also acts *emotively* to induce the hearer to share the speaker's approval. It must always be remembered, however, in the case of this and of *any* ethical term, that the emotive force may be used only to exert a *tentative* influence. It may be used not to sway the hearer, without more ado, but rather with the

22. See p. 103.

hope of occasioning a counterinfluence, that will lead to mutual self-criticism and joint deliberation.

6

THE critics of "ethical naturalism" have much to be said in their favor. They have seen that normative ethics is something more than a branch of psychology or of any other science; and they have realized that ethical judgments have a function in influencing, guiding, and remolding attitudes. But very little can be said for their views on how this remolding occurs. It is one thing to explain how attitudes are influenced and another to influence them. Metaphysical writers on ethics rarely keep these undertakings apart. To surround ethical judgments with other-worldly mystery may serve to *intensify* their influence, whether in one direction or another; but to explain it is quite another matter. An ethical judgment is not a psychological statement; that is granted. A characterization of its emotive meaning in psychological terms serves to distinguish it from a psychological statement, not to make it one. It exerts its influence upon attitudes in a much more direct way than any statement of science, and lends itself to a different sort of agreement or disagreement. But it need not therefore be considered a statement of some "nonnatural" science, with a peculiar and occult subject matter.

Perhaps some theorists may seek to accept the positive contentions of the present account and still remain "nonnaturalists." Without neglecting emotive meaning, and without ignoring disagreement in attitude, they may introduce a unique quality as well. "Good" will then be granted a laudatory emotive meaning, but simply one that is dependent on its descriptive reference to this quality. Since "All men love the good," how could its name fail to be laudatory? And "good" will lead to agreement or disagreement in attitude, but only because people's approval is attracted or not, in accordance with whether they believe that this quality is present. This is very well, so long as one can identify the quality that is spoken of. If a theorist should insist that he readily recognized some such quality in his experience (or "intuition"), and if he should insist that it is unmistakably "nonnatural"—rather than a "natural" coloring of sensations or imagery that changes with changing attitudes, as Santayana[2]

23. "The Philosophy of Bertrand Russell," *Winds of Doctrine*, sec. i (Scribner's, 1913). This article greatly influenced Russell's subsequent view on ethical analysis.

has urged—then he may be refuted, if at all, only by an elaborate study of the uncertainties of introspection. But "nonnatural" qualities are not urged on this ground. Theorists have adhered to them, as R. B. Perry says, "owing to the force of certain logical and epistemological considerations. They have virtually affirmed that good must be an indefinable quality, however elusive it be empirically."[24] In current literature, the quality is often assumed as a means of escaping the peril of Moore's "Naturalistic Fallacy." [25] This fallacy is indeed fallacious[26] if it provides no distinction between normative ethics and science. But in what way do emotive meaning and disagreement in attitude neglect this distinction? In what way do they fail to preserve the molding influence upon attitudes, which ethical judgments so manifestly have? The inadequacies of analyses that give exclusive emphasis to agreement and disagreement in *belief about* attitudes are serious; but they are not to be corrected by multiplying entities beyond necessity. Unless the "nonnatural" quality can be defended on more positive grounds, it must be taken as an invisible shadow cast by confusion and emotive meaning.

The Sophists saw much that Plato[27] did not see, but only a part of it. Refusing to be blinded by the imagined sun of Plato's realm—which would keep men blind not for some transitional period but for an eternity—they discerned, in the first stages of ordinary scientific vision, only those starker aspects of reality that romantic theory obscures. They saw in their time what so many adolescents find disheartening in our own; the tyrant or dictator shouts out "duty" and "right" to bend a gullible public to his will, and the politician shouts them out to preserve vested

24. *General Theory of Value*, pp. 34 f.
25. *Principia Ethica* (Cambridge University Press, 1903), chap. i.
26. It is not a formal fallacy, however, as William Frankena has argued in his remarkably acute article, "The Naturalistic Fallacy," *Mind*, Vol. LVIII, N.S., No. 192.
27. Throughout the present work it is assumed that Plato can be given the other-worldly interpretation that writers on his ethics have often emphasized. It may easily be the case that these interpretations are one-sided—that there is a Plato whose conceptions have a much more scientific cast than this, and whose references to the objective realm of ideas, to which his ethics seems so intimately related, are largely figurative. If this is so, the criticisms here directed to Plato apply properly only to misguided Platonists. Yet it must be granted that these Platonists have still a strong influence in ethics; and if their master can be summoned against them, rather than in support of them, that is a point which—though it is too controversial to be treated here—could be taken as a welcome amendment to the position that the present volume is defending.

interests and fill his own pocketbook. And the public shouts in its turn, branding all innovation as a violation of its moral inertia. These practices do not easily fit in with one's early dreams; and one who is shocked into seeing them may see them alone, and come to feel that moral judgments are the instruments of swindlers, used by the few to impose on the many, or by the many to impose on the few. But a full vision does not require this conclusion, any more than it requires Platonism. One may recognize a temple as the man-made structure that it is and still see more than the dirt on its floors.

The present analysis can afford no assurance that dictators and self-seeking politicians, whose skill in exhortation is so manifest, "inevitably must" fail, if left unopposed, in reshaping moral codes to serve their narrow interests. Nor can analysis in itself be expected to oppose these men; for it must retain that difficult detachment which *studies* ethical judgments without *making* them. But this much must be said: Those who cherish altruism, and look forward to a time when a stable society will be governed by farsighted men, will serve these ideals poorly by turning from present troubles to fancied realms. For these ideals, like all other attitudes, are not imposed upon human nature by esoteric forces; they are a part of human nature itself. If they are to become a more integral part of it, they must be fought for. They must be fought for with the words "right" and "wrong," else these attitude-molding weapons will be left to the use of opponents. And they must be supported with *clear-minded reasons*, else hypostatic obscurantism will bring contempt to the cause it is intended to plead. The present work, with its humble task of clarification, cannot directly participate in this undertaking; but it certainly does not confine one, after clarity is obtained, to a passive or cynical neutrality.

V

First Pattern: Method

1

THE dictum, "Matters of taste are not to be disputed," is useful so long as it is narrowly understood. For connoisseurs of food and wine it can often terminate an argument that grows tedious. When the dictum is broadened to include artistic taste, however, it encounters too many disputatious volumes of artistic criticism to be comfortably accepted; and when it is broadened still further to include all human attitudes, it must reckon with a literature that extends from the earliest days of writing to the editorials in this morning's newspaper. The reason is by no means mysterious. If a man dislikes a wine that we consider good, we have no ready verbal means of changing him, and little occasion for trying to do so. Although we may urge him to drink what he doesn't like, promising that attention and habituation will finally lead him to like it, prolonged argument on such a point would have only its labor for its pains. But if a man upholds some moral aim to which we are opposed, the matter is quite different. We are more able and more anxious to change a man's attitudes than to change the sensations of his palate. Our attitudes clash with his; and words, which are attitude-molding instruments no less than belief-molding ones, are our habitual servants in resolving the discord. Matters like these are "not to be disputed" only if one is content to survey life with passive detachment, without interest in directing its course.

There are times, of course, when people differ in their attitudes without having a sufficient motive for resolving the difference. They may feel that the difference will lead to no clash; they may be too timid, too aloof, or too economical of their time to make an issue of the matter; they may consider certain men too fixed in their ways to be changed, and others capable of leading their own lives. But that is not always the case. If one man is for war and another for peace, their attitudes may too nearly concern them to permit a quiet tolerance. One cannot live and let live so long as life itself requires concerted social action. The motives for altering attitudes—for arguing and deliberating in a way that may change disagreement in attitude to agreement—therefore become manifold. Nor are they always of the same sort. They range from the advertiser's desires to sell his products to the clergyman's desires to meet his congregation in heaven; they spring from hopes or fears, founded or unfounded, from histrionic desires for power to modest desires for anonymity, from desires for bare subsistence to desires for conspicuous waste.

We shall see far too few of these motives if we view them with Hobbes or with Nietzsche; and we shall still see too few if, reacting from these writers, we find only the ones that they neglected.

The verbal means by which influence is exerted is no less complicated than its motivation. Under certain circumstances the mere use of "ought" or "right," said in a forceful manner, may have a decisive effect. Much must have gone on before; the hearer must be habituated to the force of these terms, he must hold the speaker in esteem, he must have latent attitudes that lead him in the direction urged, and so on; but these circumstances are not infrequently present. Thus strong-minded parents may on occasion influence their children "by a word"; and leaders of all sorts may speedily redirect the attitudes of their devoted followers. The emotive terms may exert their pressure unopposed, needing no supplementary factors beyond those that the circumstances already provide. It is more usually the case, however, that the hearer demands *reasons*. He is neither so docile nor so trusting as to set the speaker up as his ultimate authority. Nor need the speaker always wish to have him do so. A man who accepts every ethical judgment we make, neither asking why nor giving reasons to the contrary, is one from whom we get nothing. Our personality does not grow in contact with his; we find that he becomes our moral dependent. Some of us like to have moral dependents, of course, and others like to be the dependents; but many of us do not care to assume either role. In consequence we often find, and hope to find, that the emotive force of our judgment serves only, in the first instance, to occasion a resistance or counterinfluence. Our hearer then gives reasons for the attitude he urges, and we give reasons for ours.

Perhaps we may end by changing him, or he by changing us; perhaps both of us may come to a middle position; or perhaps we may continue to go in divergent ways, each more confident than ever of being in the right. In any case the argument may be healthful and illuminating, leading far beyond the force of emotive words with which it began.

The reasons which support or attack an ethical judgment have previously been mentioned. Subject to some exceptions that will be noted as we proceed, they are related to the judgment psychologically rather than logically. They do not strictly imply the judgment in the way that axioms imply theorems; nor are they related to the judgment inductively, as statements describing observations are related to scientific laws. Rather, they support the judgment in the way that reasons support imperatives. They serve to intensify and render more permanent the influence upon attitudes which emotive meaning can often do no more than begin. This is possible whenever attitudes are functions of beliefs.

2

LET us examine the methods used in ethical arguments with full attention to details. The study will be continued throughout this chapter and the three that follow, always presupposing the first pattern of analysis; and a parallel study will later be presented for the second pattern. To free the account from misunderstandings, it is necessary to give preliminary emphasis to the following points:

(a) Methodology rarely confines itself to a description of methods that are in current use. It usually goes on to decide which of these are valid and which are not. Thus formal logic distinguishes between valid inferences and the actual ones, often fallacious, that people make; and scientific method distinguishes between a description of what scientists *take* as grounds for an induction and an estimate of the *validity* of such procedures.[1] In ethics, however, we shall be concerned only with a description of the methods often used, not with a discussion of their validity. The reasons for this will be considered in Chapter VII. Meanwhile it may be observed that ethics, to whatever extent its problems extend beyond agreement or disagreement in belief, may in-

1. See J. M. Keynes, *A Treatise on Probability* (Macmillan, 1921), p. 218.

volve methods that extend beyond formal logic and induction; and although we may, if we choose, call some of these methods "valid" and others "invalid," that might extend the usual sense of these terms in a misleading way.

(b) Many modern writers accept the maxim, "To understand what a sentence means, ask how you would verify it." It is not to the present purpose to inquire whether this maxim is essential to science. In ethics we shall find it useful for the second pattern, but only as a rule of thumb. For the first pattern, so long as sentences describing the "verification" of an ethical judgment are identified (as perhaps they should not be) with the reasons that support it, the maxim will be of no service at all. The ethical judgment and its supporting reasons become logically independent by this pattern, apart from exceptions that will be mentioned.

(c) The present approach will not confine its attention to what is "good as an ultimate end" or "good independently of its consequences," as distinct from "good as a means." [2] Most of the examples cited will be of the sort *usually* classified as dealing with what is "good as a means." In point of fact, means and ends are too intimately related to permit even a temporary separation. Those who, accustomed to the traditional emphasis on ultimate ends, and who derogate all other questions to "casuistry," may find the present emphasis strange, and perhaps a laboring of trivialities. But in Chapter VIII, where it is argued that the traditional emphasis represents a confused and impossible specialization, it will become manifest that ethical methodology must inevitably proceed in the pedestrian manner here adopted. Meanwhile the reader must refrain from pressing the remarks that follow into any traditional mold.

When these points are clear, the general outline of first-pattern methodology is very simple: *Any* statement about *any* matter of fact which *any* speaker considers likely to alter attitudes may be adduced as a reason for or against an ethical judgment. Whether this reason will in fact support or oppose the judgment will depend on whether the hearer believes it, and upon whether,

2. In the usage here intended, "X is good as a means" is emotively active, eliciting the hearer's approval of X on account of its (perhaps unspecified) consequences, and indicating the speaker's approval. It must be distinguished, then, from the sense that was illustrated on p. 83. In that sense "good" is emotively *inactive*, being synonymous with "effective," and neither testifies to the approval of the speaker nor influences that of the hearer.

if he does, it will actually make a difference to his attitudes; but it may conveniently be called a reason (though not necessarily a "valid" one) regardless of whether it is accepted or not.

A full psychological explanation of how a reason, when believed, serves to alter attitudes is a matter that we have seen to involve great difficulties, and must not be conceived in any hypostatic way.[3] The fact that beliefs *do* alter attitudes, however, is indubitable, nor is it a discovery of recent date. Throughout Book III of Spinoza's *Ethics* there is an elaborate discussion of just this relationship, much of which is surprisingly modern in its tenor. In Book IV, Proposition VII, Spinoza concludes that "An affect cannot be restrained or removed unless by an opposed and stronger affect." This would suggest, to speak in a contemporary idiom (though with no pretense of exactness), that beliefs alter attitudes in virtue of being intermediaries, as it were, between a given attitude and certain others. A belief reinforces an attitude, or diminishes its strength, by disclosing new objects of favor or disfavor, in such a way that several attitudes act concurrently, with a mutual modification of them all. This may help to explain why the same belief may have different effects upon attitudes, depending upon the temperament of the person who has the belief. But however this may be, we must forego any further analysis of this type, and study ethical methods in their more external aspects.

Further remarks must be in the nature of typical examples, grouped in a way that will serve to classify them, though without any expectation of securing a classification that is exhaustive. The examples are fictitious, since those of current or historical interest would less adequately isolate the several factors that require attention. It will be assumed throughout that the speakers use ethical terms in accordance with the first pattern.

Group I. The examples of this group illustrate some of the ways in which ethical methods resemble factual ones. They present *exceptions* to the rough but useful rule mentioned previously—the rule that ethical judgments are supported or attacked by reasons related to them psychologically, rather than logically.

(1) A: It would be a good thing to have a dole for the unemployed.

3. Cf. pp. 7 f.; 59 f.; and 63–67.

> B : But you have just said that a dole would weaken peo-
> ple's sense of independence, and you have admitted
> that *nothing* which has that consequence is good.

Here B attacks A's position by pointing out a formal inconsistency. In general, ethical statements, like all others that have
at least *some* descriptive meaning, are amenable to the usual
applications of formal logic. Care must be taken, of course, that
verbally seeming contradictions are not merely apparent, due
to a change in sense of the particularly ambiguous ethical terms;
and further care must be taken to avoid emotive repercussions
of otherwise innocent tautologies.[4] Otherwise, this aspect of ethical methodology brings with it no special problems.

> (2) A : It is always wrong to break a promise.
> B : You speak without thinking. There are many cases
> of that sort which you regard without the least dis-
> approval.

B's reply is an empirical assertion, but note that it contradicts
A's judgment (by the first pattern only, of course) and so is logically related to it. A must, in the interest of consistency, either
reject B's assertion, or give up his ethical judgment. (He would
be very likely to qualify his judgment, saying merely that *most*
instances of breaking promises are wrong.)

Even in this simple case, however, we must realize that on
occasion B's statement may be more than it seems. He may
speak in a tone of incredulity, as if he "simply can't believe"
that anyone is *unqualifiedly* opposed to breaking promises, even
though he may suspect that A actually is. By so doing, he may
lead A to worry for fear his attitude is socially "odd," and thus
to come to a state of mind which makes his attitude easier for
B to change.

> (3) A : It is by no means my duty to repay C.
> B : Your moral feelings really torment you for not doing
> so, as you well know. You say you have no duty as a
> feeble effort to quiet your conscience, and free the
> expression of your crude selfishness.

This example is in some respects parallel to the preceding one.
If A's statement descriptively means that he has no moral dis-

---

4. As illustrated on pp. 103–107.

approval of his not paying C, and if B's statement is a rough way of saying that A does have such a moral disapproval, then clearly, B's statement is an empirical one which logically contradicts A's, as was the case in (2) above.

It is here more obvious, however, that the logical opposition is subordinate to one of another sort. B supposes that A has conflicting attitudes—that his moral attitudes oppose what his (allegedly) crude selfishness favors. A is trying not to describe his present moral attitudes, but rather to *mis*describe them (perhaps without being aware of it), in order to weaken their force by a kind of auto-suggestion. Now B, if we are to assume that he typifies many ordinary people, is opposed to this procedure. So when he mentions the "torment" of A's moral feelings, he is far from having a perfectly calm wish to help A introspect. He is forcibly calling these feelings to A's mind, so that A will be prevented from weakening them. If we should see no more in the example, then, than that A and B are making incompatible statements, "one of which cannot possibly be true," we should ignore the main issue. The *truth about* either party's present attitudes is subordinate to their concern in determining what A's attitudes are *later to be*. The main disagreement is one in attitude, since A wants to weaken his moral feelings, and B does not want him to.

It is very often the case, as this example shows, that when people talk about attitudes (even in language which is not strongly emotive) they are less concerned with describing the existing state of attitudes than with altering them by suggestion. The error of treating language as though its function were always cognitive is almost incredibly naïve; and yet it is an error which is largely responsible for the impracticalities of traditional ethical theory.

(4) A: Their friends are all of them shamelessly immoral.
    B: Not knowing them all, you should not generalize so sweepingly.
    A: I know a great number of them, such as C and D and E . . ., and their immorality gives my judgment no little support.

This example is of interest for showing how closely an ethical argument can approximate to ordinary induction. A is arguing from specific judgments, such as "C is immoral," "D is immoral," etc., to the immorality of all members of a class in which C and D, etc., fall. But note that the specific judgments, unlike observation-sentences in science, are open to disagreement in attitude. If they are challenged and are supported by reasons in their turn, the support must ultimately involve arguments unlike (4), and may in fact involve any or all of the other methods that are here being considered. There is no use of induction in ethics that can secure agreement in attitude in the same *direct* way that it can secure agreement in belief.

One may analyze (4), alternatively, as an induction about some unstipulated *factual* characteristics of the people in question, insisting that the ethical element enters only in so far as A "tacitly" makes an adverse judgment about *anyone* having these characteristics. But for logical purposes, "tacit" judgments cannot comfortably be recognized.

Group II. In this group, and those that follow, an ethical judgment is supported or attacked by reasons that are psychologically related to it. Unlike (1) and (2) of Group I, these examples do not call into question the descriptive *truth* of the initial judgment, so long as the judgment describes (in accordance with the first pattern) merely the speaker's present attitudes. They represent efforts to change attitudes, or to strengthen them, by means of altering beliefs. Hence, although the reasons themselves are of an empirical character, and may be rendered probable or improbable by scientific methods, one must not say that they render the ethical judgments "probable" or "improbable" in the same sense. They are simply of a sort that may lead one person or another to have altered attitudes in consequence of altered beliefs, and so, thereafter, to make different ethical judgments.

(5) A: The proposed tax bill is on the whole very bad.
     B: I know little about it, but have been inclined to favor it on the ground that higher taxes are preferable to further borrowing.
     A: It provides for a sales-tax on a number of necessities, and reduces income-tax exemption to an incredibly low figure.
     B: I had not realized that. I must study the bill, and perhaps I shall agree with you in opposing it.

A has supported his ethical judgment by pointing out to B the *nature* of that which is judged. Since B is predisposed to oppose anything of that nature, he shows his willingness to change his attitude, unless, perhaps, further study will disclose matters that weigh the balance to the other side. If B were not a person predisposed to disapprove of the provisions mentioned, however, he would find A's reasons unconvincing, and the argument would probably lead to a discussion of whether these provisions are good or bad. This in turn might lend itself to a use of any of the methods that are being exemplified.

In the sense here intended, the "nature" of an object is given by means of factual, contingent statements about the object itself. In another sense, it is given by statements which, though they appear to be about an object, serve actually to *define a term*—a term which does not clearly or unambiguously designate any object until the definition is given. That is to say, the word "nature" often introduces Rudolph Carnap's "quasi-syntactical idiom." [5] Ethical reasons which are in this idiom—those, for instance, which clarify the meaning of a noun which an ethical adjective has been used to modify—do not fall within the present group. They are of particular importance when judgments use such verbal chameleons as "liberalism," "social equality," and the rest. But since the general theory of definitions and their quasi-syntactical equivalents has often been discussed by others, and since the definitions that are of peculiar interest to ethics will be discussed subsequently,[6] the topic need not be developed here.

(6) A : The proposed tax bill is on the whole bad.
　　B : I know little about it, etc.
　　A : It will put a great burden on the poor, and make little difference to the rich.
　　B : I had not realized that, etc.

This example is parallel to (5), save that A supports his judgment by pointing out the consequences of that which is judged, rather than its nature. The effect of his reason will depend on B's attitude to these consequences.

The distinction between the nature and consequences of anything is clear enough to merit a separate example for each. It must be remembered, however, that there are many border-line

5. *Logical Syntax of Language* (Kegan Paul, 1937), pp. 233–240, and 284–292.
6. Chaps. IX and XIII.

cases where such a distinction is arbitrary; and even in cases where it is readily made, the nature of something is often of interest only because of the consequences it suggests. A's reasons in (5), for instance, would probably not have been accepted by B had they not led him to suppose that the proposed bill would bring with it the consequences explicitly mentioned in (6).

There is no theoretical limit to the number of consequences that may be considered in an ethical argument. Consequences go on without end. In practice, however, they can be known with little certainty when they are remote; and the uncertainty of the remote ones, together with their very remoteness, often makes them have very little effect on present attitudes. Hence many ethical arguments confine attention to the consequence in a not-distant future. Some may wish to call these arguments "short-sighted," with condemnation; others may wish to call them "realistic," with praise. The present work must neither condemn nor praise arguments, nor judge the condemnation or praise of others; but it must be remarked that since arguments of the sort in question differ sharply from one another in many ways, any general condemnation or praise is very likely to be too general.

(7) A: The government ought to put more severe restrictions on the sale of patent medicines.
B: That would interfere with freedom of enterprise.
A: Yes, but it would certainly forward the greatest happiness of the greatest number.

Here consequences are again in question, but consequences of a broader sort.

It is a frequent practice in ethical theory to hold up some very broad kind of consequence as "the" one which determines whether anything ought or ought not be done. We shall subsequently have reason to question this procedure.[7] But however that may be, all of the familiar "ends"—whether those of the utilitarians, or the evolutionists, or the integrators of attitudes, etc.—have their place in ethical methodology as it is commonly applied; nor are they confused when taken as having a *partial* place. Any person who favors one of these broad consequences, and who comes to believe that a given X will help to bring it

7. Chap. VIII and Chap. XV.

about, will thereby be led to favor X—unless some other sort of consequence outweighs this broad one.

Group III. Like the preceding group, this deals with empirical reasons psychologically related to an ethical judgment; but it differs in that the reasons are not limited to the nature and direct consequences of that which is judged. Some of them deal with consequences of another sort, and some have little or nothing to do with consequences.

> (8) A: C's courtesy to his elder friend is admirable.
> B: Perhaps you would speak with less assurance if you knew how anxious he is to have that elderly friend take him into his business.
> A: Yes, that puts the matter in another light.

In this example B mentions not the nature or actual consequences of C's courtesy, but rather the *motives* that attend it. A's attitude to these motives alters his attitude to C's courteous actions and to C himself, so in effect he withdraws his initial judgment.

Moralists have always paid great attention to motives. One reason for this—though doubtless one among many—is very simple. A person's motives are clues to much else. They are grounds for predicting his subsequent actions,[8] and in turn the results of these. Like the nature of an action, its motivation is usually of interest for the consequences it suggests. To whatever extent moralists have been influenced by such matters, their beliefs about attendant motives have influenced their judgments of specific acts. This point has been so well made by John Dewey[9] that it will here require no further attention.

> (9) A: It is your duty to vote.
> B: No, my vote will make no difference to the final outcome.
> A: You could scarcely wish that all others should adopt your ways!

A's rejoinder, reminiscent of Kant's categorical imperative,

---

8. Note that motives, being attitudes and hence dispositions, may be called "causes" of actions only in accordance with the idiomatic use of "cause" mentioned on pp. 52 f.

9. *Human Nature and Conduct,* particularly Pt. I, chap. iii.

unquestionably has its place in common-sense arguments. How may its relevance be explained? Although it does not name any direct consequence of B's stand, it is fertile in suggesting many indirect ones. B may set a precedent to others which he will not welcome. Or he may nullify his influence in *inducing* others to vote, for people are temperamentally suspicious of those who "do not practice what they preach." Or he may develop habits of noncoöperation, which like the motives discussed in (8) may have effects that extend far beyond the present case. These observations are clearly a part of the explanation of the force of A's reason; and to continue the explanation in this way, rather than in Kant's way, seems only in keeping with the principle of parsimony.

It may parenthetically be remarked that the Kantian imperative[10] has this much to be said in its behalf. When a man judges that X is obligatory, his emotive influence extends beyond X to some class of actions into which X falls. In other words, by his very judgment itself he is in the course of making some "maxim" or latent principle[11] more generally accepted. Hence if he cannot "will" that his maxim be generally accepted, he is exerting an influence that he does not want to exert. Now in an intelligible sense (though not the sense of formal logic) this is an "inconsistency"; but it does not require us to recognize a synthetic, a priori dictate of a special faculty of reason, nor does it yield a principle that is sufficient as a basis for normative ethics. It will be obvious that a maxim, being latent, is nothing very precise, that the same action may fall under more than one maxim, and that a given maxim that is willed universal by one person may not be by another. These are difficulties for the Kantian ethics, leading to the familiar criticism that the categorical imperative can be "provided with no content." By the present views, they testify only to the fact that generalizations latent in a particular judgment must become articulate before they are precise, that articulate judgments differ in their generality, and that people disagree in attitude about classes of actions no less than about particular ones, exerting different influences. If the present work mentioning supporting reasons rather than final proofs, cannot

10. In the "first form" only, which in Abbott's translation (*Kant's Theory of Ethics*, 6th ed. p. 18) is stated: "I am never to act otherwise than so that I could also will that my maxim should become a universal law."
11. Cf. p. 95, n. 12.

promise an a priori certainty in ethics, it must be remembered that metaphysical writers, though they make more encouraging promises, do not always keep them.

> (10) A: Extramarital sexual intercourse is sinful.
> B: But only consider why you say so. You are influenced by others, who follow the authority of others still. On back in this chain of authorities there were unquestionably a great many people who were impelled to the view by a need of giving children a secure social status. But these people lived in a time when there were no effective means of birth control. With birth control, extramarital intercourse need no longer have anything to do with illegitimate children and must be viewed in a new moral light.

The position of B is in part concerned with the changed consequences of that which is judged, and to that extent the example is parallel to (6); but it is of further interest because it deals with the *origin* of the *attitude* to which A's ethical judgment testifies. Beliefs about the origin of an attitude, so far from mirroring a dead past, are often important in determining whether or not a man will allow his attitude to continue, and so may serve to alter ethical judgments. The explanation of why this is so, like all the psychological side of ethical methodology, is highly complicated; but a part of the explanation is probably this:

People who have never seriously investigated the origin of their attitudes often invent fictitious explanations. Certain attitudes are either caused by the voice of God, speaking through Conscience, or else by something equally beyond the sight of empirical inquiry. They have a seemingly supernatural sanction which makes people afraid to change them. A naturalistic explanation cuts through these fears, and makes the attitudes more subject to the ordinary causes of change. In particular, an inquiry into origins often discloses arresting parallels between ourselves and primitive peoples. If certain of our attitudes are shown to have the same origin as the taboos of savages, we may become disconcerted at the company we are forced to keep. After due consideration, of course, we may decide that our attitudes, however they may have originated, are unlike many taboos in that they still retain a former function, or have since acquired new ones. Hence we may insistently preserve them. But in the midst of such considerations we shall have been led to see our attitudes in a natural setting, and shall be more likely to change them with changing conditions. Hence anyone who wants to change a man's attitudes can prepare the way by a genetic study.

In the above example there is obviously the "other side" of the issue which B leaves unmentioned. One can easily imagine the argument continuing in this way:

A: What you say of the origin of my feelings may be quite true. But meanwhile you overestimate the effectiveness of present birth-control methods, and people's ability to make intelligent use of them. And again, you overlook all the more subtle consequences. You reckon without jealousy, and without considering that intercourse brings with it emotional ties that are not easily broken. These are matters which lead me to continue my unfavorable attitude, regardless of how my attitude may originally have been formed.

Note that although A accepts the genetic aspects of B's account, he does not reject his initial judgment, and goes on to support it by pointing to consequences as in (5). As was remarked above, a man may know the origin of his attitudes without changing them, if he has other reasons for keeping them as they are. The argument may then continue further, B in turn pointing to further consequences, or to all manner of other considerations, seeking to make a difference to A's attitudes by these means. In particular—and this must be emphasized, not being mentioned elsewhere—B may point to the consequences of the *alternatives* to extramarital intercourse; for ethical situations are often preferential, involving a choice between inevitable alternatives (whether a choice between evils or goods) where the verdict on the one alternative will influence that on the other. A may reply using the same or other methods, but with opposed efforts. Arguments which are ended by the use of one method only are comparatively rare.

As our discussion proceeds it becomes more and more apparent, particularly since many of the methods can appear in the same argument, and repeatedly, how very complicated ethical questions can become. It is partly for that reason, no doubt, that many people consider certain matters "too sacred" to be freely discussed. The factors that determine what our attitudes are to be are so multitudinous and bewildering that most of us are afraid to face them. Even those facts which tend to fortify our present attitudes become troublesomely suggestive of others that will not. A change in habitual attitudes, with all the involved consideration and readjustment that it occasions, is not obtained without cost; yet it is not easy to admit that one lacks the vitality to change with changing times. So rules "beyond all discussion," simplifying the complexities of life, give the cherished illusion that no change is needed. This remark is made not in idle cynicism, but with a full awareness of a problem. The complexities of evaluative questions are all too real, and many people are not capable of dealing with them. One of the great obstacles to the work of a practical moralist lies in finding substitutes for full arguments—methods that will simplify without too gross a distortion. And even when the desire to simplify produces fictions, we must remember, whether we accept them or not, that fictions no less than truths have played an important part throughout the long course of social history.

(11) A: Our schools ought not fail to emphasize the humanities.
       B: Why?
       A: "To seek utility everywhere is entirely unsuited to men that are great-souled and free," as Aristotle has so wisely said.[12]

In this familiar appeal to authority, the effect of the reason will depend on the hearer's respect for the authority in question. If B is predisposed to shape his attitudes in the way that Aristotle directs, he will find A's reason convincing. Otherwise he may question whether Aristotle's authority is in this case *good;* and the argument on the latter point may involve any or all of the methods that we are in the process of studying.

Here again, a consideration of the role of authority in moral history must temper any scorn with which the method of authority may be greeted. "The mass of mankind, including even their rules in the practical departments of life, must, from the necessity of the case, accept most of their opinions on political and social matters, as they do on physical, from the authority of

12. *Politics*, VIII, 3, 1338b.

those who have bestowed more study on those subjects than they generally have it in their power to do." [13]

(12) A : Education is a fine thing.
     B : For some people only.
     A : The consensus of opinion is wholly against you.

This is a variant of the appeal to authority, where the authority is not some one person or text, but rather a large group of people. It is a "band-wagon" argument, particularly appealing to those who fall in with the existent mores.

(13) A : You ought to give the speech, as you promised.
     B : That is unfortunately beyond my power. My health will not permit it.

This example deals with the consequences of a judgment's *influence*. A is endeavoring to influence B to give the speech. If B's reply is true, then whatever influence A's judgment may have on attitudes, it will not have the further consequence of making B speak. Realizing this, A will be likely to withdraw his judgment; he sees that it cannot have its intended effect. We shall later find that the old problem of "free will," so far as it relates to ethics, brings up the same considerations. [14]

In the present case A may withdraw his judgment not merely because it will fail to serve its original purpose, but because it may have effects which he, in kindness, does not desire. It may lead B to be perturbed about his disability.

(14) A : An action like his is outrageous, and deserves no clemency.
     B : But who else, in his circumstances, would have been strong enough to do otherwise? Human nature being what it is, your standards are impracticably severe.

Like the preceding one, this example has to do with the consequence of A's influence. A is building up an unfavorable attitude, hoping to prevent a certain kind of action. B, in effect, says that this attitude would be powerless to prevent actions of that sort, since human nature is so prone to them. Seeing this, A may no longer wish to persist in a judgment that is of little avail.

13. J. S. Mill, *Autobiography* (1873; Oxford World's Classics, 1924), p. 179. Cf. pp. 164 f. of the present work.
14. Chap. XIV.

B's remark may have alternative interpretations, depending on its living context. He may be prepared to acknowledge, for instance, that A's influence would be of some avail, but urge that the influence would bring so many attendant evils, in the way of inhibitions and so on, that the good of stopping the actions would be offset by the cost of the change. The argument might then continue about whether the alleged attendant evils were evils, or about whether these were outweighed by the good consequences. The decision upon this last point would depend upon whether the set of beliefs considered would or would not be collectively sufficient to make A's and B's attitudes converge.

Group IV. In this group B is less concerned with resolving disagreement in attitude than with temporarily evading the force of a disconcerting influence, or altering the means by which it is exerted.

(15)   A: You are much too[15] hard on your employees.
       B: But you, certainly, are not the one to say so. Your own factory would bear investigation far less easily than mine.

B here makes a counterattack. Finding A's judgment humiliating, and hoping to silence him, he insinuates a still more troublesome judgment in reply. He assumes that A would rather desist from his influence than be subject to one of the same kind. The procedure is recognized by many common sayings, such as "People in glass houses should not throw stones."

There may be other sides to this example. B may be appealing to the weakness of human nature, in a way reminiscent of example (14). He may wish to suggest: "You want me to be altruistic in a way that is beyond human attainment, as is shown by the fact that you yourself are incapable of such altruism." Or he may be appealing to A's sense of equality: "Who are you to condemn in me that which you yourself do?" The fact that A may be moved by this latter remark is due to his embarrassment in making an exception of himself—a matter which in turn needs explanation, but which, again in the interest of parsimony, is most plausibly explained not as Kant explained it, but in terms of a purely empirical psychology. Although a complete explanation cannot be attempted here, the following illustration may be

15. Note that "too" is often an ethical term. Here "too hard" has the meaning of "harder than you ought to be."

of interest: If a monarch extolled the virtues of domestic life, and at the same time kept several mistresses, he might in no way be moved by the charge of making an exception of himself. He might urge, and successfully, that it was the special privilege of his rank. But A, in our example, could not follow a parallel course, because, if for no other reason, he would immediately be made the object of ridicule for his presumption. It is not easy to maintain an attitude to which all others are opposed—not because the others will be led to take forcible steps to prevent it, necessarily, but because their very expression of opposition is psychologically "hard to face."

(16) A: You are shamelessly wasting your youth in idleness.
      B: You did the very same thing in your own youth.
      A: I did indeed, and my unfortunate career should be a lesson to you.

Here again B makes a counterattack; but note that it now ceases to be effective. The success of a counterattack depends on whether the opponent is more anxious to escape humiliation than to persist in his influence.

(17) A (speaking to C, a child): To neglect your piano practice is naughty.
      B (in C's hearing): No, no, C is very good about practicing. (Out of C's hearing): It's hopeless to drive him, you know; but if you praise him he will do a great deal.

Here B is not opposed to the general direction of A's influence on C, but wishes to change the manner in which it is exerted. Examples of this kind are so common, and illustrate the hortatory effect of ethical judgments so obviously, that it is difficult to understand why emotive meaning in ethics was not recognized in the earliest theories. B's last remark serves to point out the consequences of the sorts of influence exerted, much as in (13) and (14).

(18) A: You ought to vote for him, by all means.
      B: Your motives for urging me are clear. You think that he will give you the city contracts.

Here B, by showing that he "sees through" the motivation of A's judgment, hopes to put an end to A's efforts. A may continue to address the same judgment to others, but is not likely, if B's charge is obviously correct, to continue to urge B—either because he sees that the procedure will be unsuccessful or because he wishes to escape the humiliation of B's accusation.

If A's tone of voice indicates that "ought" is used in a peculiarly moral sense, B may in part be indicating that A is misdescribing his own attitude. His attitude is in fact a mere self-interest, but he masquerades it as being something else. To that extent the example would be parallel to (3).

The list of illustrations given throughout this section is incomplete, even for indicating the broad heads under which ethical methods may be classified; but a more exhaustive list would be beyond any practical need. It must be emphasized, however, that ethical reasoning need not be confined to terse, isolated supporting statements, as our simple examples may too easily suggest. An ethical judgment is often supported by the systematic presentation of a whole *body* of beliefs, in which specific (factual) conclusions are subsumed under more general ones, and each conclusion is weighed with regard to its probability. One need only turn, say, to a book which defends a particular form of government (democratic, or communistic, etc.) to see that an elaborate structure of economic and psychological theory, supplemented by conclusions drawn from history, sociology, and many other fields, may be used in its entirety as a means of strengthening or redirecting attitudes in the light of beliefs. Such structures of theory are of a scientific character, of course; but they involve applied science, rather than pure science—being utilized as supports for moral judgments, and being organized and classified, accordingly, in a way that *selects out* the beliefs that will have the greatest bearing on the attitudes that are to be guided. We shall see this more clearly in Chapter VIII. It must be remarked, meanwhile, that any such selection from scientific conclusions *need* not involve, consciously or unconsciously, the *omission* of factors that might argue against the ethical aim that a writer may have. That this actually happens, in the case of some writers, is obvious. But another possibility remains, which many writers earnestly strive to realize: that of giving the arguments which may support "the other side" their full attention, and balancing them off against those which support the aims that are advocated.

The ethical function of a systematic body of knowledge, though of enormous importance, is in the nature of the case too complicated to be illustrated here in detail. There is ground to suppose, however, that a full study of it would disclose only an elaborate interweaving of the reasons that our simple examples have presented. Except for cases like those of Group I, the relation of beliefs to attitudes would remain a psychological one, involving the *resultant* effect on attitudes of a great number of beliefs.

3

UNTIL now only the interpersonal aspects of ethical method have been considered. Reasons have been taken as instruments whereby one person supports a view that he is recommending to another, or criticizes a view that the other is recommending to him. These interpersonal aspects are of unquestionable interest, but they are not representative of all ethical reasoning. There are times when a person is faced not with the need of convincing others, or deliberating with them, but rather with a problem of convincing himself. Nor is the latter problem an easy one. People of all ages and circumstances—the schoolboy puzzled about "fair play," the adolescent perplexed about sexual morality, the mature man torn between divided responsibilities—continually find problems which are difficult to settle in their own minds. Deliberation with others, though helpful, may fail to resolve the difficulty; and whether or not they can convince others, once they have made their ethical decision, sometimes seems to them a relatively unimportant matter. Thus the following question, hitherto neglected, will require careful attention: By what methods of reasoning do people make up their own minds about what is good or bad, right or wrong?

The question is complicated in its details. People make their ethical decisions in many different ways. In outline, however, it can be answered quite simply, and in a way that follows so naturally from our previous considerations that it brings with it little novelty. To understand this let us consider how a personal decision arises.

When does a person feel the need of making up his mind about what is right or wrong? Not, certainly, when his attitudes speak with one voice, urging him in a definite direction. His mind is then already made up, and his only problem is one of execution. Rather, the need of a personal ethical decision arises from a *con-*

flict of attitudes. The individual's attitudes do *not* speak with one voice, but urge him both this way and that, with the net result of leaving him in a painful and inactive state of irresolution. Conflict and ethical indecision are the same; and indecision is replaced by decision only when conflict is resolved. John Dewey has given so much emphasis to this that perhaps it had better be put in his own words:

The occasion of deliberation is an *excess* of preferences, not natural apathy or absence of likings. We want things that are incompatible with one another; therefore we have to make a choice of what we *really* want, of the course of action, that is, which most fully releases activities. Choice is not the emergence of preference out of indifference. It is the emergence of a unified preference out of competing preferences.[16]

From this it can be seen that the personal aspects of ethics are not very different from the interpersonal ones. The former involve conflict; the latter, when they are controversial, involve disagreement in attitude. Conflict and disagreement in attitude are much the same, since conflict occurs (to speak roughly but not ineptly) when an individual disagrees in attitude with himself. So the personal aspects of ethics reveal the same opposition within an individual that has previously been seen within a group.

In personal decisions we again find reasons which are psychologically related to the judgment in which they eventuate. The resolution of conflict requires a modification of one of the conflicting attitudes, and reasons become relevant to the extent that they bring this about. A reason which a man seeks for himself, to change his own attitudes, will not be greatly different from one that he uses in arguing with a friend.

More specifically: Suppose that in time of war a man is making up his mind whether or not to be a conscientious objector. Let us assume that he respects the aim for which his country is fighting, feeling strongly "bound" to work for it, and that this attitude (which in any typical case will be reinforced by many others, such as an urge to social conformity, a desire for new experiences, etc.) presses him to serve. On the other hand, let us assume that he has a strongly developed sentiment against taking any man's life, and that this attitude (again mingled, per-

16. *Human Nature and Conduct* (Modern Library ed.), p. 193.

haps, with desires to remain with his dependents, fears of being killed himself, etc.) presses him not to serve. A conflict of attitudes is accordingly present, and his ethical deliberation will take the form of developing such beliefs as will cause one set of attitudes to predominate over the other. Perhaps, then, he will inquire more fully into the services for which he is eligible, or into the consequences of his serving, including the precedent he would establish for others, the sacrifices that his serving would require for his family, and so on. These considerations are parallel to those of Group II of the preceding section. They may elicit new attitudes, fortifying one side or the other in his internal conflict. Again: perhaps he will consider in detail just what kind of attitudes are motivating him. He may find that his opposition to fighting springs in large measure from a fear of being killed, his pride having hitherto led him to misdescribe it as an attitude of a more altruistic and humane sort. Seeing clearly the nature of his attitude, he may inhibit it out of shame. The procedure is reminiscent of example (7) of Group II, and of the remarks toward the end of (3), Group I. Alternatively: the man might consider the *origin* of some of his attitudes. He may previously have believed, or half-believed, that his dread of killing anyone was the prompting of a God-given voice, but on reflection come to believe that it was a product of natural causes. This may prepare the way for making this attitude subordinate to the others, just as has been noted in the discussion of example (10). So one might continue, showing all manner of ways in which personal decisions are analogous to interpersonal ones.

A personal decision is an extremely complicated matter, often requiring knowledge drawn from many fields of inquiry. To say that a decision is "nothing but" a manifestation of one's preferences is to speak with little discernment. It is certainly not a matter of becoming introspectively aware of one's present attitudes—for when a decision is required these attitudes have no definite direction. Rather, it is a matter of systematizing one's actual and latent attitudes in a way that *gives* them definite direction. This requires knowledge of the natural and social sciences (and their less formal, common-sense counterparts) which show the relations between the objects of one's attitudes; and it requires a thorough knowledge of one's self—of the permanence of one's attitudes, the degree to which they may be sublimated, the effects of sharply inhibiting them, and so on. When major conflicts are involved, the difficulties of making ethical decisions are enormous. That is why biographers recognize them as crucial aspects of a man's life. And that is why so many people, consciously or unconsciously trying to avoid the *turmoils* of decision, shelter themselves from new experiences, and blind themselves to such facts as may impede the routine expression of the attitudes they have socially inherited.

The intellectual processes that attend ethical deliberation are all of them concerned with matters of fact. They do not exhibit the exercise of some *sui generis* faculty of "practical reason," sharply different from some other reasoning faculty. Reasons and reasoning processes become "practical" or "ethical" depending upon their psychological milieu; when they direct attitudes they are "practical." This relational characteristic does not change their nature, nor does it free *them* from the ordinary canons of inductive logic. The process of making an ethical decision is something more, of course, than the process of formulating factual beliefs; but that is simply because reasons, in addition to their cognitive nature, have conative-affective *effects*. An ethical decision requires a full or partial resolution of conflict, and no set of beliefs can be *identical* with this, however much it may contribute to it. Here again the parallel to our previous considerations is plain: just as agreement in attitude, even when it is achieved by reasons, is not identical with agreement in belief, so the resolution of internal conflict, even when it is achieved by altering and broadening one's beliefs, is not identical with these beliefs. But it remains the case that the rational methods which are available for making ethical decisions are wholly those of acquiring and ordering beliefs, and that these beliefs need not be concerned with any esoteric subject matter.

A man who resolves a conflict with the help of beliefs is not necessarily engaged in *psychological* inquiry. He is *mentally* going *through* the processes which a psychologist *studies;* he is *using* beliefs (which may be about many subjects) to resolve his conflict, not developing other beliefs *about* how this happens. The view that normative ethics is a branch of psychology, often advanced by those who are anxious to escape a supersensible ethics, and who see no third alternative, fosters insidious confusions. In the first place, it implies that ethical conclusions can be founded on some *one* science, and so can be left to the hands of specialists; whereas we have seen, and shall later see more clearly, that moral questions may lead one to all fields of inquiry. In the second place, it overintellectualizes normative ethics, and gives a purely cognitive appearance to a subject that in fact occupies the whole of one's personality. A psychologist has only to understand; he must simply *cognize* conflicts. A man faced with a moral decision must do more than cognize; he must put his beliefs to work in reorienting his emotional life.

4

So close is the parallel between the interpersonal and personal aspects of ethics, that any effort to give equal emphasis to both would lead to tedious redundancy. Let us be content, then, to emphasize only the interpersonal ones, treating the personal ones largely by implication. This must not be allowed to suggest that the personal aspects are less important. The interpersonal ones will be emphasized only because they have so often been slighted in traditional theory, and because they illustrate, far better than the personal ones, the degree to which a proper understanding of ethics involves a proper understanding of language.

Let us accordingly turn back, and ask whether methods like those of Section 2 can hope to be definitive. The answer has been suggested previously,[17] but it will be well to present it with greater care.

When a speaker makes ethical judgments that are formally contradictory,[18] a strict refutation is possible. But note that the speaker need give up only one of his judgments, formal logic being unable to determine which. Note further that only such an indefinite *disproof* is final. Judgments which are consistent may nonetheless be rejected. Judgments which are analytic either may be rejected for their emotive repercussions,[19] or else will be devoid of normative interest. The following will instance the latter alternative: "If he ought to do it, it would be wrong for him not to do it." Such a statement is justified by logic (though not without the definitions previously suggested[20]); but its content-less nature prevents it from either indicating the direction of the speaker's attitudes or influencing that of the hearer's. It serves only as a linguistic rule. Note further that although one may con-

17. Chap. II, pp. 30 f.
18. As in (1), pp. 115 f.
19. As explained on pp. 103–107, particularly p. 105.
20. See p. 100.

struct a valid syllogism with ethical premises and an ethical conclusion, the acceptance of the conclusion will depend on that of the premises. The premises will not be guaranteed by logic alone, unless they are of the contentless sort just mentioned. In short, formal logic can provide *necessary* conditions to the rational acceptance of normatively interesting ethical judgments, but not *sufficient* ones.

When a speaker is opposed by an *empirical* reason that contradicts the descriptive meaning of his judgment—as when A, having said "It is right," is told "You really do not approve of it"[21]—there is again a *dis*proof, final to whatever extent the empirical reason is established. But the reason, if established, is sufficient to refute A only, and only at the time in question. Another person, acknowledging that A really does not approve of what he calls "right," may himself really approve of it, and insist that it *is* right. For him the reason will be unavailing; and indeed A himself may change his attitude later on, and then insist that it is right in a way that the reason will no longer truthfully attack. Thus the reason may conceivably do no more than make A withdraw his judgment for a limited time. It must be acknowledged that the reason, "X is not approved of by anyone at any time," will, if established, permanently refute any favorable judgment of X, no matter who makes it; but such reasons can be established for only a very limited number of X's.

When a speaker's judgment is supported or attacked by empirical reasons psychologically related to it,[22] it is even more obvious that no exhaustive method, convincing to all people under all circumstances, can confidently be hoped for. This remains the case no matter how many reasons are used conjointly in the same argument, and no matter how systematically they are developed. Reasons may easily convince some people, and in certain cases may eventually convince all people; but there are conceivable cases in which no set of reasons, numerous though they may be, would be convincing; nor, in such cases, need either of the disagreeing parties be making any error of fact or logic. It is possible, of course, to prove or render probable the reasons themselves—to test *them* by the ordinary procedures of inductive or deductive logic; but to prove the reasons is a different matter

21. Cf. (2), p. 116; but note the comment following (3), p. 117.
22. Like any of those in Groups II, III, and IV of Sec. 2.

from using the reasons to prove an ethical judgment. It is in regard to the latter point that finality may be impossible.

A brief explanation of *why* ethics may lack any definitive method of proof has been given previously,[23] and need not be repeated here. It may be well to recall, however, that *granted an assumption*, one may hope that ethical agreement *can* be obtained by reasons. This assumption may conveniently be restated in somewhat different terms:

Let us say that disagreement in attitude is "rooted in" disagreement in belief whenever the former can be reconciled by reconciling the latter. For instance, if A approves of X and B does not, and if they are not content merely to "differ," there will be a disagreement in attitude, regardless of its source. But if this disagreement ends when the parties reach similar beliefs about X, then it will be said to be "rooted in" disagreement in belief. The assumption in question can now be stated in this simple way:

All disagreement in attitude is rooted in disagreement in belief.

Strictly speaking, this assumption insures that rational methods will be convincing in ethics only to the extent that they, in turn, are sufficient to bring about agreement in belief; but even so one may hope, granted the assumption, that the growth of empirical knowledge will slowly lead to a world of enlightened moral accord. The assumption itself, however, must be used with caution. Since the days of Hume, who made a somewhat similar assumption,[24] we have learned how problematical any psychological generalization, even when it is less sweeping than this one, must inevitably be.

That there are *some* cases for which the assumption holds is scarcely to be doubted. When people are ignorant of the means to ends vital to them all, their divergent evaluations may easily be rooted in their beliefs. But other cases may be of a different sort. Some ethical disagreements *seem* rooted, rather, in the scarcity of what people want. Several nations may urge that their crowded and suffering populations give them the right to take a disputed territory. Others *seem* rooted in temperamental differences, as when an oversexed, emotionally independent ado-

23. See p. 31.
24. For a discussion of Hume's assumption, and a comparison of his analysis with the present one, see Chap. XII, Sec. 5.

lescent argues with an undersexed, emotionally dependent one about the desirability of free love. In these cases the growth of science may, for all that we can now know, leave ethical disagreement permanently unresolved.

To be sure, a person can always say that the disagreement is rooted in one in belief, even for these cases; and the complexity of the situations will free him from any immediate refutation. It may always be that when nations dispute a colonial right, all but one would withdraw their claims *if* the full truth were known about consequences, precedents, motives, and so on. That is possible in the sense that it cannot categorically be refuted; but its opposite is also possible. It is even possible that increased knowledge would be hostile to ethical agreement. Plato tacitly assumed so, perhaps, when he urged that the guardians should be taught not the truth about their ancestors, but rather deliberately romanticized untruths.[25] He felt that moral stability could not endure a general dissemination of knowledge, even in a utopian state.

How are we to test the assumption? The ideal procedure would be to experiment in a world where all men had the last word of factual knowledge, and observe whether any disagreement in attitude remained. This being manifestly impossible, one has only indirect procedures, based on the natural laws that seem to govern human beings in their environment. What is now known of these laws is assuredly not enough for any well-founded conclusion. In psychology and the social sciences, particularly, there can be little pretence of knowing the essential facts, and still less pretence of knowing dependable laws. Hence any assurance that may attend the assumption must be tempered by a scientific caution. One may, of course, have occasion tentatively to accept the assumption. There can be no assurance that it will *not* hold in any given case, and its adoption may be beneficial in prolonging the enlightenment of discussion. One may even cling to it in desperation, as the only hope of settling issues that may otherwise lead to serious discord. But that is not to say that it is well confirmed. A victim of a fatal disease may put implicit faith in the belief that medical research will find a cure for it before he dies. We respect the belief as he maintains it, but do not counte-

---

25. *Republic*, 389. "The rulers of the state . . . , in their dealings either with enemies or with their own citizens, may be allowed to lie for the public good." Only the rulers were to be granted this privilege, however.

nance it in a scientific text that deals with the probable developments of medicine.

It must be observed, however, that although the assumption is lacking in confirmation, it is at least free from the fantastic implications that might too easily be ascribed to it. It does not imply, for instance, that all individual differences in temperament are a product of ignorance, and that the growth of science would make men behave with monotonous uniformity. Although individual differences may sometimes prevent ethical agreement, they need not always do so. If the assumption were true, and if all men had unlimited knowledge, it might still be the case that some would be artists, others manufacturers, others athletes, and so on. Men may differ in the way they wish to lead their lives without having attitudes that clash. Both A and B, for instance, may agree in wanting A to be an artist, and agree in wanting B to be a manufacturer. Again, under the above conditions, it might be that different nations would have different forms of government. Nations C and D might agree that a nation like C ought to be democratic, and that a nation like D, facing different problems, ought to be communistic. One must not think, here, that the nations must disagree in attitude simply because each wants for itself a different form of government. When C wants democracy in C, and D wants communism in D, the restricting phrases, "in C" and "in D," keep the objects of attitude distinct, and the attitudes need not necessarily be opposed. Should C want democracy in C, and D want communism *in C*, then the attitudes would indeed be opposed; but that is another matter, and there could be differences among nations without this kind of difference. Hence the assumption we are discussing does not look to a future with drab and fantastic uniformities of conduct, but only to one in which there is a freedom from opposition and discord.

Yet an assumption that is not fantastic may nevertheless be false, nor have we any trustworthy assurance that it is true. Our conclusions about the finality of rational methods in ethics must accordingly be hypothetical:

If any ethical dispute *is* rooted in disagreement in belief, it may be settled by reasoning and inquiry to whatever extent the beliefs may be so settled. But if any ethical dispute is *not* rooted in disagreement in belief, then no *reasoned* solution of any sort is possible.

VI

Persuasion

1

WE have seen that the rational methods used in normative ethics may lack finality, even in theory. That they
are not final in practice, amid the complexities of applying them, is evident on every hand. What recourse is there,
then, for one who despairs of a reasoned solution? Must he be
content with a continued disagreement, or may he support his
ethical position in some other way? That is to say, are there any
methods of settling ethical disagreement that are "nonrational"?

That there are such methods is perfectly obvious. Their nature
and *modus operandi* can be explained in this fashion:

The resolution of an ethical argument requires a resolution of
disagreement in attitude, and so requires that the attitudes of one
party or the other (or both) be changed or redirected. One way
of changing attitudes proceeds *via* changes in beliefs. Such a
procedure is characteristic of the rational methods, as illustrated
in the preceding chapter. But there are other ways of altering a
man's attitudes—ways that are not mediated by reasons which
change beliefs. Like all psychological phenomena, attitudes are
the outcome of many determining factors, and beliefs figure as
but one set of factors among others. To the extent that the *other*
factors are subject to control in the course of an argument, and
so may contribute to changes in a man's attitudes, they both can
be and are used as a means of securing ethical agreement. Such
procedures constitute the "nonrational methods" of ethics, which
must now be studied.

The most important of the nonrational methods will be called
"persuasive," in a somewhat broadened sense. It depends on the
sheer, direct emotional impact of words—on emotive meaning,
rhetorical cadence, apt metaphor, stentorian, stimulating, or
pleading tones of voice, dramatic gestures, care in establishing
rapport with the hearer or audience, and so on. Any ethical

judgment, of course, is itself a persuasive instrument; but in the use of persuasive "methods" the effects of an initial judgment are intensified by *further* persuasion. A redirection of the hearer's attitudes is sought not by the mediating step of altering his beliefs, but by *exhortation*, whether obvious or subtle, crude or refined. For some people persuasion will have a quite transitory effect unless it is elaborately supplemented by the use of rational methods. For other people this may not be the case. It is perhaps not rash to say, however, that *any* person, no matter how reason-loving he may be, will be influenced more strongly and permanently by persuasion *and* reasons than he will be by reasons alone. That, in good measure, is why the style of normative ethical works is so different from that of scientific treatises, and why such phrases as "moral exhortation" and "impassioned moral plea" come to be familiar idioms.

Persuasion is nonrational in a sense that must be contrasted with irrational, no less than with rational. Irrational methods are rational in the sense of "reason-using," and are distinguished by the fact that the reasons themselves (as distinct from the judgments they support in turn) are defended by invalid methods. But nonrational methods go beyond the use of reasons altogether—always provided, of course, that the term "reasons" is to designate statements that express beliefs.

As additional methods that are nonrational (using "method" in a broad sense) one might recognize the use of material rewards and punishments, and also (for instance) the various forms of public demonstration and display. But for present purposes it will suffice to consider persuasive methods alone. They are particularly important because they employ, no less than rational methods, the ready-made resources of language, and so become an integral part of ordinary arguments. In many cases there is so close a wedding of persuasive and rational methods that no little discernment is needed to distinguish them. Practice in making this distinction is mandatory; for whether one wishes to use persuasion or avoid it, to accept it or resist it, one must recognize it for what it is.

2

A STUDY of persuasive methods is so largely a study of the emotive use of words, and hence subject to implicit treatment throughout the whole of this work, that it need not be developed here in any detail; but a few instances, providing opportunity for basic observations, can conveniently be listed. The numbers are a continuation of those in the preceding chapter.

Group V. This group is distinguished by the fact that the supporting statements, and not merely the initial judgments, have an effect which is predominatingly (though not wholly) emotive.

> (19) A: It is morally wrong for you to disobey him.
> B: That is precisely what I have been denying.
> A: But it is your simple *duty* to obey. You ought to obey him in the sheer interest of moral obligation.

Here there is a reiteration of ethical terms. "Duty," "ought," and "moral obligation" do not provide any additional information beyond that given by the initial "wrong" (so long as the first pattern is presupposed), but with proper emphasis they may have a strong cumulative effect on B's attitudes.

> (20) A: He had no right to act without consulting us.
> B: After all, he is the chairman.
> A: Yes, but not the dictator. He violated democratic procedure.

In important respects this example resembles (5) of Group II.[1] The mention of "dictator" and "violated democratic procedure" serves to *classify* that which was judged, thereby pointing out its nature. To that extent A's method is rational, and will be convincing to the extent that B disapproves of anything so classifiable. But obviously, "dictator" and "democratic" do not have a descriptive function only. They have an emotive meaning which, if largely dependent on their descriptive meaning,[2] is not wholly so; and the emotive meaning is not unlikely to make a difference to B's attitudes. A's method is persuasive, then, to whatever extent this emotive effect, intensified by the circumstances of utterance, *augments* the attitude-changing effect of the rational method that it accompanies.

Arguments which exemplify a mixture of persuasion and rationality are common. *Purely* persuasive methods are seldom found—and indeed our language itself militates against them, for there are very few words which have an emotive meaning only. Although emotive terms are often descriptively vague and

1. Pp. 118 f.
2. See pp. 72 f.

ambiguous, we can seldom make interjections of them without distorting language; and even if we should do so, they would continue to suggest[3] the information that we somewhat arbitrarily said they did not mean.

Just as few arguments are wholly persuasive, so few are wholly rational. What words could A have used in the above example *in place of* "dictator" and "democratic"? Substitutes might involve a pedantic circumlocution that would persuade against his contention just as much as these terms persuade for it. In some cases, of course, words will be available whose emotive meaning is negligible. In other cases this is not so, and one must, if he wishes to use rational methods exclusively, either neutralize emotive meaning by his tone of voice, or give explicit admonitions that the persuasive effect of the words must be discounted, or oppose laudatory and derogatory terms in such a way that the net emotive effect is canceled out. It will be obvious that writers and speakers seldom have occasion to isolate the cognitive aspects of an ethical argument so rigidly. (Some of the arguments considered in the preceding chapter have accordingly a slight persuasive element, in addition to the rational one they seek to illustrate.)

> (21) A: Freedom of speech is our inalienable right.
>   B: Only within certain limits.
>   A: Within *no* limits. Is the servant of truth to be imprisoned within the gray walls of popular opinion?

Persuasion is here effected by a metaphor. B will certainly not take "servant" and "imprisoned in gray walls" literally, for the dispositions that constitute literal meanings are not fully realized in such a context; but the emotive meaning of these terms, their actual effect being intensified by the descriptive meaning (even though the latter is not "taken literally"), may act to make freedom of speech become more strongly the object of B's approval.[4]

We have previously seen that a metaphor lends itself to an interpretation or interpretations.[5] In the present case a plausible interpretation would be, "If we do not have freedom of speech, popular opinion will make the discovery of truth more difficult." Shall we say that any metaphor, on account of its possible inter-

3. See p. 70.
4. See pp. 49, 73 ff.
5. P. 74.

pretations, may serve not only to persuade but also to give a *reason* for an ethical judgment? Though the question presents a border-line case of classification, there is a convenience, perhaps, in answering it in the negative. Metaphors simply *suggest* what their interpretations descriptively *mean;* and their suggestiveness is often too vague to permit them to pass as reasons. But however this may be, the possibility of giving interpretations is manifest; and in certain cases most hearers will agree in giving the same interpretations. This must serve to caution us against giving the persuasive aspects of metaphor a disproportionate emphasis, and against feeling that exhortation and information are mutually exclusive.

It must be remarked that when a sentence uses only a "sleeping" metaphor, there can be no doubt that it is to be classified as a reason, even though it may have emotive effects as well. Thus should A above have said that the suppression of free speech "throws obstacles in the way of" the discovery of truth, his phrase would retain a clear, habitually realized descriptive meaning, in spite of its sleeping spatial metaphor, and could be taken as a fairly strict synonym of "prevents." In such a case the metaphor is so frequently interpreted in a fixed way that the correlation between it and its interpretation itself becomes a special linguistic rule. The phrase becomes an "idiom," in which the component words, behaving somewhat like component syllables in one long word, are no longer fully subject to the linguistic rules that govern their use in other contexts, but have a rule which governs them as a group. Note that such phrases as "on the whole" and "by and large" likewise behave as if one long word, with their own special rules rather than those evident from their component words. But these, being idioms of a nonmetaphorical origin, do not readily suggest their composite meaning prior to a special rule; whereas idioms of a metaphorical origin do so, the special rule simply making the descriptive reference of the whole context more precise. It is always possible, of course, to "wake up" a sleeping metaphor by bringing the rules for its component words into play, letting these temporarily take precedence over the special rule—a procedure which enriches the range of further interpretations. (This has an analogue in ordinary ambiguity; it is rather like taking the word "man," in "Our leader is a man," first in the sense of "male" and next in the more richly suggestive sense of "one who has strength of character.") The use of sleeping metaphors that are easily awakened is often a subtle way of combining rational and persuasive methods; for such expressions, even in contexts that are overtly descriptive, may have no little force as a consequence of quasi-dependent[6] emotive meaning.

> (22) A (after much previous exhortation): Deception is always bad policy.
>
> B: Doesn't it sometimes succeed?
>
> A (in impressive tones): Never. It is always detected before it achieves its insidious purpose.

In this example, which belongs only peripherally to the present group, it will be obvious that A's final remark is not easily confirmed, and is likely to involve wishful thinking. Yet A's impressive tones, assisted by the general mood that he has previously built up, may induce B to accept his remark without careful criticism. Perhaps one may call this, though in an extended sense, a persuasive method for establishing an ethical judgment. But it must be distinguished from those previously illustrated. In our strict sense, a method is persuasive to the extent that it supports a judgment by means that go beyond the mediation of articulate beliefs. Here the support of the judgment *is* mediated by an articulate belief, and it is the belief which is persuasively supported.

(23) We must now consider an example which cannot be developed in detail; and indeed, a proper analysis of it would require an extended study. But let us deal with it to the extent that space will allow.

Suppose that a writer is in full, altruistic sympathy with a certain minority group in his country, whose rights he feels to be neglected. He cannot easily make known their needs, since their way of living is one with which most people are totally unfamiliar. A bare, external description of them would be imperfectly understood. So he presents his views in the form of a didactic novel. He succeeds in recreating typical aspects of their life, leading his readers imaginatively to live among them, and encounter their problems. The readers can then more readily understand the minority group in question, drawing from a kind of introspection that has been extended through *einfühlung;* and they may be able to learn more in this way than ever they could from a formal, sociological study.

How shall the writer's methods, used to support his didactic

6. See pp. 78 f.

aim, be classified? In certain respects they seem clearly to be rational. No matter what means the writer used in *communicating* beliefs to his readers, no matter how much the beliefs may have been fashioned by einfühlung, they will remain empirically true or false, and open to the usual tests. We need only recall a distinction that is often made in scientific method. The psychological route by which a hypothesis is reached is usually quite different from the steps that confirm or disconfirm it; and any peculiarities in its origin, provided it is confirmable, do not deprive it of a scientific status. Similarly for the present case. The beliefs which the writer communicates to his readers will support his didactic aim in the way that reasons do, regardless of the einfühlung on which their origin depends.

In certain other respects the methods will differ from rational ones. Some of the beliefs that are in question, for instance, may be very faintly suggested by the language used, rather than crystallized in a literal way. It may then be misleading to say that "reasons" are being given, as we have just seen in the case of metaphor.[7] And some of the beliefs may be presented *along with* praise or condemnation. The einfühlung which attends them may have a double purpose, first of enabling the beliefs to be communicated, and second of altering the readers' favor or disfavor, *independently* of beliefs, to the issues that are being discussed. To the latter extent the methods will be persuasive.

But even when einfühlung is used solely to forward rational methods, we must remember that it will require, on the part of the writer, far more than a use of descriptive meanings. It will require, as well, an attention to emotive and pictorial meanings, and to the phonetic factors that contribute (always in conjunction with meanings) to rhythms and cadences in style.

A didactic novel, then, clearly illustrates how the several aspects of language can coöperate, all in support of an ethical judgment. And in particular, it illustrates how the nondescriptive aspects of language need not always be persuasive, but can actively forward the use of rational methods.

(24) A: Our race deserves to have special privileges.
B: Why?
A: Because there are unperceivable forces in the universe that are struggling to make us dominate all others.

7. P. 143.

The supporting statement apparently gives *information* about the race in question, which might in turn lead B to share A's attitudes. Thus the method *seems* rational. And indeed, there would be no doubt about its being so—since it would be rational (i.e., "reason-using" but not necessarily "valid") whether or not the reasons were true, and whether or not it had any *actual* effect on B's attitudes—if the force mentioned were "unperceivable" in some sense that implied only the limitation of our present ability to perceive, or in some sense that permitted, if not a direct perception of the force, at least a set of indirect observations which tested its presence or absence. But suppose that the force is alleged to be unperceivable in the very nature of the case—to be of the kind that makes no possible difference to our experience. The supporting statement then becomes suspect, according to the views of many contemporary empiricists and some historical ones, of having no descriptive meaning at all. It has the appearance (they would urge) of a descriptive meaning, due to its verifiable analogues; but in fact it has only confused meaning, together with emotive meaning dependent on confused meaning and perhaps pictorial meaning,[8] and so does not exemplify a reason. Such in effect is the currently familiar contention, and as applied to the present case it is not likely to meet with much opposition. There are, however, certain metaphysical statements which resemble A's in being transempirical, but which are by no means obviously confused. The status of their meaning is still a matter of controversy.

A resolution of this controversy would have a bearing on the present work. The question "Has X's remark a descriptive meaning or a confused one?" is perplexing in part because "descriptive" and "confused" have not been sharply enough defined. Even so, the issue cannot receive attention here. The precise definition of "descriptive meaning," which in turn requires a precise definition of "cognitive," is a matter of great difficulty.[9] This term, like all others, cannot profitably be made precise unless the purposes for which it is used are fully clarified; and this in turn (there being "no immaculate conception of purposes") requires a detailed investigation into the many specific and problematic situations with which the term is expected to deal. Unable to undertake this complicated task, the writer must be content to

8. See pp. 78 ff.
9. Cf. pp. 62–67.

remain silent on the controversial points. So long as only the status of this or that reason is in question, the matter will not be of great importance to ethics. When certain other aspects of ethics are in question, however—as when the *ethical terms* are alleged to refer to a supersensible realm—the matter becomes too vital to be neglected. Here the charge of confusion will continue to be made, and will be provided, it is hoped, with an adequate defense. Limited to this special class of unverifiables, the problem becomes more workable; nor will it require a tedious refutation of all the extramundane theorists. The constructive aim of this study—that of setting up a practicable analysis of ethics without departing from the world of experience—is itself a partial answer to those who claim that another course is necessary.

For sentences whose meaning is confused beyond any reasonable doubt, as example (24) may be presumed to illustrate, there will usually be no little emotive meaning dependent on confused meaning. It is accordingly convenient to recognize such sentences as persuasive, and similarly, we must recognize sentences that express quasi-myths, somewhere between beliefs and daydreams, imperfectly distinguished. But we must guard against any precipitous or impatient use of "persuasive" which suggests (like the corresponding use of "emotive") that all persuasion is confused, or which damns a statement as confused before making evident that a confusion exists.

3

IT was previously observed [10] that methodology must consider not only how people proceed to convince others, but also how they make up their own minds on ethical issues. Although we must usually treat the latter question by implication, it is not feasible to do so in the case of persuasive methods. At first thought it may appear that persuasive methods have nothing to do with personal decisions—that they are purely interpersonal devices, finding no counterpart in one's private deliberations. Is this actually the case, or must we recognize a kind of "self-persuasion" as well?

The answer cannot be long in doubt. It is true that when persuasion becomes a markedly social phenomenon—when it is used by political orators, religious revivalists, tabloid editorialists,

10. Chap. V, Sec. 3.

propagandists,[11] and the like—it is more likely to arrest our attention. But these cases do not exhaust, or even typify, the many forms that persuasion may take. If we look to less conspicuous instances, we shall find that persuasion is as ubiquitous as choice, and finds its place, as a kind of auto-suggestion, in almost all of our personal deliberations.

Let us look first to the motives of self-persuasion. A conflict of attitudes, from which ethical reflection proceeds, is a disquieting, half-paralyzing state of mind. However much our several wants may oppose one another, we definitely do want to resolve this opposition. There is thus an urgency toward making a decision quickly, and the process of making it with painstaking care, by purely rational methods, is often too slow to content us. Or perhaps we must make a "forced decision"—one that must be made immediately if the decision is to have practical importance. Or again, prolonged deliberation may fail to resolve the conflict, there being so much to be said on both sides that an accumulation of evidence simply maintains the old impasse on a more complicated level. Or deliberation may only half-resolve the conflict, leaving a predominating force of our attitudes in a definite direction, it is true, but so hampered by dissenting ones that our subsequent actions lack vigor and incisiveness. In all of these cases there are obvious motives for making the decision in one way or the other, if only to put an end to conflict. A continual, perplexed state of mind will fail, so most of us think, to bring anything that we desire; but a definite decision opens more attractive prospects. Even if we later regret the decision, it may at least lead us, when acted upon, to acquire a fund of instructive experience. So we often hasten our decision, supplementing or replacing rational methods by a vigorous self-exhortation—a kind of persuasion in soliloquy which shames certain impulses into quiescence, and gives to the others increased activity. The attitudes that are predominant, at any one stage of deliberation, are given greater strength by a counterpart of literary expression.

There can be no doubt that words or other symbols play a part in private deliberation, in whatever way it is that we "think in words" without saying the words aloud. Thus the same labels and slogans that the orator uses, though often in more subtle form, are likely to reappear in our personal meditations. Certain

11. For a discussion of the meaning of "propaganda" see Chap. XI.

of our attitudes prompt us to actions that are "courageous," "independent," and "liberal," and these are the expressions of our "true self"; but these impulses are held in check by others, foreign to our true self, which urge in the direction of "timid docility." Or, should the decision be inclining the opposite way, with the general circumstance otherwise the same, we find that certain attitudes are in the direction of "prudence," "respectful considerateness," and "sound conservatism," but are held in check by those that pull in the direction of "rash presumption." These words are not wholly emotive, not wholly devoid of descriptive content; but when they work their way into private deliberations, it is scarcely to be thought that their function is exhausted in characterizing the alternatives before us with scientific detachment.

The use of self-persuasion is evidenced by the way in which certain people project their deliberations into some pretended social setting. They fancy themselves arguing with some superior, or old friend, or revered teacher, and in the course of this mental dramatization find themselves apt in epigram, and masters of declamatory prose, until their opponent ends with an enthusiastic endorsement of their now decisive resolution. Obviously, this imaginary argument is not always a rehearsal for an argument that they expect later to take place; for it may occur even when their respected opponent has long forgotten who they are, or when he is dead. Nor is it wholly an effort to fashion themselves in his pattern, or to reconstruct what he would adduce from his richer stores of information as reasons for or against their decision. Rather, they make their opponent a fictitious character in a play, who lends them mainly the dignity of his name; and the epigrams and declamations which so effectively sway him are in fact serviceable in swaying themselves, with all the vigor of improvised narrative.

But it is not necessary to turn to arguments which people imagine; for actual arguments often illustrate self-persuasion no less clearly. When a man exhorts another, it is not always the other whom he wishes to convince. His urgency may symptomatize an internal conflict, and his hearer may serve only to remind him of tendencies of his own which he is in the course of trying to strengthen or repress. He is an orator whose oration convinces himself.

In this respect self-persuasion is comparable to "rationalization." It is well known that when a man's decision resolves his conflict imperfectly, leaving contrary urges that make him hesitant or ashamed of it, he will often misrepresent the considerations that guided him. He will disguise selfish considerations as altruistic ones, or pretend that *indubitable* consequences of his choice, unpleasant in nature, were really only faintly probable ones; and he will disguise the alternative he rejected in the opposite fashion. In part this rationalization is addressed to others, as a means of evading their censure; but this overtly social aspect of the process is not its only function, nor need it be the predominating one. In great measure the man is bent upon making his decision seem admirable to himself. He must allay the promptings, so damaging to his self-respect, of the frustrated attitudes that fall among his personal ideals. Some of these struggling attitudes may be a product of social pressure; but since they may persist long after the factors which engendered them have been forgotten, and long after society has moved on to new mores, they are not to be confused with overt fears of public disapproval. Thus much of rationalization presupposes no audience. It is *self*-deception, seeking to appease attitudes that have no social object, but which, still partly uninhibited or unsublimated, remain to perturb one with their dissenting voices.

It will be evident that rationalization, being self-deception, is not the same as self-persuasion; for deception implies false beliefs, whereas persuasion does not. And those of us who are ashamed of self-deception, once it is pointed out to us, are perfectly free to feel unashamed or even proud of certain kinds of self-persuasion. But the two have a parallel function. In both cases there is an effort to quiet certain attitudes that impede the expression of other ones. All the resources of one's personality are brought to bear in the resolution of conflict—truths very often, but also lies and errors, and persuasive utterances of varying kinds and of varying degrees of utility. Even if there were not an abundance of direct evidence for self-persuasion, one might plausibly have surmised its presence from its functional resemblance to rationalization.

Self-persuasion, like all persuasion, is seldom used alone, but habitually goes along with much else. Perhaps it will be well to cite an instance in which it combines with other factors quite intimately:

In the course of hastening a decision a man may single out only the agreeable consequences of one alternative, presenting them vividly to his imagination; and immediately thereafter may single out the disagreeable consequences of the other alternative, representing them with equal vividness. Now should he believe that he has considered *all* the consequences that have a strong bearing on the decision, he will very probably be rationalizing; though a great many of his beliefs, so far as they go, may be true. To that extent he is using reasons, whether false or true ones; though some of his reasons may be exaggerated to a point of myth-making, involving matters that he would explicitly reject if a question were clearly put to him. Meanwhile a use of self-persuasion is quite evident—not, necessarily, from his use of emotive terms, but rather from his manner of presenting his reasons. The sharp contrast in which he places the two sets of consequences makes the attractiveness of the one alternative and the unattractiveness of the other stand out with greater force. This is a persuasive factor which must be distinguished from the subject matter introduced into his deliberation, even though it presupposes the use of subject matter. Just as Tolstoi alternates the passages about Anna and Vronsky with those about Kitty and Levin, so any man, in the lesser artistry of his private decisions, may make use of dramatic contrast. And just as Tolstoi's use of this device must be distinguished from the fidelity of his character drawing, so any lesser use of it must be distinguished from the truth or falsity of the beliefs which it attends. We must separate the several aspects of ethical method in attention, but mainly in order to discern their complicated interrelatedness in fact.

Thus there is a place for persuasion in private decisions. In this respect, as in all others, the personal and interpersonal aspects of ethics are closely analogous.

VII

Validity

1

THE preceding chapters have dealt with the nature and effectiveness of methods that are in fact used in common life. Such a study is not the same, if we are to go by parallels to deductive and inductive logic, as a study of what methods are *valid*. People often use invalid methods, and these sometimes help them to win arguments. Common acceptance does not imply validity. Hence there would seem to be a further part of ethical methodology, as yet only touched upon, which has to do with correcting or validating the methods that are usually employed. It has been suggested[1] that this further problem may, contrary to appearances, have no special place in ethical methodology; but this must now be considered with more care.

There are certain aspects of ethical arguments—and very important ones—to which questions about validity are obviously relevant. If an ethical argument applies formal logic, as in example (1), page 115, it will be valid or invalid in whatever sense the logic is valid or invalid. If it uses empirical reasons, the inductive support given to *them* in their turn (as distinct from the support given *by* the reasons *to* the ethical judgment) may be called valid or invalid in whatever sense the empirical methods used are valid or invalid.[2] Thus when ethics uses the methods of logic or science *directly*, the ordinary canons of validity remain in full operation.

On the other hand, validity has *nothing* to do with persuasive methods. It is cognitively nonsensical to speak either of "valid" or of "invalid" persuasion. If one is led by the excitement of persuasion into making logical errors, it is the logic, and not the

1. Pp. 113 f.
2. It will be assumed here that one may speak of "valid" and "invalid" inductive procedures, though of course an inductive argument will not be *demonstratively* valid.

persuasion, that is invalid. One may, of course, call a certain kind of persuasion "invalid" in order to reject it—to indicate that it is objectionable or ineffective; but the emotional impact of a military band could be "invalid" in the same way. Clearly, this figurative way of speaking is not to the present interest.

So far the role of validity in ethics is beyond serious dispute. There is a further aspect of the question, however, which requires a little more attention. One of the peculiarities of ethical arguments lies in the inference from a factual reason to an ethical conclusion. The use of such a step does not exemplify persuasion, for persuasion is not mediated by articulate beliefs; and at the same time it does not exemplify any inductive or deductive procedure—so long, that is, as the first pattern is presupposed, and apart from exceptions such as (2) and (3), pages 116–117. It has been repeatedly illustrated in Groups II–IV of Chapter V. Now in a valid ethical argument, must *this* step, no less than the steps in confirming the reasons, be valid? Or does the term "valid" here introduce an irrelevant consideration? That is: if "R" and "E" stand respectively for a set of reasons and an ethical conclusion, related neither deductively nor inductively, then is it of interest to ask whether an inference from R to E is valid?

Clearly, the inference will be neither *demonstratively* nor *inductively* valid, by hypothesis. By these standards of validity, it will always be *invalid*. But this is a triviality. When an inference does not purport to comply with the usual rules, any insistence on its failure to do so is gratuitous. We have marked out the step between R and E as different from any found in logic or science, and cannot expect it to be valid in the same way.

The only interesting issue is of another sort. Granted that demonstrative and inductive validity are irrelevant to this step, is there not some *other kind* of validity, peculiar to normative arguments, that deserves equal emphasis? Perhaps the usual rules for demonstrative and inductive inference need to be *supplemented* by special rules for inferences from R to E—rules which are enough like the others to be said, generically, to mark off *valid* inferences, but which are enough unlike the others to mark off a distinct *kind* of validity.

The term "validity" is not free from vagueness, and so can be defined in several alternative senses without "unnatural" distortions of language. One might, accordingly, devise some broad definition of the term in which certain inferences from R to E could be called "valid." It seems wholly impracticable and injudicious, however, to sanction such a sense. The grounds for saying this will be elaborated later in the chapter, but in brief they are as follows:

No matter how else we may define "valid," we shall very likely want to retain a sense which is intimately related to "true." The precise way in which the terms are to be related, and the precise meaning of them both, may occasion no little perplexity; but we shall in any case want to say that a "valid" method is more conducive to establishing truths, or probable truths, than any "invalid" one. Should anyone deny this, we should usually insist that he must be using either "valid" or "true" in some other sense than the perhaps poorly defined but still roughly intelligible one that we prefer. But if "valid" is to be applied to the step from R to E, then—as we shall see in a moment—the word could not have its accustomed connection with "true." Such a sense, which would almost certainly persist *in addition to* the truth-related sense or senses, might foster a misleading ambiguity, and keep people from making the requisite distinctions between reasons in ethics and reasons in logic or science. In the interest of clarity, then, it will be expedient to deny the word any application to the ethical cases in question.

But why will "valid," applied to an inference from R to E, be deprived of its connection with "true"? The answer must not depend on the contention that ethical judgments "cannot sensibly be called either 'true' or 'false.' " This is not so, even for the first pattern of analysis; for although the emotive meaning of an ethical judgment has nothing to do with truth or falsity (subject to a qualification to be made in Section 5), its descriptive meaning, which refers to the speaker's attitudes, may be true or false in the ordinary way. The point is rather that, for the step in argument we are considering, the reasons *do not establish or call into question* the truth of an ethical judgment's (descriptive) meaning. This can be made clearer by example: Suppose that A declares X to be good, and B declares it to be bad. And suppose that A supports his contention by pointing out the consequences of X, as in (6), page 119. A is not thereby calling into question the truth of B's ethical judgment; for B has said (according to the first pattern, and ignoring emotive meaning) only that he disapproves of X. So far from denying this, A may be presumed to believe it; and he is certainly free to do so, since between A's own judgment—which descriptively means that he, A, approves of X—and B's judgment—which descriptively means that he, B, disapproves of X—there is no logical contradiction. The opposition is in attitude, not in belief. What A is trying to do is not to question the truth of what B has said about his attitudes, but rather, as we have repeatedly seen, to *redirect* B's attitudes. Acknowledging that B began with the attitudes to which his initial judgment testified, A is pointing out the consequences of X in order to make B have different attitudes to X later on. This in no way questions the truth of B's initial judgment;[3] nor does it prove the truth of A's initial judgment, which was descriptive only of A's attitudes.

In general, when E is supported or opposed by R, R neither proves nor disproves the truth of the descriptive meaning of E. So unless "valid" is to have a misleadingly extended sense, the question, "Does R permit a valid inference to E?" is devoid of interest. One may, if he likes, say that such an inference is always "invalid" by the rules of formal logic or induction; but as we have seen, this is not to point out some inadvertency—some failure to observe rules that the inference might have been expected to follow. If anyone sought to make it follow these rules, he would deprive it of its distinctive function.

These remarks will require careful qualification, but in a general way they can be seen to proceed naturally from the foregoing chapters. The notion of validity retains its accustomed application to any aspect of an ethical argument that is concerned wholly with establishing *beliefs*. Illogicalities do not become logical, and lies do not become true, simply because they occur in a broader ethical context. But wherever these matters are in question an ethical argument is factual, its methodology falling within the widely studied fields of logic and scientific method. For the steps which go beyond these, and use beliefs in their turn to alter *attitudes*, questions about validity, in any helpful sense

3. For the first-pattern sense here in question, the ethical term of B's judgment refers only to his attitudes *at the time of speaking*. This was discussed in Chap. IV, p. 93. His initial judgment is more strictly speaking his initial *utterance* of "X is bad"—that which began the argument. The importance of singling out specific utterances in this way will be evident from Sec. 4 of the present chapter.

of the term, are irrelevant. In sum, wherever ethical methodology must be *distinguished* from logic and scientific method, validity presents no problem at all.

2

A DISMISSAL of validity, even in this partial way, risks opening the way to certain misunderstandings in the course of guarding against others. The validity of a method stands out as the most conspicuous ground for choosing it; hence when certain methods, or aspects of them, are denied any connection with validity, one may feel that no ground for choice between them remains. Or if such a ground is recognized, it may seem to involve only a crude, forensic success. So long as one's opponent is impressed (a hasty critic may suppose), one method is as good as another; for the whole purport of ethics is to sway attitudes. Where Plato and Kant sought eternal principles of reason, are there merely the empty rules of rhetoric? After this one is likely to envisage disillusionment and chaos, and the many other disturbing "implications" which objective theorists so habitually attribute to their opponents.

Viewed with circumspection, these apparent implications can be seen to have nothing to do with the present views. There are any number of grounds for choice between methods; and if in certain cases these do not depend upon validity, it does not follow that they depend on oratorical strategy. We have seen that whenever validity has any relevant application, it is wholly available for the moralist's purposes. Whenever it does not have application, there are other considerations, equally available to the moralist, that free his choice of methods from any necessity of callousness or caprice.

If a man's ethical judgment has failed to impress his hearer, shall he support it by methods that are predominantly persuasive or predominantly rational? The former will have nothing to do with validity, and neither will the latter, *so far as* it involves steps from factual statements to the judgment; but he may choose between them on other grounds in such a way as this: Certain factors may incline him to use persuasive methods. Perhaps his hearer is blinded by wishful thinking to all reasons which undermine his present attitudes, and persuasion is a necessary preliminary to making him "listen to reason." Or perhaps the judgment concerns the immediate future, and persuasion alone can decide the matter quickly enough. Or perhaps the hearer, being unusually meditative, has let his reflective habits devitalize his emotional ones, and persuasion will assist, whereas rational methods will actually hinder, any quickening of his practical attitudes. On the other hand, certain factors may incline him to use rational methods. He may believe that the attitudes of the hearer, if directed to objects of whose nature and consequences he remains ignorant, will express themselves in actions of a blundering, disorganized sort. Reasons may remedy this ignorance, whereas persuasion may conceal it. Or, looking still further ahead, he may wish to build up in the hearer an inquiring habit of mind, conducive to his making all future ethical decisions, and not merely this one, in the light of full knowledge. The speaker's own use of rational methods may serve to recommend them by example. (This is often the explicit aim of teachers— those who feel that education should not indoctrinate students, but rather should teach them how to make ethical decisions for themselves.) Or again, he may use rational methods because his own attitudes, prompting the judgment, are not free from conflict and hesitation. He may fear that an imperfect knowledge of the object judged is directing his attitudes, and causing him to influence the hearer's, in a way that both will later come to regret. So he chooses rational methods largely to open the way to a counteruse of them. He hopes that the hearer will criticize his reasons, or supplement them with others, with a result of mutual enlightenment.

These are only a few of the many considerations which, singly or in combination, may guide one in deciding what methods to use. Among them, of course, the forensic "effectiveness" of a method must be given its proper place. But it would be a gross distortion of people's motivation to say that this factor is always the decisive one. In the case last mentioned above, for instance, where rational methods were selected in the hope of a *mutual* redirection of attitudes, all blunt coercion, exerted without regard to the further effects of one's procedure, is wholly absent. An effort to reach convergent attitudes may be no less a coöperative, modest enterprise than is an effort to reach convergent scientific beliefs. If not all ethical arguments are so motivated, that is a fact about certain human beings which all are free to note and none is required to copy. Whenever validity cannot enter, then, the choice of methods need not be guided by the method's sheer impressiveness. Choice is a complicated matter, and the grounds for choosing a method are no less complicated than those for choosing anything else.

It will now be clear that the whole question about the choice of methods, and the "available grounds" for choice, does not constitute some isolated division of ethics, involving an analysis that is foreign to the remainder of this work. On the contrary, any decision about what methods are to be used, if it cannot be made with reference to validity, is itself a normative ethical matter. This becomes quite obvious when the question is phrased in ordinary ethical terminology. To ask "What method shall I choose?" is in effect to ask "What method *ought* I choose?" Any argument about the question will involve disagreement in attitude; and the considerations which one adduces as "grounds" for choosing one method or another are simply the "reasons" (like those mentioned in ChapterVI, Groups II–IV) by which an ethical judgment—here a judgment about the way *another one is to be supported*—is itself supported.

To evaluate or recommend an ethical method (whenever validity can have no bearing on the case[4]) is to moralize about the ways of moralists. Ethical judgments may be made about innumerable actions, and the procedure of supporting a judgment, being itself an action, is open to judgment in its turn. When a man makes a judgment, E^1, which is about X, we may make a judgment, E^2, which is about his way of supporting E^1. Our way of supporting E^2 will then be open to the judgment E^3; and so on.

There is nothing vicious about this series of judgments. It would be vicious only if we had to begin at "the other end" of it,

4. There may be normative questions about methods even when the methods raise the ordinary considerations of validity. Thus it may be asked whether a scientist, in the interest of popularizing certain of his conclusions, is morally justified in defending them by superficially plausible methods which he himself knows to be invalid. But this, being obvious, is not of great concern to us. For the scientist, validity still remains as a possible ground for choice; whereas for the moralist, so far as he goes beyond purely logical and scientific inferences, it does not.

Some may wish to contend that "validity" *itself*, even in the conventional sense that applies to logic and science, is a *normative* term; but the writer suspects that any such contention would involve a misleading use of either the term "validity" or the term "normative." A logician who points out an inference as valid is not exhorting anyone to use it; he is simply saying that if anyone does make such an inference, using true premises, his conclusion, being contained in the premises, must also be true. This point is discussed implicitly in Sec. 5 of this chapter, and certain parts of Chap. XIII will have a bearing on it.

the series by its very nature having no "other end." In point of fact, we usually and quite feasibly begin right at "this" end. We do not withhold all expression of approval until having first decided whether we approve of approving of approving . . . of this kind of expression of approval. We simply *find* ourselves approving, and using certain methods to defend what we approve; and we call our procedure into question only when there is a practical likelihood of conflict or disagreement.

It is a consequence of these views, of course, that the use of an ethical method, whether it is selected out of habit or more self-consciously, will always be open to *possible* criticism. The goodness or badness of certain methods may be a topic of much argument; and the disagreement in attitude that it involves may at times, apart from a heuristic assumption to the contrary, be irreconcilable. Disagreement about the value of methods is like any other ethical disagreement. It can be reconciled by rational methods only if the disagreement in attitude is rooted in disagreement in belief, and if the disagreement in belief is itself practically reconcilable. It can be resolved by persuasive methods only if the persuasion which people decide to use will be sufficiently moving. To say this is simply to specify the factors which could cause or fail to cause an agreement on ethical methods to come about; it is to view controversy about ethical methods with ethical *neutrality,* studying (though in a very general way) under what circumstances, hypothetical or actual, people will come to approve of the same methods, but without in any way taking steps to actualize or change these circumstances, and thus without explicitly trying to alter what ethical methods people may agree to accept. It is just this detachment which the greater part of the present volume, as a working limitation of its subject matter, wishes to preserve. However—and here it is necessary to emphasize, with application to the special case of making judgments about methods, the more general remarks that concluded Chapter IV—this must in no way be permitted to suggest that the reader, having for purposes of analysis been led to suspend any participation in normative controversy, must avoid any such participation forever afterward. A judgment about ethical methods, as distinct from a description of them, may be of great social importance; nor is it predestined to dogmatism or ineffectuality.

Should anyone feel, for instance, that persuasive methods are too frequently used by moralists, there is nothing in the present analysis to prevent him from making urgent ethical judgments to that effect. He will do well, of course, to support his own judgment largely by rational methods—for persuasion to end persuasion, like war to end war, is a disconcerting matter, even though in strictness of logic it is not a contradiction; but in any case there are many methods at his disposal. If he should feel that his ethical judgment, even of this sort, would still be a blind, egotistical effort to impose his preferences on others, contrary to his ideals, the answer is very simple. His effort will be blind and egotistical only if he makes it so, and his protestation of ideals to the contrary is itself evidence that he will not. An effort is usually called "blind" when it proceeds without knowledge of the factual situation, particularly the more remote consequences, with which it deals; and it is usually called "egotistical" when it is an expression of vanity. Hence if a person, in his efforts to make one method more widely used than another, does so in the light of much knowledge, and if his motives in propagating his attitudes are uncolored by vanity, his efforts will be neither blind nor egotistical in any usual sense. And should his efforts, if successful, lead people to be satisfied and thankful for his influence, they at any rate will not say that he has "imposed" his preferences on them, nor will they reproach him with any other abusive term.

But although an effort to judge ethical methods may be of unquestionable importance, the present work does not propose to join in the undertaking, save in passing. The methods of ethics must for the present be seen, all praise or condemnation of them being withheld.

3

A WORD of explanation must now be inserted, or else the analytic detachment here professed may seem an impossibility. Although analysis is concerned with observing and clarifying, as distinct from judging, it cannot pretend to sever its studies from all evaluation whatsoever. The reason for this is that analysis, like any other inquiry, must introduce certain evaluations (though they will not be peculiarly "moral" ones) in the course of marking off its field of study. No one can inquire without being motivated, whether by idle curiosity or by a more practical urge. Since an inquirer seldom leaves his motives uncriticized, he may be presumed to have decided whether his inquiry is *worth* pursuing; and if he refuses to disclose the considerations that might lead others to agree in attitude with him about its worth, then (unless this agreement can safely be presupposed at the outset) he will restrict himself in a wholly artificial way. The truth of his results will be a consideration distinct from their value, but if he neglects their value they may in the end seem "true but trivial" both to himself and to others. The same considerations arise when an inquirer is deciding which aspects of his study are *worth* developing in full, and which ones *deserve* only passing mention.

This point (which many writers have stressed) leads to a further one, more closely relevant to our discussion of methods. Whenever an inquirer defends the importance of his work, he is in the course of altering certain attitudes of those to whom he addresses himself. In so doing he must himself inevitably *use* methods—methods which may be persuasive or rational, and, if rational, may be of all sorts, employing reasons which in their turn are supported validly or invalidly. Now the value of these methods, so far as their application to his *special problem* under his *special circumstances* is concerned, is a matter on which he quite obviously cannot be neutral. If "detachment" implied neutrality on such a matter as this, it would name an impossibility.

No inquiry, then, can divorce itself from the evaluative considerations that directly concern and guide the process of inquiry itself; nor is ethical analysis an exception to this general principle. But ethical analysis can, no less than science, mathematics, and logic, limit itself *solely* to those evaluations which are essential to the pursuit of its descriptive and clarificatory studies. It is this degree of "detachment" (and no higher degree is possible) at which the present work will usually aim; and it will do so on the ground that such an effort, highly specialized though it is, is important as a prolegomenon to normative ethics, freeing it from its often stultifying confusions. To evaluate for purposes of analysis is not to take sides in the many other evaluative issues of men. These other issues—even those that concern important aspects of method, such as the social value of persuasive methods, or the value of finding convenient, deliberately oversimplified rational methods—can here only be touched upon, in passing digressions from the topics of central interest.

It is quite possible that analysis may have *indirect* bearings on a number of broader issues. But so does any study, no matter how detached it may be. The most impartial of historical studies may make a great difference to our aims for the future; and astronomy, seemingly so remote from practical influences, has served to foster humility, and allay superstitious fears. This is only to say that any descriptive statement may be used as a *reason* by others in support of *their* judgments. The conclusions of analysis may be used in the same way. And with regard to a descriptive study of methods, it is particularly likely that analysis may make a difference to the procedures that people may subsequently wish to adopt. But it is one thing to look with temporary indifference on this effect, even if it varies with different people, and leads some to use methods (to emphasize only this aspect of the matter) that the analyst disapproves of; and it is quite another thing to strive to promote enlightened agreement on the value of various methods. The latter undertaking, which could be permanently forwarded only by a detailed and diversified knowledge of many fields, specially organized to have a bearing on the issue, will usually be beyond the aim of the present work, nor does the present writer feel fully competent to deal with it. One who makes a sculptor's chisel may inadvertently contribute to the making of a deplorable statue; but he will not always do well, on that account, to leave his trade and become a sculptor.

There is a certain pedantry, however, in circumscribing an inquiry too narrowly. An evaluation of methods, in certain of its aspects, is greatly facilitated by a description of their nature and *modus operandi;* hence it will sometimes be undertaken, partially and briefly, in later chapters.[5] And perhaps it will be advisable, without delay, to make a judgment which may counteract another that the reader, should he temporarily forget the purpose of analysis, may feel that the present work "requires" him to make. A few words will be said, though they will of necessity be very general, about the value of persuasive methods.

At the present time there are a number of people who have suddenly become sensitive to emotive language, and have seen how widely it enters into seemingly factual discussions. These same people have also become sensitive to "propaganda," whose emotional effect so frequently proves successful in leading people this way or that, often contrary to their own interest. Putting

5. Particularly in Chap. XV.

two and two together, but without making four, some of them
seem cynically to conclude that all emotive language, and indeed,
all persuasion, exhortation, rhapsodic enthusiasm, and the like,
are open to suspicion, and should give place to the cold, fact-
loving language of science. That is to say, moved by one particular word, namely, "propaganda"—for "propaganda" is a word
often used to *derogate* this or that kind of mass persuasion[6]—
they become frightened of all emotive words whatsoever. All
persuasion is somehow a kind of propaganda, and so bad and
shameful, regardless of its motivation and its aims.

Such a contention can represent only an inadvertency. It is
one thing to say that persuasive methods are often used for
thoroughly bad purposes, and in cases where rational methods
would serve a crying need. With this judgment the writer is in
full sympathy. Nor can one tolerate, among those who pretend
to think for themselves, and lay the foundations for morality,
that grotesque *confusion* of persuasive and rational methods
which so often protests a philosophical profundity. But it is
quite another thing to make a wholesale condemnation of persuasion. No reflective person could condemn on such a scale. In
practice we never have occasion to decide whether to reject all
persuasion, or accept it all. The difficulty is always one of deciding *which* persuasion to reject and which to accept. One must
say, then, in judging persuasive methods, what must be said on
so many general issues—and the judgment is of use only in correcting a propensity to generalize too broadly: Persuasion is
sometimes good and sometimes bad, depending upon the circumstances.

Any total repudiation of persuasion would be palpable in its
absurdity, save that the effort of imagining society without it
is too great, and we only half-imagine it. If we always inhibited
any expression of enthusiasm, avoiding all strongly emotive
words, mitigating the emotive effects of other ones by a colorless
tone of voice, scrupulously avoiding any impressive cadence of
words, and striving to convey only those truths that the hearer's
preëxisting wants made him interested in hearing—if we did
this, our emotional lives would derive so little exercise that life
would be unbearable. There is a kind of apathy into which we
fall when our attitudes are not socially and articulately mani-
fested, quickened by the resistance or concurrence of other

6. See Chap. XI for a further discussion.

people. Detached reasoning may end by causing our attitudes to work together, and make a great difference to our lives; but there is a limit to the intensity of feeling that it permits. For the full, vigorous attitudes, without which little is accomplished, there must be the contagion of directly expressed enthusiasm. Persuasion is unquestionably a tool of the "propagandist" and soapbox orator; but it is also the tool of every altruistic reformer that the world has ever known. We must not banish all doctors to rid the world of quacks.

The value of certain kinds of persuasion—indeed, the inevitability of it—depends in good measure on the way it is bound up with authority and leadership. The greater number of people, bewildered by the complexities of moral decisions, resolve their difficulties by deferring to others—either to the combined authority of public opinion, or to the authority of some text or institution, or to that of some person whom they believe to have acquired knowledge beyond their own limited understanding. At times these authorities are consciously selected; at other times they come, as it were, with one's birthplace. But however blindly people may sometimes accept their authorities, or however much certain individuals may feel the need of rebelling from all authority in order to think things out for themselves, no one could wish to recommend, as a general social policy, that people be scornful of all moral leadership. How, then, may one who is held as an authority support the ethical judgments that he makes to his followers? Certainly not by giving all his detailed reasons —for these reasons are often too complicated for the followers to understand, and they have been content to be followers, rather than leaders, partly on that account. Persuasive methods must here of necessity supplement those few reasons which the followers can take into consideration.

Who are the *rightful* authorities? Who *ought* to guide others by their exhortation? These are precisely the questions which amateur moralists debate over the cracker-barrel; and their work is often more practical than that of philosophers by profession. Since the issues are complicated normative ones, they can be advanced only a little by broad generalities, and advanced not at all when they are divorced from the concrete situation out of which they spring. Unless a man is wholly content to abide by the authorities of his birthplace, and is fortunate enough to find that their advice does not conflict, he must at least decide for himself in choosing what authority to follow, or discuss the matter with others on equal terms. The issue arises out of such specific decisions, and although broad principles may help its solution, the principles may be more difficult to establish than a judgment about a special case. Questions of this sort would lie too far afield to be debated here, even if there were occasion to debate them.

It will be enough, in this slight digression into evaluative matters, to point out that broad judgments are often rash, and that judgments about the evils of *all* persuasion are more than usually so.

4

IT has been explained that "validity" introduces nothing novel into ethics, and that no chaotic implications (such as "One method is as good as another, so long as it impresses people") need be feared from this conclusion. For practical purposes the discussion could now end; but since the discussion of "validity" in Section 1 was somewhat rough, technically minded readers may desire a more rigorous analysis. For them it may be well to go into details. The discussion will be mainly of interest in clarifying certain confusions about the use of "true" and "false" in ethics, which are a little more troublesome for the first pattern than they will be for the second.[7]

Let us begin in a seemingly indirect manner. Note that the phrase,

(a) " 'I approve of X' said by A at time t"

designates a certain utterance[8] of A's. The whole of (a) designates the utterance, not merely the part in single quotation marks, for "said by A at time t" serves to distinguish this utter-

7. For the logical aspects of the analysis that is to follow, the writer is greatly indebted to Nelson Goodman. See chap. xi of his doctoral dissertation, *A Study of Qualities*, available in typescript in the Widener Library, Harvard University.

8. The term "utterance" is here used as a convenient synonym for Peirce's term, "token," which he contrasts with "type." See *Collected Papers of Charles Sanders Peirce*, edited by Hartshorne and Weiss (Harvard University Press, 1933), Vol. IV, par. 537. Instead of "type" and "token" Peirce sometimes uses the terms "legisign" and "sinsign." The distinction is simply this: If a man repeats the same sentence ten times over, he has spoken only *one* sentence if we mean *type* sentence, but *ten* sentences if we mean *token* sentences or utterances *of* the type sentence.

ance of "I approve of X" from other utterances of it—those made at other times or by other people.[9] Similarly, the phrase,

(b) " 'I approve of X' said by A at time t + n"

designated a further utterance of A's. It will be evident that (a) and (b) will both designate true utterances *only if* A approves of X *both* at t *and* at t + n.[10] In much the same way, the phrases,

(c) " 'I disapprove of X' said by B at time t"

and

(d) " 'I approve of X' said by B at time t + n"

designate utterances of B's. The utterances may both be true, but only if B's disapproval of X at t has changed to approval by t + n. Note further that the utterances designated by (a), (b), (c), and (d) are logically independent of each other.

Each of the utterances in question preserves the descriptive meaning, though not the emotive meaning, of some corresponding ethical utterance. Thus (a) designates an utterance which has the same descriptive meaning as "X is good," *provided* that the latter is said by A at time t. And so on, for the others. Since emotive meaning is irrelevant to considerations of truth or falsity,[11] it follows (the first pattern being presupposed throughout this discussion) that two ethical utterances which sound alike will not necessarily have the same truth-value. "X is good," for

9. It must be assumed in this account that the variables used may uniformly be replaced by constants, *whether or not* they occur within quotation marks. Although this convention is inconvenient for certain aspects of logic, it here greatly simplifies exposition.

10. Goodman (*op. cit.*) has pointed out that whenever "indicator" terms are in question (like "now," "I," and verbs whose temporal reference is relative to "now") the several utterances of a given (type) sentence need not be logically equivalent, and "true" and "false" must accordingly be predicated of the separate utterances, rather than of the (type) sentence itself. Thus the utterance of "I am tired" that a man makes *before* resting may be true, whereas the utterance that he makes of it *after* resting may be false. On the other hand, for sentences like "all bodies attract each other in inverse proportion to the square of their distance," which contain no indicator words, the tense of the verb being omni-temporal, the several utterances will all (assuming a language unambiguously understood by everyone concerned) be equivalent; hence it is there convenient to predicate "true" and "false" of the (type) sentence itself, without bothering about which specific utterance of it is in question.

11. Subject to the qualification of Sec. 5.

instance, may be true for the utterance of A at t, but false for the utterance of A at t + n, just as (a), above, may designate a true utterance and (b) a false one. This will in fact be the case if A approves of X at t, and no longer does so at t + n. Similarly, "X is good" may be true when said by A and false when said by B, just as (b) may designate a true utterance, and (d) a false one. This will happen if A approves of X (at t + n) and B does not.

Let us now take a case where A says "X is good" and B says "X is bad," both speaking at roughly the same time, t; and where A proceeds to support this contention by the reasons, R—reasons which are related to his judgment psychologically, like those of Groups II–IV of Chapter II. If descriptive meaning only is considered, the argument is equivalent to one in which the designatum of (a) above is opposed to the designatum of (c). Since these utterances are logically independent, the disagreement so far is *not* in belief. In fact, so long as methods like (2), page 116, are not used, each person may be presumed to *accept as true* what the other says about his attitudes. So when A uses the reasons R, he is not defending the truth of his initial utterance nor is he questioning the truth of B's initial utterance. Instead, A uses R in the hope of *changing* the attitude which B's initial utterance (so both may be presumed to believe) *truthfully* described, and to defend himself from having to change the attitude which his own initial utterance truthfully described. To change an attitude, or keep it from changing, is not to refute an utterance which truthfully described it as it was at a given time. Hence A's assertion of R has nothing to do with the truth of the initial utterance of either A's or B's ethical judgment.

There is an indirect way, to be sure, in which A's reasons may be relevant to the truth of *subsequent* ethical utterances. Although R has nothing to do with the truth of A's utterance of "X is good" made at t, or of B's utterance of "X is bad" made at t (these being respectively equivalent to the designata of (a) and (c)), it may have a bearing on the truth of similar-sounding utterances made by either A or B at t + n (e.g., on those equivalent to the designata of (b) and (d)). For suppose that A, by use of R, finally convinces B at t + n. Both of them will then approve of X; hence if either makes an utterance of "X is good" at t + n (which will be descriptively equivalent to the designatum of (b) or of (d), depending on who speaks) *that* utterance will be true. And the reasons R will have helped to make it true. For without R, which changed B's attitude from what it was at t, B could not have made any truthful utterance about his approval of X at t + n; and much the same holds for A, who without R to defend his initial contention, might no longer have approved of X at t + n. In short, A's reasons may be instrumental in making "X is good," said by either person at t + n, a true utterance.

Shall we say, then, that A's reasons, in virtue of this indirect connection with the *truth* of ethical utterances, may "validly" or "invalidly" (in some permissible sense) lead to the t + n utterances of "X is good"? Obviously not; for although A's reasons are related to the truth of certain ethical utterances, they are related in a way that makes the use of "valid" wholly inappropriate. They do not *show* that any ethical utterance *is* true, but rather alter attitudes, by means of beliefs, in a way that *makes* the utterance true. This is best understood by analogy; Speaking to a child, A remarks, "If I say 'You are laughing' five minutes from now, I shall be telling the truth." He then tells amusing stories that make the child laugh, so that five minutes later, when he does say "You are laughing," he tells the truth. It is clear that A's amusing stories are related to the truth of this utterance; they bring about the situation which the utterance describes, thus making it true. It is equally clear that A's stories do not establish the truth of the utterance by "valid" methods. It is one thing to talk in a way that *causes* a subsequent utterance to be true, and another thing to use valid methods in *proving* it true. The relation of A's stories to his utterance (however trivial the example may be) is of the same causal nature as the relation, in the preceding ethical example, between R and the t + n utterances of "X is good." If it is misleading to use "valid" in the one case, it will be equally so in the other.

The discussion thus far may now be summarized: If an argument includes reasons which support or attack an ethical judgment, but which are related to it neither demonstratively nor inductively, the reasons do not call into question the truth of the initial utterance of the judgment; and although they may be relevant to the truth of later utterances of it, they are relevant only because they *bring about* the situation which these later utterances describe. Since the terms "valid" and "invalid" elsewhere have a quite different relation to truth, it is not feasible to use them in the present connection.

5

THE above remarks must be supplemented by mention of an idiomatic sense of "true" that might otherwise confuse the issue. In the example,

A: X is good.
B: Yes, that's true.

we should *not* be likely to take B as saying the equivalent of,

(a) "Yes, when you uttered 'X is good' you really did approve of X."

although that was the way "true" was used in the preceding section. We should be more likely to take B as saying the equivalent of,

(b) "Yes, X *is* good."

In other words, B may use "That's true" in order to repeat A's words after him, as it were, to signify agreement—but where the agreement would be in attitude, rather than (as it would be for usage (a)) in belief. Using "true" in this way, one may properly say that reasons *do* relate to the truth of an ethical judgment. Except in this sort of ethical context, however, such a use of "true" is most unusual. As we shall see presently, it is not a sense that we shall want to be related to the terms "valid" and "invalid." Hence our decision to reject the latter terms, in any peculiarly ethical application, need not be altered.

The sense of "true" that is translatable as in (b) is not unusual merely because it has the effect of repeating another man's words after him. Such a usage is by no means uncommon, as may be seen in the example,

A: Crows are always black.
B: That's true.

Here B's reply is equivalent to a repetition of A's words—equivalent to B's having asserted, "Yes, crows *are* always black"—and one does not feel that "true" is being used in any unnatural sense.[12] The ethical usage, as previously illustrated, is unusual

12. This illustration must not suggest, however, that "true" has no other function. See the view propounded by Frank Ramsey (*Foundations of Mathematics*, pp. 142 f.) and A. J. Ayer (*Language, Truth and Logic*, pp. 122 f.). Most of those who espoused this view are now more inclined to ac-

only in that it is tantamount to repeating a man's words after him in a *particular way*—a way that changes their descriptive meaning[13] and retains their emotive effect. When B uses "true" with the effect of repeating A's remark, "X is good," he is not talking about A's approval, as A was, but rather about his own; so their respective utterances of the words have different descriptive meanings. And B may use "true" in this context in a way that keeps some of the emotive effects of "good." This usage, being possible only when the rather colloquial indicator terms are used, is not found in science; and indeed, is of no use unless agreement in attitude (or some analogue of it[14]) is in question.

It will be obvious, however, that this sense of "true," though foreign to science, is useful in ethics. We cannot easily change our common idioms, so had better recognize the sense, and devote our efforts to emphasizing how it differs from others. On the same grounds, it may at first seem that an unusual sense of "valid" should also be accepted. Inferences from R's to E's[15] are to be called "valid," it may be suggested, if they are of the sort conducive to reaching E's that are true in the nonscientific sense of "true." To this it must be answered that such a sense of "valid," unlike the parallel one of "true," is not strongly sanctioned by our common idiom. But apart from this linguistic point, we must realize that such a sense would not provide, for ethics, a study of "validity" parallel to that found in inductive or deductive logic. It is the latter point that requires particular emphasis.

Suppose that a theorist should *tabulate* the "valid" inferences from R's to E's. It is difficult to see how he could be doing any-

cept an alternative like that presented by Alfred Tarski in "The Semantic Conception of Truth," *Philosophy and Phenomenological Research* (March, 1944).

13. This is not always so for second-pattern senses of the ethical terms.

14. Such an analogue can be found in cases where there is agreement "in locus assigned to experienced qualities." Thus if A says, "That picture has a well-balanced look," he may be using an elipsis for "That picture looks well-balanced *to me*"; and if B replies, "That's true," he may be saying the equivalent of "It looks well-balanced *to me* also." Here "true," which in effect reiterates words with a change in the reference of the indicator term, "me," has the usage above discussed. The agreement is not the same as agreement in attitude, but is rather like it; and it certainly is not agreement in belief. Although it is not to the present purpose to analyze the statements of aesthetics, it may be remarked that many of them lend themselves to this type of analysis.

15. As before, R is assumed to be related to E psychologically.

thing more than specify what R's he thereby resolves to *accept* as supporting the various E's. He would maintain, "The inferences from these R's to these corresponding E's are valid because if the R's are true, the E's will be true." Now "true," as he predicates it of any E, will only testify (for the nonscientific sense in question) to the attitudes that lead him to maintain E; hence his recognition of any R as "validly" leading to the E will reflect the sort of consideration (R) that has a potential bearing on his attitudes. Under the name of "validity" he will be selecting those inferences to which he is psychologically disposed to give assent, and perhaps inducing others to give a similar assent to them. This might be of interest, but would seem to be different from the more impersonal study in which students of validity in science and logic—so at least they usually insist—are engaged.

The point would not require so much attention were it not that validity is perplexing elsewhere. In scientific methodology (so Hume, in effect, has asked) does not our distinction between valid and invalid methods reflect our psychological habits? When we characterize a certain induction as valid, what more are we doing than resolving to accept it, and acting to induce others to do the same? If there is no answer to Hume, the unusual sense of "valid" considered above would have a status not far different from the scientific sense. Our decisions about invalid inferences from R to E would reflect our approval or disapproval; but in a similar way, our decisions about valid inductions would reflect our habits of belief or disbelief.

This can be no place to deal with Hume's question. It will be sufficient to deal with the consequences upon ethics that may attend its solution, one way or another:

Perhaps Hume will be answered by a tenable theory that divorces scientific validity from any dependence on psychology. If so, it does not seem likely that a similar explanation can replace our psychological one about the relation of R to E. Should the theory refer to a Keynes-like probability,[16] there would seem

---

16. See J. M. Keynes, *Theory of Probability*, Pts. I and III.

It may be mentioned that current analyses of probability can be classified into three main groups, each of which (rather surprisingly) is reminiscent of a corresponding type of analysis of the *ethical* terms. Thus Frank Ramsey's "subjective" theory (*Foundations of Mathematics*, Paper VII) makes "probable" indicate the degree of the *speaker's* inclination to believe, much as the present account makes "good" indicate the *speaker's* attitudes; though of course Ramsey adds much about the *consistency* of partial beliefs. Further, the many who espouse frequency theories of probability (clearly sum-

little hope of extending it to ethics. Probabilities as guiding "rational beliefs" have at least an initial plausibility, but it is difficult to see how a counterpart of probability could guide "rational attitudes." If in the light of full knowledge people should still have different attitudes—and that could happen if disagreement in attitude were not rooted in disagreement in belief—whose attitudes would be the "rational" ones? Or again, should the answer to Hume deal with the prerequisites of communication —with the contention that the canons of inductive confirmation are essential to preserve the meaningfulness of synthetic statements—then again, a similar view is not mandatory for ethics. If scientists disagreed radically about what observations would serve validly to confirm "a" given scientific theory, we might, no doubt, conclude that they had different theories in mind, expressed by the same words; but if men disagreed about the R's that would "validly" support a given E, we could readily take E as following the first pattern of analysis, unambiguously, and ascribe the disagreement to differences in temperament or training. Thus an E might be mutually intelligible even though no R's were agreed upon as the ones which would support it.

Perhaps, on the other hand, Hume's question will prove to be unanswerable—or rather, will be shown to require no answer. The quest for certainty in regard to method may prove to be as aimless there as elsewhere, and philosophers will have the task of making clear that its impossibility has no suicidal consequences for the intellect. In that event, should "valid" and "invalid" be retained to characterize inductive arguments, they would reflect the psychological habits of the man who made them—and this very statement about the habits could be validated only relatively to the theorist's habits of studying habits.

marized in Ernest Nagel's "Principles of the Theory of Probability," in the *International Encyclopedia of Unified Science,* Vol. I, No. 6, University of Chicago Press, 1939) treat probability on an intersubjective, empirically testable basis, in a way that naturalistic ethical theories, like R. B. Perry's, treat "good." (Thus conceived, the estimate of probabilities presupposes the validity of induction, hence cannot be used in "justifying" it.) And those who, like Keynes, take "probable" as designating something unique, recall to mind the unanalyzable ethical quality of G. E. Moore and his followers. These parallels lend point to the familiar contention (as preserved in the old trinity of "the true, the beautiful, and the good") that logic is essentially normative. Although the present writer is not sympathetic to such a contention (see p. 158, n. 4), he must acknowledge that no analysis of ethics can pretend to be completely adequate unless it goes beyond the present one, examining parallel problems in other fields.

"Validity" in inductive logic would to this extent resemble the "validity" of inferences from R to E. This partial similarity, however, must not blind us to points of difference:

It is possible helpfully to classify inductive inferences with regard to the logical form of the statements used, and thus to handle them quite generally, without going into the elaborate details of their subject matter;[17] and even if the propounding of inductive canons reflects only a *resolution* to accept them, it reflects one that is likely (judging inductively, by the same resolution) to be shared by all others who trouble to understand them. In ethics a parallel situation cannot be hoped for. One may, of course, indicate certain specific inferences from R's to E's which he resolves to accept; but it is not practicable to classify them with regard to logical form. And apart from this, temperamental differences in people's aspirations might lead to insoluble controversies about the methods proposed. So even if Hume's question requires no answer, there will be sharp differences between "validity" in induction and "validity" in inferences from R's to E's. These differences suggest that the term will be misleading in its extended application, and that when any theorist urges that a given reason should always be accepted as a support for a given ethical judgment, his contention is itself to be classified as an ordinary evaluative one.

To summarize this section: There is a sense in which "That's true" signifies agreement not in belief but in attitude. Although not found in science, this sense is useful in ethics, to whatever extent the first pattern is useful. It may accordingly seem feasible to recognize a corresponding sense of "valid," in which a reason, if true in the ordinary sense, may "validly" establish an ethical judgment as true in this special sense. But this suggestion, though it is not to be repudiated simply on dictionary grounds, will not provide a sense in which a study of ethical "validity" will parallel studies of validity in deductive or inductive logic. According to certain possible views about induction, there will be great differences between ethical and scientific "validity"; and according to others, there will be, in spite of some analogies, differences that prevent the fields from being open to a similar type of inquiry.

17. Thus Keynes (*op. cit.*, Pt. III) requires no other vocabulary for his discussion of induction, apart from the symbol for probability, than that provided by formal logic. Though not "formal" in the sense of "deductive," inductive logic makes use of the logical forms.

VIII

Intrinsic and Extrinsic Value

1

THE preceding chapters have been developed in connection with common-sense examples, of a sort that some may wish to deprecate as casuistic. No effort has been made to single out judgments about *intrinsic* value, and the very distinction between intrinsic and extrinsic has for the most part been disregarded. This topic must now be studied, with particular attention to its consequences on methodology.

In the sense here in question, "intrinsically good" is roughly synonymous with "good for its own sake, as an end, as distinct from good as a means to something else." Since an object may obviously be *approved* for its own sake, as distinct from a means to something else, this sense will not require us to depart from the first pattern of analysis, or in any way to ignore attitudes. And as we shall progressively come to see, it will not introduce any considerations that minimize the place of beliefs in ethics. The *relationship* between beliefs and attitudes, here no less than elsewhere, will be of central importance.

There are a number of philosophers who take judgments about intrinsic value (in a sense of "intrinsic" which, if not always precisely like that to be used here, is roughly similar to it) to have an importance that is beyond question. They distinguish between intrinsic and extrinsic value (or "ultimate ends" and "means"), in the first pages of their work, and from there on emphasize the former. Now why does this emphasis seem to them warranted? Perhaps the answer is largely this:

They hold, in effect, that normative ethics admits of a division of labor. Philosophical moralists can limit their attention to intrinsic values, since these are issues to which the "speculative" methods of philosophy are suited. Questions about extrinsic value, being about things which derive their goodness at second hand, can safely be left to others—to the statesmen, social scientists, psychologists, and so on, who, taking their views about what is intrinsically valuable from the philosophers, will be able to work out the involved pattern of cause-and-effect relations upon which all decisions about extrinsic value will then depend.

This division of labor is not envisaged by all, or in a uniform way. Dewey is emphatic in declaring it to be impossible;[1] and Morris Cohen maintains that ethics "clarifies the choice of ends" only because it "enlightens us as to the necessary means." [2] Indeed, there are many other exceptions that might be cited. Yet it will be acknowledged that a preoccupation with intrinsic values, or "ultimate ends," presumed to be ascertainable without any consideration of means, is not at all infrequent in current academic ethics. The situation has not been greatly different throughout ethical history. If the early writers, being lovers-of-wisdom in general, recognized no division of labor between moralists and scientists, considered as isolated groups of men, they often recognized the possibility of isolating moral and factual questions, and of making questions about intrinsic value an independent study. One could presumably decide about the ultimate ends in advance of finding the means of obtaining them. The emphasis that philosophers have given to the *summum bonum* will be a testimony to this. Whatever may be the meaning of this term (for like other ethical terms, it is not well defined), it has almost always been taken to imply intrinsic value. It is worth having, "for its own sake," not as a means to something else.

If such a conception of ethics were feasible—and hereafter it will be convenient to call it the "specialist's" conception—the task of systematizing ethical methodology would be greatly simplified. Many of our observations in Chapter V would be superfluous; and indeed, they would be needlessly diffuse even for the ethical arguments—which so manifestly extend beyond the considerations of intrinsic value into a consideration of means—that we encounter in daily life. Since this point is essential to an understanding of the importance and relevance of the present chapter, let us examine it more closely.

In the following argument,

1. See, for example, *Human Nature and Conduct*, particularly the Introduction, and Pt. I, sec. 2. The present chapter has been greatly influenced by Dewey, as will be evident throughout.
2. *Reason and Nature* (Harcourt, Brace, 1931), p. 442.

> Objects of sort M are the only ones intrinsically good, and
> those of sort N the only ones intrinsically bad
> X leads to a preponderance of M's over N's
> Therefore: X is on the whole good

the conclusion follows from the premises by formal logic, granted appropriate definitions; hence any further support of the conclusion requires only a support of the premises. The support of the second premise may be presumed to depend on well-known scientific methods. Only the support of the first premise, then, introduces methods that are characteristically ethical.

Now by the specialist's conception of ethics, the support of *any* ethical conclusion, provided that it is not itself about intrinsic value, would be reducible to a similar form. One might always isolate a purely scientific premise, relating some given X to some M or N. And one might always isolate a purely ethical premise about the *intrinsic* value of M or N. A philosophical moralist, limiting himself to the defense of such a broad, basic premise as the latter, could pardonably be ignorant of the causes of M's and N's. For by the specialist's conception these would have nothing to do with intrinsic value, and, figuring only in the second premise, could be left to others, along with the demonstrative inference to the work-a-day judgment about the value of the given X.

Such a view would have this important implication for the methodological problems that have previously concerned us: All that is *peculiar* to ethical arguments could be studied with reference to judgments about *intrinsic* value alone. The rest would be logic and scientific method. In particular, the inferences in which, by the preceding chapters, a reason is *psychologically* related to an ethical judgment, could be taken as demonstrative ones in which a first premise, about intrinsic value, is tacit. Thus the inference, "X leads to Y; therefore X is good," might be held as incomplete unless some judgment about the intrinsic value of Y (or of something to which Y led in turn, etc.) were implicitly presupposed; and methodology might be taken as having no concern with it save for making the implicit presupposition explicit. Eventually, one would come to judgments about intrinsic value; and although these would then present a peculiar problem, it would be a problem neatly isolated from the logical and scientific problems that surround it.

But the specialist's view, with this conveniently simple conception of method, cannot be allowed to pass without question. Although its errors may at first seem slight, they become particularly misleading when they serve to excuse philosophical moralists for an ignorance of science. The penalties of scientific ignorance are suggested, to be sure, by quite direct considerations. One who, ignorant of means, proceeds to recommend intrinsically valuable ends, may recommend ends which are impracticable because unobtainable. Yet to this a ready answer is often given: An end, even if unobtainable, may serve as a goal to be *approximated*, and may be practical to that extent. If we are to criticize the specialist's conception, then, we must argue on other grounds. Now such grounds are in fact provided by the first pattern of analysis itself. We must accordingly develop its central conceptions—with renewed emphasis on agreement and disagreement in attitude—in a way that makes these implications more apparent. There may be occasion, in so doing, to enter into passing digressions, moralizing about the ways of moralists; but on the whole the present chapter will continue to study the "mechanics," as it were, by which ethical methods operate.

In brief: our present problem is one of determining whether the first pattern can sanction an emphasis on intrinsic value, and whether it can recognize a practicable division of labor between those who recommend ends and those who study means.

2

LET us first subject "intrinsic" and "extrinsic" to workably clear definitions. Since the terms will be of present interest only when related to attitudes, we may define them in such contexts:

"I approve of X intrinsically" has the meaning of "I approve of X when I disregard all of its consequences upon other objects of my attitudes."

"I approve of X extrinsically" has the meaning of "The consequences of X meet for the most part with my approval, and so I approve of X when I consider it with exclusive regard to its consequences."

The term "disapprove," or any other term designating an attitude, may uniformly replace "approve" throughout, the definitions being general to that extent.

Following the first pattern of analysis, we may now say that "X is intrinsically *good*" asserts that the speaker approves of X intrinsically, and acts emotively to make the hearer or hearers likewise approve of it intrinsically. So, *mutatis mutandis,* for "extrinsically good," "intrinsically bad," and "extrinsically bad." Two points are to be noted: (1) Judgments that declare X to be extrinsically good or bad remain emotively active; they *evaluate* X with regard to a full range of consequences, and do not merely indicate that it leads to some specified and unevaluated Y.[3] (2) The term "intrinsically good" will be assumed to influence the *hearer* to have an intrinsic attitude (like the speaker's), and not just to have any sort of favorable attitude. Though this assumption is overly precise, in view of the rough influence that judgments have in daily life, it is convenient in suggesting that people do not *agree* on the intrinsic value of something unless *both* approve of it intrinsically. (Much the same could be said of any other ethical expression in which either "intrinsically" or "extrinsically" occurs.)

These definitions do not exclude the possibility of saying that something is good *both* intrinsically *and* extrinsically. If a speaker approves of X when he disregards its consequences, he may also approve of it when he regards them exclusively; and thus his generic approval of X will be all the stronger. To say that X is good both intrinsically and extrinsically (always following the first pattern) simply testifies to this double approval, and recommends it to the hearer. On the other hand, a speaker may consistently affirm that X is good intrinsically but bad extrinsically, or vice versa. And a speaker who acknowledges that X is intrinsically good may nevertheless insist that X is on the whole bad; for his approval of X, independently of its consequences, may be outweighed by his disapproval of it when he takes its consequences into account. That is to say, he may find that X excludes too many other things of which he intrinsically approves, or that it fosters too many things of which he intrinsically disapproves. The remaining logical relations between the terms will become clearer as we proceed.

It will be convenient to interchange "intrinsically" and "extrinsically" with "as an end" and "as a means." The latter terms

3. It is this which distinguishes "extrinsically good" from the purely descriptive use of "good means," synonymous with "effective means," that was illustrated in Chapter IV, p. 83. Cf. p. 114, n. 2.

lend themselves to convenient idioms so long as "good" is in question. They will not do for contexts involving "bad," however, for "bad as a means" would inevitably suggest "inefficient means," which is by no means synonymous with "extrinsically bad"; and "bad as an end" suggests "bad for others to take as an end," which is not synonymous with "intrinsically bad." It is particularly important that "end," when it abbreviates "that which is approved intrinsically," be distinguished from another usage, not here employed, in which it refers to a broad, focal aim, predominating one's conscious attention. Such a focal aim *may* be an end in the present sense, but *need* not. It may be valued as a means to many other ends. For example: a legislator's focal aim may be to strengthen a democratic form of government; but his approval of doing so may be extrinsic—arising from the many effects that it will have on the people who are governed.

Let us now return to our problem, as stated in the preceding section, and break it up into manageable divisions.

The plausibility of the specialist's conception of ethical method depends largely on certain assumptions which, before they are attentively studied, may seem wholly innocent. They can be stated as follows: agreement on intrinsic value

(1) is presupposed by, and
(2) does not itself presuppose,

any other type of ethical agreement. The term "presuppose" is here used in a special sense. One sort of agreement, T, will be said to "presuppose" another, U, when and only when the attainment of U is one of the *steps* necessary to the attainment of T. "Presupposed by" designates the converse relation, as usual.

The bearing of these (tacit) assumptions on the specialist's conception of ethics is readily seen. If agreement on intrinsic value, by (1), is presupposed by every other type of ethical agreement—i.e., if agreement on the worth of X always implies an agreement either that X itself, or some Y accepted as a consequence of X, is good as an end—then agreement on ends will be indispensable to *any* mutually accepted judgment, and will provide moralists with their only peculiar problem. And if, by (2), agreement on intrinsic value presupposes no other sort of ethical agreement—i.e., if agreement that Y is good as an end does not imply any evaluation of the means of securing it, or of the consequences which Y itself may have—then it becomes feasible, and indeed highly convenient, for philosophical moralists to attend to ends exclusively, leaving other ethical questions to those who engage in the scientific study of what will bring the ends about. Should (1) and (2) fail to hold, on the other hand, any specialized attention to ends might prove to be relatively uninteresting, or impossible in the nature of the case.

It may be presumed, roughly but serviceably, that a criticism of the specialist's conception requires no more than a criticism of these assumptions.

3

LET us begin with assumption (1). Is it the case that agreement on intrinsic value is presupposed by every other type of ethical agreement?

The question is best approached indirectly. We must first classify the kinds of agreement in attitude that can arise, letting the principle of classification rest on whether the attitudes in question are intrinsic or extrinsic. This will readily enable us, with only a little further attention, to see which sorts of agreement are presupposed by others.

So classified, there are four "basic types" of agreement in attitude, as follows:

Type I. A and B may both approve of X intrinsically. In this event they need *not* agree that X is "good on the whole," as we have seen. But they will at least agree that X is intrinsically good; and if no other factor will make a difference to their attitude to X (as we may now assume, to make the case as simple as possible) then they will agree on the value of X without qualification.

Type II. A and B may agree on the intrinsic value of Y, and thus, if both believe that X leads to Y, may agree that X is good extrinsically, being a means to their common end. They need not do so, of course, if they believe that X leads to *other* consequences than Y which would serve to alter their approval of X; but if again we assume that there are no other factors beyond those indicated, we may conclude that X will be accepted as good by both, though not as an end.

Type III. A may approve of X as an end, and B, although indifferent to it as an end, may approve of it because he believes it is a means to Y. So long as no other factors enter, A and B will agree that X is good, generically speaking, even though it is neither a common end for both nor a common means.

Type IV. A may approve of Y intrinsically but be indifferent to Z, and B may approve of Z intrinsically but be indifferent to Y. If they believe respectively that X leads to Y and to Z, then, so long as no other factors enter, they will agree that X is good—good as a means to their divergent ends.

BASIC TYPES OF AGREEMENT IN FAVORABLE ATTITUDE

TYPE I.

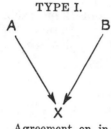

Agreement on intrinsic value of X.

TYPE II.

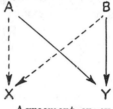

Agreement on extrinsic value of X, arising from agreement on intrinsic value of Y.

TYPE III.

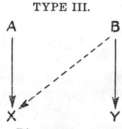

Diverse agreement on value of X.

TYPE IV.

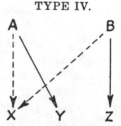

Agreement on extrinsic value of X, independent of agreement on intrinsic value.

Key to diagrams: A and B are persons; X, Y, and Z are objects of possible approval. Both A and B believe that Y and Z (wherever they occur) are consequences of X. The unbroken arrow indicates "approves intrinsically," and the broken arrow, "approves extrinsically."

Before relating these types of agreements to our central problem, let us see how each might be concretely illustrated. The illustrations must of necessity be a little artificial, since the types themselves are abstractions—being serviceable, like the "frictionless" or "perfectly rigid" bodies of physics, to isolate in attention the aspects of a problem that cannot be isolated in fact. But when this is allowed for, the illustrations are easily given.

Suppose that A and B agree that racial survival (X) is intrinsically good. To that extent their agreement will be of Type I. If they assign no added value to racial survival because of its consequences on something else (as is thoroughly unlikely, but will do as an artificial supposition) then their agreement on its value will be *exclusively* of Type I.

Suppose that the agreement of A and B on racial survival (now taken as Y) is exclusively of Type I. If they believe that a centralized form of government is a means to this end, their agreement on the means (X) will to that extent be of Type II. If they assign no further value to the government—if neither approves of it as itself an end, and if neither approves of it as a means to some further end which the other does not accept—then their agreement on its value will be exclusively of Type II.

The next type can be illustrated by introducing assumptions into the old story about Menenius, the friend of Coriolanus. Suppose that the sole end of the patricians is the survival of their own class (X), and the sole end of the plebeians is the survival of their own class (Y). So long as the plebeians see no connection between the patricians' survival and their own, they do not recognize it as good. But when Menenius, with his fable of the state and the human body, leads them to see that the survival of the two classes is interdependent, they come to approve of the patricians' survival as a means to their own. Here there is no common end, for the patricians take as an end what the plebeians take as a means; but there is nevertheless a convergence of approval, and agreement of Type III.

The final type can be illustrated by assuming that each person of a given society takes *his own* survival as his *sole* end (Y being A's survival, Z being B's survival, and so on). Since the survival of one person is not identical with that of another, there will be nothing commonly accepted as an end. But if each person believes that peace rather than war is a means to his personal survival, all will agree that peace is good. The agreement will be of Type IV, where there is a generally accepted means to ends which are wholly divergent.

It may be noted that, so far as logical possibilities are concerned, a given society can be totally free from disagreement about what is good, even though all agreement is of Types III and IV exclusively. That is to say, these types do not necessarily purchase agreement on X at a cost of disagreement elsewhere; for although they do imply a *difference* elsewhere (namely, a difference of ends), this difference does not entail *opposition*, and so does not entail *disagreement*.[4]

Our diagrams and illustrations deal only with agreement on what is good; but it will be obvious that similar distinctions hold for agreement on what is bad. Diagrammatic representations of the latter can be secured by drawing a line, indicating *dis*approval, through each of the arrows, broken or unbroken, that appear on page 181. The four types may then conveniently be called types of "negative" agreement—which, being agreement in unfavorable attitude, must not be confused with disagreement. We may continue to ignore negative agreement, since it so obviously raises the same issues as "positive" agreement, or agreement in favorable attitude.

Having now distinguished the four types of agreement, we may easily deal with our more central issue. Assumption (1), page 179, which we are in the course of examining, stipulates that agreement on ends is presupposed by every other sort of ethical agreement. This would hold true if all ethical agreement were of Types I and II; for agreement of Type I (on Y) is clearly presupposed by that of Type II (on X), and if there were no other types, assumption (1) would immediately follow. When Types III and IV are recognized, however, the matter stands in a different light. With either of these types there may be ethical agreement without agreement on ends. A's end may be B's means, or A and B may accept common means to divergent ends. Although no one person can approve of anything as a means without approving of something else as an end, it remains possible for people to *agree* in approving of something without *agreeing* on ends. This latter possibility is the one to which Types III and IV testify— a possibility which becomes quite obvious when the nature of agreement in attitude is clearly envisaged. It follows that agreement of Type I, sought by judgments about intrinsic value, is *not* an indispensable step in securing agreement of all the other types. In other words, agreement on intrinsic value is not presupposed by every other sort of ethical agreement. Assumption

4. Cf. pp. 4 f.

(1), which is in part to measure the tenability of the specialist's conception, proves on examination to be false.

This conclusion holds, however, only if assumption (1) is interpreted as excluding the very *possibility* of Types III and IV. Perhaps it need not be interpreted so stringently. If III and IV remain possibilities, but ones that are never actualized, then agreement will fall under types I and II so far as it is in fact obtainable. The assumption may in that form be tenable, it will be urged, and a specialized attention to ends proportionally vindicated. So we must consider whether III and IV promise to be of real interest.

The question demands an elaborate inquiry into the nature and direction of people's attitudes, and any attempt to give a definitive answer would be rash; but it will be enough to answer roughly. Types III and IV become important to whatever extent there are forces which make people pursue divergent ends. Among these forces (as will have been suggested by the preceding illustrations) we must recognize ordinary egoism; for when each man's ends are uniquely related to himself, *common* aims cannot be ends. It will not do to pretend that egoistic ends never exist nor is it easy to believe that they will ever be done away with.[5] Now so far as egoistic ends can lead to convergent attitudes at all, they must do so after the manner of III and IV. If all men were wholly egoistic, and unalterably so, *all* agreement in attitude would *have* to be of these types; but one does not have to accept this extreme view, which may even out-Hobbes Hobbes, to see that they are important. If *some* men are *preponderately* egoistic on *some* issues, and in a way that is *practicably* unalterable—and this is assuredly a condition that is actual—Types III and IV retain an importance which, though partial, is not negligible. It may be added that egoism is only one of the factors to be considered; there are many others, as will be apparent from subsequent remarks.

For some cases, then, we may conclude that Types III and IV not only conceivably may but actually must replace Types I and II, if there is to be any ethical agreement at all. Assumption (1) fails, no matter whether it is taken as a principle of logic or as an observation about how moralists can feasibly proceed.

Although the assumption may hold true for *some* cases, the fact that it does not hold for *all* is of much consequence. Its fail-

5. Herbert Spencer is interesting in this connection. See *Data of Ethics* (1879), chaps. xi, xii.

ure shows that the attempt to establish common ends, so attractive to philosophers, can at times be dispensed with, without prejudice to moral stability. And its failure shows that unless such efforts *are* dispensed with, or widely supplemented, there will be cases where ineffectuality will take the place of practical moral efforts. This will be true even if the work of philosophical moralists is extended by that of scientists, so long as both are content with rigid specialization. The pure philosopher, limiting his judgments to ends, will secure only agreement of Type I, to the limited extent that that is possible; and should he turn his established ends over to the pure scientist, who is to discover the means of obtaining them, this will lead, indirectly, only to agreement of Type II. Who, then, is to deal with the issues where Type I, and hence Type II, are unobtainable, and where Types III and IV are alone the practicable ones? These will be shunned by the pure philosophical moralist as tainted by science, and by the pure scientist as tainted by morality. Yet they may be issues that are not beyond solution. The peculiarly evaluative aspects of ethics are not exhausted by an effort to establish common ends, however consoling it may be to the "pure" philosopher to believe the contrary.

With Types III and IV the relation between directing attitudes and establishing beliefs is inseparably close. The issues cannot there be handled by separate groups of men each ignorant, or half ignorant, of the detailed development of the other's work; for although the issues are evaluative, a knowledge of means is essential to *every* step of debating them. An isolable premise, purely about intrinsic value (like that illustrated on page 176), simply does not occur. A moralist who *himself* possessed scientific knowledge—one who organized and applied it, making generally known the common means to divergent ends, and who supplemented his procedure by any other methods, including the persuasive ones, that he saw fit to use—could hope effectively to cope with such issues; whereas the moralist who specialized, failing to establish agreement of Type I, would have no conclusion likely to interest the scientists, or to guide them in selecting what means-end relations to study. Nor will the scientists, left to their own devices, promote agreement of Types III and IV automatically. Their conclusions are often in a necessarily general form, requiring careful application to any case at hand; they organize their knowledge for quite different purposes than the moral ones; and they do not call their conclusions to people's attention at just the time that attitudes must be altered. A scientifically minded moralist must of course be expected to *draw* from the work of the scientists, but an application of their conclusions to moral issues must be his own. To this extent an effectual moralist cannot delegate the use of scientific reasons "to others"—unless, indeed, he is content with methods that are for the most part persuasive, or with reasons that found ethical agreement on falsehoods.

A specialized attention to ends is not, to be sure, entirely discredited by these observations. It is not predestined to failure in all cases—or at least our discussion has not yet been able to show that it is—and to whatever extent it can lead to common ends, there being then no occasion to make use of Types III and IV, it will serve its purpose. But we may readily see, even at this early stage of our discussion, that judgments about ends must not be ascribed an exaggerated importance. They are not indispensable to all other ethical agreement; and they are unlikely, in view of egoism, to provide the broad, complete basis for ethics which philosophical moralists desire.

4

WE have so far dealt only with the first of the assumptions that are to be criticized. Before turning to the second, we must give further attention to the sorts of agreement in attitude. This will serve to correct certain oversimplifications in what has preceded, as well as prepare for the sections that are to follow.

The diagrams on page 181 isolate the basic types of agreement on what is good, but no actual case, found in daily life, need represent one of them to the exclusion of the others. The types may occur simultaneously, in combination. One kind of combination can be illustrated as follows:

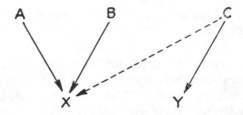

Here A, B, and C all agree in approving of X, but the agreement of A and B is of Type I, whereas that of A and C (or B and C)

is of Type III. Any of the types, and any number of them, may enter into such combinations. It would be possible, for instance, to have a general agreement on the value of X, in which that of A and B, say, is of Type I, that of C and D is of Type II, that of A and C is of Type III, and that of C and E is of Type IV.

In the case diagrammed above, the agreement between any pair of men is of only one type, but there is a combination in that different pairs of men exemplify different types. When the types are combined in this fashion, let us say that the general agreement is of a "compound" nature. There is another kind of combination, however, which must sharply be distinguished from this. It occurs when agreement exemplifies two or more types simultaneously, with regard to the same object, for a *single pair* of men. This we may call "complex" agreement. In the following diagram, for instance,

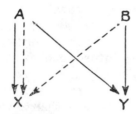

the unbroken arrow from A to X, with the broken arrow from B to X, indicate agreement of Type III, whereas the broken arrows to X indicate Type II. The possibility of having both sorts of arrow from A to X has been shown on page 178, where it was explained that something may be approved both intrinsically and extrinsically. The complex cases, like the compound ones, can become quite involved. It would be possible, for instance, to have an agreement between A and B on X that was partially of all four types. Both men might approve of X as an end, but also approve of it as a means to other ends, some of which would be common ones and others disparate.

There can be cases where agreement is both compound and complex—where at least two pairs of men agree in different ways, and where those of at least one pair agree in more than one way.

Compound agreement is an obvious possibility that need not greatly concern us. Complex agreement, however, is of no little theoretical importance. It is particularly interesting for calling attention to a psychological situation which we may call "reinforcement."[6] Such a situation is illustrated by the attitudes of A in the diagram just above, whose intrinsic approval of X is "reinforced" by his extrinsic approval of it. One may also say that his extrinsic approval is reinforced by his intrinsic one. In general, reinforcement occurs simply when the same man approves of something both as an end in itself and as a means to some further end, or else when he approves of it as a means to several ends. (The latter alternative, not suggested by the above example, permits one to say that a man's approval of X as a means to Y may be reinforced by his approval of X as a means to Z, even though X is in no part an end.

Reinforcement must be contrasted with conflict. The latter occurs when X is the object of the same person's extrinsic approval and intrinsic disapproval, or vice versa, or when X is the object of his extrinsic approval so far as it leads to Y, and of his extrinsic disapproval so far as it leads to Z. The effect of conflict is to weaken or nullify the resultant force of a man's attitudes, whereas that of reinforcement is to strengthen it.[7]

The prevalence of reinforcement is readily illustrated. There are all sorts of things which, as we say, are "valued in part for their own sake," or "are in part their own reward," but which are also valued as a means to other things. Walks on sunny afternoons, hearing music, talking with friends, eating a luxurious dinner, working with complete absorption, helping those in distress, and so on, may all be ends—valued apart from their consequences on the objects of other attitudes. Yet they are not valued *only* in that way. All of them *have* consequences, and if we did not value them further on that account they would seem relatively unimportant to us. A man may value walking on a sunny afternoon both as an end, and as a means to health, and as a means of reaching his destination; and similarly for the other examples. This is in effect to say that an intrinsic attitude

6. The term has other uses which must not be confused with the present, arbitrarily selected one.

7. Some of the writers who speak of "integration" of attitudes may be referring to the state of mind (often obtainable, in varying degrees of approximation, by intelligent foresight and sublimation) in which there is a minimum of conflict and a maximum of reinforcement. Such a definition would require careful qualification, but is perhaps a convenient point of departure for clarifying a term that shows promise of being useful.

is often reinforced by an extrinsic one—and there will usually be several extrinsic attitudes, each arising from a different consequence, and each reinforcing the others.

We have seen that reinforcement and complex agreement are intimately related. More specifically, whenever a man's attitudes to X are reinforced, his agreement with any other man about the value of X is extremely likely to be complex. (It is certain to be unless both men value X *wholly* as a means, and as a means to *wholly* common or *wholly* divergent sets of ends—in which case there will be a repeated exemplification of Type II only or Type IV only.) Hence if reinforcement is very common, we may expect complex agreement, for the cases in which agreement actually occurs, to be only a little less so. That is why a study of complex agreement is so important to ethical methodology.[8]

We can now understand why the concrete illustrations of the four basic types, as given on pages 181 and 182, were of necessity artificial. Complex agreement is so prevalent that it is difficult (and perhaps impossible) to find any ordinary case that exemplifies some one of the four types without at the same time exemplifying another. Yet the basic types are essential to a clear analysis. Here, as is so often the case, an isolation of certain aspects of a problem in attention goes beyond any real separation of them in their concrete manifestation; nor is an isolation of them any the less important on that account.

Ethical literature abounds with judgments of the form "X is good as an end." It is quite likely, however, that the writers who defend such judgments are not taking X to be end, primarily —so long as "end" is understood in the present sense—but rather are taking it to be a focal aim.[9] That is to say, they do not hope for agreement on X that is exclusively, or even primarily, of

8. As before, the account has been simplified by ignoring *dis*approval. It will be obvious, however, that there could be complex cases of negative agreement (see p. 183) which would involve reinforcement of disapproval—i.e., a situation in which the same man *dis*approved of X both intrinsically and extrinsically, or disapproved of it both on account of its effect Y and its effect Z.

A more thorough treatment of disapproval would introduce what could be called "agreement with partial conflict." This occurs when at least one of the agreeing parties has *repressed* attitudes that lead in the direction of disagreement. For instance: A may approve of X in all respects, both intrinsically and extrinsically, whereas B, though approving of X on the whole, and so agreeing as to its generic value, may approve of it extrinsically while disapproving of it intrinsically.

9. "Focal aim" has been defined on pp. 179 f.

Type I, but hope only for a *complex* agreement on it, and one of such strength that it will lead to further agreement on a great many objects that are a means to X. Yet these writers often suppose that they must show X to be an end, and wholly an end, in a sense not far different from the present one. This leads to methodological confusions that are quite serious, as we shall later have occasion to see.[10]

In emphasizing the prevalence of complex agreement, we have been working on a tacit premise—that it is possible for the same man to have more than one end. For without plurality of ends there can be no reinforcement, and without reinforcement there can be no complex agreement. Can the premise be defended?

There would be no doubt about the answer, perhaps, if we were fully accustomed to see behind the broad, abstract terms by which ends are so often designated. The doctrine of psychological hedonism, for instance, is sometimes stated: "Each man has an intrinsic desire for his own pleasure, and for nothing else." Would it follow that each man has only one end? A moment's thought will show that pleasure, the "one" end, need not be taken as a concrete entity whose unity "transcends temporal diversity." Any man is capable of many separate pleasures, and it would be more natural to say that each constitutes a separate end. Even for psychological hedonism, then, one can recognize a plurality of ends, with reinforcement as a possible consequence. In particular, we should expect desires for Bentham's "fecund" [11] pleasures to be reinforced, these being desired both as ends and as a means to further ends. All ends would fall into the one *class* of pleasures by such a view; but that is another matter.

Psychological hedonism is mentioned, to be sure, only for purposes of illustration. "As a psychological theory it was killed by Butler," who "pointed out clearly and conclusively the ambiguities of language which made it plausible." [12] There is no occasion here for reviewing Butler's contributions, or for entering into the work that has been done subsequently. But let us

10. Cf. pp. 202 f.
11. *Introduction to the Principles of Morals and Legislation*, chap. iv, par. 2.
12. C. D. Broad, *Five Types of Ethical Theory* (Harcourt, Brace, 1930), p. 55. Broad's account is no less interesting for his own work on the problem than it is for his presentation of Butler's.

note that when A desires X, it is usually X which is called the *object* of his desire. Now it is true that if A attains X, his desire is "satisfied," and to that extent he experiences pleasure (though the pleasure may be offset by factors that were unexpected). In other words, X can never be desired without being a *potential cause* of pleasure. But it does not follow that a pleasure must always be the *object* of desire. To say so would be to say that X, whose attainment *causes* a pleasure, is always *itself* a pleasure—a statement that sounds plausible only when the cause is confused with the effect.

This criticism has entirely to do with the word "object," and so holds for intrinsic desires no less than for extrinsic ones. Only one comment need be added: If the phrase, "A's intrinsic desire for X" purported to designate a desire that would persist even though X had *no* consequences—not even potential consequences on A's pleasure—then the phrase would be useless. There could be no desire whose object was not a potential source of pleasure; and if pleasure, even, were itself desired, it would have to be the *cause* of a *further* pleasure that attended the desire's satisfaction. So literally nothing could be desired intrinsically. But as defined on page 177, "intrinsically" gives rise to no such implication. If A desires X intrinsically, he may consider it as potentially satisfying his desire, and so giving potential pleasure. All that "intrinsic" requires is that A should continue to desire X apart from considering its consequences on other things so far as these are taken as *objects* of *other* desires. It certainly does not require that the objects of intrinsic desires are to be identified with the pleasures of satisfying them.

Once these confusions are cleared away, the possibility, and indeed, the actuality, of a plurality of ends becomes readily evident from common-sense observations. Any man will have ends of all sorts, each desired apart from its consequences. Few if any of these, however, will be ends *exclusively*. Intrinsic desires will be reinforced by extrinsic ones, as we have seen, and extrinsic desires will reinforce each other whenever an object is a means to several ends. Accordingly, much of ethical agreement, wherever it is possible, will be complex; and no theory of ethics can be acceptable which leaves complex agreement out of account. This conclusion will have an important bearing on the observations that are to follow, which in turn will serve to strengthen it.

5

WE may now proceed with our central question—whether philosophical moralists can leave questions about means to others, and limit their judgment to ends. We have seen that this roughly depends on the soundness of two assumptions, namely: agreement on intrinsic value

(1) is presupposed by, and
(2) does not itself presuppose,

any other type of ethical agreement. The first of these has been considered in Section 3, and found false. Our conclusions there were developed only for the four basic types; but it will be obvious without further discussion that they can be related to any combination of types, whether compound or complex. We may accordingly turn to the second assumption.

At first glance assumption (2) may seem indisputable. Whenever agreement on intrinsic value (Type I) is sought, and only that, questions about means appear foreign to the issue. One may, of course, use judgment about means to *reinforce* an intrinsic attitude; but will not reinforcement simply introduce complex agreement, and so types *other* than I? If so, it will show only that one can go beyond Type I, not that the attainment of I *presupposes* the attainment of the other types. How, then, is assumption (2) open to criticism?

So far as (2) points out a logical possibility, it is indeed unassailable. One can *conceive* of a world in which agreement on ends is obtained without considering means at all. But not all conceivable situations are actual. If (2) is to be of interest, it must point out not merely a logical possibility but a realizable one. Otherwise it will have little to do with what concerns us— it will not show that the specialist's conception of ethics is *practicable*. We must interpret it, then, as maintaining that one who strives to promote agreement on ends does not *in fact* need to deal with means. So understood, (2) becomes untenable. In spite of initial appearances, we shall be led to quite the opposite conclusion.

To understand this, let us begin by noting that intrinsic attitudes are not an immutable part of each man's nature, predestined by his germ cells to be just as they are. (If they were, by the way, any effort of a moralist to alter them would be futile, and judgments limited to intrinsic values could be discredited without further ado.) Without denying that a man may have hereditary dispositions to acquire certain attitudes, we must realize that the actual development of them will depend upon many environmental factors—social, geographical, and so on.[13] This general point being scarcely disputable, we may proceed to the central contention of the present criticism.

Among the factors that determine intrinsic attitudes we must recognize *habituation*—the sheer "getting used to" something. Habits of approval, once formed, become fixed, and may outlast the circumstances that brought them into being. So when a man becomes used to striving for something, for no matter what reason, he will tend more and more to take it as an end in itself. Extrinsic approval comes progressively to be *reinforced* by intrinsic approval, as a part of the general adaptability of human nature. In brief: What is first favored as a means may on that very account grow to be favored as an end.

From this it readily follows that when men first *agree* that something is valuable only as a means, they may later come to *agree* that it has value as an end. An agreement initially of Type IV, for instance, may in time become complex, involving Type I as well—the extrinsic approval of the agreeing parties being reinforced, as a consequence of habituation, by an intrinsic one. And there may be no other way, in certain cases, in which agreement of Type I can arise. We may accordingly draw this conclusion: An effort to establish commonly accepted means, even to divergent ends, can be a step that is necessary—not logically, of course, but practically—to establishing commonly accepted ends.

Now this is the full contradictory of assumption (2), which must accordingly be repudiated.[14] Our conclusion shows that agreement of Type I, to which judgments about intrinsic value are conducive, can be obtained by *first* securing agreement of the other types. A moralist who neglects the other types, hoping thereby to keep to fundamentals, half-unwittingly gives up this important procedure; hence he risks ineffectuality even in the pursuit of his chosen task.

Such is the criticism of the specialist's conception, so far as assumption (2) is concerned; and stated in this brief form it is

---

13. Cf. Dewey, *Human Nature and Conduct*, Pt. II.
14. It must be remembered that the term "presuppose," as used in the formal statement of assumption (2), has been defined in a semitechnical sense. See p. 179.

extremely simple. It is quite another thing, however, to provide the criticism with a more detailed defense, and to show the full range of its ethical implications. To these latter matters we must now turn, treating them in order in the two sections that follow.

6

OUR rejection of assumption (2) has depended upon a key psychological premise, namely: What is first favored as a means may on that very account grow to be favored as an end. The present problem, accordingly, becomes one of providing this premise with empirical proof, drawing upon such common-sense observations as are available.

The premise is not easily denied. It fits in so readily with daily life that many have recognized its truth, even though they have not recognized its full importance. J. S. Mill, for instance, defends it by citing a well-known example: In many cases, he urges, an object of desire is

originally a means, and . . . if it were not the means to anything else, would be and remain indifferent, but . . . by association with what it is a means to, comes to be desired for itself, and that too with the utmost intensity. What, for example, shall we say of the love of money? There is nothing originally more desirable about money than about any heap of glittering pebbles. Its worth is solely that of the things which it will buy; the desires for other things than itself, which it is a means of gratifying. Yet the love of money is not only one of the strongest moving forces of human life, but money is, in many cases, desired in and for itself; the desire to possess it is often stronger than the desire to use it, and goes on increasing when all the desires which point to ends beyond it, to be compassed by it, are falling off.[15]

If Mill then goes on to "logic-chopping," vainly hoping to reconcile this passage with his other views, the very laboriousness of his effort shows how indubitable he took the passage to be.

Common-sense examples are easily multiplied. When parents encourage their children to be honest or considerate, they often point out that these qualities lead to social approval or to success in after life. Initially, this recommends the qualities as a means to egoistic ends; but with habituation it may be a factor which makes them ultimately valued for themselves, cherished, at least in some degree, in circumstances where the more indirect

---

15. *Utilitarianism*, chap. iv, par. 6.

rewards are known to be lacking. In somewhat the same way, a musician who first desires technique only as a means to artistic expression may later value it in part for its own sake. If he does not, he is unlikely to develop enough technique to forward his artistic aims. (Thus technique, like so many other things, must in part become an end if it is adequately to be cultivated as a means. Nature has been kind in making this possible, and becomes a "stepmotherly nature," not in all cases, but only when the means become so much an end that other ends are neglected.) Similarly, a professor who first tolerates his teaching as incidental to his research may grow to like it for its own sake; a lawyer who first defends his clients in order to forward his career may find that a skillful defense has become an end in itself; and so on.

Such examples cannot, to be sure, establish a probability comparable to that of well-controlled experimental techniques. They introduce many irrelevant factors that cannot be held constant. But they point to our key psychological premise with no little insistence. In Santayana's phrase, there is a "tendency of representative principles to become independent powers and acquire intrinsic value"—a tendency which, if "sometimes mischievous," leading to "idolatrous veneration," may also produce "the finest flower of human nature."[16]

Among contemporary psychologists, this view has been strongly supported by G. W. Allport, in his theory of the "functional autonomy of motives."[17] He gives many examples analogous to those above, and cites a number of experiments on animals, all pointing to the conclusion that "what was once an instrumental technique becomes a master-motive." Allport makes clear, of course, that the theory is an old one; it is only his name for it and defense of it that are new.

There are unquestionably some practical difficulties in testing such a theory, but not fatal ones. Let us pause to consider the most important of them. The principle here in question,

X, first sought as a means to Y, may later become an end,

16. *Sense of Beauty* (Scribner's, 1896). Ed. of 1936, p. 26.
17. *Personality, A Psychological Interpretation* (Henry Holt, 1937), chap. vii. Allport's views are summarized and criticized by David C. McClelland, "The Functional Autonomy of Motives as an Extinction Phenomenon," *Psychological Review*, Vol. 49, No. 3 (May, 1942).

usually operates in close connection with a different principle, namely:

X, first sought as a means to Y, often promotes, unexpectedly, some further end, Z; and thereafter X may be sought as a means to Z no less than to Y.

Let us hereafter refer to the first of these as "Allport's principle"; and let us refer to the second as "Wundt's principle"— for it was Wilhelm Wundt who most emphasized its importance. We shall later see that his principle lends itself to a more interesting interpretation, but the interpretation above will serve a temporary purpose.[18] So understood, Wundt's principle points mainly to the plurality of ends, and the possibility of increased reinforcement with increased knowledge. But its importance, for the present purpose, lies in suggesting the need of caution in using the examples that support Allport's principle—both the examples that Allport himself gives and those that have been given here. When X, first desired as a means to Y, continues to be desired independently of Y, one must not conclude that X is to this full extent desired intrinsically; for X may be desired in part as a means to the originally unforeseen Z, to which Wundt's principle calls attention. Thus the virtuoso who first develops technique as a means to musical expression, and continues to develop it beyond the point that expression requires, even flaunting it about at the expense of music, is not shown, in just that degree, to value technique for its own sake. He may have come to desire it as a means of impressing others with his skill—a factor which may have been accidental to his original motives.[19]

18. Wundt called it the "law of the heterogony of ends." His treatment of it will be evident from the following quotations from his *Ethics* (1886). English trans. by Titchener, Gulliver, and Washburn (Macmillan, 1897).

"The effects of . . . action extend more or less widely beyond the original motives of volition, so that *new* motives are originated for future action, and again, in their turn, produce new effects." (I, 330.) "The official who serves the State perhaps does his duty in the first instance merely because he finds it to his own advantage. The worker in industrial arts who benefits the public by a technical application of some useful discoveries may have an eye, first of all, to his own personal interest. But ultimately neither of them can ignore the wider results of his activity. And so the universal end [accidentally] attained becomes one of the motives of action. Later, under the influence of practice, it may even become the ruling motive." (III, 102 f.) "It is one of the most wonderful things about moral development that it unites so many conditions of subordinate value in the accomplishment of high results." (*Idem*, p. 66.)

19. McClelland (*op. cit.*) uses somewhat similar examples in criticizing Allport.

In this as in so many examples, intrinsic and extrinsic attitudes are so closely connected that it is practically impossible (though of course logically possible) to devise well-controlled operational techniques for separating them. But we shall conclude too hastily if we suppose that Wundt's principle requires us to dismiss Allport's, or that there is no evidence for the growth of means into ends at all. If the examples cited are taken as suggesting a multitude of others, it becomes difficult to believe that Wundt's principle alone—though it is unquestionably operative, and complicates the test of Allport's—is sufficient to account for the extraordinary way in which admittedly outmoded means continue to be the objects of veneration (as in "cultural lags"), or for the way in which new means, even when proved as efficient to accepted ends, are not greeted with full favor until after a period of habituation. This, together with the evidence of introspection —which however loathsome it may be to experimental psychologists, is our only guide over the vast regions of human conduct which are too complicated for experimental techniques—seems strongly to indicate that Wundt's principle does not supplant Allport's, but only supplements it. That is to say, when X is first desired as a means to Y, X may later be desired, in part, *both* as an end in itself *and* as a means to some originally unforeseen Z.

If it will now be granted that the two principles operate conjointly, we may proceed to an extension of Wundt's principle, as previously interpreted, which in some ways makes it closely resemble Allport's, and makes it doubly interesting in its implications for ethics. Suppose that X, repeatedly sought as a means to Y, is found always to have the incidental consequence Z. And suppose that Z is at first greeted with indifference. It may then happen that Z gradually ceases to be indifferent, and becomes an additional end. Habituation to it, arising by a kind of accident, arouses latent intrinsic desires, which without habituation would never have developed. If Z, in turn, has incidental consequences, the process may repeat itself; and so on.

It is not insisted that Wundt's principle operates in this broader way exclusively. Wundt himself seems sometimes to have in mind the narrower operation of it that was stressed in the preceding paragraph—where Z is not initially indifferent, but fully desired from the first, being neglected in the original pursuit of X only because X and Z were not then known to be causally related. But the extended interpretation of the principle, enabling it to account for the development of *new* intrinsic desires, seems to preserve an essential part of Wundt's meaning; and indeed, the view itself has no little plausibility. It remains distinct from Allport's principle; for that holds that means may themselves become ends, whereas Wundt's principle, as now interpreted, holds that the incidental, originally indifferent *consequences* of a given means may become ends.[20] But the principles agree in recognizing that ends arise and change in the course of discovering and developing means; and that is precisely the point which the present discussion seeks to establish.

It must not be thought that the principles operate with an inevitability. Habituation is not the *only* factor that modifies intrinsic attitudes, and other factors often nullify its effects. But the principles operate with sufficient constancy and strength to deserve marked attention.

7

HAVING now sought to establish the view that means pass into ends, which in turn justifies the rejection of assumption (2), let us look to the repercussions on ethics. Although these were briefly sketched in Section 4, they deserve more emphasis.

It will be convenient to begin with an example. A moralist is contending that X is intrinsically good—his judgment, accordingly, being one which seeks to establish agreement of Type I. Not all of his hearers at first agree with him, so he feels the need of providing his judgment with support. How may he proceed?

One method would be to point out the consequences of X upon some Y which his hearers already accept as an end. If sufficient, this procedure will not, of course, immediately establish agreement of Type I, since it recommends X only as a means. The agreement of the moralist with his hearers will be of Type III,[21] and that of any of his hearers with any other will be of Type II. But by contenting himself with the latter types of agreement temporarily, the moralist may achieve a general agreement of Type I later on. By the operation of Allport's principle, his hearers may come to take X as an end in consequence of having

20. It may be added that the incidental consequences of a given end may become further ends.

21. It will be complex, of course, involving both Type III and Type II, if the moralist takes X not only as an end but as a means to Y as well. But the whole of this example assumes that the *initial* attitudes to X (and to Y) are not reinforced—an assumption whose artificiality has previously been pointed out, but which is now serviceable in simplifying exposition.

been led to take it as a means. If he proceeds in this way, the moralist can hope to forward his aims; though his success, as always, will be conditional to the circumstances, and to the kind of people whom he is addressing.

As a further method, the moralist might find some W which had X as an incidental consequence, and proceed to defend the value of W by any of the ways suggested in Chapter V. Directly, this would lead to no agreement at all on the value of X; but indirectly, through the operation of Wundt's principle, in its extended interpretation, it might cause X to be generally accepted as an end. Again the moralist may hope for effectuality, though subject to the same restrictions as above.

Now if the moralist wishes to use either of these methods, it will be clear that he must reject the specialist's conception of ethics. He must himself—unless he is to invent falsehoods, and capitalize on his hearers' ignorance—have a full knowledge of the causal milieu into which his influence is introduced. For even though he is supporting judgments about intrinsic value, promoting common ends, his very process of doing so requires intervening steps in which the recommended ends are seen as causes or effects. Indeed, he must be the very opposite of a specialist. We have only to complicate the above example, realizing that there may be not one Y or one W but a whole group of them, to see that the causes and effects in question may lie in all manner of fields. Certain studies, such as psychology, sociology, history, and economics, may be of particular importance to him; but there is no field of study whose conclusions are without a potential bearing on ethical orientation, and so no field of study which he can be content to neglect. He will do well, moreover, to give full exercise to his imaginative and emotional habits, whether in cultivating the arts or in meeting the practical decisions of a varied life. This will preserve his mental health, essential to the acquirement and organization of knowledge itself; and it will give him vitality in communicating his opinions to others, and in putting his opinions to work in the service of his aims.

But what if a moralist, eager to abide by the specialist's conception, should reject these methods? What if he should still hope —scorning to soil his hands with practicalities—to establish common ends by some procedure in which a consideration of means had no part? It is then very difficult to see how he could make use of rational methods at all. If intrinsic attitudes are not redirected by a knowledge of the factual situation which confronts them, they are not directed by knowledge. A reason can have force only by relating the recommended object to the object of some preëxisting attitude, thus serving, by the operation of Allport's principle or of Wundt's, to alter intrinsic attitudes indirectly.

For a *direct* alteration of intrinsic attitudes, only one procedure is available—and that is the exclusive use of persuasion, whether overt or concealed, clear or confused. The "specialist on ends" must compensate for his ignorance of means by the vigor of his pronouncements. Now we have seen that persuasion has its place in ethics, and must not hastily be scorned. Yet it is not to be supposed that a specialist would commit himself to this method exclusively, if he were aware of what he was doing. Nor is persuasion, isolated from all use of reasons, likely to be effective in producing permanent results. No attitude, not even an intrinsic one, can be deeply ingrained into a person's nature unless it is reinforced by others, and has a place in the economy of his multiple aims.

In an interesting passage in Plato's *Republic*, Adeimantus abuses the moralists for defending the conventional virtues as a means, insisting that this procedure produces only a semblance of virtue. He urges Socrates, who has "admitted that Justice is one of that highest class of goods which are desired indeed for their results, but in a far greater degree for their own sakes," to "praise" justice in the latter capacity alone.[22] But Adeimantus, in neglecting the growth of ends through habituation to them as means, neglects the most important way in which "virtue can be taught." Had Socrates followed the advice, his "praise" of justice could have been only that. And indeed, Adeimantus himself quickly veers in his request, asking to know what justice and injustice "do to the possessor of them." To that extent he asks not about intrinsic value but about the *effects* of just practices on a given individual; he testifies to the inevitable need of looking to the consequences of a given end, even in the course of establishing it.

It may be objected that the rational methods are not exhausted

22. II, 363–367. The quotation is from 367, as translated by Jowett. We shall find in the following chapter that "justice" is a word that raises its own problems; but for the present context we may assume that it is mainly a descriptive term, designating the instances of which Socrates and Adeimantus would both predicate it.

by means-ends relationships—that one may defend the value of X without mentioning any Y or W with which X is causally connected. In a limited sense this is true. Example (10) of Chapter V,[23] for instance, illustrates a method which points out not the ends to which X is a means but rather the origin of the *attitude to* X. We can readily see, however, that although this may avoid reference to the consequences of X, it does not avoid all considerations of cause and effect. One must still consider the causal milieu out of which the ethical controversy arises; and any moralist who does this must still abandon the specialist's conception. Perhaps it is not impossible that a moralist, though illinformed about matters of fact, may give partial support to a given end by the clarity of his statement of it. But even this is far from a likelihood. As Dewey has remarked, "Only as the end is converted into means is it definitely conceived, or intellectually defined, to say nothing of being executable. Just as an end, it is vague, cloudy, impressionistic. We do not *know* what we are really after until a *course* of action is mentally worked out."[24]

We may conclude that a study of means is wholly indispensable to ethics, if moral judgments are to have effective support. So inevitable is the conclusion that it becomes difficult to see why philosophical moralists should ever have been content to deny it. But perhaps there has been more denial of it in words than in actual practice. Some, with Kant, have said that "every empirical element is not only quite incapable of being an aid to the principle of morality, but is even highly prejudicial to the purity of morals."[25] Yet the native urges of common sense have a way of breaking through the artificialities of theory, and of making theorists wiser than they know. Each tentative application of a principle becomes a secret test which guides its formulation. If that were not the case, the study of the a priori moralists would be (as it is not always, in fact) a kind of "mental archeology."

An implicit concern with means, in spite of theories to the contrary, can be found in nearly all the ethical traditions; and perhaps it deserves a more detailed illustration:

The defenders of utilitarianism, though sensitive to the importance of consequences, often speak of them only in connection

---

23. P. 123.

24. *Human Nature and Conduct*, pp. 36 f. Yet this quotation must be understood with caution; for Dewey is not making a clear distinction, perhaps, between an "end" (as here defined) and a focal aim.

25. *Metaphysic of Morals*, p. 54. Trans. by Abbott.

with the *practical application* of their principle, rather than in connection with the establishment of the principle itself. Indeed, both Bentham and Mill acknowledge that their central principle, "which is used to prove everything else [in ethics] cannot itself be proved."[26] "Questions of ultimate ends are not amenable to direct proof. Whatever can be proved to be good, must be so by being shown to be a means to something admitted to be good without proof."[27] Here it seems clear, particularly so for Mill, that the writers feel they must recommend social happiness as the sole *end*, and that they must accordingly give up as impossible any purported proof that shows it to be a *means* to other ends. An appeal to the consequences is deemed irrelevant, so far as the proof of their central principle is concerned.

But it will not do to leave so important a principle without some manner of support. For that reason, perhaps, both Bentham and Mill give attention to "sanctions"—to the factors which induce a man to act in accordance with a principle, or which deter him from violating it. Now the sanctions of the utilitarian principle, if they do not "prove" it, are essential, so long as lip-service is not enough, to making it accepted. In fact the sanctions are simply consequences which certain *reasons* for the principle, as the present work uses the term "reasons," may serve to point out. And clearly, if a man espouses the principle on account of its sanctions, he takes the general happiness as a *means* of obtaining the rewards, whether "internal" or "external," or as a means of avoiding the penalties, which the sanctions bring with them. An appeal to consequences, seemingly dismissed, reappears in another form.

In this respect the utilitarians exemplify a mixture of confusion and discernment that is extremely common in ethics. They suppose themselves to be recommending general happiness as the *sole end*, understanding "end" in much the same sense that is here used. But if they were really doing this, they

26. Bentham, *Introduction to the Principles of Morals and Legislation*, chap. i, par. 11.
27. J. S. Mill, *Utilitarianism*, chap. i, next to last paragraph. Mill goes on to recognize a "proof in a broader sense," which he considers available. This is essentially a matter of stating the principle in a way that frees it from misinterpretation, perhaps. Or it may be that Mill was anticipating the formal proof he provides in chap. iv—but the latter is obviously confused; and even if it were acceptable, it would not be a "proof in a broader sense," but only a straightforward logical and empirical proof.

would be committed to ineffectuality from the start. We have seen that each man has many ends, innumerably many; and although the altruistic end of the utilitarians may be among these, the others could not possibly be obliterated. So the utilitarians, their common-sense habits breaking through their artificial conceptions of method, cannot avoid striving, in actual fact, to support a judgment which is far more practical. As our remarks about sanctions will indicate, they in effect recommend the general happiness not as the *sole* end, but simply as *an* end which is also a means to many divergent ends. They recommend it as what has here previously been called a "focal aim"—as an end which is also such an exceptionally important means to so many divergent ends that if anything else is not, in its turn, a means to this, it will be without predominating value.[28] Taken in this way (as, in sanity, it must be taken) the utilitarian contention has a hope, at least, of being practical. Whether or not it would in fact be accepted, in the light of full knowledge, is another matter; but *if* it would be, it would provide a centralizing generalization, giving better organization and coherence to the many specific judgments of daily life. It could be no more than a rough principle, admitting of only an uncertain application, and subject to many exceptions; but what more can one hope for amid the varied problems of normative ethics? Meanwhile, it would give rise to no methodological difficulties, save those of sheer complexity, and the uncertainties that attend the support of ethical judgments in general—for it would be open to support by a full appeal to the consequences. It is unfortunate that the utilitarians, misled by linguistic and methodological difficulties, should have appealed to the consequences only covertly, and so have left their principle without the more adequate support which, whether acceptable or not, would unquestionably have led to illuminating discussion.

The distinction between ends and focal aims, simple though it is, has perhaps more important implications on ethical philosophy than any other that our study has introduced. The topic

28. Cf. pp. 179, 189 f. And note that the importance of taking the utilitarian ideal as a focal aim, rather than an end, is not offset, but actually increased, by Allport's principle. The operation of this principle might make the greatest happiness of the greatest number more and more an end, but never the *only* end. It tends to increase the number of ends, not to decrease them.

cannot be developed here; but in a later chapter,[29] where methodology will be reviewed from a different point of view, it will be given its proper attention.

Of the specialist's conception in general, little more need be said. It has nothing in its favor, and is so contrary to common sense that those who maintain it in words must reject it in practice. There has been occasion to refute it, but only because the effect of faulty theory, even though it cannot wholly obstruct our native wisdom, can yet retard it, and prevent its full development.

One may specialize, beyond any doubt, to the extent that he seeks to advance knowledge in some selected branch of science. And one may specialize to a certain extent in the linguistic and methodological aspects of a subject, including ethics—as the present work, it is hoped, does not wholly fail to indicate. If specialization is not obtained without cost, even in these fields, the cost is often less than the gain. In normative ethics, however, with its practical task of setting up and defending standards of moral conduct, there can be no such thing as specialization. There all things are in question. An emphasis on ends to the neglect of means is an emphasis on conclusions to the neglect of reasons. It must either exploit ignorance or countenance futility.

8

LET us now briefly summarize this chapter—but with a somewhat different emphasis, that will relate it to the chapters on method that have preceded.

By the specialist's conception of method, any argument will always have an isolable first premise, whether implicit or explicit, that is about intrinsic value. All else being logic or science, it will then be feasible, presumably, to simplify ethical methodology by considering judgments about intrinsic value alone.[30] Our problem has been to subject this view to careful examination, looking to the assumptions that underlie it.

Our criticism of assumption (1) has shown that such a first premise is not always isolable.[31] To whatever extent Types III and IV are in question (either exclusively, or as the principle

29. Chap. XV.
30. Cf. pp. 175 f.
31. Cf. Sec. 3, particularly p. 185.

aspects of an agreement that is to be complex) there will be no effort to agree on ends, and no need *at all* for a judgment about intrinsic value. Each party in the argument will have ends, but it is not they which will be called into question.

Our criticism of assumption (2) leads to a stronger conclusion. Even if a judgment about intrinsic value should be easily isolable—even if it should be effective in producing agreement of Type I, strong enough and widespread enough to be the basis of much agreement of Type II—there would be no gain in centering a discussion of ethical methodology about it. The support of "X is intrinsically good" is in no way simpler than that of any other ethical judgment, for it leads to the same consideration of means. Indeed, it is more complicated, involving the principles of Allport and Wundt.

In no case does an emphasis on intrinsic value permit one to ignore the use of reasons about matters of fact, which in their *psychological* relationship to ethical judgments, constitute the peculiar aspects of ethical methodology.

It is on this account that the present work, departing from a much too current procedure, has taken "good," rather than "intrinsically good," as central to an analysis of both meanings and methods. The generic term, "good," may lead to agreement of any of the four types, and to the combinations of them, involving complicated reinforcement, that we find in daily life. The central topics arc most conveniently introduced by it; and any elaboration of them, into which the present chapter has entered, forms an essential part of the superstructure of ethical analysis, rather than of its foundations.

IX

Second Pattern of Analysis: Persuasive Definitions

1

THE first pattern of analysis has now been presented, apart from some details that can conveniently be left until later. Let us accordingly turn to the second pattern.

The differences between the patterns have been explained in Chapter IV, at the beginning of Section 3; hence they will need here only a very brief restatement. Two patterns are required because the ethical terms, as used in everyday life, are vague. Whenever a term is vague there is no sharp distinction between its strict descriptive *meaning* and what it *suggests*. If an analyst makes such a distinction, in the hope of bringing clarity to ordinary discussions, he will not do well to insist that the distinction *must* be made in one way, to the exclusion of all others. It is more important to understand the flexibilities of common words, and the varieties of meaning they may "naturally" be assigned, than to insist on some one meaning that they *should* be given. The first pattern deals with only a few of the many analyses possible—those in which descriptive reference is limited to the speaker's attitudes, all else being "suggested but not strictly meant." Since the ethical terms can readily be assigned more complicated meanings—meanings which are often insisted upon, and give rise to problems that are much in need of clarification—the second pattern is designed to study them. In both patterns the ethical terms are considered as emotively active, for in other cases[1] there is no peculiar linguistic or methodological problem. And in both patterns there is an emphasis on disagreement in attitude. The distinguishing features of the second pattern, then, lie solely in the added descriptive meaning that it provides, and the complications of methodology that arise as a consequence.

---

1. As illustrated on p. 83 f.

The following typifies the general form which any second-pattern analysis of an ethical judgment will exemplify:

> "This is good" has the meaning of "This has qualities or relations X, Y, Z . . . ," except that "good" has as well a laudatory emotive meaning which permits it to express the speaker's approval, and tends to evoke the approval of the hearer.

The following points are to be noted: (1) As usual,[2] the emotive meaning must be separately "characterized," as distinct from being preserved by the defining terms. (2) Reference to the speaker's attitudes, so important in the first pattern, is now left without explicit mention—though it will be "suggested," of course, by the presence of emotive meaning. One could readily preserve it by a suitable substitution for one of the variables ("X," say); but since this would introduce the complication of an indicator term (the "I" in "I approve"), whose nature has received sufficient attention in Chapter VII, let us simplify matters by assuming that no such substitution will be made. (3) The above is not a definition of "good," but rather a formal schema for a whole set of definitions; for there is no definition until the variables are replaced by ordinary words.[3] A schema is just what is wanted, since the second pattern deals with many definitions, differing from one another in that the variables give place to different sets of constant terms. Schemata for terms other than "good" may be given in a parallel way, and need not be separately mentioned.

What sort of definitions may be instances of the second pattern? That is to say, by what constant terms may the variables of the schema be replaced? It will not do to admit of any substitution whatsoever. If that were done, "good" would be a possible synonym for any term in the language which has both a laudatory and a descriptive meaning; and although "good" is vague, it is not so vague as that. Our linguistic habits are well enough established to rule out certain descriptive meanings as "unnatural," particularly for extreme cases. Thus the schema

2. See pp. 82 f.
3. By the present conventions, substitutions for the variables may be made regardless of whether or not they occur in quotation marks. Cf. p. 166, n. 9.

for the second pattern is not complete. It requires a qualifying clause that keeps the constants replacing "X," "Y," "Z" . . . within certain boundaries—boundaries between which descriptive meanings of "good" may be expected to fluctuate, and beyond which they are unlikely to extend. For present purposes, however, these boundaries will only be mentioned; no effort will be made to specify what they are. The reasons for this omission will grow clearer as we proceed. Meanwhile it may be observed that the boundaries for the "natural" meanings that may be assigned to "good," as is true of any vague term, are so shadowy and unstable that it is difficult to specify them even in a rough way. And there would be little gain if this were done; for confusions arise not from inattention to the boundaries, but from inattention to the many possible senses that lie between them.

The unformulated boundaries of common usage are unquestionably wide enough to permit great numbers of second-pattern definitions. Suppose, for instance, that a man says, "By a 'good' college president I mean one who is an industrious executive, honest and tactful in dealing with his faculty, and capable of commanding universal respect for his intelligence and long-sighted aims." This makes the little word "good" say a great deal, and we should doubtless hesitate to take the remark as strictly a definition. Yet for the purposes of a given context and conversation, we might readily be content to do so. The word would then, so to speak, be granted a local, temporary sense, and for other purposes quite different senses would be necessary; but one of the chief functions of vague words is that they can be adapted to this or that specific purpose, as occasion requires. It must be granted that any such specialized sense of "good," when singled out to the exclusion of others, and isolated from a living context, is likely to seem a little odd. We should feel the same oddity if "middle-aged man" were defined as "man who is between the ages of 44 and 58." A definition of a vague term almost always renders its meaning *less* vague, temporarily; and this seems capricious so long as the change is made without some definite purpose in mind. But in the "sample" definitions that must here be studied, the oddity will vanish if we allow for the artificial conditions of analysis, and imaginatively reproduce the practical situations in which words are at work.

There are many possible definitions which are less specific than the one above; and among them are those which refer to the broad aims which normative theorists so often recommend. For instance: if we tacitly remember the difference in emotive meaning, we may define "good" to have the meaning of "conducive to the greatest happiness of the greatest number." Such a definition will make the principle, "Anything is good only if it leads to the greatest happiness of the greatest number" an analytic one; but if that is to be a source of objection, the objection cannot be based on purely linguistic grounds. In the same way, "good" may be defined in terms of the "integration of interests," or "universal love," or "survival," and so on. It may seem rash to tolerate so many senses, in the face of the many controversies they have stirred; yet if we look solely to linguistic proprieties, and bear in mind the great flexibilities of language, it will be clear that any of them is permissible, and that none, at least for the language of sophisticated circles, extends the word beyond the boundaries of its vagueness. When any normative principle comes to be an accepted doctrine, "good" may come habitually to *suggest* it; and it is then by no means unnatural to define "good" with explicit reference to the principle. Vagueness always permits this procedure. We shall soon see, to be sure, that there may be urgent reasons for rejecting a definition, even though language allows it. A definition may be linguistically permissible and still fail to serve certain purposes—purposes which in ethics will require particularly careful study. But it remains the case that many senses of "good" are equally possible so long as we look to the dictates of common usage alone.

Throughout the pages which follow it will be necessary to emphasize this general point: The great variety of meanings which the second pattern recognizes, as compared with the first, and the greater "content" which it seems to provide, end by making no essential difference to the nature of normative ethics. Ethics becomes neither richer nor poorer by the second pattern, and neither more nor less "objective." All the considerations of the first pattern reappear, and the task of analysis is simply to discern them in their new linguistic guise. Perhaps this will not be initially obvious. With increased descriptive meaning, ethical judgments are open to a more direct use of empirical and logical methods, and thus seemingly more amenable to the ordinary considerations of proof and validity. We shall see, however, that this is a wholly unimportant matter, without any results upon the possibility or impossibility of reaching ethical agreement.

The importance of the second pattern lies not in revealing new ethical "content," but rather in revealing new complexities of language; and perhaps it is chiefly of interest in calling attention to a much used but too little studied type of definition. Definitions are usually studied as a propaedeutic to science, logic, or mathematics, with emphasis on the way they clarify common notions or make convenient abbreviations. One is likely to think, then, that definitions have the same function in ethics, and that the selection of any defined sense, from the many that the second pattern recognizes, will be guided by purely descriptive interests. In point of fact, this is rarely the case; description is usually a secondary consideration. Ethical definitions involve a wedding of descriptive and emotive meaning, and accordingly have a frequent use in redirecting and intensifying attitudes. To choose a definition is to plead a cause, so long as the word defined is strongly emotive. For the first pattern, attitudes are altered by ethical judgments; for the second, they are altered not only by judgments but by definitions. Thus the disagreements evinced by contrary *predications* of the ethical terms may also be evinced by contrary contentions about their *meaning*. Disagreement in attitude may be debated over the dictionary. It is this characteristic of second-pattern definitions that brings back all the considerations that the first pattern has introduced.

Any further steps in analysis must accordingly be prefaced by a study of the "persuasive definitions," as they will be called, which the second pattern so habitually involves. Since these definitions are not ethically neutral, and since analysis must strive to be so, the present work will not defend any one of them to the exclusion of others; but it will be possible to study typical instances of them in a way that indicates their nature and function.

2

IN any "persuasive definition" the term defined is a familiar one, whose meaning is both descriptive and strongly emotive. The purport of the definition is to alter the descriptive meaning of the term, usually by giving it greater precision within the boundaries of its customary vagueness; but the definition does *not* make any substantial change in the term's emotive meaning. And the definition is used, consciously or unconsciously, in an effort to secure, by this interplay between emotive and descriptive meaning, a redirection of people's attitudes. These remarks will suffice to indicate the technical sense in which "persuasive definition" will here be used.

Further explanation can best proceed by example, and at first the examples will be taken from terms that are, so to speak, only semi-ethical—terms which are not usually given the unqualified ethical status of "good," "right," "duty," and "ought," but which introduce many of the same considerations. Let us suppose, then, that A and B are discussing a mutual friend, and that their remarks take this form:

A: He has had but little formal education, as is plainly evident from his conversation. His sentences are often roughly cast, his historical and literary references rather obvious, and his thinking is wanting in that sublety and sophistication which mark a trained intellect. He is definitely lacking in culture.

B: Much of what you say is true, but I should call him a man of culture notwithstanding.

A: Aren't the characteristics I mention the antithesis of culture, contrary to the very meaning of the term?

B: By no means. You are stressing the outward forms, simply the empty shell of culture. In the true and full sense of the term, "culture" means *imaginative sensitivity* and *originality*. These qualities he has; and so I say, and indeed with no little humility, that he is a man of far deeper culture than many of us who have had superior advantages in education.[4]

It will be obvious that B, in defining "culture," was not simply introducing a convenient abbreviation, nor was he seeking to clarify "the" common meaning of the term. His purpose was to redirect A's attitudes, feeling that A was insufficiently appreciative of their friend's merits. "Culture" had and would continue to have, for people of their sort, a laudatory emotive meaning. The definition urged A to stop using the laudatory term to refer to grammatical niceties, literary allusions, and the rest, and to use it, instead, to refer to imaginative sensitivity and originality. In this manner it sought to place the former qualities in a relatively poor light, and the latter in a fine one, and thus to redirect A's admiration. When people learn to call something by a name

4. From here on the present work incorporates, though with many changes, omissions, and additions, the material in the author's paper, "Persuasive Definitions," *Mind,* Vol. XLVII, N.S., No. 187 (July, 1938).

rich in emotive meaning, they more readily admire it; and when they learn not to call it by such a name, they less readily admire it. The definition made use of this fact. It sought to change attitudes by changing names.

The word "culture" readily lent itself to such a purpose. Its emotive meaning, it is true, may have been partly *dependent* on its descriptive meaning, and to that extent subject to variation with varying descriptive senses; but in part it was independent —established in such a way that it would persist even though its descriptive meaning did not. The definition could effect a change in descriptive meaning, then, which left the emotive meaning substantially unaltered. Since the change seemed rather "natural," thanks to vagueness, the hearer was not sharply reminded that he was being influenced, and so not emotionally stultified by being made self-conscious. The practicability of the definition lay partly in this, and partly in the fact that it made its results permanent by embedding them in the hearer's linguistic habits.

The definition was "persuasive" in a not unusual sense. Like most persuasive definitions, it was in fact doubly persuasive, taking away emotive meaning here, and adding it there. It at once dissuaded the hearer from any exclusive admiration of one set of qualities (the "outward forms," which are denied the more laudatory appellation) and induced him to admire others (imaginative sensitivity and originality). The speaker wished to attain both of these ends, and was enabled, by his definition, to work for both at the same time.

It must not be thought, of course, that *all* definitions of emotive terms are persuasive, or that they need always have an inadvertent persuasive effect. A speaker whose purposes are mainly descriptive can neutralize the effects of emotive meaning by intonation or explicit admonition. At times even this is unnecessary, for if the general situation is one which militates against persuasion, or if the speaker and hearer concur on the relevant evaluative matters, the actual emotive effects may be without practical bearing. The definition can then proceed as though the term were emotively neutral, and may serve a primarily descriptive purpose. It remains the case, however, that a great many definitions of emotive terms are persuasive, in intent and in effect. Our language abounds with words which, like "culture" have both a vague descriptive meaning and a rich emotive meaning. The descriptive meaning of them all is subject to constant redefinition. The words are prizes which each man seeks to bestow on the qualities of his own choice.

Many literary critics, for instance, have debated whether Alexander Pope was or was not "a poet."[5] The foolish retort would be, "It's a mere matter of definition." It is indeed a matter of definition, but not a "mere" one. If the word "poet" is to have an unusually narrow sense, Pope will become, beyond any doubt *for such a sense,* no poet. This, so far from being an idle conclusion, has important consequences; it enables the critics to deny to Pope a laudatory name, and so to induce people to disregard him. A persuasive definition, tacitly employed, is at work in redirecting attitudes. Those who wish to decide whether Pope was a poet must decide whether they will respond to the influence of the unfavorable critics—whether they will come to dislike Pope's work enough to allow him to be deprived of an honorary title. This decision will require an intimate knowledge of literature and of their own minds. Such are the important matters which lie behind the acceptance or rejectance of the tacitly proposed, narrow definition of "poet." It is not a matter of "merely arbitrary" definition, then, nor is any persuasive definition "merely arbitrary," if that phrase is taken to imply "suitably decided by a flip of a coin."

Persuasive definitions are often recognizable from the words "real" or "true" employed in a metaphorical way. The speaker in our first example, for instance, was telling us what "true" culture was, as distinct from the "shell" of culture. Similarly: "Charity," in the true sense of the word, means the giving not merely of gold, but of understanding. True love is the commun-

---

5. Thus Samuel Johnson wrote: "It is surely superfluous to answer the question that has once been asked, Whether Pope was a poet? otherwise than by asking in return, If Pope be not a poet, where is poetry to be found? To circumscribe poetry by a definition will only show the narrowness of the definer, though a definition which shall exclude Pope will not easily be made." See *Lives of the English Poets* (Everyman's), II, 230. To W. L. Bowles, however, the answer was not so obvious, requiring several distinctions. See his first letter to Byron. More recently, A. E. Housman, in his *Name and Nature of Poetry,* stood as kind of Bowles. He was an exception to the trend indicated by a contemporary scholar, who writes. "In the nineteenth century critics could dispute as to whether he (Pope) was really a poet at all. Since the beginning of the present century there have been many indications that the tide of taste has turned the other way." See R. K. Root's *The Poetical Career of Alexander Pope* (Princeton, 1938), Introduction. It will be clear that these writers sense the evaluative nature of the issue, and are not so undiscerning as to consider it "purely verbal."

ion between minds alone. Real courage is strength against adverse public opinion. Each of these statements (if we take the last two as being in quasi-syntactical idiom) is a way of redirecting attitudes, by leaving the emotive meaning of a word laudatory, and wedding it to a favored descriptive one. In the same way we may speak of the true or real meaning of "sportmanship," "genius," "beauty," and so on. Or we may speak of the true meaning of "selfishness" or "hypocrisy," using persuasive definitions of these derogatory terms to blame rather than to praise. "True," in such contexts, is obviously not used literally. Since people usually accept what they consider true, "true" comes to have the persuasive force of "to be accepted." This force is utilized in the metaphorical expression "true meaning." The hearer is induced to accept the new meaning which the speaker introduces.

Persuasive definitions are too frequent to have escaped attention, and although much neglected in academic ethics, they are sometimes stressed in other fields. Or rather, if little is said about persuasive *definitions,* much is said about the broad head under which a study of them would fall: the interplay between emotive and descriptive meanings in determining linguistic change, and its correlation with attitudes. Leonard Bloomfield gives a particularly clear example:

The speculative builder has learned to appeal to every weakness, including the sentimentality, of the prospective buyer; he uses the speech forms whose content will turn the hearer in the right direction. In many locutions "house" is the colorless, and "home" the sentimental word. Thus the salesman comes to use the word "home" for an empty shell that has never been inhabited, and the rest of us follow his style.[6]

And an extremely penetrating account is given by Aldous Huxley, in his *Eyeless in Gaza:*

But if you want to be free, you've got to be a prisoner. It's the condition of freedom—true freedom.

"True freedom!" Anthony repeated in the parody of a clerical voice. "I always love that kind of argument. The contrary of a thing isn't the contrary; oh, dear me, no! It's the thing itself, but as it *truly* is. Ask any die-hard what conservatism is; he'll tell you it's *true* socialism. And the brewer's trade papers: they're full of articles about the beauty of true temperance. Ordinary temperance is just gross refusal to

6. *Language* (Henry Holt, 1933), p. 442.

drink; but true temperance, *true* temperance is something much more refined. True temperance is a bottle of claret with each meal and three double whiskies after dinner . . .

"What's in a name?" Anthony went on. "The answer is, practically everything, if the name's a good one. Freedom's a marvellous name. That's why you're so anxious to make use of it. You think that, if you call imprisonment true freedom, people will be attracted to the prison. And the worst of it is you're quite right."

These last quotations illustrate a blatant use of persuasion, and one may be tempted to let them cast a general disparagement on persuasive definitions. But we must remember the remarks that were made in Chapter VII. The practical question is not *whether* to reject persuasion, but *which* persuasion to reject. Not all persuasion is that of the mob orator; and the evaluation of persuasion, like the evaluation of anything else, is not a matter that lends itself to hasty generalizations.

An interesting parallel to persuasive definitions is found in the perplexities that emotive terms sometimes introduce into science. Should a scientist define an emotive term for some technical purpose, he is likely to *seem* to persuade, and provoke disagreement in attitude, even though this is no part of his intentions. Thus F. W. Taussig remarks:

The opinion of many of the earlier writers on economics especially the English writers from Adam Smith to John Stuart Mill . . . was that only such laborers as turned out material things were productive; all others were unproductive. . . .

This distinction between productive and unproductive laborers was early attacked and long debated. It was pointed out that it seemed to affix some sort of stigma—an accusation of uselessness, of being in need of support from others—on whole classes of persons whose work was admitted to be honorable and often seemed to be indispensable.[7]

The seeming "stigma" was in part due, no doubt, to a simple ambiguity. Certain readers may have thought that "unproductive" labor, in this technical sense, was of necessity "unproductive" in some more familiar, wider sense. But the emotive derogation of "unproductive," not easily altered by technical definition, must also have played its part. A definition which was presumably not persuasive in its intention was interpreted as being so.

7. *Principles of Economics* (Macmillan, 1925). 3d ed. revised, I, 16.

Such confusions arise quite frequently in economics, where scientific detachment is so hard to preserve. Gide, for instance, writes that

The "sterile classes" in Physiocratic parlance simply signifies those who draw their incomes second-hand. The Physiocrats had the good sense to try to give an explanation of this unfortunate term, which threatened to discredit their system altogether, and which it seemed unfair to apply to a whole class that had done more than any other toward enriching the nation.[8]

Again, a number of economists—including, though perhaps with qualifications, Adam Smith and Ricardo—espoused "labor theories" of value.[9] Few will suppose that these earlier writers sought by this means to plead the cause of the workingman, but they opened that possibility to subsequent writers. Thus Haney summarizes Proudhon, the socialist economist, as

mocking the economists for attempting a science while professing that there is no absolute measure of value. To him the matter is simple. "The absolute value of a thing, then, is its cost in time and expense." A diamond in the rough is worth nothing; cut and mounted it is worth the time and expense involved. But it sells for more than this;—that is because men are not free. Therefore, "society must regulate the exchange and distribution of the rarest things, as it does that of the most common ones, in such a way that each may share in the enjoyment of them." Value based upon opinion (or utility) is delusion and robbery.[10]

This, like "Marx's idea that labour alone created value, and that consequently profit and interest constituted a theft"[11] draws such a vast ethical implication from what is in effect a definition of "value," quasi-syntactically expressed, that an element of persuasion in the definition can readily be discerned. It would be presumptuous for the present writer, with his severely limited knowledge, to minimize the scientific contributions which social-

8. C. Gide and C. Rist, *A History of Economic Doctrines* (London, Harrap, 1915), p. 14.
9. See L. H. Haney, *History of Economic Thought* (Macmillan, 3d ed. 1936), pp. 219, 287. And see p. 131 for a reference to Petty and Locke in this connection.
10. *Idem*, p. 436.
11. Gide and Rist, *op. cit.*, pp. 184 f.

istic or communistic economists may have made; but since persuasion is not being ascribed to them only, but to anyone who proceeds from detached science to the emotive pleading of a cause,[12] and since persuasion is not being indicated as an exclusive factor, but only as *a* factor among many scientific ones, there can be no presumption in pointing out the emotive impact which "value" can so easily have. The word is not readily compliant to detached theory; and Pareto seems to sense its susceptibility to persuasive definition, as compared to an emotively more neutral term, when he writes:

Jevons in his day very wisely dispensed with the word "value" which from being stretched in this, that, and every direction, and from having countless meanings, ended by having no meaning at all; and he proposed a new term, "rate of exchange," of which he gave an exact definition. Literary economists did not follow him along that road; and they are to this day still dilly-dallying with speculations such as "What is value?" . . . They are strictly dependent on words capable of arousing the sentiments that are useful in convincing people; and that is why literary economists very properly are so much concerned about words and much less about things.[13]

It would be a pity if Pareto, or anyone else, served to dissuade economists from influencing attitudes; for they, beyond many others, have the information which gives their influence an illuminating support. It would be equally a pity, however, if economists should obscure the distinction between their work as scientists and their work as reformers. Some may wish to reject the reforms and accept the science. Others may wish to accept the reforms, on grounds of their own, and reject the science. And of those who accept the reforms on account of the science, many might think again if they realized that the reforms depended not upon the science alone, but upon the redirection of attitudes that might or might not ensue in the light of it.

12. The examples here cited are all from historical writers, since their procedures can more easily be seen in perspective. It is not difficult, however, to find examples in contemporary speeches and articles. A word like "inflation," say, will often be defined in an extended sense, so that its application to a given measure, in that usage, seems obviously correct. The stigma of the term, still persisting, is then used as a device for condemning the measure.
13. Vilfredo Pareto, *The Mind and Society.* Trans. by Bongiorno and Livingston (Harcourt, Brace, 1935), Vol. I, pars. 117, 118.

3

WE may now return to the second pattern, looking to the terms that ethical writers are more accustomed to stress. The possibilities of persuasively defining "good" will be obvious. The word is both strongly emotive and vague. And we are particularly habituated to using it in this or that special sense—as the fifteen and more columns which the *New English Dictionary* devotes to it will amply testify. Thus whenever, with suitable context, there is occasion to use the emotive force of "good" to plead a cause, our language enables us to do so in the form of a definition, without hindrance from the rules of common usage. The dictionary, for all its columns, simply gives samples of the more frequent senses. In short, any second-pattern definition of "good" —any substitution for the variables in our schema, page 207—is unlikely to represent detached, neutral analysis. It is less likely to *clarify* normative ethics than to *participate* in it. The effect of the definition is to give emotive praise to whatever the definiens designates; and had one, instead, synthetically *predicated* "good" of these designata, using the term as in the first pattern, the result would have been essentially the same. If this is not always so—persuasion depending as much upon the living context as upon the words that are used—it is so often enough to deserve careful attention.

If "good" is *defined* as conducive to the preponderance of happiness over unhappiness for society as a whole, the effect of the definition is, among other things, to support democratic ideals. It urges us to consider the happiness of *each* man, equally and without exception, allowing nothing else the laudatory force of the ethical term. The fact that so many of us are partially willing to respond to this persuasion, and to employ it, must not blind us from seeing that it is persuasion. There will be others, with different ideals, who will insist on defining "good" with reference to the happiness of some privileged racial or social group. Their ideals clash with ours, if we are utilitarians; and we shall be unlikely to make them abandon their persuasive definition unless we support our own by the many considerations that determine changes in attitude.

As this last remark suggests, it is quite possible to use reasons to support persuasive *definitions*, just as it is possible to use them to support first-pattern *judgments*. An initial persuasion need not be supported exclusively by further persuasion, regardless of the pattern that is used. But this is a point that must be developed in the following chapter.

What has been said of "good" may be said of the other ethical terms. Some of them have rather narrower boundaries between which the descriptive meaning can "naturally" vary; and some (like "ought," perhaps) are a little resistant to persuasive definition altogether, seeming more "natural" when analyzed by the first pattern. But all are subject to persuasive definitions in greater or lesser degree.

Bentham adapted a number of terms to his aims. When interpreted in accordance with the principle of utility, he writes, "the words *ought,* and *right* and *wrong,* and others of that stamp, have a meaning: when otherwise, they have none."[14] And " 'Justice,' in the only sense that has meaning, is an imaginary personage, feigned for the convenience of discourse, whose dictates are the dictates of utility applied to certain particular cases."[15] No doubt these definitions sought to clear away hypostatic confusions; but that could have been only a part of their aim, as we have seen above.

The term "justice," long a source of confusion, will be a convenient one to emphasize throughout the remainder of the present discussion.

Henry Sidgwick begins a patient and inconclusive chapter with the following remark:

It is the assumption of the Intuitional method that the term "justice" denotes a quality which it is ultimately desirable to realize in the conduct and social relations of men; and that a definition may be given of this which will be accepted by all competent judges as presenting, in clear and explicit form, what they have always meant by the term, though perhaps implicitly and vaguely.[16]

This is not a comfortable beginning. By the first half of the assumption he recognizes that "justice" must designate something "desirable," which is in effect to recognize its laudatory emotive meaning. This opens the possibility of persuasive definitions; and rival ones will be an obstacle to any meaning "accepted by all competent judges," which by the last half of the assumption is what the theorist must discover. Or such will be the case, at

14. *An Introduction to the Principles of Morals and Legislation,* chap. i, par. 10.
15. *Idem,* chap. x, par. 40, n. 2.
16. *Methods of Ethics* (Macmillan, 1874). In 7th ed. p. 264.

least, so long as men have opposed attitudes, and so long as one who dissents from a definition is not called an "incompetent judge" solely on that account. Thus it is not surprising that Sidgwick, whose careful analytic habits could not long ignore the turmoils of language, tacitly abandons the assumption as he proceeds, finding that "the attempt to map out the region of Justice reveals to us a sort of margin or dim borderland, tenanted by expectations which are not quite claims and with regard to which we do not feel sure whether Justice does or does not require us to satisfy them."[17] The hope of finding "the true definition of Justice"[18] gives place to a number of tentative proposals, differing for the several typical contexts in which the word may be used; and for the several "kinds" of justice which are accordingly recognized—such as "Corrective Justice," "Criminal Justice," "Retributive Justice," "Conservative Justice," and "Ideal Justice"—no common genus is provided.

Sidgwick's discussion is of exceptional interest for examining the many definitions that may be given; but these are not all vague gropings for the *same* sense, nor is it possible to *select* a sense while maintaining the emotional detachment for which he strives. In spite of himself, he implicitly acknowledges the evaluative, as distinct from the clarificatory, nature of the definitions, and their variation with varying ideals, when he writes that "our notion of Justice furnishes a *standard* with which we compare actual laws," and that "there seem to be two quite distinct conceptions of it, embodied respectively in what we have called the Individualistic and Socialistic *Ideals* of the political community."[19]

What sort of procedure can here be advocated as an alternative to Sidgwick's?

The essential step lies in making a clear distinction between the *purely* linguistic and the moral aspects of the issue. And with regard to the linguistic aspects, one must begin by heeding the sage observation of Aristotle—that "both 'justice' and 'injustice' have several senses, but, as the different things covered by the common name are very closely related, the fact that they are different escapes notice and does not strike us, as it does

17. *Idem*, p. 270.
18. *Idem*, p. 265.
19. *Idem*, pp. 265, 293. Italics not his.

when there is a great disparity."[20] That is to say, there must be no thought, in defining such a term as "justice," of finding "the" quality which people "have always meant by the term, though perhaps implicitly and vaguely"—nor is this a peculiarity of any one language. So far as common usage is concerned, an analyst can do not more than indicate a *range* of meanings to which the term is susceptible. Sidgwick does this implicitly, to some extent; but his avowed procedure always hampers his actual one.

Even in indicating the *range* of senses, there must be no hope of a definitive treatment. The problem itself (and this is particularly true for "justice") is an interesting and legitimate one when properly conceived. We do not use "justice" in a way that designates *any* virtue, but always a little more narrowly;[21] and one may wish to know *how much* more narrowly. Yet the answer cannot be precise, since the boundaries of a vague term, particularly when it is subject to persuasive definition, are themselves vague. An answer must often take the lexicographical form of exemplifying numerous definitions and typical contexts—a procedure which, even at best, takes one only a small step in developing or reëstablishing that bewilderingly complicated set of habits that are called "a feeling for the language." One may, alternatively, proceed in a more general manner—mentioning that the senses of justice have "something to do" with the *distribution* of commodities or opportunities, or with equality, or with law, and so on. But there is not always a uniform direction in the force that these considerations exert upon the term; and in the end one must acknowledge that the senses have only (in Wittgenstein's phrase) a "family resemblance."

The present account, somewhat regretfully, must for the most part ignore the boundaries for the meaning of "justice," much as it has previously ignored them for "good." [22] The problem lies amid many philological details, which could be more adequately treated by other hands; and perhaps a study of it, however fascinating in itself, would make only a minor contribution to the task with which alone we can here be concerned—that of freeing ethics from the confusions that are most prevalent and central.

20. *Nicomachean Ethics*, V, 1, 1129a. Trans. by F. H. Peters.

21. Note Bentham's reference, as quoted above on p. 219, to the way that "justice" is "applied to certain particular cases." Cf. p. 225, n. 25, on the different range of meanings for the corresponding term in Greek.

22. Cf. pp. 207 f.

Let us be content to emphasize that there *is* a range of meanings, hoping that a general sensitivity to this will serve for most practical purposes.

When the range of the term's meanings has been considered, and when this is supplemented by a study of its emotive meaning, the clarificatory aspects of the problem are virtually ended. Although one may be interested, more specifically, in understanding how the term is used by some particular historical author, this author will himself usually vary within a range of possible senses. There will still be a range, albeit a narrower one. For the rest—when a specially defined sense is singled out and recommended for exclusive use—the matter becomes an *evaluative* one. The definition is persuasive. Those who select a sense as the "true" sense may exert a deep and important influence as moralists, but they have ceased at that point to be analysts.

It is often the case, to be sure, that a writer wishes to *combine* the functions of analyst and moralist. This was doubtless the case for Sidgwick, whose work has prompted this discussion. And it will be obvious that the functions can, so far as the possibilities go, be quite happily combined. If the present writer does not seek to combine them, that is not to be taken as a precedent binding upon all others. But any combination of the functions must always be attended with this caution: Analysis is a narrow, specialized undertaking, requiring only close distinctions, careful attention to logic, and a sensitivity to the ways of language. Evaluation, on the other hand, is by no means a specialized undertaking—as we have seen in preceding chapters and shall see again in the following one. Should anyone, then, combining the functions of analyst and moralist, suppose that the habits of mind conducive to clear analysis are also adequate to the task of defending a moral standard, his work would lead to serious confusions. It is these confusions which are most conspicuous in the writings of Sidgwick and his British followers. They are no more serious—and perhaps they are less so—than those of writers whose analytic habits of mind are overridden by their moral zeal; and yet they have had, on the whole, an influence which is far from fortunate.

Ultimately, analysis and evaluation must be brought together; for the former is of use only so far as it gives discipline to the latter. But they must not be forced together prematurely. They must carefully be distinguished before they can profitably be combined.

Before leaving Sidgwick, and the observations to which he has led us, we must look to another passage from his work. This will illustrate an exceptional case in which a definition does *not* serve to influence attitudes, *even though the emotive meaning of the definiendum is quite strong.* By a "just" man, Sidgwick writes, we seem to mean "an impartial man, one who . . . does not let himself be unduly influenced by personal preferences." [23] Such a definition has but little normative import. But the reason is readily seen: An "impartial" man is one who does not favor any party more than he *ought* to; and a man is not "unduly" influenced by his personal preferences (presumably his self-regarding rather than his socially regarding ones) when he is not influenced by them more than he *ought* to be. The implicit force of "ought" in the *definiens* has a way of making any disagreement in attitude center about *it*, rather than about the definiendum. The disagreement is not, so far, in the course of being resolved, but is simply transferred from one set of terms to another. Indeed the seeming definition serves rather as a schema, helping to delimit the *boundaries* of the meanings of "justice" by relating them to those of "impartial" and "undue." No issue is likely to arise about the range of senses that these boundaries mark off, for people's attitudes are sufficiently similar to let them find, somewhere within it, a meaning they are willing to associate with the laudatory term. Hence an evaluative issue is postponed by this type of definition, but will reappear (and Sidgwick, with his excellent but puzzled common sense, is not insensitive to this) when the definiens is itself applied to concrete cases.

Apart from such exceptions, which extend the present account without greatly qualifying it, it may be conjectured that all writers who seek "the" meaning of justice, selecting it from the wide range of possibilities that the second pattern recognizes, have in part been pleading a moral cause. We often say, colloquially, that a writer has a "low conception" of justice or a "high" one. By this we indicate that his sense of the term, with its wedding of emotive and descriptive meaning, upholds ideals which clash or concur with our own—those that we are in the very course of defending.

23. *Op. cit.*, p. 268.

4

PARTICULARLY instructive examples are found whenever persuasive definitions take their place within an elaborate philosophical framework. In this respect the works of Plato, who so carefully theorized about the nature of definitions, and insistently emphasized their importance in ethics, are more than usually deserving of careful attention.

The first book of the *Republic*, it will be remembered, is largely taken up with an argument between Socrates and Thrasymachus. Socrates is the victor, and yet he is not content. "I have gone from one subject to another," he says, "without having discovered what I sought at first, the nature of justice. I left that inquiry and turned away to consider whether justice is virtue and wisdom, or evil and folly." [24]

Was the argument about the "virtue or evil" of justice really an unwarranted digression? In the light of our previous discussion we cannot agree that it was. The argument had the important function of determining whether or not "justice" was to retain its laudatory emotive meaning; and this was essential to the subsequent development of the dialogue. When a man is about to give a persuasive definition (and we shall see in a moment that Socrates was) he must make sure that the emotive meaning of the term defined is well established. Otherwise a definition which was intended to illuminate a descriptive meaning under a laudatory title will end by obscuring it under a derogatory one. The word "justice," a little too stern to be wholly pleasing, is in danger of becoming derogatory, and particularly so when men like Thrasymachus are using their oratorical ability to *make* the word derogatory. Socrates must praise justice, then, before he defines "justice."

The question about the meaning of "justice" reappears in the fourth book. The two intervening books have redirected our attitudes by a moving description of the ideal state. These new attitudes must be rendered more permanent. This can be done by dignifying the more significant aspects of the state under laudatory names. Of the four laudatory terms which Socrates mentions, "wisdom," "courage," "temperance," and "justice," the first three are readily made to serve this purpose, without any great change in their descriptive meaning. The remaining

24. 354, Jowett.

term must be reserved for whatever else needs dignity. And so the definition of "justice" is found. "Justice of the state consists of each of the three classes doing the work of its own class." [25]

The persuasive character of this definition—the fact that it forms a part of a spirited plea for a class system, a beautiful and moving appeal for a special kind of aristocracy—can scarcely be denied. The usual meanings of "justice" must give place to the "true" one, to the meaning which needs the dignity of a laudatory name.

This account differs materially from any that Plato himself would have given. Yet if we examine his own account, with severe reinterpretation, we shall find instructive points of analogy.

Plato would have agreed that the common conceptions of justice are vague and divergent. He was clearly not seeking to indicate merely the rough, common usages of the word. The definition of "justice" must be fashioned not after the common conceptions of it, but after justice itself—after the eternal Idea of justice, which we have beheld in a life before birth, and can now know only through careful *recollection*. Definitions based on common usage would disclose merely the several imperfect recollections of the Idea, as grasped by men bound to the world of opinion.

His recognition of the vagueness of common conceptions, although similar to the present account, seems greatly outweighed by the theory of recollection. But let us look more closely, asking how Plato determined whether his recollection was correct. Did he consider it correct when he reached a conception which satisfied his deepest, inmost aspirations? Did the dialectical method serve only to clarify his mind, so that his aspirations could be directed by articulate, consistent beliefs? It is difficult to think of any other answer. Plato aspired to the Ideas; but this was not

25. 441, Jowett. If the definition seems odd to English ears, that is due, no doubt, to the different range of meanings of the corresponding Greek term. Aristotle recognizes both "justice in that sense in which it is a part of virtue," and in that sense in which it "is not a part of virtue but the whole of it." (*Nicomachean Ethics*, V, 1 and 2, 1130a.) Such a range is not common, of course, for the English term. Classical scholars have often remarked that the abstract terms in Greek, slowly developing through an extended use of more concrete ones, are far more flexible than any ordinary English translation can indicate. They must be treated, perhaps, by means of the "multiple definitions" which I. A. Richards exemplifies in translating from the early Chinese. See Richards' *Mencius on the Mind* (Kegan Paul, 1932) particularly chap. iv.

a consequence of some miraculous power of attraction which the Ideas possessed. It depended on a linguistic resolution. Anything which was not an object of his aspirations was not to be called an Idea. If this is so, the present account is again close to his. If he had consciously been giving a persuasive definition, he would still have selected, as the descriptive meaning of "justice," the object of these same aspirations. Nothing else would have been granted the laudatory name. We have retained the factors which led Plato to give his definition, without retaining the poetic realm of the Ideas, whose function, indeed, was only to adorn his procedure, not to alter its outcome.

If Plato's work had been less Utopian, more satirical, he would have had recollections not from one realm of Ideas but from two. The first realm would have been the dwelling place of the gods, as described in the *Phaedrus;* and the second the dwelling place of the "author of evil" who makes his unexpected appearance in the tenth book of the *Laws.* Just as aspirations would be the criteria for correct recollection from the first realm, so aversions would be the criteria for correct recollection from the second. His theory of definition would then be less closely confined to the laudatory terms. Recollection could function for derogatory terms, like "injustice" and "evil," which need not then be defined indirectly, in relation to their opposites. But it would be of vital importance, in defining the derogatory terms, to confine the recollection to the second realm. The most serious philosophical errors would come from a failure to recollect from the "correct" realm, where the correctness of the realm would depend on the emotive meaning of the term defined.

It is curious to note that Plato—and he is only one of a great number of writers that could be cited—was earnestly perturbed by the vagueness of ethics, and sensed out the opposition of attitudes, and consequent persuasion, that its issues involve. He sought to avoid this by defining his terms, hoping to give greater rigor and rationality to his inquiries. Yet, ironically enough, these very definitions involved the same persuasion; and in a way that veiled and confused it, by making it appear to be purely intellectual analysis. The reflective elements in Plato's ethics are to be found not in his definitions themselves, but in the wealth of illustrative material that supports them.

X

Second Pattern: Method

1

IT has been remarked that the second pattern differs from the first in its external aspects alone. The old factors have only to be recognized in their new form. In the present chapter this contention will be established in detail, with particular attention to methodology. It will be shown that our previous conclusions, as developed for the first pattern, can be extended to the second without essential change.

Let us begin by emphasizing a point which, although apparent in all that has preceded, has not been explicitly stated:

The effect of any persuasive statement lies in the *combined* use of both emotive and descriptive meanings. This is true not merely because persuasion is so habitually accompanied by reasons, or because emotive meaning is so often dependent on descriptive meaning; it is true quite independently of that. For when emotive meaning praises or condemns, descriptive meaning must indicate the object on which praise or condemnation is *bestowed*. Without both sorts of meaning, acting together, the persuasion will lack either force or direction. Although a persuasive statement need not give new information about any object, it must at least center the emotive influence on an object that is descriptively designated.[1] The verbal form of the statement which combines the meanings is not of great consequence. All that is required, for persuasion, is that the meanings be combined by some device or another.

This observation helps us to see, first of all, why second-pattern definitions are persuasive and first-pattern ones are not. In the

1. There are exceptions, of course. One may persuade without using any emotive term, so long as an emotive *effect* is secured by gesture or intonation. And one may persuade without strictly designating the object praised or condemned, so long as the object is evident from the general situation, or from the interpretation of a metaphor. But these exceptions are so obvious that we may here conveniently neglect them, for simplicity.

second pattern a combination of descriptive and emotive meaning is effected by a definition itself. The vague emotive definiendum is given the more precise descriptive meaning of the definiens. This immediately persuades, for it directs the emotive force of the definiendum to the defining qualities that are provided for it. In the first pattern, however, no significant combination of emotive and descriptive meaning is effected *by a definition itself*. There is, to be sure, a wedding of an emotive definiendum to the descriptive meaning of "I approve" or "I disapprove"; but note that the "I" in these phrases refers to *any* speaker, and that the phrases indicate no particular object which *is* approved or disapproved. The definition does not, then, bring about any combination of emotive and descriptive meaning in which the latter gives *direction* to the former. That is why a first pattern definition, unlike a second pattern one, is neutral.

These remarks must bear their usual qualifications. One may not characterize a definition as either persuasive or neutral without looking beyond the words that are used—without considering the living context in which the words are at work. We have noted in the preceding chapter that under certain circumstances a second-pattern definition may have no real persuasive import.[2] And it may be added that certain second-pattern definitions, which do have persuasive import, are not greatly different from first-pattern definitions. Thus the definition:

> "X is good" has the meaning of "I approve of this, having carefully reflected on the matter," except that "good" has a more strongly laudatory emotive meaning

recalls the first pattern quite strongly. Yet it may be persuasive, preëmpting the emotive meaning of "good" for attitudes that arise upon reflection, and deterring anyone from using the word to forward his temporary whims. (Whether it will in fact do this will depend, as usual, on the circumstances, and on whether it is given as a "sample" definition or as "the" definition.) In such a case the explicit use of "approve" and of the indicator term, "I," raise the problems that have been discussed in connection with the first pattern; but the potential persuasiveness of the definition make it more suitably classified as a second-pattern one. Its precise classification matters but little, however, so long as its nature is understood.[3] There are other exceptions,

2. P. 212. The point will be fully illustrated in Chap. XI.
3. It may be mentioned, in this connection, that a persuasive interpreta-

and seeming exceptions, that might be mentioned. They are not so frequent, however, as to render our conclusions seriously inaccurate, and if their possibility is kept in mind they will not require further attention.

Let us now proceed, emphasizing this simple but central point: The difference between the definitions that typify the two patterns, marked though it is, has no bearing on the nature or outcome of ethical arguments. In such arguments there is more than a detached *study* of the ethical terms; there is a *use* of them— an effort, even if only an initial, tentative one, to exert an influence. Now if the second pattern permits this persuasive effort to be mediated by definitions, whereas the first pattern does not, it remains the case that for every second pattern *definition* there is a first pattern *judgment*, the latter being the persuasive counterpart of the former. That is to say, instead of *defining* "good" in terms of X, Y, and Z, as in the second pattern, one may use "good" in a first-pattern sense and simply *predicate* it of X, Y, and Z. Either procedure will be persuasive, and either will be equally open to counterpersuasion. We have seen that persuasion is effected by a combination of emotive and descriptive meaning, the latter giving direction to the former. The verbal mechanism by which this is done is only an incidental matter. Hence either definition or predication will do. If the wedding of the two sorts of meaning is *not* established by definition, the initial persuasion will be diverted to subsequent contexts—to the judgments in which this or that is declared (by ordinary predication) *to be* good. If the wedding *is* established by definition, the persuasive task of subsequent contexts will be proportionately reduced. So a change from the first to the second pattern simply reapportions the attitude-molding aspects of ethics to different contexts, in no way augmenting or diminishing it.[4]

tion of a first-pattern definition—though one arising from a confusion—was implicitly in question in Chap. IV, pp. 102 ff. The objection there answered, which held that the first pattern fostered an "irresponsible egotism," depended for its plausibility on a persuasive element suspected to underlie the definition—as if the definition sought to make all others accept the attitudes of the speaker. We have seen that the definition would not be so understood, apart from confusions about the indicator terms; but the example is of interest in showing how plausible logical errors can be, when a background of emotive language is provided for them.

4. The term "persuasive method" was used in Chap. VI to indicate not the effect of an initial judgment but only that of a supporting one. The term "persuasive," by itself, is now being applied to *any* moving statement. To avoid a possible confusion it may be well to reiterate the remark that was made on pp. 139 f.: "Any ethical judgment, of course, is itself a persuasive

This conclusion has some immediate implications on methodology, as will be clear from the examples that follow. The examples will be slightly artificial, suggesting that people are self-conscious, in ordinary discourse, of which pattern they are following. Actually, people are given to talking in a vague way that imperfectly distinguishes the patterns, leaving it undecided whether certain of their remarks are to be taken as definitions or judgments. But an artificial assumption to the contrary will do no harm, and will simplify exposition.

Suppose that a man affirms: "An action is good only if it contributes to human survival." By the second pattern this can be made true by definition; by the first pattern it cannot. Does the second pattern, then, make the assertion indubitable, and immune to criticism? Clearly not. A critic who acknowledges, by the second pattern, that the statement is true *in the sense of* *"good" which the speaker used,* may nevertheless reject the statement on account of its emotive repercussions. He may accuse the speaker of distorting the "real, deeper" sense of the term, and insist, in this deeper sense, that an action may be good *without* contributing to human survival. Thus the assertion would be rejected through the mediation of a rival persuasive definition. The effect would have been the same if, in first pattern manner, the critic had simply made a counterjudgment, without any mention of a persuasive definition. (As has been implied above, people often do not decide whether their statements are to be taken as analytic or synthetic; and for the purposes of exerting an influence this is no great oversight, since the statement will serve to combine descriptive and emotive meanings in either case.) In ethics, unlike science, the analytic character of a judgment is not sufficient to establish it; much depends as well on the attitude molding effect of the terminology in which the analytic statement is expressed. We have seen this even for the first pattern.[5] For the second it becomes more obvious.

Much the same considerations reappear in showing that the second pattern, with its more complicated descriptive meaning, does not provide ethics with a richer "content." A man who *defines* "good" with reference to benevolence, honesty, altruism, and so on, may seem to manifest a richer mind than one who

instrument; but in the use of persuasive "methods," the effects of an initial judgment are intensified by *further* persuasion."
5. Cf. pp. 104 f.

defines it in the colder manner of the first pattern. But surely, so long as these characteristics are the objects of a man's aspirations and exhortatory aims, it can make no difference whether he indicates this by definition or by some other means. If the man, following the first pattern, declares that these characteristics *are* good, his nonanalytic judgment will manifest neither more nor less richness of mind than the corresponding analytic one which the second pattern one would provide. Any "content" which the first pattern seems to omit can always be made to reappear; and this may be done either, as above, by explicitly mentioning it as the subject of an ethical judgment, or else by mentioning it in a reason that supports the judgment.

2

WE must now consider the way in which second-pattern judgments can be supported by reasons. We have seen that they may need support even if they are analytic, and it will be obvious that they may need support if they are not. The discussion can be confined to one typical but extended example, since the parallels to the first pattern will everywhere be evident.

Let us suppose that A and B are in disagreement about whether some object, O, is good, each using that term in some second-pattern sense. The several forms which their argument may take must be considered in order:

(1) Assume that A, who says that O is good, and B, who says that O is not good, both use "good" with the same descriptive meaning, namely: *conducive to the consequences X, Y, and Z.* And assume that X, Y, and Z are open to empirical tests. It will be immediately evident that the *reason*, "O leads to X, Y, and Z," will be logically equivalent to A's judgment, and that its negation will be equivalent to B's.[6] Hence the empirical confirmation or disconfirmation of this reason, logically related to the judgments, will be sufficient to decide the argument, one way or another.

It will not always happen, however, that both men use "good" in the same sense. We have seen that the word is subject to rival persuasive definitions, and hence to divergent senses. So let us consider a further possibility:

(2) Assume that A, in saying that O is good, uses "good" to refer to X and Y; and that B, in saying that O is not good, uses

6. It is assumed that logical relations are wholly unaffected by emotive meaning.

"good" to refer to Y and Z. It is possible, in such a case, for the argument to proceed and terminate without either party's being aware of the discrepancy in terminology. For suppose that B, defending his position, should immediately give the reason, "O does not lead to Y." This reason will contradict A's judgment and logically imply B's; hence if B can establish it, he will establish his position. But this is obviously not the only possibility, and we must look to another:

(3) Make the same assumptions as in (2), but suppose that B, *admitting* that O *does* lead to Y, still contends that O is not good. He now gives the reason, "O does not lead to Z"—holding (correctly, for the sense of "good" that he uses) that this logically implies his initial judgment. In that case A will immediately notice the divergence in terminology, and perhaps will demur at B's sense of "good." But quite apart from settling the meaning of "good," A may be content to refute B's reason, showing that O does lead to Z. If he succeeds, he will fully overthrow B's position; for B has admitted, previously, that O leads to Y. "You are refuted," A will say, "even granted your faulty conception of goodness."

This case raises a point of particular importance. A does not refer to Z in his initial statement, and B tries to support *his* initial judgment by reference to Z alone. So A's initial judgment is at no time logically contradicted. Yet A will feel, even after the discrepancy in terminology is clearly seen, that he was opposed from the very beginning. He will wish to refute B's statement, as though this were necessary to support his own. Why is this the case?

In the light of the previous chapters the answer cannot be long in doubt. We have only to look beyond disagreement in belief, which has temporarily been emphasized, and consider disagreement in attitude. Although A's initial judgment was not logically contradicted by B's, it was *emotively* opposed by it. The use of "good" and "not good," whatever descriptive meaning they might have, indicated that one man was in favor of O and the other was not. X, Y, and Z were relevant, of course, but became so because agreement in belief about these matters might cause disagreement in attitude to end. A was not content merely to prove the descriptive truth[7] of his initial judgment; he wanted as well to

7. The word "truth" is used in the ordinary scientific sense throughout; the "nonscientific" sense, mentioned in Chap. VII, pp. 169 f., will not be considered.

make B share the attitude to which it emotively testified. Z was relevant to B's approval; and that is why A, though at first not mentioning it, had later to take it into consideration.

Disagreement in attitude is most easily seen in cases like (3), but a moment's consideration will show that it was equally present in cases (1) and (2). The use of the laudatory term, "good," in the earlier cases, indicated that they too were concerned with whether or not O was to be favored. The reasons there used had the appearance of being definitive, for they served both to contradict one man's judgment and imply the other's. But these logical relations would have been ethically inconsequential, had not the judgments themselves indicated the *attitude* each speaker would have, provided the descriptive assertion of his judgment could be maintained. A, for instance, would approve of O if and only if it led to X and Y; for if he were otherwise disposed, he would reject his sense of "good," persuasively defining the term in another way. The same can be said of B, with regard to Y and Z. That is why the argument was ethical, rather than purely factual. Hence the reasons used in (1) and (2), even though they happened to be logically related to both judgments, had a function analogous to that of the reason in (3). They served to alter a disagreement in belief in which disagreement in attitude was rooted. Case (3) differed mainly in that the topic for disagreement in belief, not being common to both speakers' initial judgments, was a little more difficult to locate.

These remarks prepare us for a further case:

(4) Suppose, as before, that A uses "good" to refer to X and Y, and that B (who denies that O is good) uses "good" to refer to Y and Z. And suppose that both have fully established that O does lead to X and Y, but does not lead to Z. A's judgment is acknowledged to be correct, then, in asserting that O leads to X and Y; and B's judgment is equally correct in asserting that it does *not* lead to *both* Y and Z. They have as yet located no point of disagreement in belief, nor is there the possibility, as in (3), of one man's refuting the other "even granting a faulty conception of goodness." Yet they may still argue about whether O is good. The emotive effects of "good" and "not good" are indicative of a disagreement in attitude.

This case is of particular methodological interest. It represents a disagreement which rational methods may (subject to later qualification) be wholly powerless to resolve.

This will be clear if we again consider, at the expense of partial repetition, why rational methods *were* decisive in cases (1), (2), and (3). In each of the earlier cases the initial judgment of one man was false. This was guaranteed either by the law of contradiction or by explicit hypothesis. Each man, moreover, would have a favorable attitude to O if and only if he believed that "good," in his sense, was truthfully predicable of it; for otherwise he would have used the laudatory term with a different descriptive meaning. (As we have seen above, if one man had favored O in spite of its lacking a certain property, he would have persuasively defined "good" to exclude that property, and so would have enabled himself to say, with both factual truth and laudation, that O was good.) For these reasons the men could look exclusively to the truth or falsity of one of their initial statements, and this would lead them to have the same kind of attitude. The disagreement in belief, in which their disagreement in attitude was rooted, concerned something which at least one of the opponents had falsely expressed in his initial statement. Rational methods, by upsetting this belief, would likewise resolve the disagreement in attitude.

In case (4), however, the initial statements of the opponents are both of established truth. The men are disposed, as above, to grant or withhold their approval of O in accordance with whether "good," in the disparate senses which they employ, is or is not truthfully predicable of it; but rational methods serve only to support both of their judgments. Hence A will continue to call O "good," with approval, and B to call it "not good," without approval. Their disagreement is not rooted in some belief which either has expressed in his initial judgment, and may be due to a fundamental difference in temperament. Since rational methods alter attitudes only through altering beliefs, how can they be used to resolve this disagreement?

It is immediately clear that rational methods have not the same direct application in (4) that they had in the earlier cases. Yet we shall conclude too hastily if we say that there is no room for them here at all. Let us examine further.

If case (4) continues to be disputed, persuasive definitions, which hitherto have been involved in the argument only tacitly, will come to play a more overt and important role. Each man, in order to influence the other's attitudes, will insist upon his own definition. They will argue about whether O is good in the *true* sense of "good." Unless they agree upon the sense of the word they will not agree upon their fundamental issue, namely, whether O can be described by a name that indicates their praise.

Rational methods, however unavailing they may be in refuting the descriptive assertions which the speakers first made, may re-appear as a means of supporting their persuasive definitions. For there is manifestly such a thing as giving *reasons* for accepting or rejecting a second-pattern definition, and in such a procedure many properties may be mentioned, and relevantly so, which differ from the X, Y, and Z that the definition directly involves. For example: Suppose that B is led to see that Z, which he has been seeking to include in the definition of "good," has the further consequences, C_1, hitherto unknown to him. If he has an unfavor-able attitude toward these consequences, this may be transferred to Z itself, and he may no longer wish to define "good" in terms of Z. Similarly, if he is led to see that X has the further conse-quences, C_2, toward which he has a favorable attitude, he may decide to define "good" in terms of X. In other words, guided by reasons which refer to C_1 and C_2, B may come to accept the persuasive definition upon which A has been insisting. The men will then "agree" on the definition, which is in effect to say that they will agree quite significantly in attitude. And this agreement, it must be noted, will not have been obtained by the emotive im-pact of persuasive definitions alone, but by the aid of reasons. Any disagreement in attitude to X, Y, and Z, between A and B, was rooted in belief about C_1 and C_2. With a resolution of the latter comes a resolution of the former. The initial issue about O will also be settled; for since O has been shown (by hypothesis) in (4) to lead to X and Y, but not Z, and since both parties now agree in favoring X and Y, but not Z, their attitude to these fac-tors will be transferred to O, extrinsically. (It is being assumed, of course, that nothing beside X, Y, Z, and the C's is relevant to the issue.)

Thus a second-pattern argument need not stop short, or aban-don rational methods, simply because, as in (4), an examination of the opponents initial statements, and the reasons which logi-cally imply them, discloses no disagreement in belief. The dis-agreement in attitude which pervades the argument may still be rooted in disagreement in belief—not in these initially stated beliefs, to be sure, which concern whether O leads to X, Y, and Z, but rather in *other* beliefs, which concern the relation of X, Y, and Z to the C's.

When C_1 and C_2 occur in the reasons which support one side or another in the argument, the reasons are related to the initial judgments neither logically nor inductively. (Clearly, the relation of O to X, Y, and Z may be established independently of the relation of the latter to C_1 and C_2.) They do not call into question the descriptive truth of the initial statements, but operate, rather, to change the descriptive sense in which the initial terms are used. This does not introduce irrelevancies, or confuse the point at issue. The issue centers about disagreement in attitude, which, regardless of divergent descriptive senses, will be indicated by emotive meaning.

We have encountered in the second pattern reasons of the same sort as those in the first—reasons which give psychological rather than logical support to an emotive statement. For the second pattern these reasons support persuasive definitions; for the first they support ethical judgments. Since we have seen that a second-pattern definition has much the effect of a first-pattern judgment, serving to combine descriptive designata and emotive meaning, the methodological parallel is not surprising.

The only point that needs emphasis is that *two* sorts of reason may occur in the second pattern. There is the sort that introduces reference to the C's as just mentioned, and which supports or attacks a persuasive definition. There is also the sort that deals only with X, Y, and Z, and which supports or attacks an initial judgment without questioning a persuasive definition. The latter sort of reason is *logically* related to the judgment. It is of a sort that sometimes occurs even in the first pattern, as example (2), page 116, will testify. In the second pattern such reasons are much more frequent, and indeed, cases (1), (2), and (3), above, exemplify them exclusively.[8] They do not, however, give second-pattern methodology any superior finality. Logically related reasons, if themselves well proved, may serve to prove or disprove the *descriptive truth* of a second-pattern judgment; but an opponent who accepts the descriptive truth need not—as case

8. But reasons of the nonlogical sort, about the C's, might have been introduced in these cases, and would have made a difference. They were omitted only for simplicity.

(4) illustrates, and as is apparent from the remarks on analytic judgments in the preceding section—accept the judgment. He may reject it because of its emotive language and the relation that it thereby bears to attitudes. The relation between beliefs and attitudes is psychological, and a change in patterns can make no difference to it. It may be added that the *logical* relations between belief-asserting statements are also analogous for the two patterns. The difference lies in whether the beliefs are asserted in an ethical judgment itself or subsequently. A reason which contradicts an opponent's second-pattern judgment, for instance, will also contradict a counter-reason that the same opponent would have considered indispensable in supporting a corresponding first-pattern judgment.

We have seen that cases like (4), no less than cases like (1), (2), and (3), can be resolved by rational methods. But our discussion was based on the assumption that agreement in belief about X, Y, Z, and the C's would lead to agreement in attitude. Without this assumption, the ethical issue might be insoluble. We reach our old conclusion: Rational methods can resolve ethical disagreement if and only if it is rooted in disagreement in belief. The conclusion is perfectly general. Our outline of second-pattern methodology has become complicated with regard to *which* beliefs were at the root of the disagreement in attitude— whether there were any, and if so, to what extent they were expressed in the initial judgments or the reasons that logically implied them. Such considerations throw a needed light on the ways of language, but end by revealing the central issues with which we have become familiar.

What has been said of "good" might have been said of any other ethical term, and indeed, of any term that is subject to persuasive definition. What has been said of consequences (for X, Y, Z, and the C's were limited, for simplicity, to consequences of O) might have been said about the *nature* of O, or the *motivation* of some action, and so on. Clearly, the C's may be extended to include any of the considerations that were mentioned in Chapter V; and if X, Y, and Z cannot easily be extended beyond the boundaries of conventional usage, they may still range quite widely. With regard to the subject matter of the reasons that may be used—which is unlimited—the two patterns do not differ in the least.

3

THERE are three basic respects in which our account of the second pattern remains incomplete. Nothing has been said about (a) personal decisions, (b) intrinsic value, and (c) persuasive *methods*. Let us consider them in order.

(a) Little need be said about personal decisions, for the parallel between the two patterns, and the equally close parallel between personal and interpersonal decisions,[9] will make the matter almost self-explanatory. One who is making up his mind about a second-pattern judgment must first decide upon the sense in which he is to use an ethical term. This will depend upon how his attitudes are directed to certain factors (X, Y, Z . . .) that are to be given the emotive praise or blame of the definition. Any conflict in his attitudes to these will be open to the same considerations, and manner of reconciliation, that were mentioned in connection with the first pattern. He may be led to revise his attitudes to them in the light of reasons like C_1 and C_2, which will affect his own decision in much the same way that, in the preceding section, they were taken to affect that of a hearer. And it is not necessary (here or in any other case) that his personal decision should be made *apart* from an interpersonal argument.[10] In the ordinary course of discussion one may revise a persuasive definition in the light of his own reasons, convincing himself by words that ostensibly are used to convince others. The rest of a personal decision, once the definition is established, raises no peculiar methodological problem. Any predication of the defined term of some O will involve only the ordinary methods of establishing a descriptive judgment.

It must be acknowledged, however, that these last remarks are a little artificial. They imply that there can be a strict separation between selecting a definition of a partly emotive term and predicating the term of some O. To speak more accurately—and this qualification holds not only for the personal cases but for the interpersonal ones previously discussed—the distinction is one that is usefully imposed on ordinary examples, for the purpose of clarifying them, rather than one that can immediately be discerned there. It is not a distinction which people always make, for language is often left vague. A man will often be un-

9. As explained in Chap. V, Sec. 3.
10. Cf. pp. 149 f. What is said there for persuasive methods holds equally true for rational ones.

certain whether certain qualities are to be included in his definition or whether they are simply to serve, like the C's, as considerations which indirectly lead him to modify the definition.
And even when the distinction is sharply made, there will be no
full separation, in point of time, between revising a definition
and revising a judgment in which the definiendum is used. Suppose, for instance, that A has *tentatively* defined "good" with
reference to X and Y, and proceeds to decide whether O is good in
that sense. His very inquiry may disclose certain C's (or other
facts about O, X, or Y) that make O abhorrent to him, even
though O is unmistakably found to lead to X and Y. This unexpected discovery may lead him to define "good" in some more
complicated way. The inquiry, beginning in a way that seems
only to concern whether "good" can be predicated of O, may end
by altering the term's meaning. The present chapter, by temporarily ignoring these matters, has obtained a convenient simplicity. This has not been secured without artificiality; but if the
artificiality is now allowed for, there should be no serious misunderstanding.

(b) The term "intrinsically good" does not readily lend itself
to a second-pattern definition, being more typical of the first
pattern. This must be explained, since it may not be immediately
obvious. Suppose that the generic term, "good," has persuasively
been defined in terms of the *qualities* X, Y, and Z. And assume
that the speaker's approval of X is wholly intrinsic, whereas his
approval of Y and Z are wholly extrinsic. It would then be roughly
plausible to say that the term "intrinsically," qualifying "good,"
had the effect of eliminating Y and Z, serving to restrict the
descriptive reference of "intrinsically good" to X. But the assumptions which lead to this conclusion are of no practical use.
Any man's attitudes are likely to be reinforced,[11] and reinforced
so widely that there will be no X for which his approval is
wholly intrinsic. Intrinsic attitudes enter as aspects of a complicated interplay of attitudes, from which they may be ab-
stracted but not concretely isolated.[12] Second-pattern definitions
do not, in themselves, permit this abstraction to be indicated.

It is easy to see, however, that although the distinction between
intrinsic and extrinsic cannot be made by means of second-

11. As defined on p. 188. The prevalence of reinforcement was discussed
on pp. 189 ff.
12. Cf. p. 189.

pattern definitions, it will appear elsewhere in the second pattern. Suppose, as above, that the generic term, "good," has been defined persuasively in terms of X, Y, and Z. And assume, now with more plausibility, that X, Y, and Z exhaust the speaker's focal aims.[13] So far as the speaker's attitudes to these factors are extrinsic, they will be conditional to certain beliefs about consequences, say C_1. Hence a reason, if it leads him to change his beliefs about the relation of Z, say, to C_1, may lead him to revise his persuasive definition. The reason will operate in exactly the way we have considered in the previous section.[14] On the other hand, so far as the speaker's attitude to Z (or X or Y) is intrinsic, no reason could have this direct bearing on his definition. Yet it could have an indirect bearing. By the operation of Allport's principle, or Wundt's,[15] the reason might serve to change his intrinsic attitudes as a consequence of changing his extrinsic ones (etc.), and cause him to alter his persuasive definition by that procedure.

Thus in the second pattern the discussion of intrinsic and extrinsic value cannot be made to center on the *definition* of the terms "intrinsically good" or "extrinsically good"; but the same considerations reappear in new phraseology. The difference between the patterns, here as elsewhere, is only of linguistic interest. It has no bearing on the nature of ethical disagreement or on the extent to which it can be resolved.

(c) In discussing persuasive *methods* in the second pattern we must distinguish between the persuasion of an initial statement, leading to an argument, and the further persuasion that may then ensue. Only the latter will be considered under the name "method." [16] We may assume that the initial persuasion is exerted by a persuasive definition—for although it may also be exerted by a judgment (either analytic or not) in which an ethical term, implicitly defined in a given way, is simply *used*, this latter alternative will introduce nothing that will now require explanation. The problem accordingly becomes one of seeing how a persuasive definition can be supported by further persuasion.

The matter presents no difficulty. Suppose that a speaker, having defined "good" in terms of X and Y, should find that his

13. Focal aims were discussed on pp. 189 f., and again on pp. 202 f.
14. Cf. p. 235.
15. See pp. 194–198.
16. Cf. p. 229, n. 4.

opponent is on the point of dissenting. To support his persuasive definition, the speaker may use any persuasive device that will serve to make X and Y seem more attractive. Perhaps he will employ metaphors. X will become the cornerstone of our civilization, and Y its most decorous ornament. Extolled in this way, the properties may seem more worthy of being christened by the name of "good." It will be obvious that other devices will be open. Indeed, the persuasive support of a second-pattern definition will be no different from that of a first-pattern judgment, as the identity in function between the two sorts of statement readily permits us to see. The conclusions of Chapter VI can be extended to the present question without reservation.

One of the most interesting aspects of second-pattern persuasion, not hitherto mentioned, lies in the *multiple* use of persuasive definitions. Suppose, for instance, that a speaker has defined a "good" man as an "honorable" and "upright" one. The latter words are not free from vagueness and emotive meaning of their own, hence they may in turn be persuasively defined. If the terms which *they* are defined are also emotive and vague, the process of definition may repeat itself, until some final, relatively definite set of terms (let us again represent them by X, Y, and Z) is reached. In such a procedure, X, Y, and Z will be the effective defining properties of "good," and will stand under its emotive light. But they will also stand under the light of all the *other* emotive terms which the series of definitions has introduced. The cumulative effect of so many emotive terms will exert a stronger persuasion, very likely, than any which could have been obtained by defining "good" directly in terms of X, Y, and Z, without the mediating definitions.

The use of persuasive definitions, and of multiple persuasive definitions, might have been mentioned in first-pattern methodology, and was omitted in Chapter VI only because such definitions had not then been studied. If a first-pattern *judgment* must, by its very nature, be free from wide shifts in descriptive meaning, that is not so for the supporting *reasons* that attend it. Whenever the reasons contain terms that are both emotive and vague, these may be subject to a persuasive definition, or a series of them, in the usual way.

It will now be clear that persuasion need be neither more nor less common in the second pattern than in the first. And the patterns have been shown to be parallel in all other central respects. We may conclude that the choice of one pattern in preference to another is a choice between forms of language; and whichever form of language is adopted, there will be the same possibilities in the information that can be conveyed, and in the influence that can be exerted.

This conclusion must be qualified, however, in a not unimportant way. Although both patterns reveal the same central issues, a choice between them will be arbitrary *only* if we assume that the flexibilities of ethical language, and its emotive repercussions, are clearly understood. This is by no means an assumption that can safely be brought to everyday discussions. When we look beyond our simplified examples, considering the complicated normative situations in which the ethical terms and methods are at work, we shall find that one pattern may often be more useful than another because of its comparative freedom from confusion and misunderstanding.

It is not easy, however, to *generalize* about which pattern will be preferred on this ground—not even if we charitably suppose that people are anxious to avoid confusions rather than exploit them. Both patterns are open to confusions, and the comparative degree of confusion will vary with the particular ethical terms that are used, the psychological habits of those who use them, and the nature of the issue in question. Some people, for instance, are easily impressed by a display of definitions, considering them very "logical" and "scientific." Second-pattern definitions may seriously mislead them, and cause them to think that an issue has been definitively settled when in fact it is highly controversial. On the other hand, first pattern procedures may be equally confusing. When persuasive definitions are replaced by first-pattern judgments, there is less outward display of rigor. Those who are impressed by the display may be disconcerted by its absence, and may, in reaction, yearn for some "ultimate proof" that is beyond possibility.

Thus the choice of patterns becomes difficult, if confusions are to be avoided, and must often be made in a spirit of compromise. There is no ready antidote to confusion, nor can there ever be, so long as the Idols of the Market-place "wonderfully obstruct the understanding."

XI

Moralists and Propagandists

1

A MORALIST, as it will appear from the preceding chapters, is one who endeavors to influence attitudes. He often does so indirectly, succeeding mainly because his judgment is supported by reasons; but he may also use persuasion or "exhortation." Now much the same can be said of other men, with whom the moralist may seem to keep strange company. In particular, it can be said of propagandists; for propagandists, whatever else may be true of them, seek to exert an influence. How, then, are moralists and propagandists to be distinguished?

The answer to this question, half-suggested in Chapter VII,[1] can now be developed more fully. It is concerned with *definitions* of "moralist" and "propagandist." Perhaps these definitions, like so many others, will prove to be persuasive. We must take care, in that case, to reveal the full complexity of the issues that are involved.

The possibility of persuasively defining the terms will be manifest. In ordinary usage neither term is emotively neutral, "propagandist" carrying a stigma, and "moralist" a note of comparative respect. On the whole, though not without marked exceptions for this or that group of people, the terms are emotive antonyms.[2] At the same time, both terms are vague, and vague in a way that leaves precision only to the *generic* aspects of their reference—their common reference to men who exert *some sort* of influence. *What* sort of influence is "moral exhortation," and what sort "propaganda," is not, in common usage, made descriptively precise. If we cut through this vagueness, then, drawing a line between "moralist" and "propagandist," we shall not be *discovering* a distinction that is clearly implicit in our lan-

1. Pp. 162 f.
2. Cf. T. W. Arnold's remarks on "polar words," in *The Folklore of Capitalism* (Yale University Press, 1937), chap. vii.

guage. Nor shall we, unless we make particularly strong efforts to do so, be sharpening a classification that will serve cognitive purposes alone. Rather, we shall be apportioning descriptive meanings to the emotive antonyms that we use. We shall ourselves be acting, by our persuasive definitions, to influence the way in which others exert an influence. Those whom we call "moralists" will be praised or tolerated, and those whom we call "propagandists," condemned.

As has elsewhere been remarked, however, no definition can safely be called "persuasive" when it is torn from the living context in which it is at work. With regard to "moralist" and "propagandist" it is of particular importance to bear this in mind. Of the many writers who seek to define these terms, not all are engaged in a moralizing or propagandizing of their own. Some are striving, not without success, to preserve a complete detachment. If we neglect the work of such men, we shall exaggerate the extent to which persuasive definitions are prevalent.

Let us begin, then, by considering definitions that are *not* persuasive—or which at least need not be—giving particular attention to the term "propaganda." This will throw the definitions that *are* persuasive into proper relief, and permit them to be studied subsequently with a just emphasis.

2

AN instructive compilation of various definitions of "propaganda," taken from current writers, has been made by F. E. Lumley.[3] His study shows beyond any doubt that "the definers do not agree"—that "there is no *the* way in which propaganda 'is in practice recognized,' but a baffling confusion of 'ways.'" Now among the many definitions which Lumley quotes, there are some of this sort:

"I would define propaganda as the dissemination of interested information and opinion."

"Propaganda is the deliberate effort to affect the minds and emotions, chiefly the latter, of a group in a given way for a given purpose."

Propaganda means "any effort to persuade and win people to the acceptance of some particular proposal or support of a cause."[4]

3. *The Propaganda Menace* (Century, 1933), chap. ii.
4. The sources of the quotations, as indicated by Lumley, *op. cit.*, pp. 23 ff.,

These definitions, which are roughly equivalent, stand off from many others that Lumley mentions in that they are very broad, permitting the term "propagandist" to be applied to a great variety of men. All advertisers, for instance, would be propagandists in such a sense; and so would all missionaries and clergymen; and so would editorial writers and columnists; and so would teachers who imbue their students with ideals of citizenship. Lincoln's Gettysburg Address, and Washington's Farewell Address, considered as indispensable reading for all American schoolboys, would mark each of these statesmen as propagandists of great power. It is not to be thought that scientifically minded theorists, using this broad sense of "propaganda," have any intention of stigmatizing such men—certainly not *all* such men. They use it in the hope that it may become, for their purposes, a colorless term, useful in marking off a selected topic of study in which any sheep-and-goats division is deliberately avoided. Having begun their studies, perhaps, using "propaganda" in some narrower but ill-defined sense, they extend the term to cover a broader field, which to the eyes of a scientist remains homogeneous.[5]

If "propaganda" is to lend itself to a scientific usage, its emotive meaning must be neutralized. We have seen this in Chapter IX, for the parallel examples taken from economics;[6] and we have seen that a neutralization of emotive meaning is by no means easily secured. Yet it is not beyond all possibility; and in spite of the difficulties, it may occasionally be the most convenient alternative that our language affords. Emotive meaning can be neutralized, for instance, by letting the tone of the whole context stand as a compensation for it, or by balancing a particular laudatory term with a particular derogatory one, or by giving explicit admonitions that emotive effects are to be resisted.[7] Some of the writers whom Lumley quotes are properly cautious about these matters. They insist that "propaganda," as they use the term, designates something which they sometimes consider *good*. Such a statement helps to make the term emotively neutral,

are respectively: R. Wreford, "Propaganda, Evil and Good," *Nineteenth Century* (April, 1923), pp. 514–524; M. K. Thomson, *The Springs of Human Action*, p. 451; and C. C. North, *Social Problems and Social Planning*, p. 117.

5. The broad sense may have a "re-emphatic" function. See Chap. XIII, Sec. 3.

6. Pp. 215 ff.

7. Cf. pp. 78, 142.

counteracting the usual derogation; and if supplemented by other efforts, may make way for a study that is wholly detached.

In any use of "propaganda" that is at once broad and colorless, one may acceptably say that all moralists are propagandists. (And if "moralist" is broadened and emotively neutralized in a corresponding way, one may acceptably assert the converse— that all propagandists are moralists.) But it is impossible to overemphasize the caution that must attend any such statement. To certain ears it will sound like the bitterest cynicism, and may continue to do so in spite of all explanations and protestations to the contrary. "Are all moralists, then, really nothing more than propagandists? Has man no other guide than bias and prejudice? If this is the teaching of social science, or of analytic philosophy, then let us have none of it, and base our own theories on higher things." This sort of remonstrance will always be a possibility, so long as people refuse to look behind their words. It requires only a little attention, however, to see that the phrases, "nothing more than" propaganda, and "bias and prejudice," are irrelevant to the issue. They emphasize a derogation that the critic has been accustomed to associate with some narrower sense of "propaganda," and which he insistently retains for the broad and potentially neutral sense, heedless of any admonitions that might moderate his linguistic inflexibility. He finds persuasion where none is intended, and enters into a confused counterpersuasion.

Yet it remains the case that a theorist who strives for scientific detachment may succeed, by exercising care, in making "propaganda" a neutral term; and if his care is extremely great, he may mislead none save those whose propensity to misunderstand is willful.

So far we have considered only the possibility of neutralizing a *broad* sense of "propaganda." The term may also be neutralized for narrower senses; and although these raise much the same questions, we shall find it profitable to consider them.

The number of narrower senses that are available, if we limit attention to those that are most important, will depend on the number of ways in which those who are engaged in influencing attitudes can profitably be classified. And it will be obvious that such men may be classified in this way or that, depending upon the distinctions that need emphasis for this or that purpose. Some men exert influence by methods that are mainly persuasive, others by methods that are mainly rational. And of those who use rational methods, some include deliberate lies among their reasons, and others do not; some include only a carefully selected part of the truth—that which is most likely to sway the hearer in the desired direction—and others try to "present both sides." Again, some exert an influence for selfish motives, others for altruistic ones. Some conceal their motives, others reveal them. Some are agents of an elaborate organization, others are not. Some influence attitudes of a certain sort only, such as those connected with a sense of sin and remorse, whereas others influence attitudes of all sorts. Some may be directly and intimately concerned with changing a form of government, or altering the outcome of a war, whereas others may be politically less conspicuous. And so on.

Any of these distinctions, singly or in combination, may be important for some given inquiry, and the words "propagandist" and "moralist" can readily be defined in a way that preserves them. It may be that the definitions will temporarily seem "odd." Certain men will be included among the "propagandists" who might with equal naturalness, in some other possible sense, be included among the "moralists," and vice versa. But this is only to be expected, for there can be no perfect fidelity to common usage when common usage is vague and ambiguous. Definitions based on any of the above distinctions will be as conventional as any others; and indeed, nearly all the distinctions appear, with particular reference to the differentiae of "propaganda," in Lumley's compilation of definitions.[8]

Must these narrower definitions always be persuasive? The question is complicated by the fact that "propagandist" and "moralist" are not used interchangeably in preserving the distinctions. People are so accustomed to reserve "propaganda" for what they condemn that any assignment of generally esteemed characteristics to it, in any exclusive way, will more than strain the limits of linguistic flexibility. One would not specify that propagandists must, by definition, be people who try to tell the whole truth; but to say this of moralists—though it would indeed pick out an extremely narrow sense of the term—might be linguistically less surprising. In any narrow definition, then, there is the likelihood that "propaganda" will be made to designate what most people despise or fear, and "moralist" the opposite.[9]

8. *Op. cit.*, particularly pp. 25, 27, 28, 29, 31, 33, 37.
9. There are those who become so disillusioned with the "old-school"

There will be a strong appearance of persuasion in this—a seeming effort to intensify or render more permanent the usual direction of people's attitudes.

And yet the definitions *need* not be persuasive. In selecting narrower senses, no less than the broader ones, a theorist can make efforts to neutralize emotive meaning (or at least, all but dependent emotive meaning) and leave the terms free for detached description. If he uses the terms consonantly with the usual direction of people's attitudes, as just mentioned, he may do so purely in the interest of making the terms easily understood. He may suppose, that is to say, that the usual emotive use of the terms has served as a philological factor in decreasing their natural range of *descriptive* meanings; and taking this as a *fait accompli,* may apportion descriptive meanings to them accordingly. Having done this, he may proceed to neutralize the emotive meaning, putting any suggestion of praise or blame to one side. Such a procedure can be successful, when carefully handled, in yielding narrow senses that are without any element of persuasion.

The present account, in emphasizing emotive meaning, has by no means maintained that the emotive terms are fated to a non-scientific use. It has insisted, however, and must continue to insist, that emotive terms are great obstacles to detachment, and that their use in science, where detachment is needed, must always be attended by great caution.

3

IF many definitions of "propaganda" (or of "moral exhortation") are detached, it must not be forgotten that many others are persuasive to a high degree. This is not an inadvertency, but something which many writers are urgently, and sometimes honestly and overtly, trying to achieve. Those who *expose* propaganda, or *warn* people against it, or point out its *subversive menace,* are by no means trying to neutralize the term's emotive meaning. They are not pure scientists, even though they may be meticulous in their applications of science. Their effort is to build up a counterinfluence, undermining that of the "propagandists"; hence they must define "propagandist" in a way that limits its derogation to their opponents.

moralists that the word "moralist" itself becomes tainted for them. This is a marked exception to the laudatory, or at least not derogatory, use of the term that is in question throughout this chapter.

A man who is innovating sharp changes in the mores may be called by his opponents a "propagandist against the accepted order," and by his sympathizers a "leader of a new moral crusade." It is quite possible that both the opponents and the sympathizers, by careful choice of definitions, can make their statements descriptively true—but true only in persuasively defined senses, which themselves will become the points of contention.

Let us not forget that those who use the term "propaganda" to decry their opponents are not always to be decried in their turn. *They* will be decried only by those who sympathize with the alleged "propaganda."

Persuasive uses of "propaganda" are not limited to those who define the term, but are more typical, perhaps, of those who define it half-metaphorically, or not at all. This is a point of particular interest; it helps to account for the inadvertent overpersuasion which, as briefly noted in Chapter VII,[10] breeds suspicion of all other persuasion. Vaguely used, the term "propaganda" can forward an emotional plea for emotional apathy, confusedly suggesting that the emotive terms, because they are sometimes abused, must wholly lose caste in our "scientific age."

Inadvertent overpersuasion can be found even in writers whose work is otherwise illuminating. It may arise, for instance, from the method of propaganda analysis that has been developed by Albert and Elizabeth Lee.[11] These writers reproduce several radio addresses given by the Reverend Charles E. Coughlin, interspersing his text with ideographic symbols that make a running commentary on the persuasive methods used. Each vague and laudatory word that Father Coughlin uses is followed by a pictorial symbol of a glittering jewel; each vague and derogatory word, by a symbol of a hand pointing thumbs down; each arresting metaphor, or similar figure, by a mask indicating emotive transfer; each effort to ingratiate the speaker into the audience's sympathies (suggesting that he is a "simple citizen, like them"), by a symbol of an old shoe; and so on. (There are other symbols which are less concerned with emotive meaning than with the misrepresentation and distortion of evidence; but these need not here concern us.) The use of these symbols, which the authors find that they can scatter through Father Coughlin's re-

10. P. 163.
11. *The Fine Art of Propaganda* (Harcourt, Brace, 1939).

marks by handfuls, is highly instructive. By no other device can an analysis of persuasive methods be presented so specifically, briefly, and graphically; and it is to be hoped that the method will come into more general use.

The inventors of it cannot so heartily be commended, however, for their care in avoiding misinterpretation. They are avowedly exposing the "tricks of the trade," and although they sometimes remark that not all the "tricks" of propaganda are to be deplored, this latter point receives little emphasis. Excitable readers may come to feel, then, that Father Coughlin is being damned not because of the direction of his influence, or his motivation, or the untenability of his supporting reasons, but purely and simply because he utilizes the emotive terms—as if the use of any glittering-jewel word, or thumbs-down word, and so on, betokens linguistic treachery.

In point of fact, the symbols that the Lees have developed are susceptible to a wide variety of applications, and can be sprinkled quite plentifully throughout the works of all politicians, reformers, religious leaders, journalists, educators, novelists, and poets—many of whom neither the Lees nor any of their readers would wish to deprecate. Several of the present writer's students have actually applied the symbols in this way, using material that varied from the most revered works of philosophers and reformers to columns of "advice to the lovelorn"; and some took pleasure in applying them to explanatory passages in the Lees' own book. The symbols had a ready application in every case. There is nothing surprising or alarming in this. It shows only the ubiquitousness of persuasion. It shows anew what we have elsewhere observed: to point out persuasion is not to condemn it; the practical problem is not to avoid all persuasion, but to decide which to avoid and which to accept. There is little doubt that the Lees realize this, but their failure to emphasize it is unfortunate. It may lead the undiscerning into a kind of linguophobia, and make them so wary of any expression of the emotions that they will become confused nonparticipants in the issues of political and social life.

Walter Millis, in his article entitled "Propaganda for War," [12] has become more than usually sensitive to the dangers of this overpersuasion. After pointing out that "there are countless definitions of propaganda," which have nearly destroyed any fixed

12. *Southern Review* (autumn issue, 1939).

meaning altogether, and made the term largely an epithet, he remarks: "The concept of propaganda is an incomparable propaganda device." It will not do to press this epigram uncharitably, for, indeed, it presents in succinct form the essentials of the present view. But precautions are necessary even for those who are in the course of recommending them; so let us temper Millis' epigram (though with fidelity to the spirit of it) by insisting that not *every* use of "propaganda" is propaganda. The concept of propaganda may also be an incomparable *moral* device.

These remarks will be sufficient to disclose the kind of issue to which a distinction between propagandists and moralists may sometimes give rise. It is simple enough in principle, but like all issues that are evaluative, it must be seen amid the full milieu of human attitudes and beliefs.

Must we, for present purposes, actually make the distinction, clearly defining the terms? If emotive meaning is not neutralized, and the definitions become persuasive, it must be the special aim of analysis to *avoid* making the distinction. Persuasive definitions have an important function elsewhere, but analysis must study them without making them. If emotive meaning is neutralized, then in the particular case of "propaganda" there will again be no need of selecting a definition. We shall have no further occasion to use the term, which was introduced only as an example for analysis; hence the selection of any particular sense is best left to those who use it for more detailed cognitive purposes.

The term "moralist," may conveniently be retained for present use, and will be employed in a wholly neutral and very broad sense. It will designate those who purposefully (though the purpose may be unconscious) influence attitudes in some specified direction—beyond the requirements of pure cognition, though not, of course, in a way that need be divorced from rational support. Any more specific sense can easily give place to the broad one qualified by an adjective. Thus one may be said to exert a "peculiarly" moral influence if he influences only those attitudes that are correlated with a sense of guilt, sin, or remorse, and so on; one may be called a "conventional" moralist if he renders more permanent the usual standards of society. Further possibilities will be obvious. The qualifying adjectives can often be omitted, being evident from the context.

This procedure can be recommended to all theorists, even

though they may wish, as many do, to supplement their analysis of ethical judgments with judgments of their own about (other) moralists. Instead of using "moralist" as a term of praise, it is less misleading to speak of "good" moralists, where "good" can readily be used in first-pattern fashion. And instead of using it as a term of reproach, as those who rebel from the conventional moralists sometimes do,[13] it is less misleading to speak of "bad" moralists. The use of "good" and "bad" will serve to make the theorist's own influence manifest, and help to keep it from being confused with his analysis.

In using "moralist" in a neutral sense, we must continue to exercise all the care upon which this chapter has insisted. Anyone who uses an ethical judgment will speak in the capacity of a moralist; and anyone who condemns the judgment as "immoral" (or "unethical") will also be a moralist, saying nothing that is incompatible with the present analysis, or in any way opposed to it.

4

ALTHOUGH this chapter has simply applied the present analysis to a special case, it may be well to summarize its conclusions:

The terms "propagandist" and "moralist" need not be persuasive terms, provided care is used in neutralizing their emotive effects. But they readily lend themselves to a persuasive usage, and sometimes overpersuade, inadvertently. When the terms are *completely* neutralized, one may say with tranquillity that all moralists are propagandists, or that all propagandists are moralists. Either statement can be made true by definition, without violence to the boundaries of conventional usage. It is equally possible, for other senses, that they should be false. In any case, the "moralists" and the "propagandists" will be neither abused nor praised. On the other hand, if the words are used with rhetorical emphasis, with their full emotive effect, they will serve less to preserve cognitive distinctions than to plead a cause. A statement like "All moralists are propagandists," even though it is made true by definition, may by its emotive meaning serve to exert an influence which discredits the influence of others. This effect may be a part of the speaker's intentions, or contrary to them.

13. Cf. p. 247, n. 9. The motives for reversing the emotive meaning in this way will be considered in Chap. XIII, Sec. 1.

XII

Some Related Theories

1

THE second pattern of analysis is often useful as a tool for clarifying and criticizing the several trends of ethical theory. We have seen this in Chapter IX, with reference to Plato, Bentham, and Sidgwick. Let us now consider some other writers, paying particular attention to those to whom the present work is indebted. For there are several theorists whose views are very close to the present ones—so much so that it becomes interesting, amid the points of resemblance, to make clear the precise points of difference.

The greater part of our attention must be given to John Dewey, whose work in ethics as in every field is worthy of respectful study.

How does Dewey distinguish between evaluative terms and descriptive ones? He answers rather carefully in *The Quest for Certainty*,[1] where he contrasts "desired" with "desirable," "admired" with "admirable," "esteemed" with "estimable," and so on. In each pair of terms the first serves "to make a statement about a fact" or to give "a mere report"; whereas the second is used to make a "judgment as to the importance and need of bringing a fact into existence; or if it is already there, of sustaining it in existence." Only the latter terms, which indicate that something is "to be prized and cherished, *to be* enjoyed," mark a "genuine practical judgment." And a page or two later the same distinction is reiterated:

Propositions about what is or has been liked are of instrumental value in reaching judgments of value, in as far as the conditions and consequences of the thing liked are thought about. In themselves they make no claims; they put forth no demand upon subsequent attitudes and acts; they profess no authority to direct. . . . A judgment about

1. Chap. ix, particularly pp. 260–263 (Minton, Balch, 1929).

what is *to be* desired and enjoyed is, on the other hand, a claim on future action; it possesses a *de jure* and not merely *de facto* quality. . . . It is, in effect, a judgment that the thing "will do." It involves a prediction; it contemplates a future in which the thing will continue to serve; it *will* do. It asserts a consequence that the thing will actively institute; it will *do*.

Let us see whether these remarks can be likened to the present views. One factor that accounts for the "*de jure* quality" of evaluative judgments is their predictive nature. They "contemplate a future." This is compatible with the second pattern of analysis; since the variables of its schema (the "X," "Y," and "Z" of page 207 can readily be replaced by terms designating the consequences of an object judged. And obviously, there often *will* be this reference to consequences. So far Dewey's views are not foreign to the second pattern; though he expressly *requires* what the second pattern simply *recognizes* among the many linguistic possibilities.

But are the predictive aspects of an evaluative judgment *sufficient* to mark off its "*de jure* quality"? It would not seem so; for even if all evaluative judgments were predictive, it could scarcely be held that all predictive statements are evaluative. To predict rain is not to evaluate; or if it is urged that in a sense it is, since the prediction has potential effects on choice and action, then it must be remarked that *all* judgments will be *de jure*, leaving no room for the *de facto* ones—for there is no judgment (as we have previously seen,[2] and as Dewey would be the last to deny) that is without potential effects on conduct.

So prediction is not *enough* to characterize a *de jure* function in any distinctive sense. There is little doubt that Dewey realizes this, and intends to refer to a special *kind* of prediction. Perhaps his view can be summarized in the following way: An evaluative judgment is one which makes predictions that are quite heterogeneous in their subject matter, but which have in common a particularly intimate bearing on people's attitudes to the object that is evaluated. In other words, a value-judgment will differ from a scientific one only with regard to the selection and classification of the consequences predicted. A scientific term classifies consequences for the purpose of systematizing cognition, where one's approval or disapproval of the object studied

2. Cf. pp. 62–66, and 162.

is held temporarily in abeyance, subordinate to the aim of predicting as much about it as possible. In that way scientific knowledge is made available for forwarding many different and divergent aims.[3] An evaluative term cuts across these scientific classifications, and selects out consequences that may have little else in common than the effect which a knowledge of them will have in redirecting or intensifying approval. Evaluation (or "appraisal," as Dewey says) is not pure science but science *applied* and organized for the special purpose of altering attitudes.

There is much in Dewey's writing that bears out this interpretation. He frequently compares normative ethics with such applied sciences as engineering and medicine.[4] In the latter subjects, of course, there must be a grouping of predictions which cuts across that of the pure physicist, pure chemist, or pure biologist, just as the grouping of the moralist's predictions must cut across many pure fields. And the role that he assigns to attitudes, amid this selective application of science, is often clearly stated:

Men *like* some of the consequences and *dislike* others. Henceforth (or till attraction and repulsion alter) attaining or averting similar consequences are aims or ends. These consequences constitute the meaning and value of an activity as it comes under deliberation.

Moral science is not something with a separate province. It is physical, biological and historic knowledge placed in a human context where it will illuminate and guide the activities of men.

The alternative, here as elsewhere, is not between denying facts in behalf of something termed moral ideals and accepting facts as final. There remains the possibility of recognizing facts and using them as a challenge to intelligence to modify the environment and change habits.

What is objected to in the current empirical theories of value is not connection of them with desire and enjoyment but failure to distinguish between enjoyments of radically different sorts. . . . Values

3. But there can never be science divorced from *all aims*. This would certainly be Dewey's view. The present writer's opinions on the subject will briefly be developed in Chap. XIII.

4. See, for example, "Theory of Valuation," *The International Encyclopedia of Unified Science*, II, No. 4 (Chicago University Press, 1939), 22. Evaluative statements are there taken as "rules for the use, in and by human activity, of scientific generalizations," and specifically compared to engineering.

. . . may be connected inherently with liking, and yet not with *every* liking but only with those that judgment has approved, after examination of the relation upon which the object liked depends . . . its connections and interactions.

The previous discussion does not point in the least to supersession of the emotive [i.e., emotional] by the intellectual. Its only and complete import is the need for their integration in behavior—behavior in which, according to common speech, the head and the heart work together.[5]

Dewey does not always write in a way that lends itself to one and only one interpretation; but we may safely conclude that his emphasis on prediction, which so repeatedly characterizes his remarks about evaluative judgments, bears an important restriction: the predictions are selected and used in an effort to guide attitudes.

If this is what Dewey means, his views continue to be compatible with the present ones. We have seen that the second pattern permits ethical judgments to be predictive; and if moralists use the judgments in the course of resolving disagreement in attitude, we may expect them to select out the predictions that are most relevant to attitudes. The predictions will be quite heterogeneous, as Chapter VIII of the present work has indicated—no less so than Dewey would insist. With regard to *descriptive* meaning, then (for "descriptive" is not opposed to "predictive" but includes it) Dewey provides a special instance of the several sorts of analysis that the second pattern recognizes.

But what shall be said of the quasi-imperative aspect of ethical terms, which the present analysis has preserved by emotive meaning? Is this wholly ignored by Dewey? There are times when he seems to recognize it; or rather, he comes very near to doing so, and then backs away. This is a matter that we must consider in detail:

Dewey often says that judgments like "X is good" and "X is desirable" indicate that X is *to be* prized or *to be* desired.[6] What does "to be" mean? There is a familiar sense, of course, in which it is used predictively. "There *is to be* a solar eclipse tomorrow"

---

5. The first three quotations are from *Human Nature and Conduct*, pp. 225, 296, 301 f. The fourth is from *Quest for Certainty*, pp. 260, 264; and the fifth from *Theory of Valuation*, p. 65.

6. This is instanced by the quotations given on p. 253 f.

just means that there *will be* a solar eclipse tomorrow. But there is another sense in which "to be" behaves like the Latin gerundive, which is less predictive than hortatory. When a man says to his assistant, "This work *is to be* finished and in my hands again by five o'clock," the remark is in effect an imperative. Now when Dewey uses "to be," in an effort to explain the *"de jure"* function of an ethical judgment, the expression always seems to carry with it the quasi-imperative force; and perhaps it is on this account that his equating of "desirable" and "to be desired" sounds so plausible. But this quasi-imperative force seems to be utilized tacitly, without receiving explicit mention. Although Dewey states that "morality is largely concerned with controlling human nature," [7] he gives no overt emphasis to the effect of imperative or quasi-imperative statements in exerting this control. The hortatory "to be's" are absorbed into an elaborate conjunction of predictive ones.

It is here that the present account conspicuously diverges from Dewey. He tacitly identifies the quasi-imperative function of ethical judgments with their predictive function; and the present account, although granting that the two factors often occur together, insists upon a distinction. Now *if* emotive or quasi-imperative functions *could* be absorbed into predictive ones, Dewey's manner of doing so would be less misleading than that of any other ethical theorist; for Dewey singles out the kind of prediction that roughly approximates to emotive meaning in its practical effect. He does not quite identify emotive meaning with descriptive meaning, if we abide by the terminology that was suggested in Chapter III. Descriptive meaning must be something kept relatively precise by linguistic rules,[8] and most of the predictiveness that Dewey recognizes for ethical judgments is too vague to be so classified. Rather, he identifies a word's emotive meaning with what it predictively *suggests*. In other words, he tacitly takes all emotive meaning to be quasi-dependent emotive meaning,[9] and does not distinguish the latter from the cognitive suggestions *on* which it depends. This would be the most plausible identification, if any were possible; but a brief examination, emphasizing previous remarks, will show the grounds on which it must be criticized:

7. *Human Nature and Conduct*, p. 1.
8. Cf. pp. 68 ff.
9. Cf. pp. 78 f.

Let us suppose, for the sake of analogy, that we were asked to analyze an overt imperative,[10] such as "Please close the door," and that we responded by saying that it is synonymous with an elaborate conjunction of predictive statements, such as, "There is a draught, and closing the door will be a means of stopping it," "If the door isn't closed, we may both catch cold," "Closing it will be easier for you than for me, since you are right next to it," and so on. It will be obvious that the latter statements, if we look only to this special situation, realizing that a quite different "analysis" would be needed for a different situation, may be no less effective in directing the hearer's actions than the overt imperative, and that for many purposes they would be functionally interchangeable with it. It will be equally obvious that the predictive statements can be called an "analysis" of the imperative only in an extended and perplexing sense. In present terminology the so-called "analysis" would rather be a list of *reasons* that might be given to support the imperative—reasons which reinforce its directive effect *by another means*, and which may replace it only when they are themselves sufficient to guide the hearer, the more direct hortatory appeal being a gratuitous addition. Dewey's procedure in ethics is somewhat comparable to this. He preserves what could readily be recognized as *reasons* for an ethical judgment, but insists that they exhaust the *full meaning* of the judgment. In certain respects, to be sure, the analogy is not exact. One would strongly demur at having an imperative analyzed in a way that included the meaning of its supporting reasons, but would not always demur (as the remarks on the second pattern have shown) at having an ethical judgment do this. And it is to be assumed that Dewey would consider an ethical judgment as "containing" the "meaning" of its supporting reasons only in a vague way—much more vaguely than explicit definition can indicate. But an important parallel remains. In identifying the *whole* meaning of the judgment with its supporting reasons, Dewey explains *away* the characteristically hortatory, quasi-imperative meaning, as distinct from explaining it; he overintellectualizes the emotive urgency of the ethical terms, just as the parallel here considered overintellectualizes the direct psychological impact of the imperative.

We have previously found the need of making a simple distinction between two methods of directing attitudes: those which

10. Cf. Chap. II, Sec. 1.

proceed *via* changes in belief and those which do not. The fact that these methods are so often used together does not trivialize the distinction, since there is a more-or-less independent variation in the *extent* to which one predominates over the other. It is to this distinction that Dewey gives too little attention.

And yet Dewey retains a substitute, as it were, for emotive meaning. So perhaps it may seem that his analysis is accurate enough for all practical purposes. Even if a distinction *can* be made between the predictive and quasi-imperative force of a judgment, why does the distinction need emphasis—why is it more than an idle subtlety? This is to ask why emotive meaning requires special attention in ethics, and although the answer has been suggested elsewhere, let us review it for this special case. Dewey might be criticized simply because he obliterates a distinction that is important to the study of language. There are certain fields, such as literary criticism, where the trifold distinction that is here recognized—that between a word's emotive meaning, its descriptive meaning, and what it (quite vaguely) suggests—promises to be useful. Any effort to absorb one into the other would be needless and clumsy. So long as the distinction must be developed for other purposes, there can be no gain in simplicity in trying to avoid it in ethics. But this is not a vital consideration; it is subordinate to a further, indirect effect of Dewey's procedure—that of underemphasizing disagreement in attitude, of *seeming* to absorb (whether he really meant to do so or not) all disagreement in attitude into disagreement in belief. This is always the effect of dwelling on the descriptive aspects of language, and it leads to serious confusions about methodology:

In the first place, it gives no explanation of the emotional contagion that may attend ethical arguments—the use of persuasive methods to produce a direct, unquestioning enthusiasm, and to cut through apathy with greater force or finesse than rational methods ever permit. Even if persuasive methods were wholly to be repudiated (a contention that is not at all practicable) an analyst must take them for what they are, rather than confuse them with their nearest intellectual approximation. In the second place, the procedure tempts one to ascribe too great a finality to rational methods. Dewey has explicitly stated that "appraisals of courses of action as better or worse . . . are as experimentally justified as are nonvaluative propositions about impersonal subject matter."[11] This is a ready consequence of his emphasis on prediction. It is subject, to be sure, to a cautious qualification: "A moral theory based on the realities of human nature and a study of the specific connections of these realities with those of physical science . . . would not make the moral life as simple a matter as wending one's way along a well-lighted boulevard. All action is an invasion of the future, of the unknown."[12] But this qualification shows only the uncertainty of *all* prediction; it *seems* to maintain (although again, Dewey may not wish it to be so construed) that normative ethics is uncertain because all *beliefs* about the future are uncertain, and for no other reason. Granted that empirical confirmation is always partial and difficult, ethical judgments are open to it no less *directly* than are scientific ones. The present account cannot accept this conclusion, as will be apparent if we briefly recall the analysis of the preceding chapters.

The initial inadequacy of accepting a *direct* empirical confirmation of ethical judgments is that their predictive aspects, if we take them as "implicit" in ordinary usage, are so vague that the speaker will not himself have decided what observations will verify them. This can be remedied by *defining* the ethical terms in second-pattern fashion. But any definition which draws out the predictive aspects into a definite, testable descriptive meaning is likely, for the important issues on which disagreement in attitude is prevalent, to be a persuasive definition. Different speakers may insist on different definitions, and so may use their *emotively* opposed judgments to make *compatible* sets of predictions. More specifically, the judgment "X is good," said by A, may be fully confirmable in experience; but so may "X is not good," said by B—as we have previously seen.[13] If we let ethical methodology end with scientific methodology, we could say no more than that both parties might be correct. Dewey does not discuss this, tacitly assuming, it would seem, that divergent predictions will not occur. (Such an assumption could scarcely have contented him, had he taken care, in emphasizing that ethical predictions are relevant to the direction of attitudes,

11. *Theory of Valuation*, p. 22.
12. *Human Nature and Conduct*, pp. 11 f. (Although this work was written seventeen years before the *Theory of Valuation*, there seems little reason to suppose that Dewey's views have undergone significant change during the interval.)
13. Cf. Chapter X, p. 233.

to specify *whose* attitudes were in question, and to give clearer *instances* of *what* predictions he had in mind.) By the present views, divergent predictions are not excluded; and this has the indirect effect of showing that scientific agreement (or any sort of agreement in belief) might not be sufficient to end ethical disputes. Even though A and B agree on all predictions, and know it, they may disagree in attitude, and will verbally indicate their disagreement so long as A weds certain predictions to a term of emotive praise, and B refuses to. This discloses an uncertainty in ethical arguments that may exist *in addition* to the general uncertainty of prediction that Dewey recognizes. The added uncertainty must always be reckoned with, so long as one cannot be sure that all disagreement in attitude is rooted in disagreement in belief.

So far we have seen that the present account differs from Dewey with regard to emotive meaning, and with regard to the precise role of empirical methods. There is an additional difference that has been mentioned in passing, but must now be emphasized. Dewey holds that ethical judgments are always predictive, whereas the present analysis simply recognizes this as one linguistic possibility among others. For the first pattern, ethical judgments are not in themselves predictive, any prediction being left to the supporting reasons; and for the second pattern, prediction receives no exclusive stress, and in any case need not be so involved and complicated as Dewey would require. The present procedure, preferable on linguistic grounds, suggests a further point of interest:

Dewey, unlike the present writer, does not wish to isolate the special tasks of analysis; he wishes to supplement his analysis by exerting an influence of his own. In good measure he moralizes about the moralists. Deploring the shortsighted, capricious dogmatism and rhetoric of many moralists, he declares, in effect, that their methods *ought* to be altered. This influence is mediated by his emphasis on prediction; for by insisting that the ethical terms *are* predictive he serves by suggestion to *make* them so, barring the way to any other usage. Emotive meaning, unrecognized but still present, is preempted for predictive terms; hence nothing is to be called "good" unless its consequences are examined. In effect, his analysis embodies vigorous and well-defended persuasive definitions, pleading that moralists make greater use of rational methods. He does not *quite* give persuasive definitions of the ethical terms, since he specifies no exact definitions at all, but only a *range* of predictive meanings; but in insisting on just *this* range of meanings, he specifies the sort of descriptive meaning to which he will grant the emotive dignity of ethical terminology. Those who wish to exert an influence independently of any prediction must confine themselves to the use of less impressive terms. We *ought* to make "the head and the heart work together."

Let us remember that a plea for the full use of knowledge is not unbecoming in a philosopher; and Dewey's plea is no mere rhapsody, but is supported by the light of that very knowledge for which it pleads. If in his eagerness to praise the scientific aspects of ethics he has overemphasized them, it is also true that the traditional moralists have too frequently ignored them, and have earned their reputation for vacuity on that account. Yet Dewey's ethics would have gained in clarity if his plea had been mediated in some other manner than by persuasive definitions. Let us see why this is so.

There are obviously a great many people whose ethical judgments have little to do with prediction, and much to do with a mirroring of their old, socially inherited attitudes. Dewey wishes, understandably, to take such judgments only as raw material, to be shaped into a finished product. He engages in the double task of clarifying the judgments and of inducing people to support them with richer stores of information. But the component aspects of this double task must be kept distinct. A plea for the use of full knowledge is not committed to any one way of clarifying the ethical terms, but is compatible with definitions that are extremely simple. Dewey is not content, however, to let any part of his work lose touch, even temporarily, with such a plea; hence he urges, in effect, that the only "real" senses of the ethical terms are predictive ones. This leads to a seeming dilemma. If he acknowledges the full range of meanings that the ethical terms *can* have, including the simple ones, he will obscure the importance of science; and if he refuses to acknowledge it, he will obscure the nature of language. The dilemma, of course, is wholly artificial. The full range of meanings can be emphasized in analysis, and the plea for wider knowledge be emphasized later. This possibility is not evident when analysis, seeking only clarity, uses definitions which are also persuasive; for persuasive definitions, even when they encourage people to be more rational, may too easily be confused with the definitions that are required for analysis itself.

The present account, by talking *about* persuasive definitions as distinct from employing them, is enabled to recognize linguistic flexibility. Although this does not in itself have the direct result of reforming the moralists, and making them feel an obligation to take the sciences more seriously, it is certainly not incompatible with that result; and it undertakes the preliminary task, which Dewey himself has so often declared important, of surveying and clarifying the situation out of which any improvement must arise.

Although these criticisms of Dewey are of consequence, they do not repudiate the central aspects of his work. He has emphasized the function of ethical judgments in *redirecting* attitudes, and has thereby brought ethics into closer contact with the earth. There the present writer concurs, and must express deep indebtedness.[14] The main differences occur largely on the degree to which ethical language is recognized as vague and emotive, and on the degree of finality that must, in ethics, be granted to empirical methods. Even on these points, perhaps, the present account has less occasion to reject Dewey's broader insights than to round them out and qualify them.

In view of these broad similarities, one wonders why Dewey, whose views so readily suggest a quasi-imperative element in ethics, and whose efforts to build attitudes upon prediction and knowledge could not arise from any artificial quest for certainty, should have been so neglectful of emotive meaning. His section on "Value Expressions as Ejaculatory," in *Theory of Valuation*, leads him to make no significant qualification of his earlier conceptions. Some may wish to account for this by saying that Dewey found nothing in emotive meaning that he had really neglected. He is not an easy author to interpret, and perhaps his seeming omission of emotive meaning is rather a failure to abstract it out and emphasize it. The present contention is that he absorbs emotive meaning into predictive suggestion, but one might also say that he absorbs predictive suggestion into emotive meaning; or, to speak less paradoxically, it may be that Dewey preserves both the notion of prediction and of emotive force, as those terms are

14. A further indebtedness has been acknowledged in Chapter VIII. Although the present writer's views on means and ends may differ from Dewey's in the manner in which they are developed, the general similarities will be obvious.

here understood, but always as aspects of his own broader ("instrumental") sense of "prediction." The writer is inclined to accept this interpretation as a possible one. Yet Dewey will be open to criticism, even so. There will still be different *kinds* of "prediction" in his sense, requiring more disparate treatment than they receive. The same objections will reappear in another terminology.

A particularly interesting way of accounting for his views is suggested by the kind of normative problem that he most emphasizes. His references to attitudes are largely taken up with a study of *conflicts*, and this leads him to stress what are here called personal decisions, as distinct from interpersonal arguments. (The present work has reversed this emphasis, though without wishing to ignore either aspect, partly in order to make clearer how Dewey's work must be corrected and supplemented.) Now in personal decisions emotive meaning is not conspicuous. Self-exhortation certainly exists, as we have seen,[15] but it intrudes upon the attention less strongly than does the manifest interpersuasiveness of social discourse. What *does* become conspicuous in personal decisions—particularly for highly rational theorists, who may then credit others with the states of mind that they discover in their own introspection—is the great difficulty of taking full account of an action's consequences. Moreover, a man's prediction of these consequences seems to him to have a *direct* relation to his conflict; for the psychological effect of his beliefs upon his attitudes, which makes the relation indirect, usually occurs without conscious scrutiny. It may be that Dewey's imperfect separation of the hortatory and predictive aspects of ethics has arisen (though only partially, to be sure) from these tempting sources of introspective error. This does not temper our criticisms of his analysis, even for personal decisions; for we have seen that in these cases, no less than in others, emotive meaning remains important, and rational methods remain indirect. It shows, rather, that Dewey might have altered his conclusions had he viewed personal decisions in the light of analogies to interpersonal ones. Perhaps Dewey has departed, inadvertently, from a maxim that he himself has so admirably defended: the moral terms must be studied when they are at work—in the full variety and complexity of their living contexts, both individual and social.

15. Chap. VI, pp. 148–151.

2

LET us now turn from Dewey to some other contemporary writers. In the past decade or two philosophical analysts have given increasing attention to emotive meaning, and several have emphasized it in ethics. Their views have found some adherents, but a rather larger number of opponents. A. J. Ayer's analysis has provoked heated discussion.[16] Bertrand Russell, whose most recent views on ethical analysis[17] are almost identical with Ayer's, has not, in this connection, been so widely discussed—perhaps because the old-school moralists, after their previous attacks on him, have become too exhausted to repeat them. Rudolph Carnap has devoted several brief pages to the imperative and expressive functions of ethical statements;[18] and C. D. Broad has summarized an emotive view,[19] drawing from an unpublished paper of A. E. Duncan-Jones. An earlier account was given by Ogden and Richards in *The Meaning of Meaning,*[20] and several

16. *Language, Truth, and Logic,* chap. vi. In the present writer's opinion, Ayer has managed, in his very brief compass, to speak with clarity and much discernment. Yet he has been repudiated by some with a fervor that borders on melodrama. Martin D'Arcy, writing on "Philosophy Now," in *Criterion,* 1936, ends with the following remark: "Under the pretence of ultimate wisdom it [Ayer's book] guillotines religion, ethics and aesthetics, self, persons, free will, responsibility and everything worth while. I thank Mr. Ayer for having shown us how modern philosophers can fiddle and play tricks while the world burns."

17. *Religion and Science* (Henry Holt, 1935), chap. ix. Russell writes, for example: "Questions as to 'values'—that is to say, as to what is good or bad on its own account, independently of its effects—lie outside the domain of science, as the defenders of religion emphatically assert. I think that in this they are right, but I draw the further conclusion, which they do not draw, that questions as to 'values' lie wholly outside the domain of knowledge." "[Ethics] is an attempt to bring the collective desires of a group to bear upon individuals; or conversely, it is an attempt by an individual to cause his desires to become those of his group. . . . When a man says, 'This is good in itself,' . . . he means . . . 'Would that everybody desired this.' . . . [Such a statement] makes no assertion, but expresses a wish; since it affirms nothing, it is logically impossible that there should be evidence for or against it, or for it to possess either truth or falsehood." These views were foreshadowed, though not so clearly, in Russell's earlier book, *What I Believe* (Dutton, 1925), particularly pp. 29 ff.

18. *Philosophy and Logical Syntax* (Kegan Paul, 1935), pp. 22–26. For some more recent remarks by Carnap, see his letter to R. Lepley, quoted and discussed in Lepley's *Verifiability of Value* (Columbia, 1944), pp. 137 f., n. 14.

19. "Is 'Goodness' a Name of a Simple, Non-natural Quality?" *Proceedings of the Aristotelian Society,* 1933–34.

20. See the quotation at the beginning of the present volume.

others have contributed to the view in this or that detail.[21]

The criticisms that have been leveled against these views have shown more impatience than understanding. They have usually assumed that an emotive analysis represents an effort to "discredit ethics"—and indeed that very phrase was used even by so astute a critic as W. D. Ross.[22] But the writers above mentioned have certainly been free of such sinister intentions. They have obviously repudiated all trans-scientific ethical *subject matter*, and have suggested that the philosophers who defend it say nothing that is salvageable. But it is one thing to attack certain writers on ethics, and another to discredit ethics. To compare ethical judgments to imperatives is not to deny that imperatives have an important use. To say that ethical judgments express feelings is not to imply that all feelings are to be inhibited. To say that ethical judgments are "neither true nor false" is not to maintain (as will be clear from the parallel remarks on "validity" in Chapter VII) that they are to be made capriciously, in ignorance of one's self, or the nature and consequences of the object judged.

It must be granted, however, that certain of the writers mentioned have thrown themselves open to such misinterpretations. They have been eager to show that normative questions are quite different from scientific ones; and have sometimes given the impression—due, perhaps, to the brevity of their remarks—that ethics is thereby being swept aside. Carnap is particularly unguarded in this respect. He remarks, to be sure, that

the non-theoretical character of metaphysics would not be in itself a defect; all the arts have this non-theoretical character without losing their high value for personal as well as for social life. The danger lies in the *deceptive* character of metaphysics; it gives illusion of knowledge without actually giving any knowledge. That is why we reject it.[23]

But only a few pages before he has made metaphysics include

21. In particular see Karl Britton, *Communication* (Harcourt, Brace, 1939), pp. 8 f., and chap. ix; W. H. F. Barnes, "A Suggestion about Values," *Analysis* (March, 1934) ; Helen Wodehouse, "Language and Moral Philosophy," *Mind* (April, 1938) ; Abraham Kaplan, "Are Moral Judgments Assertions?" *Philosophical Review* (May, 1942). And for a study which, though it does not mention emotive meaning, is close to the conceptions of methodology which emotive meaning suggests, see Charner M. Perry, "The Arbitrary as a Basis for Rational Morality," *International Journal of Ethics* (January, 1933).

22. *Foundations of Ethics* (Oxford, 1939), p. 38.

23. *Op. cit.*, p. 31.

all value statements.[24] One can scarcely avoid the inference that ethical statements, unlike artistic forms of expression, are to be rejected. Whether they are to be rejected from the pure sciences only, or rejected altogether, is not made sufficiently clear. Now it would be strange if ethical judgments, simply because they have deceived certain philosophers, must be banished from all human affairs. The thousands of ethical problems that attend daily life, even though they may be confused in this or that particular, are not confused beyond hope of clarification. They may occasion disagreement in attitude; but if this differs from disagreement in the pure sciences, it is not therefore indicative of "pseudo-problems" in any sense that hints at intellectual debauchery. Manifestly, so long as it is taken for what it is, disagreement in attitude is something which each of us, in the course of ordinary living, does and must engage in with absorbing seriousness. Carnap would not wish to deny this; but he would have avoided much hostile criticism had he expressly and clearly affirmed it.

Yet the present work finds much more to defend in the analyses of Carnap, Ayer, and the others, than it finds to attack. It seeks only to qualify their views—partly in the light of Dewey's—and to free them from any seeming cynicism. It hopes to make clear that "emotive" need not itself have a derogatory emotive meaning. And in particular, it emphasizes the complex descriptive meaning that ethical judgments can have, in addition to their emotive meaning. Descriptive meaning is not eliminated even in the first pattern (though it could have been), and for the second it is recognized quite freely. Such a procedure avoids any dogmatism about "the" meaning of ethical judgments, and tempers the paradoxical contention that ethical judgments are "neither true nor false." This latter remark is wholly misleading. It is more accurate and illuminating to say that an ethical judgment *can* be true or false, but to point out that its descriptive truth may be insufficient to support its emotive repercussions. It will be recalled, moreover, that Chapter VII has pointed out a particularly broad sense of "true"[25]—a sense whose application could be extended, as will be obvious, even to ethical judgments in which the predicate is taken as *purely* emotive. In addition to

24. *Op. cit.*, p. 26: "Value statements . . . have, here as elsewhere, no theoretical sense. Therefore we assign them to the realm of metaphysics."
25. Pp. 169 f.

these considerations about meaning, the present work seeks to give full attention to ethical methodology, emphasizing the *interplay* between emotive and descriptive meaning, dispelling any impression that a moralist must be irrational or dogmatic, and indicating the general circumstances under which ethical arguments can be resolved by scientific means. Some of these points are suggested by the writers mentioned; but in ethics, where detached analysis is so rare and misinterpretation so prevalent, it is particularly important to replace all suggestions by definite statements. It may be added that the present analysis differs further from other emotive theories (again going more in Dewey's direction) in that it gives diminished importance to the distinction between "good as a means" and "good as an end."

These are the main points of difference between the present views and the other "emotive" ones that are now current; but the differences must not cause us to overlook the similarities.

3

THE work of R. B. Perry,[26] with its careful attention to "interests" (attitudes), has exerted a great influence on current theory. Let us briefly compare his analysis with the present one. The basic differences are all implied in what has preceded,[27] but there are several points which require emphasis.

There can here be no repudiation, but only an indebted recognition, of Perry's study of the psychology of interests; but the present work must make its usual objection to any unqualified identification of ethical judgments with psychological statements *about* interests. That this can be done for certain usages, where emotive meaning is rendered inactive by the context, has been previously acknowledged;[28] but it neglects the ethical senses that theorists have found most troublesome. By passing over agreement and disagreement in attitude, giving exclusive emphasis instead to agreement and disagreement in belief about attitudes, Perry makes normative ethics a direct branch of natural science, and so gives an illusory certitude to ethical methodology. Although he is sensitive to the "mutation" or

26. *General Theory of Value*, particularly chaps. v and xviii–xx.
27. Particularly in the remarks on Richards, whose analysis is similar to Perry's in many respects. See pp. 8–11 of the present work. But these remarks were provisional, and what is here said of Perry must be taken as implicitly qualifying them.
28. Cf. pp. 83 f.

change of interests, and even to the effect of an active expression of one person's interests in altering those of another,[29] he does not properly emphasize the role of the emotive ethical terms in initiating such changes.

The misleading implications of Perry's procedure are most apparent when he discusses "the measurement of comparative value."[30] He recognizes *several* factors which determine whether one object is "better or worse" than another, but we can simplify the present discussion by considering only his criterion of "inclusiveness,"[31] which "takes precedence over the others."[32] The term "inclusiveness" refers to the *number* of interests that an object satisfies, and this in turn being partially a function of the number of people who have an interest in the object, Perry is led (for instance) to make the following remark: "An object which is loathed by L and M is worse, other things being equal, than an object which is loathed only by L, or only by M."[33] Now in its cognitive aspects this statement is immune from criticism; for since the ethical terms have flexible meanings, "worse" can be understood in a way that makes it true by definition. It will be obvious, however, that the statement has a normative force, a tendency to support democratic ideals, that no *emotively inactive* analytic statement could have. Indeed, Perry's procedure immediately takes its place beside the several others that we have studied. In implicitly defining "worse," he has not neutralized the term's emotive meaning, but has associated it (subject to an "all else being equal" clause, of course) with whatever the *greater number* of people have a loathing for. Thus if anyone favors anything that the majority loathe, he will receive emotive discouragement from being told that he favors the "worse" rather than the "better." In effect, "worse" has been persuasively defined in support of the majority, its derogation being reserved for "inclusive" loathings, not for the loathings of the dissenting minority.

Perry introduces many important extensions and qualifications of his views as here summarized, but these only complicate the present criticism without weakening its general purport. The *other* criteria of comparative value that he mentions (and these

29. *Op. cit.*, chaps. xviii, xix, particularly pp. 524 ff.
30. *Idem*, pp. 615–625; and chap. xxi.
31. *Idem*, pp. 617 f.
32. *Idem*, p. 656.
33. *Idem*, p. 621.

include not only "intensity" and "preference,"[34] but the aspects of "inclusiveness" that deal with several interests in the same person[35]) make his democratic aims take on a broadened, novel form. Yet it remains the case that these other criteria too are wedded to an emotive term, and so have a status that will be apparent from the above remarks. And the positive terms, such as "better," and "more valuable," will obviously raise the same considerations as "worse," with emotive meaning reversed. Thus the whole set of normative conclusions which Perry embodies in this part of his work—his *standards* for comparing values—are conditional to one's acceptance of his persuasive definitions.

These remarks must not be misconstrued. It is acknowledged that *if* Perry's persuasive definitions of "better" and "worse" are accepted, he has provided a standard of comparative values which has the advantage over many others in being intelligible, and applicable to concrete cases—not applicable in any simple or wholly rigorous way, of course,[36] but at least in a way that may be roughly practicable. It must further be observed that his definitions are not capriciously persuasive, but derive no little rational support from the study of interests that accompanies them. It may well be the case that many people will gladly accept his definitions, both for his reasons and for others that might supplement them. His work accordingly serves the purpose of making articulate an important type of ethical norm. To say this, however, is to recognize Perry's place as a *moralist*, and in no way compromises with the above criticism of his work as an *analyst*.

The writer's indebtedness to Perry will be evident in several parts of the present work. In Chapter VIII, for instance, the conception of reinforcement[37] is similar (though only from a personal, as distinct from an interpersonal, point of view) to Perry's conception of inclusiveness. But note that the present work makes use of it only in explaining how, as a matter of psychological fact, people are often led to decide what they will call "good." To do this—to describe how people make ethical deci-

34. *Idem*, pp. 616 ff.
35. *Idem*, pp. 617 f.
36. Perry has himself noted some serious difficulties about the commensurability of his three criteria. (*Idem*, 653–658.) And clearly, any effort to measure degrees of intensity and preference raises the usual difficulties about intensive magnitudes. There is the further difficulty, particularly pressing for "inclusiveness," of specifying what will be called "one" interest.
37. Pp. 188–191.

sions—is not to make an ethical decision. Perry goes on to make an ethical decision of his own, saying that an object becomes better when, all else being equal, someone's attitudes to it become more strongly reinforced. He is fully privileged to do so; but at that point he leaves analysis and becomes a moralist. Much the same considerations arise in a further connection. An increase in (interpersonal) ethical agreement, as here conceived, will lead to an increase in inclusive interests. But to say this simply clarifies the nature of ethical agreement; it does not evaluate anything, nor does it oblige anyone who disagrees with the majority to refrain from doing so. Evaluation comes only when, with Perry, the objects of inclusive interests are judged (all else being equal) to be better than others.

Throughout Perry's work the analytic and psychological aspects of ethics are confused with the normative ones—a confusion which at once distorts analysis and hampers well-defended evaluations. But it is often possible to separate the confused elements and recombine them. When this is done, Perry's work affords many suggestions, interesting to analysts and practical moralists alike.

4

LET us now briefly consider the work of G. E. Moore. Although his theories have been mentioned previously,[38] they will have a renewed interest when seen from the viewpoint of the second pattern of analysis.

The central contention of Moore's ethics can be presented in a sentence: "Propositions about the good are all of them synthetic."[39] In other words, given *any* ethical judgment of the form "N is good," where "N" stands for a naturalistic term and "good" is used in any typically ethical sense, the judgment will never be analytic. From this it immediately follows that "good," for any typically ethical sense, cannot be *defined* in naturalistic terms; for otherwise one need only replace "N" by the definiens, keeping "good" in the typical sense in question, and an analytic judgment would result. (For present purposes "naturalistic" may be taken as synonymous with "scientific." Moore doubtless had some broader sense in mind, but that will not be important to the present criticism.)

38. Pp. 25 f., 108 ff.
39. *Principia Ethica*, p. 7.

The present work, quite obviously, does *not* hold that "N is good" must be synthetic. All of the senses that have been mentioned have a *descriptive* meaning that is exhaustively definable in naturalistic terms; and if the analytic or synthetic character of a statement depends wholly on its descriptive meaning, each of these senses will permit corresponding analytic judgments. In this respect the present work is wholly opposed to Moore. Yet in another respect the opposition is not so serious. Although the present account permits "N is good" to be analytic, it does not therefore declare it trivial, or urge that it should provoke no opposition. An ethical predicate (as we have repeatedly seen) does not merely reiterate the subject, but adds an emotive mean ing. Moore has intellectualized this emotive meaning into an indefinable *quality;* but at least he recognizes an added factor which the purely scientific analyses of ethics are accustomed to ignore. He is perfectly right, then, in looking askance at analytic ethical judgments, and in abusing those who "foist upon us . . . an axiom," which they declare to follow from "the very meaning" of "good."[40] No analytic judgment of the form "N is good" can be held up as an incontrovertible axiom, for one can always disagree in attitude with the persuasive definition that *makes* it analytic.[41] In an indirect and imperfect way Moore must have been sensitive to something like this; and if his preoccupation with the cognitive aspects of language distorted his conceptions, and led him to be unintelligible on crucial points of meaning and methodology, his errors are no more serious—and perhaps they are more provokingly instructive—than those of writers who insist that normative ethics is a branch of psychology or biology.

Almost all of those who now emphasize the emotive aspects of ethics (including the present writer) have at one time been greatly under Moore's influence. It is not easy to believe that this is an accident.[42] The parallel between his views and the

40. *Idem*, p. 7.
41. For a parallel situation in the first pattern, see pp. 103 f.
42. It is interesting to note that in Moore's most recent publication on ethics, he is himself half-inclined to accept an emotive view. When men disagree on ethical matters, he writes, "I feel some inclination to think that . . . [they] are *not* making incompatible assertions; that their disagreement *is* merely a disagreement in attitude . . . and I do not know that I am not *as much* inclined to think this as to think that they are making incompatible assertions. But I certainly still have some inclination to think that my old view was true and that they *are* making incompatible assertions."

present ones—which in spite of all the differences remains surprisingly close—will be evident from this observation: Wherever Moore would point to a "naturalistic fallacy," the present writer, throughout the many possible senses which the second pattern recognizes, would point to a persuasive definition.

5

IN concluding this chapter it will be of interest to turn back from contemporary writers, and consider the ethical theories of David Hume. Of all traditional philosophers, Hume has most clearly asked the questions that here concern us, and has most nearly reached a conclusion that the present writer can accept.

Hume summarizes his views on ethical meanings and methods in this way:

The hypothesis which we embrace is plain. It maintains that morality is determined by sentiment. It defines virtue to be *whatever mental action or quality gives to a spectator the pleasing sentiment of approbation;* and vice the contrary. We then proceed to examine a plain matter of fact, to wit, what actions have this influence. We consider all the circumstances in which these actions agree, and thence endeavour to extract some general observations with regard to these sentiments. If you call this metaphysics, and find anything abstruse here, you need only conclude that your turn of mind is not suited to the moral sciences.[43]

These brief remarks must be qualified and interpreted in the light of other parts of his work. The term "approbation" refers not to *all* favorable attitudes, but only to "benevolent" ones, for "all passions vulgarly . . . comprised under the denomination of *self-love,* are here excluded from our theory . . . not because they are too weak, but because they have not a proper direction for that purpose."[44] The term "spectator" is not always emphasized in Hume, and perhaps it here replaces the more general term, "person" (though this is conjecture) in order to suggest

(See *The Philosophy of G. E. Moore,* edited by Schilpp, pp. 546 f.) The writer hopes that the present account, particularly that of the second pattern of analysis, will help to dispel Moore's still lingering doubts. We have seen that it is quite possible for opposed ethical judgments to make incompatible assertions *and* to express disagreement in attitude. An indefinable quality is not at all necessary in explaining how this can happen.

43. *An Enquiry Concerning the Principles of Morals,* Appendix I. (See *Hume's Enquiries,* edited by L. A. Selby-Bigge [Oxford, 2d ed. 1902], p. 289).
44. *Idem,* Sec. IX, Pt. I, p. 271.

that a spectator can better distinguish between his "approbation" and "self-love" than can any person more directly concerned in an ethical issue. In referring to "a" spectator, Hume seems to mean *any* spectator. This would be paradoxical if different spectators would experience approbation in opposed ways, but such a possibility is excluded by an explicit assumption that underlies Hume's whole work: "The notion of morals implies some sentiment common to all mankind, which recommends the same object to general approbation, and makes every man, or most men, agree in the same opinion or decision concerning it.[45] Hume could not possibly mean to assume, however, that all "or most" men will have the same sort of approbation so long as some are ignorant of the "facts of the case," for "in order to pave the way for such a sentiment, and give a proper discernment of its object, it is often necessary, we find, that much reasoning should precede, that nice distinctions be made, just conclusions drawn, distant comparisons formed, complicated relations examined, and general facts fixed and ascertained."[46] Thus we must assume that only the approbation of the factually informed is in question. In accordance with these several remarks we may rephrase Hume's definition as follows:

"X is a virtue" has the same meaning as "X would be the object of approbation of almost any person who had full and clear factual information about X."

So long as the judgment is insured this meaning, Hume's unqualifiedly empirical conceptions of ethical methodology come as a consequence.[47]

45. *Idem*, p. 272.
46. *Idem*, Sec. 1, p. 173.
47. In this condensed summary there can be little effort, of course, to consider alternative interpretations. In the *Treatise* Hume writes: "When you pronounce any action or character to be vicious, you mean nothing, but that from the constitution of your nature you have a feeling or sentiment of blame from the contemplation of it." (See Selby-Bigge's edition of *Hume's Treatise* [Oxford, 1896], p. 469.) This definition sounds more "subjective" than the one we have extracted from the later *Enquiry*. And elsewhere in the *Treatise*, Hume seems very close to acknowledging the quasi-imperative effect of moral judgments, though he veers off, feeling that he is criticizing only the a priori moralists: "Morals excite passions, and produce or prevent actions." "If morality had naturally no influence on human passions and actions, 'twere vain to take such pains to inculcate it; and nothing wou'd be more fruitless than the multitude of rules and precepts, with which all moralists abound." (Selby-Bigge, p. 457.) The interpretation given above, however, seems most consonant with the body of Hume's work. Nothing will

It will be observed that Hume's underlying assumption—that factually informed people will have approbation for the same objects—is parallel to the assumption mentioned here—that all disagreement in attitude is rooted in disagreement in belief.[48] But the present account treats the assumption in a different way. Hume fully accepts it, whereas we have seen that it is doubtful; and he implicitly embodies it in the meaning of moral judgments, whereas we have seen that it is more suitably mentioned in connection with methodology. What would happen to Hume's ethics in the failure of his assumption? Given his manner of defining the moral terms, a surprising number of moral judgments would be false. Indeed, if the assumption failed seriously—if there were *nothing* for which all or most informed people would have a similar approbation, people being temperamentally different in this respect—then *nothing* would be a virtue and *nothing* a vice. Now we must not be saved from this result merely by a poorly confirmed assumption. People would continue to make moral judgments even if they thought the assumption unwarranted. Instead of forcing their words into possible falsehoods, we had better recognize, as Hume does not, a number of senses in which their judgments would be less foolish. In the present account such senses are provided by either pattern. Hume's assumption must still be considered with attention; for wherever it fails, ethical disputes will have no *scientific* solution. But issues must not be dismissed from ethics just because they are scientifically insoluble. They must be recognized as distressing but real possibilities.

It will be obvious that Hume, like so many others, emphasized not disagreement in attitude but disagreement in belief. Normative ethics deals with a "plain matter of fact"—with what informed people would take as the object of their approbation. This has no strikingly paradoxical consequences so long as his assumption is granted, for the assumption insures that disagreement in attitude (or rather, in "approbation"[49]) will take care

be said here of Hume's form of utilitarianism, for that enters into his normative conclusion, not into his analysis.

48. Pp. 136 ff.
49. Hume does not assume that full information would eliminate the opposition of *all* attitudes, but only the opposition of approbation. Self-love might take precedence over approbation, and lead a man deliberately to prefer something which was an object of disapprobation. In asking whether a man could be dissuaded from this, Hume remarks, "I must confess that . . . it would be a little difficult to find any [reasoning] which will appear to him

of itself if people have true beliefs. When the assumption is given a revised status, however, disagreement in attitude requires explicit attention. And Hume would not be wholly free from criticism even if the assumption were granted. By neglecting disagreement in attitude he oversimplifies and overintellectualizes the arguments that occur between people who are not yet factually informed, and provides no place for persuasive methods.

As we have repeatedly seen in this chapter, those who make normative ethics a natural science have a seeming success only because they give a persuasive definition at the outset. This general rule holds for Hume no less than for other writers, though it is complicated by the assumption discussed above. Hume's manner of defining the moral terms makes such a statement as "Anything is good if and only if the vast majority of people, on being fully and clearly informed about it, would have approbation for it" an analytic one. Like so many other analytic statements in ethics, this retains an emotive force. It excludes any sense of "good" (and the same may be said of "virtue," etc.) with which one might *oppose* the vast majority of informed people's attitudes, and so is persuasive. And—unless Hume was simply pointing out a linguistic possibility, rather than showing partiality for the sense in question—his definition is persuasive in a further respect: it reserves the emotive meaning of ethical terms for the *benevolent* attitudes of "approbation," as distinct from the selfish ones. Here, as usual, we must not let our sympathy with his persuasion prevent us from recognizing it as persuasion.

On the whole, however, Hume seldom distorts analysis in the interest of exhortation. His persuasion seems inadvertent, arising not from a misplaced attempt to plead a cause, but from his eagerness to cut through ethical obscurantism, and to "introduce the experimental method of reasoning into moral subjects." In this we must admire the spirit of his work, however much we may quarrel with its details.

satisfactory or convincing." (*Enquiry*, Selby-Bigge, p. 283.) But Hume thinks that these cases will be extremely rare.

XIII

Further Observations on the Function of Definitions

1

AN understanding of the second pattern requires little more than an understanding of persuasive definitions. These have been illustrated in abundance, and if they were as readily discernible in all cases as they have been in our selected examples, they would require no further attention. But it is not always easy to recognize them, or to be clear about their distinguishing characteristics. There are a number of cases in which persuasive definitions might be confused with persuasive statements of another sort, or with definitions of a more neutral character. So it will be well to make some additional distinctions. The remarks of this chapter are not indispensable to ethical analysis, but may help to dispel misapprehensions, and to throw light on the several uses of language.

Let us begin by distinguishing persuasive definitions from statements that produce a similar effect by opposite means. It will be recalled that persuasive definitions alter attitudes by changing only the descriptive meaning of an emotively laden term, allowing emotive meaning to remain roughly constant. Clearly, the inverse procedure is equally important and prevalent: the emotive meaning may be altered, descriptive meaning remaining roughly constant. When emotive meaning is altered in a way that neutralizes it, there need be no persuasion, but rather (as explained previously in the remarks on "propaganda"[1]) an effort to avoid it. When emotive meaning is intensified, however, or changed from praise to blame, or vice versa, the effect may be no less persuasive than that of persuasive definitions. In fact the same persuasive force can often be obtained either by the one linguistic change or the other.

In our earlier example of "culture,"[2] for instance, the second

---

1. Particularly pp. 245–248.
2. Pp. 211 f.

speaker used a persuasive definition, defining the term with reference to imaginative sensitivity and originality. He might equally well have reiterated such statements as this: "Culture is only fool's gold; the true metal is imaginative sensitivity and originality." This procedure would have permitted "culture" to retain the *descriptive* meaning that his opponent (in the friendly argument) assigned to it, but would have tended to make its emotive meaning derogatory; and it would have added to the emotive force of "imaginative sensitivity" and "originality." The same purpose would have been served in this way that was served by the persuasive definition. The qualities the opponent designated by "culture" would still be placed in a poor light, and imaginative sensitivity and originality in a fine one; but this would have been effected by a change in emotive meaning, rather than in descriptive meaning.

Cases of this sort do not exemplify persuasive definitions, in spite of their similar function. They involve a linguistic change which is mediated not by definitions, but rather by gestures, tones of voice, or rhetorical devices such as similes and metaphors. It is convenient to restrict the term "definition" to cases where descriptive meaning alone is being determined, or where, at least, that aspect predominates. Thus the above example involves no definition, but only what may be called (for temporary brevity, and in want of a better term) a persuasive quasi-definition.

Apart from the kind of linguistic change that is involved, it will be evident, without further illustration, that persuasive definitions and quasi-definitions may receive parallel treatment. In either case there is a rewedding of the two sorts of meaning, with consequent redirection of attitudes.[3]

We have been speaking freely of a "change" in emotive meaning; but it must be remembered that emotive change cannot be marked off so precisely as descriptive change, since it is not made exact by formal linguistic rules. Changes in emotional *effects* are easily recognized, but these will not represent a change in emotive *meaning*, necessarily. They may represent only a change in the way the constant meaning (disposition) is *realized*. One cannot specify *which* change is in question without specifying which factors comprise the attendant circumstances of the meaning-

3. Cf. p. 227.

disposition and which do not. As we have seen elsewhere,[4] it is not possible, in practice, to do this in a rigorous way. Hence persuasive quasi-definitions, which initiate "changes" in emotive meaning, can be distinguished only in a rough way from statements that make no change in meaning at all, but simply use words under attendant circumstances that strengthen or modify their usual emotional effect. The roughness of this distinction will not be a serious disadvantage, so long as it is not forgotten. A sharp line would be needed only if the doubtful cases and the obvious cases gave rise to different problems, and for the present range of considerations that is not the case.

Let us now turn to an intermediate sort of persuasive statement. A persuasive definition changes descriptive meaning without substantially changing emotive meaning; and a persuasive quasi-definition changes emotive meaning without substantially changing descriptive meaning. In either case only one kind of meaning undergoes marked change. Now there are many instances which fall under neither heading, since they involve changes in both kinds of meaning. If the changes were *successive*, we should have only a combination of the procedures that have been mentioned.[5] In many cases, however, the two sorts of change are not successive but simultaneous, or so closely related that no one remark stands out either as a persuasive definition or as its inverse. Statements which persuade by this means must be classified under a separate head, and may temporarily be called "mixed." They are very frequent, perhaps more so than the others.[6]

The persuasive effect of "mixed" statements can be illustrated by the following passage, taken from a newspaper summary of a sermon:

Today, as it seems to have been throughout the years, our conceptions of honor are widely divergent in their viewpoint. That is the reason the majority of people are misled by a fundamental fallacy in regard

4. Pp. 55.
5. Successive change has been illustrated previously, though without being expressly labeled as such. See the example on p. 224, where Socrates first praises justice and then defines "justice."
6. The "multiple persuasive definitions," as mentioned on p. 241, might alternatively be classified among the "mixed" statements; but only if the series of defining phrases serves to change the emotive meaning, no less than the descriptive meaning, of the original definiendum.

to their conception of honor. Many people consider honor as a material thing, much in the same way you consider your money, job, and home as material things.

Honor, however, is not like that. You can be deprived of your money, your job, and your home by someone else, but, remember, that no one can ever take away your honor . . .

After all, what is honor? It is your own personality, and true honor depends on the standards which a man will set up for himself and by which he will endeavor to live.[7]

The mention of "true" honor, and the need of selecting it from "widely divergent" conceptions, seems to promise a persuasive definition—though the references to the immateriality of honor, its identity with one's own personality, and its relation to self-erected standards, do not provide the differentiae that one is inclined to expect. For the rest, the passage serves by its general tone to give "honor" an added laudatory emphasis, serving to praise any range of referents that the hearers (now that the "fundamental fallacy" of their conceptions has been guarded against) can be entrusted to supply for themselves. There is here an approximation both to a persuasive definition and to a persuasive quasi-definition but no clearly separable use of either.

A more arresting and complicated example is to be found in the novel, *Sanine*, by M. Artzibaschef.[8] The title character, Vladimir Sanine, suspects that his sister is about to be seduced by a libertine. Now Sanine is himself cynical about the accepted moral standards, and in a half-brooding, half-independent way is more inclined to approve of seduction than to condemn it; but the present case puts his theories to a severe test. So he addresses the suspected seducer, Sarudine, in this fashion:

"Blackguards are the most fascinating people."

"You don't say so?" exclaimed Sarudine, smiling.

"Of course they are. There's nothing so boring in all the world as your so-called honest man. . . . With the programme of honesty and virtue everybody is long familiar; and so it contains nothing that is new. Such antiquated rubbish robs a man of all individuality, and his life is lived within the narrow, tedious limits of virtue. . . . Yes, blackguards are the most sincere and interesting people imaginable,

7. *New York Times*, December 5, 1938, p. 20, col. 2.

8. See the last several pages of chap. iii. Trans. by Pinkerton (Huebsch, 1914). The passage here quoted is much abridged.

for they have no conception of the bounds of human baseness. I always feel particularly pleased to shake hands with a blackguard."

He immediately grasped Sarudine's hand and shook it vigourously as he looked him full in the face. Then he frowned, and muttered curtly, "Good bye, good night," and left him.

For a minute Sarudine stood perfectly still and watched him depart. He did not know how to take such speeches as those of Sanine; he became at once bewildered and uneasy.

This passage is conspicuously marked by its reversal of emotive meanings. "Honesty" and "virtue" become as if derogatory, whereas "blackguard" becomes as if laudatory. At the same time the descriptive meaning of the terms shifts somewhat, partly to make the emotive change have an appearance of being dependent; "blackguard" takes on something of the descriptive significance (as well as the emotive force) of "sincere," and "virtue" is denied any reference to a man's "individuality." The double shift in meanings (characteristic of all "mixed" persuasive statements) indicates so startling a variance from conventional moral standards that Sarudine cannot help but suspect a furious irony; and yet he knows, perhaps, that Sanine is reputed to express in full seriousness views that are equally cynical. Thus Sarudine is left "bewildered and uneasy"; and the reader, no less than he, cannot be certain that Sanine's irony is free from a bitterly conflicting earnestness.

No further examples will be needed to show that persuasive definitions, even though they give a partial account of how changes in meaning produce changes in attitude, are far from giving the whole account. They take their place beside statements that exert influence by another means. There is a continuum, as it were, in which persuasive definitions shade gradually into "mixed" statements, which in turn shade gradually into persuasive quasi-definitions; and both the latter (as will be evident from the remarks on pages 278 and 279) shade gradually into ordinary persuasive statements, where emotive meaning is active without involving change of meaning at all.

It may be added that there is another continuum, which will need only this passing attention, in which persuasive definitions (like all definitions) shade gradually into statements whose quasi-syntactical nature is doubtful, and from there into statements which, although they serve to *change descriptive* meanings, do so not by definitions, but by using words in ordinary contexts that make the change indirectly evident.

It is not always possible, then, to say with precision whether a given statement is to be called a persuasive definition or one of its border-line analogues. But the absence of any sharp dividing line must not lead us to dispense with dividing lines altogether. The term "persuasive definition" can still serve the useful purpose of marking off, albeit roughly, a group of statements whose persuasive character is most likely to escape attention.

2

WE have seen how persuasive definitions are related to statements that persuade without defining; let us now see how they are related to statements which define without persuading.

It will be obvious that no definition, however severely intellectual and detached it may be, can be wholly divorced from certain bearings, direct or indirect, upon human inclinations or purposes. Thus Russell, writing not of ethics but of logic and mathematics, has remarked: "A definition usually implies [i.e., leads one to suspect] that the definiens is *worthy* of careful consideration. Hence the collection of definitions embodies our *choice* of subjects and our judgment as to what is most important." [9] Now a choice of what is judged important or worthy of attention is a reflection of the speaker's attitudes, and may serve to redirect the attitudes of the hearer. If this is the usual effect of any technical definition (and Russell's observation seems beyond intelligent objection) then how are persuasive definitions to be distinguished from others? References to a redirection of attitudes will not be adequate for this purpose. It will be obvious, then, that the burden of the distinction will rest quite heavily on emotive meaning.

Now if the distinction must rest on emotive meaning, it cannot be made precise. Emotive meaning is largely a matter of degree. Although a great many scientific terms are *almost* free from emotive meaning, even they tend to acquire a certain scientific prestige, and so, when defined in a new way, may make a very gentle *plea* for the value of talking about the new designata. We cannot specify that nonpersuasive definitions be free from *these* emotive repercussions, else they will constitute a trivial

9. A. N. Whitehead and B. Russell, *Principia Mathematica* (2d ed.), I, 11. Italics not theirs.

class with virtually no members. We must specify, rather, that emotive meaning be "practically negligible" in them, or rendered "practically negligible" in its realization. But the term "practically negligible" is not free from vagueness. Hence persuasive definitions will shade gradually into nonpersuasive ones, with many border-line cases. Here is another continuum, to be added to those of the preceding section.

To a certain extent this source of vagueness will be unavoidable. It is possible, however, to make some observations that help to prevent its being troublesome:

Let us refer to the most familiar of the nonpersuasive definitions—those which are usually discussed in logic—as "detached."[10] If we now subject obvious instances of persuasive and detached definitions to comparison, we shall find that the latter, though they may serve to alter certain interests or attitudes, do so by a mechanism that is more indirect. They serve initially to guide the hearer's *attention,* and lead him to consider the objects of attention as *important* largely by that means. Since their emotive effect is "practically negligible," they exert little further pressure on attitudes, whether of inducement or coercion, beyond that which the factors mentioned in the definition, or the scientific evidence that has preceded it, themselves supply. In other words, they redirect attitudes much in the way that *reasons for* an ethical judgment redirect them, rather than in the way an ethical judgment itself redirects them. Yet they may obviously have an effect on one's estimate of what is "worth speaking of"; and that is why they still have a semblance of imperative force, even though they involve no conspicuously emotive term. The first point of difference, then, between persuasive definitions and detached ones, lies in the directness or indirectness of the way in which attitudes are influenced—a point that simply emphasizes what has previously been implied.

The second point of difference lies in the *nature* of the attitudes that are influenced. We have seen that persuasive definitions may be used to alter all manner of attitudes, directed to all manner of objects. Now detached definitions affect attitudes whose range of objects is much more limited. They influence what is judged important as a part of knowledge, not what is judged important or desirable in other respects. In science, for

10. It is not convenient, however, to take the detached definitions as exhausting the nonpersuasive ones, as we shall see in the following section.

instance, detached definitions influence only what a scientist will want to take account of in the course of pursuing his theoretical inquiry. This remark is subject, to be sure, to a type of qualification that will now be familiar. *Any* definition, no matter how detached, may help to clarify a given statement, and the statement may be used in its turn as a reason for a moral judgment. In this remote way the definition may have broad ethical bearings. But the same can be said of all aspects of theory, as we have previously seen.[11] For present purposes we need be concerned only with the immediate, *controlled* effects of detached definition. In their remote effects they may lead this man to this ethical ideal and that man to that; so they do not advocate, like persuasive definitions, some one of the broad ideals rather than another. They exert a controlled influence, then, on attitudes of a relatively narrow range.

The second point of difference does not, like the first, divide persuasive and detached definitions into classes which (apart from vagueness) are mutually exclusive. It is to be taken as stipulating a condition that *must* hold for definitions that are to be called "detached," and so distinguishes them from *many* that are to be called "persuasive"; but it does not distinguish them from *all* that may be called "persuasive." This can be made clear by example: If a theorist defined a "legitimate" theory as one which treated its subject mathematically, he would, presumably, be influencing only the attitudes which directly govern what is judged important for knowledge. If this were a final test, the definition would be detached. But in fact it is more convenient, so long as the emotive force of "legitimate" is more than "negligible," to classify the definition as persuasive. The burden of any mutually exclusive distinction, then, still rests on emotive meaning. Yet it can be said, analytically, that detached definitions are *limited*, in their controlled effect upon attitudes, to a narrow range of them, whereas the same cannot be said of persuasive definitions; and this remains as a helpful, if partial, way of distinguishing them.

Let us pause to say a little more about the "narrow range" of attitudes with which detached definitions are concerned. It will be convenient to refer to such attitudes as "interests in knowledge," using that expression to include not only broad interests

___

11. Cf. p. 162, and more generally pp. 160 ff., where points are mentioned that are intimately related to the present ones.

in knowledge of any sort, but also more specific ones, such as desires to emphasize this aspect of a field rather than that, or to classify certain material in a given way. These interests must be contrasted with the approval or disapproval of the subject matter *about* which knowledge is obtained. It often happens that theorists share the former attitudes without sharing the latter. Thus a number of anthropologists, studying the customs of a primitive society, may agree on what customs are *important* to an *understanding* of the society; and yet some of them may admire these customs and others detest them.

Interests in knowledge must not, of course, be thought of as "compartmentalized." They are related to many other attitudes —to desires for power, security, social conformity, and so on. An engineer, for instance, may be interested in certain aspects of mathematics because he wants to build a bridge; and this want will in turn be related to others. If certain native urges of "curiosity" pervade much theorizing, these are initially transient and ubiquitous. They attain their strength and direction by being reinforced,[12] and the factors that lead to their reinforcement may be innumerable. But the relationship which such attitudes bear to others in no way serves to obliterate their *identity* as interests in knowledge. Knowledge, in this or that aspect, will still be their object, even though it is sought as a means to other ends. In general, an attitude to X as a means to Y is still an attitude to X, distinct from one to Y. It involves activities that are directed specifically to X; whereas an attitude to Y, per se, need involve no actions specifically directed to X at all, and even when it does, will almost always involve many additional ones. Thus interests in knowledge, however varied their reinforcement, remain as a small subclass of all attitudes. The restriction which limits the controlled effect of detached definitions to this subclass is by no means a vacuous one.[13]

There will remain some border-line cases, however, where a

12. Cf. pp. 188–191.
13. By the operation of Allport's principle, or of Wundt's, interests in knowledge often become strong intrinsic ones. That is why a social scientist, for instance, having begun his studies in order to forward a desire to make certain reforms, may continue as a pure scientist, even though he knows that others may use his results to *oppose* his reforms. His final desire for knowledge outweighs the desires that originally gave birth to it. Scientists are sometimes condemned as shirking "moral responsibility" on this account; yet it must be remembered that their work produces a fund of knowledge without which the "responsible" moralist would be an unenlightened one.

definition may be called either "persuasive" or "detached" at will. Although many definitions will be unmistakably persuasive, since their emotive influence extends beyond interests in knowledge, certain others, exerting an influence that does not extend beyond interests in knowledge, will be classifiable either as detached or persuasive, depending upon whether or not emotive meaning is taken to be "practically negligible." It seems preferable to countenance this vagueness rather than to remove it in some artificial way; hence the distinction between the two sorts of definition may be allowed to rest at this point.

Meanwhile, our discussion borders on a broader topic—one that was mentioned in passing in Chapter VII.[14] There are certain evaluative issues that are integral to the very process of organizing knowledge. Interests in knowledge may be opposed, leading theorists to disagree about what is *worth* speaking of, or what distinctions are *important*, or what schemes of classification are *suitable*. These issues are not always factual ones in disguise, concerned with what sort of organization will serve a stipulated purpose; for there may be disagreement about the purpose to be served. They may be genuinely evaluative issues, requiring the use of methods like those we have examined in ethics. How else can a theorist give reasons for considering a given distinction, say, as important, unless by pointing out the consequences, etc., of making it? And how can his proof be convincing unless these consequences themselves are objects of interests in knowledge for other theorists? At times these evaluative aspects of theory can center about *detached* definitions, just as ethical ones may center about persuasive ones. For detached definitions may serve, in their indirect yet controlled manner, to alter interests in knowledge, and so the organization of knowledge. Or if they serve more to *evidence* an opposition of interests in knowledge than to resolve it by their own pressure, they may be points of contention even so. If a theorist finds that another accepts his central definitions, with the distinctions and classifications that they help to preserve, he will feel confident that the other agrees in attitude with him on what aspects of his study are important.

Now we have seen that a resolution of evaluative issues is complicated, involving many uncertainties. Yet in spite of this the evaluative issues that arise in the organization of knowledge,

14. Pp. 160 ff.

though sometimes serious, usually do not reach, in our own day, very alarming proportions. They are subject to a more widespread agreement, among those who feel competent to judge the question, than are a great many of the broader moral issues. It will be of interest to inquire into the reasons for this.

When evaluative issues arise about the organization of knowledge, the attitudes involved are limited to interests in knowledge. Within this range there is no little similarity in attitudes, especially the attitudes directed to knowledge in its immediately practical aspects. The common needs of men here lead to common interests. This may at first seem surprising. Since interests in knowledge are widely reinforced, and since the attitudes that lead to their reinforcement may be opposed, it may seem that interests in knowledge will be opposed to an almost equal extent. But this is not so, as we may see by example:

Suppose that A and B are both trying to start a revolution. Both will be interested in knowing what factors will bring the revolution about, since this knowledge will be a means to their common end. So when their *other* attitudes *converge*, their interests in knowledge tend to take on a similar direction. But it is also the case—and this is the more interesting point—that their interests in knowledge may take the same direction even though their other desires are *opposed*. Thus if A is trying to start a revolution and B to *prevent* it, both will still want to know what will cause the revolution. The knowledge will be instrumental, for each, to their now *hostile* aims. A must know the causes if he is to bring them about, just as B must know them if he is to remove them; and each must have a knowledge of the weapons, as it were, that are at the other's disposal. Hence interests in knowledge may come to be reinforced, and have a similar direction, regardless of whether other attitudes are convergent or opposed. That, in part, is why a similarly organized reservoir of knowledge tends to arise in such a variety of circumstances. Since men may have similar interests in knowledge even when they are acting against each other, they tend to emphasize the same parts of it.

This tendency is only a rough one, holding mainly for the immediately practical aspects of knowledge; but it is nonetheless of interest. If it were false—if interests in knowledge were basically dissimilar, being reinforced almost exclusively in this specific direction for one man, and almost exclusively in that for another—there would be so much divergence in emphasis that commonly accepted classifications would be unobtainable; and this, reflecting itself in language, would frustrate those feeble desires to communicate that might still remain.

There is need, here, of an explanatory remark. Although opposed social aims are compatible with, and may actually bring about, similar interests in knowledge, it is by no means the case that they will bring about similar desires for *disseminating* knowledge. When A, trying to start a revolution, desires that he possess knowledge, and B, trying to stop it, desires that *he* possess knowledge, neither will wish the *other* to have the knowledge. That is one of the respects in which social discord stands in the way of free exchange of information, and so, indirectly, in the way of intellectual advance. But this determines whether a man will keep his knowledge secret, not whether he disagrees with another on the way it is to be organized; so it is irrelevant to the present question.

We have been speaking only of a broad tendency that governs the immediately practical aspects of knowledge. What shall be said of the cases in which this tendency is offset, or of the aspects of knowledge for which it does not operate? Here, manifestly, there is a source of evaluative controversy. But its seriousness must not be exaggerated. There is often less an *opposition* between desires for knowledge than a mere *difference* of them. Difference does not imply opposition,[15] for the latter introduces an effort to *redirect* attitudes, whereas the former need not. Now when men have dissimilar desires for knowledge, they frequently have no motive for resolving the difference, for one man's desire need not prevent the active expression of the other's. One may seek knowledge in this field and the other in that, or one may organize his material with this emphasis, and the other with that; and each may be content to let the other proceed as he will. It is partly for this reason that there is no little tolerance, among theorists, of divergences in emphasis and classification. To be sure, there is not a complete tolerance. A theorist will sometimes insist that his manner of classifying material is the *only* practicable one—either because he believes that others, if they understood the purpose for which the classification is serviceable, would immediately share them, or because he has motives of professional jealousy that make him dogmatic, or for many other

15. Cf. pp. 4 and 138.

reasons. But on the whole, particularly in modern times, there is much tolerance of interests in knowledge; and this diminishes the controversy to which the ordering of knowledge would otherwise be subject.

Perhaps "tolerance" is not quite the proper term. There is actually a tendency for theorists to *accept,* temporarily, the interests in knowledge that another may have, even though these are not his usual ones. For clearly, there is no *one* set of interests in knowledge that pervades all of a man's life. With varying practical problems come varying immediate aims; and with the latter come varying interests in knowledge. If certain of these interests habitually predominate, leading to a similarly organized *reservoir* of knowledge, certain others change about, and lead to alternative organizations. We have observed that in *applied* science one must work with multiple classifications—those of the pure fields from which he gets his basic information, and others of his own, which he can adapt more closely to his immediate purpose.[16] Now in practical life we are constantly in the course of applying science, though the science is usually that which is a part of common sense, rather than some technical extension or refinement of it. So we are habituated to working with many classificatory schemes, each guided by the specific sort of interest in knowledge that a given practical problem will require. Nor can we be certain, in advance, what our next interest in knowledge, and the classification to which it will guide us, will be. That is one of the reasons why a theorist will temporarily fall in with the interests of another. He may be little inclined, at the moment, to use the classification which these interests bring with them, but may be glad to have it developed; for later on he may have use for it. In other words, there is often more than a tolerance of divergent classifications; there is a positive welcoming of them. When theorists propose different schemes of classification, they need not debate which is *the* important one, but can agree that *each* is important, when seen in relation to the problem to which its use will be limited. In these cases there is no issue which prevents the organization of knowledge from being socially recognized in its several forms.

Let us now sum up these remarks, and emphasize the conclusion to which they point. There is unquestionably a possibility that interests in knowledge should be opposed, and lead to

16. Cf. pp. 185 and 254 f.

evaluative controversy, within science itself, about what is worth speaking of, or what classifications or distinctions are worth making. At times these issues are complicated enough to stand in the way of scientific agreement, and must be debated by many of the methods that we have illustrated for ethics. But there is no occasion for philosophical fear, on this account, that science totters. The evaluative aspects of science involve only interests in knowledge, and these constitute a limited range of attitudes in which opposition is relatively infrequent. They tend to converge on certain aspects of knowledge, since they come to be reinforced, and take on a similar direction, even when other desires are opposed. And when this tendency does not operate, a tolerance of divergent interests in knowledge, or an actual welcoming of them, may lead to classifications that are of generally accepted importance in their variety.

There is accordingly reason to hope, though there can be no full certainty, that the evaluative issues of science will not grow more serious than they now are, but will progressively grow less serious. One may hope as much, of course, even for *moral* problems; but there, where a broader range of attitudes is in question, the hope cannot be so confident.

3

WE have seen that detached definitions, unlike persuasive ones, exert an influence that is limited to interests in knowledge, and do so by altering attention, rather than by emotive pressure. Now there are certain definitions which usually resemble the detached ones in these respects, but which redirect attention so forcibly that they stand very close to persuasive ones. It will be well to give them brief attention, since they are extremely frequent.

The definitions in question, which can conveniently be called "re-emphatic," are usually in quasi-syntactical form, and have an effect in pointing out differences and analogies, and so an effect on interests in knowledge, by making use of a temporary element of paradox or surprise. Wittgenstein, Wisdom, and Malcolm,[17]

17. Wittgenstein, unfortunately, has published nothing on the subject, but gave much attention to it in his lectures at Cambridge, during 1932–33. For John Wisdom's remarks see particularly "Metaphysics and Verification," *Mind*, XLVII, No. 188 (October, 1938), pp. 454 ff. Norman Malcolm has discussed the subject in sec. iii of his paper, "Moore and Ordinary Language," as published in *The Philosophy of G. E. Moore*, edited by P. A. Schilpp.

among others, have cited many instances of their use in philosophy.

In mathematical texts, for example, it is sometimes remarked
that "infinity is not a number." This expresses a decision to use
the word "number" in a narrow way. In a broader sense of the
word, infinity *will* be a "number"; nor is there any serious objection to the broad sense, since "finite number" remains as a possible substitute for the narrow sense. It will be clear, however,
that for certain purposes the narrow sense may be temporarily
preferable. Suppose that a student has been accustomed to confuse infinity with some vast (finite) number. When told that it
is not a number at all, he will be led somewhat urgently to attend
to distinctions. He will say, in effect: "I used to think that infinity
was a number; so if it really isn't, infinity must be far different
from whatever else I have been calling a number. I had better
give the matter closer attention." The narrow sense has a certain
"shock-value," then, whose re-emphatic effect can be utilized even
in the disciplined pedagogy of mathematics.

In this example the only attitudes that are redirected—in a
controlled way, that is—are interests in knowledge; and there is
no active part played by emotive meaning, since an emotive use
of "infinity" and "number" is rare in modern mathematics, being
confined to metaphorical contexts. But the narrowing of the sense
of "number" is reminiscent of a persuasive definition in that its
quasi-imperative force can at times be rather strong. It has the
effect of saying, "Be more interested in noting the *differences*
between the proposed definiens and that which it excludes from
your old, broader one." A persuasive definition, neither wholly
similar nor wholly dissimilar, usually has the effect of saying
"Approve of that which the definiens designates."

For a further example let us take the remark: "All empirical
statements are hypotheses." The initial effect of such a remark
is paradoxical, for "hypothesis" is ordinarily used more narrowly
—designating only those empirical statements which lack a high
degree of confirmation. It is scarcely to be supposed that "Stones
exist" is a "hypothesis" in any narrow, problematical sense. To
avoid absurdity, one immediately takes the above remark (often
without being aware of doing so) as quasi-syntactical, used in
giving "hypothesis" a broader sense. Those who make the remark
have manifestly re-emphatic intentions. They suspect that many
people exaggerate the differences between hypotheses in the

narrow sense and statements that "give the facts." So they broaden the sense of "hypothesis" in a way that calls attention to analogies. People are likely to say: "I used to think that only some empirical statements were hypotheses; but if they *all* are, there must be many similarities that I have overlooked. Perhaps empirical statements do not differ sharply from each other, but only in degree." Thus the remark has the quasi-imperative effect of saying, "Pay more attention to similarities," just as that of the preceding example had the effect of saying, "Pay more attention to differences."

The re-emphatic uses of language are too varied to permit any simple rule about them, but the following may be suggested as a working rule of thumb, holding for many cases: An insistence on a *narrow* sense of a common, vague term tends to emphasize *differences*—differences between the proposed definiens and the broader ones that are also possible. Conversely, an insistence on a *broad* sense tends to emphasize *analogies*. This effect is due, in part, to a temporary confusion on the part of the hearer, and his consequent efforts to free himself from it. Hearing the remark, "A is not B," or "A is C," which he ordinarily would not have made, and temporarily supposing that the statements serve to state facts rather than to change meanings, he is led to note differences or analogies, and ultimately to change his meanings and classifications in the light of further thought, as a means of avoiding a paradox. Cautiously used, the device can be serviceable to exposition and theory; for although it temporarily exploits confusions, it may help to remove greater ones.

The examples just cited illustrate definitions that are markedly re-emphatic, being little concerned with emotive meaning and much concerned with interests in knowledge. They may be contrasted, in spite of certain similarities, with definitions that are markedly persuasive, being much concerned with emotive meaning and little concerned with interests in knowledge. There are other definitions, however, in which re-emphatic and persuasive functions combine, and which may be called, without change in our previous terminology, *both* re-emphatic *and* persuasive. Since re-emphatic definitions are marked off by an element of paradox and surprise, and persuasive ones by emotive meaning, it is possible for the two classes of definitions to overlap—i.e., to have common members.[18] A few examples will serve to illustrate this:

18. The class of detached definitions, on the other hand, does not overlap

Suppose that the word "art" is defined in a way that excludes photography from the arts. This relatively narrow sense might be used to emphasize certain differences between photography and the (other) arts. At the same time it might serve to depreciate photographers, denying their work the laudatory title of "art." The definition would then be both re-emphatic and persuasive. Note that the two functions might be intimately related; for the distinction that is emphasized could later be helpful in supporting the persuasion by reasons.

Or again, consider the remark: "All human actions are selfish." In order to be at all acceptable, this statement must be taken as quasi-syntactical, serving to broaden the sense of "selfish"; for there is obviously a narrower sense of "selfish" in which only *some* human actions are selfish. Perhaps the broad sense may be used to place re-emphatic stress upon analogies, breaking through any artificial compartmentalization of selfishness and altruism. But it can also serve, by directing the *derogation* of "selfish" to all actions, rather than some, to encourage a general cynicism or misanthropy. In the history of ethical theory the broad sense seems usually to be more re-emphatic than persuasive in its *intention;* but the example is of interest in showing how an injudicious use of verbal therapy can defeat its own ends. It is only too easy (though less easy in the world of practice than in the half-unreal world of grandiose speculation) to take "All actions are selfish" not as quasi-syntactical but as an empirical contention—a contention which for the *narrow* sense of "selfish" would grossly misdescribe human nature, and mark the contender as blind. And even when this confusion is avoided, the re-emphatic effect of the statement becomes so much involved with its potentially persuasive one that any efforts to counteract the persuasion, by neutralizing the emotive meaning of "selfish," may be unavailing. The confusion need not be confined to the critics of the remark, of course; its propounders may be misled by their own words.

It must be remarked that a great many persuasive definitions are also re-emphatic. In the examples of Chapter IX, for instance, a dual function will often be discernible. Critics who define "poet"
the class of persuasive ones; and it is convenient, as well, to specify that it does not overlap the class of re-emphatic ones. There will be the usual borderline cases, since the boundary between the detached and the re-emphatic or persuasive definitions is vague; but overlapping and vagueness are wholly distinct considerations.

to exclude Pope are not expressing an adverse attitude alone; they are also using the narrow sense to emphasize the way his work differs from that of others. And so for some of the other examples, including those from economics.

The importance of singling out the re-emphatic factors will be obvious from this consideration: In the controversies that attend pure theory, persuasive definitions are often brushed aside as irrelevant, or unsuitable for forwarding the topic in question. This is particularly true for the many definitions whose influence extends beyond interests in knowledge. Statements which have a re-emphatic effect, however, cannot so readily be dismissed. They may be objected to when their quasi-imperative effect is not supported by reasons, but otherwise may have a recognized place, even in the most severely cognitive inquiry. Hence when a persuasive definition is also re-emphatic, one must take care not to reject it prematurely; for the new emphasis may be of use, however irrelevant the persuasion may be. Much caution is needed, for instance, in dealing with the positivistic contention (now often much softened and qualified) that all nonverifiable statements are "nonsense." This statement usually serves as a quasi-syntactical means of broadening the term "nonsense"; and when the emotive derogation of the term is not neutralized, it may be strongly persuasive, damning a great number of metaphysicians to whom, in its broad sense, it becomes applicable. Such an effect is not a part, perhaps, of what the more distinguished positivists have consciously sought; and they might agree that it is irrelevant to the theoretical issue in question. But amid these persuasive aspects there are re-emphatic ones—efforts to stress the distinction between verifiable and nonverifiable statements, and to prevent the one sort from being confused with the other. Few will care to question the legitimacy of this latter aim; and if there is room for much debate on the *degree* to which the distinction needs emphasis, and a need of much *support* for judgments which declare it to be relatively important or relatively unimportant, it must be granted that the re-emphatic aspects of the definition of "nonsense" have been helpful in locating a crucial philosophical problem.

4

AMONG the many definitions which resemble persuasive definitions, or constitute special sorts of them, we must pay particular attention to those which raise problems for ethics. The most important instances of these occur in legal cases, when a judge or jury must decide on the meaning of a term that the law has left vague. The definitions given for the term will often determine how the case is decided; and the *modus operandi* of the definition, though it resembles that of a persuasive one, is sufficiently different to require special mention.

Suppose, for example, that all who own dwelling places in a given town are required by law to pay a tax. Vehicles, however, are not subject to a local tax. It so happens that many motorists drive to a camping spot, which the town provides, and live there for long periods in trailers. The question arises, accordingly, as to whether they are to be taxed; and this in turn will depend upon whether trailers are to be considered "dwelling places" or "vehicles." Now if the laws of the town date from a time prior to trailers (as we may assume), there can be little hope of depending on the "intention of the legislators." Their terminology was simply too vague to cover this border-line case, and was left so because they had never imagined one like it. Nor will any precedents be likely to have a unique bearing on the issue. The question of definition, then, will be inextricably bound up with an ethical one, namely: Ought those who live in the trailers be taxed, or oughtn't they? The definition of "dwelling place" or "vehicle" will reflect or articulate a decision on *this* issue, and lead to the corresponding legal action.

It will be obvious that such definitions resemble persuasive ones, save that the function of emotive meaning is replaced by something more elaborate—by the full mechanism of the law. They wed new or more definite descriptive meanings to the terms that call these mechanisms into play, and so direct the mechanisms to this or that range of application. *Which* range of application will depend on which one is judged, by those who define the term, to be *just*. In much the same way, persuasive definitions wed new or more definite meanings to terms which bring emotive effects into play. Emotive effects do not have the material sanctions that lie behind the legal mechanisms; but the two are similar in making any word associated with them an important ethical instrument, on whose definition a great deal may depend.

Legal definitions of the sort in question often give rise to judicial law-making, though in a way that makes it appear to be something else. Justice Cardozo (among many other legal theorists) has fully recognized this. He writes:

I take judge-made law as one of the existing realities of life. . . . Interpretation is often spoken of as if it were nothing but the search and the discovery of a meaning which, however obscure and latent, had none the less a real and ascertainable pre-existence in the legislator's mind. The process is, indeed, that at times, but it is often something more. The ascertainment of intention may be the least of a judge's troubles in ascribing meaning to a statute. . . . "The difficulties of so-called interpretation arise when the legislature has had no meaning at all; when the question which is raised on the statute never occurred to it." . . . The judge . . . must then *fashion* law for the litigants before him.[19]

Further examples of the essentially ethical character of certain legal definitions can easily be cited. The most familiar one is the definition of "insanity." In its everyday use this term has the vagueness of all psychological terminology, together with an additional vagueness that is a result of its emotive meaning, which makes it used as an epithet, or causes it to be pulled this way and that by rival persuasive definitions. But in law the term takes on a particularly important role, for the manner in which a court defines it may serve to determine whether a given individual will be subject to the usual penalties. The problem is often one of deciding whether or not a man, shown to have mental peculiarities that could be called either "insane" or "sane but queer" at will, *ought* on this account to receive special indulgence —a decision that usually rests on an enormous variety of considerations, including the example that full punishment would provide for others, the probability that the man will thereafter be free from similar spells of "insanity," and so on. Legal precedent may have little bearing on the given case. Indeed, even when precedent is the determining factor, it operates not through some supernatural power, but much like any other *ethical reason;* it is compelling to the extent that it modifies the attitudes of those who are judging, and has its great force because the attitudes of jurists (since they wish to keep the law uniform and predictable, or since they fear public censure, and so on) are so largely determined by it. The testimony of psychologists, so com-

19. *The Nature of the Judicial Process* (Yale University Press, 1921), pp. 10, 14 f., and 21. Italics not his.

monly introduced into cases where insanity is pled, may clear up many facts of the case; but it cannot wholly determine, though it may do much to enlighten, the *evaluative* question as to whether a man, being in the state of mind that the psychologists describe, ought to have this or that penalty inflicted upon him. It need scarcely be added that many decisions about the sanity or insanity of a man, as they actually are made in courtroom procedure, depend in great measure upon the comparative skill of the attorneys in impressing the jury with persuasive techniques.

These examples introduce few considerations that the preceding remarks have not led us to anticipate, but they show in an arresting way the folly of taking definitions as trivial or "merely" verbal. There are some definitions, of course, that are of little consequence, so far as the sound of the proposed definiendum is concerned. The distinction to be made, or the topic to be discussed, may be recognized as important by all, and require nothing more than a convenient, easily pronounced label. But many definitions—the persuasive ones, the re-emphatic ones, and the legal ones that have just been illustrated, to say nothing of the detached ones that clarify concepts or preserve and call attention to important classifications—may be central to the formulation and outcome of highly important issues.

XIV

Avoidability; Indeterminism

1

IN evaluating conduct people usually limit their judgments to actions which they consider *avoidable*, or subject to voluntary control. They tend to regard unavoidable actions as neither right nor wrong, but immune from judgment altogether. Why is this the case?

The question belongs to ethical methodology, as will be evident when it is stated in another way. In an example such as,

A: You ought not to have permitted that
B: But I couldn't help it; it was unavoidable

we must inquire why A will usually accept B's reply, if established, as a *reason* for *withdrawing* the judgment that he has made of B's action. The answer must take the form of a commonsense psychological explanation of how the reason and the judgment are related; hence it will be parallel to the explanations of Chapters V and X. Indeed, the present topic could have been developed there, and has been delayed only because it requires extended treatment. Although simple enough in itself, it often becomes involved in the controversy about freedom and determinism of the will. This controversy, as we shall see, presents no permanent difficulty to ethics, being largely a product of confusions—and confusions which writers of the past and present have repeatedly pointed out. But this must not cause us to believe that the confusions are wholly dispelled, or that ethical analysis can be content to neglect them.

Let us first of all make clearer the meaning of "avoidable," defining it in this way:

"A's action was avoidable" has the meaning of "If A had made a certain choice, which in fact he did not make, his action would not have occurred." [1]

1. When the reference is to the future, the definition becomes: "A's proposed action is avoidable" has the meaning of "If A makes a certain choice,

When a man's action is avoidable in this sense, the man is "at liberty," as Hobbes put it, and "is not hindred to doe what he has a will to." [2] Or in Hume's phrase, the man has liberty as opposed to *constraint*, which must be distinguished from liberty as opposed to *necessity*.[3] Thus the notion of avoidability has often received attention; but it may be helpful, even so, to point out what the above definition implies.

"A's action was avoidable" is by no means synonymous with "A's action sprang from an *indetermined* choice." [4] Avoidability is concerned with what would have happened *if* a choice that was *not* made *had* been made. Since the if-clause is manifestly contrary to fact, it does not deny that the *actual* choice may have been wholly determined by the preceding events. When we say, "If water contracted on freezing, ice would lie at the bottom of lakes," we do not deny that the actual behavior of water is determined. Just as the contrary-to-fact condition in this state-

his action will not occur." For past references, the if-clause will always be contrary to fact, but for future ones it may or may not be. In what follows references to the future will be treated only by implication.

It will be assumed, throughout, that the phrase "made a choice" cannot meaningfully be predicated of insensible objects, and hence that avoidable is restricted in a corresponding way. It would have been possible, however, to drop this restriction, replacing it by the following one: The if-clause in the definiens, when contrary to fact, must not be contrary to the general laws of nature; its falsity must be ascertainable only by an inquiry that relates more specifically to the case in question. Should a person idly speculate, then, about whether a tree would have stopped growing *if* it had *chosen* to, one could acknowledge that his speculation made sense, but still hold that it had nothing to do with avoidability; for the falsity of such an if-clause is evident from the general laws of nature alone. A rigorous statement of this qualification, requiring that "general" be replaced by a less vague term, would be difficult to formulate; but we need not trouble about this, since a rough formulation is sufficient for what is to follow.

2. *Leviathan*, Pt. II, chap. xxi, pars. 1 and 2.
3. *Enquiry Concerning Human Understanding*, chap. viii, end of Pt. I. Hobbes had spoken, in much the same way, of the liberty that is opposed to "opposition."
4. "X is determined" has the meaning of "There are laws of nature, and causal factors, from a *complete* knowledge of which the *exact* nature of X could be predicted. "X is indetermined" denies this, though the denial need be only "partial," as will be explained later on. The *general* doctrine of determinism asserts that *all* X's are determined, whereas the *general* doctrine of indeterminism asserts that at least some X's are indetermined. Most writers use the terms in approximately this manner, and for present purposes the definitions need not be pressed more closely. A more rigorous analysis has been given by C. D. Broad, in *Determinism, Indeterminism, and Libertarianism* (Cambridge University Press, 1934). The present chapter has an indebtedness to Broad, even though it sharply repudiates his puzzled conclusions about the relation of determinism to ethics.

ment about water does not imply indeterminism in physics, so the corresponding one in the statement about choice, included in the definition of "avoidable," does not imply indeterminism in psychology. It is a general characteristic of sentences of the form, "If X had taken place instead of Y, then Z would have taken place," that they say *nothing* about the factors that may have determined Y, but say rather that X, all else being equal, is the kind of factor that determines Z.[5] Thus the avoidability of a man's actions has nothing to do with the *causes* of his *actual* choice; it has to do with the *effects* that would have attended a *different* choice. So far from being synonymous, "A's action was avoidable" and "A's action sprang from an indetermined choice" are sharply different, the first neither implying nor denying the second. The ambiguous way in which "free" has been connected with both statements is responsible, according to a number of writers, for many of the perplexities to which the "free will" controversy is heir.[6]

In an exhaustive account the word "choice," as it occurs in the above definition, would require careful definition in its turn; but that need not here concern us. In fact "choice" will be used, by a convenient metonymy, to typify any instance of "selecting," "trying," "striving," "exercising will power," and so on. There is unfortunately no simple, general term which designates the various phenomena that the older writers seem to have referred to as "manifestations of the will"; hence it will be convenient to

5. Little more can be said about the contrary-to-fact or "subjunctive" conditional than this. As W. V. Quine has remarked in his *Mathematical Logic* (Norton, 1940), p. 16: the subjunctive conditional is "not directly identifiable with any truth-functional mode of composition, but calls for a more elaborate analysis." To the present writer's knowledge this "more elaborate analysis" has never adequately been worked out, though Carnap's references to "P-derivability" make suggestions that are helpful. See *Logical Syntax of Language*, pp. 180 ff., 184 ff.

So long as this aspect of logic remains problematical, contrary-to-fact conditionals must be used with caution; but since they pervade our common speech, in a way that is practically understood, there is no occasion for trying to avoid them altogether. The same may be said of the dispositional predicates mentioned in Chapter III, which when analyzed more closely present similar problems.

6. Hume has remarked, "All men have ever agreed in the doctrine both of necessity and liberty, according to any reasonable sense which can be put on these terms; and . . . the whole controversy has hitherto turned merely upon words." (*Enquiry Concerning Human Understanding*, chap. viii, par. 3.) For a modern presentation of much the same view, see *Knowledge and Society*, by G. P. Adams and others (Appleton-Century, 1938), chap. vi.

extend "choice" to serve that purpose. So used, the term will be vague—as, indeed, is the term "manifestation of the will." But it is helpful in suggesting the relation of the present account to the older controversies, and its vagueness will do no great harm —none that cannot subsequently be eliminated. The confusions of the "free-will" controversy, so far as they relate to ethics, center less about the terms that designate psychological events than about the terms that refer to their *causes and effects*. Thus so long as "choice" (and the other terms that it will be taken to typify) refers to something that may have causes and effects, and to something which is not too far removed from the customary range of its referents, a closer analysis will not be urgently required.

It is not necessary, moreover, tacitly to presuppose a definition of "choice" that runs counter to the general spirit of any current school of psychology. A behavioristic definition will suffice, for instance, so long as one's small-scale behavior in "choosing" is distinguished from the large-scale behavior that may *result* from the choice. And it will suffice even if a choice of an action, X, is identified with the formation of a disposition to do X—though in that case the choice will *cause* X only in the sense mentioned in Chapter III, page 52, and there must be criteria for determining the presence of the choice that differ from X itself, or the criteria for X. On the other hand, an introspective definition will serve our purposes equally well.[7] The definition can be left undecided within extremely broad limits—greater precision lying beyond the present needs.[8]

2

LET us now turn directly to our central question, namely: Why is the statement, "A's action was unavoidable," so frequently

7. If "choice" is defined as an introspectable class of feelings, it must be assumed that these feelings can sometimes *cause* a person to perform the chosen act. This in turn seems to prejudge the old "mind-body" question in favor of interaction; but in fact it need not. One can accept a regularity view of cause, which requires only that the choice (together with other factors) must lawfully precede the chosen action. Clearly, there might be this regularity for either parallelism or epiphenomenalism. C. D. Broad has suggested this in *Mind and Its Place in Nature*, p. 96, with particular reference to parallelism.

8. From here on the present work incorporates, though with many changes, omissions, and additions, the material in the author's paper, "Ethical Judgments and Avoidability," *Mind*, Vol. XLVII, N.S., No. 185 (January, 1938).

accepted as a reason for withdrawing an ethical judgment of A's action?

The answer will depend in no little degree upon this preliminary observation: Although we all of us make judgments and influence attitudes for mingled, complicated purposes, a part of our purpose, and usually an essential part, is to control how people will subsequently act. In particular, we try to control actions of the kind that we judge. For example:

We tell a man that he oughtn't to steal in order to keep him from stealing. Our immediate influence on his attitudes is simply a step toward this further aim. If we thought he was beyond all reform, we should abandon this way of deterring him, and perhaps inform the police instead. Or if we thought that stealing was wholly and permanently foreign to his habits, we should spare ourselves the trouble of admonishing him. Our motive is much the same when we make ethical judgments of something which has already been done. If the man has stolen something, we tell him that he ought not to have done so. We are not, to be sure, trying to do anything about that particular action, which is past and gone. We are trying to prevent similar actions in the future. The emotive meaning of "ought" enables us to build up in the man an adverse attitude to his act, making him recall it, say, with an unpleasant feeling of guilt. This feeling, and all its correlates in behavior, becomes associated not with the past act alone, but with others like it.[9] It deters the man from stealing anything else.

Other cases are only slightly more complicated. We often make ethical judgments of character from a novel. By building up in the hearer, through unfavorable judgments, an adverse attitude to an imaginary character, we are preventing the hearer from taking this character as a model for his own subsequent conduct. Or perhaps we have a more personal aim; we may be strengthening a resolve that *we* will not take the character as a model. Or again, we may be judging, under the name of this character, many persons whom he typifies, and whom we expect to encounter in daily life.

It will be clear, then, that ethical judgments look mainly to *future actions*. Even when they are made of past or imaginary acts, they still serve a dynamic purpose—that of discouraging (or encouraging) similar acts later on. Although this conclusion

9. Cf. p. 95.

will later be qualified, the qualification will not affect its bearing on our problem.

We are now in a position to see how ethical judgments become related to avoidability. Ethical judgments are used to modify the actions that are judged. But not all actions can be modified in this way. Judgments often induce men to give money to charity, but never make men add a cubit to their stature. If we tell a man that he ought to give more freely to charity, our judgment may serve its purpose, leading him to give more freely in the future. If we tell him that he ought to add to his stature, our judgment will not serve its purpose. Since we are unwilling to talk aimlessly, we confine our judgments to actions of the first sort, to those which judgments are likely to modify. But only *avoidable* acts, in the sense defined, are likely to be modified by ethical judgments. Hence only they are likely to be judged. In other words, the statement, "A's action was unavoidable" indicates that a judgment will not serve to *control* actions like A's, and on that account usually causes any judgment of the action to be withdrawn.

This account must be expanded, of course, with particular attention to its main premise. We must consider why ethical judgments may control avoidable acts alone. Let us do so by example:

An army officer has failed to win an engagement. His commander is deciding whether or not to censure him. Now suppose that the commander knows that the failure was *avoidable*—that a different choice on the part of the officer would have prevented it. From this it follows, granted uniformity of nature, that failure will in fact be prevented, in any future cases of the same sort, if the officer then makes the requisite choice. Of course no future cases will be *exactly* of the same sort as the past one, but some may be roughly so; and in these it is *probable* that the officer will not fail if he is led to choose differently. But what will cause the officer to choose differently? Perhaps the commander's adverse judgment will do so. His judgment of the officer's past failure will make the officer ashamed of himself, and induce him to modify his choice in any roughly similar case that may arise. To generalize: a judgment of an avoidable act is likely to control actions of the kind judged.

Suppose, however, that the failure was unavoidable, the officer having been confronted with overwhelming odds. By steps of reasoning like those above, it follows that failure will probably occur, in future cases of roughly the same sort, even if the officer chooses differently. An ethical judgment will *not* serve to prevent subsequent failures. It can have this effect only through the mediating step of controlling the officer's choice;[10] but since a change in the choice will not, in its turn, prevent similar failures, the judgment will not have its intended effect. To generalize: a judgment of an unavoidable act will not control actions of the kind judged.

Let us now put these remarks together in a way that will crystallize them. When an ethical judgment is successful in controlling the kind of action judged, it has its effect not directly, but always through mediating steps. By altering a man's attitudes, it alters his choice, and this in turn alters his subsequent action. The judgment can be a factor in controlling the action, then, only if the choice is a factor in controlling it. But the choice will be such a factor only if the action is avoidable. This is evident from the definition of "avoidable," and from the force of the contrary-to-fact condition (showing that the choice makes a difference to this kind of action) which the definition introduces.[11] Hence the judgment can control the action only if the action is avoidable. Now our main purpose in judging an action is to control it, or to control a future one that is like it. So our judgment will serve its main purpose only if the action judged is of a kind that is avoidable. In other words, a judgment of an *un*avoidable act will *fail* to serve its main purpose. That is the essential point to be proved, since the rest is readily seen. In everyday life we usually do not persist in a judgment when we learn that it will fail to serve its main purpose. And seeing, by a kind of common-sense wisdom, that judgment of an unavoidable action will be of this relatively purposeless sort, we usually suspend judgment of an action when its unavoidability is called to our attention. The question that is central to this chapter can be answered, in its essentials, in this simple way.

The account is still tentative, however, and must be qualified. Some of the qualifications will appear as we proceed, but two of them must receive immediate attention:

10. So we may assume, remembering that "choice" here typifies several other terms, as mentioned on p. 300. This assumption will be discussed later.
11. Cf. pp. 299 f.

It has been maintained, just above, that whenever a judgment serves to control the sort of action judged, it does so through intermediate effects on attitudes and choice. Now why is it necessary to mention *both* attitudes and choice in this connection, or why, indeed, is the whole reference to choice not a redundancy? In the extended sense of "choice" that is here employed, typifying any "manifestation of the will," it is difficult to see how a choice can be considered anything more than an attitude actually at work—i.e., an attitude considered in its specific bearing upon a given action.[12] It seems to be more than this, it may be urged, only because the term hints at some unique faculty of volition, hypostatically conceived.

This contention is plausible; but we can readily see that it does more to strengthen the present account than to attack it. If "choice" is understood in the proposed way, then although there will be a redundancy in speaking of attitudes *and choice,* the redundancy will be an inelegance rather than an error. Meanwhile, since attitudes are obviously a mediating link between ethical judgments and the actions they control, it will be indubitable that "choice" conceived as an attitude at work, will have the same status; and the present account requires no more than that.

The main reason for using the word "choice," in addition to "attitude," is that it permits us to avoid discussing a point that is beyond the present interests. If anyone wishes to understand "choice" as referring to some unique psychological phenomenon —insisting that only in this sense will the present account have a bearing on traditional issues and common-sense practices—he can readily do so without rejecting the essential features of the above explanation. Such a person must, of course, still give "choice" a broad sense, and must let the term designate something which can be *guided by* attitudes. More generally, he must give the word "avoidable," which is defined in terms of "choice," a sense which permits one to say that only avoidable acts can be controlled by ethical judgments. But this requirement is not unnatural if "choice" and "avoidable" are to have a meaning which makes them have a full bearing on the ethical issues that

---

12. Cf. Hobbes, *Leviathan,* Pt. I, chap. vi, p. 28: "In *Deliberation,* the last Appetite, or Aversion, immediately adhaering to the action, or to the ommission thereof, is that wee call the WILL; the Act, (not the faculty,) of *Willing.*"

have traditionally been discussed in connection with "the will." And it is not so stringent a requirement as one which specifically limits the reference of the terms to attitudes.

Let us now proceed to a second qualification. In our example of the commander and officer it was assumed that the commander's motive, in making an adverse judgment, was to prevent this very officer from failing in similar circumstances later on. Now clearly, the commander may have had more complicated motives. He may have wished to let his judgment give warning of a general *precedent,* effective in preventing similar failures in *any* of his officers. Or he may have used his judgment as a means of wholly discouraging the officer, and of causing him, as soon as military conditions permit, to resign his commission. In the latter case his judgment will not lead the officer to act differently "in similar circumstances later on," but rather will keep him from *encountering* such circumstances. These matters complicate our account, but do not alter its import. The commander's motives remain forward-looking, and will still require him to judge only an avoidable failure. The precedent established by judging an *un*avoidable act would carry over, for the most part, to *other* unavoidable acts. It would be an *ineffective* warning to the rest of his officers, terrifying them about matters which they were powerless to control. And the humiliation produced in the officer judged, if it were not wholly outweighed by indignation, would scarcely lead him to resign his commission; for knowing that the failure was unavoidable, he would have little or no reason to suppose that his successor could do better in preventing failures, and so would find resignation pointless. Only for avoidable acts will a judgment serve as a means of control.

3

OUR study of avoidability has introduced little novelty into the present analysis of ethics. We must observe, further, that it introduces little novelty into traditional philosophical theory. For although the relation between avoidability and *ethical judgments* has never (to the writer's knowledge) been analyzed in quite the present way, a parallel analysis has repeatedly been given with regard to avoidability and *punishment.* Reformative and preventive theories have long made clear that punishment of unavoidable acts would fail to serve an important purpose. All that has been overlooked is that ethical judgments, being quasi-

AVOIDABILITY; INDETERMINISM 307

imperative, have also a reformative and preventive function. Theorists have been blinded to this by their almost incredible overemphasis on the cognitive aspects of language.

The parallel between this aspect of ethical analysis and theories of punishment is instructively close. A brief development of it will help to round out the preceding account.

Preventive and reformative theories are notably forward-looking, emphasizing the function of punishment, so long as it is confined to avoidable actions, in providing a source of social control. This control may be exerted on the man punished, either by making him act differently thereafter or by preventing opportunities for such actions; or it may be exerted on others, through warning of a precedent. We have just seen that an adverse ethical judgment can exert the same control, and in the same way. Indeed, an adverse ethical judgment is a kind of blame, and since blame is a kind of verbally mediated punishment, our observations about avoidability and ethical judgments are literally a special case of what can be said of avoidability and punishment quite generally.[13] This is particularly obvious when an adverse judgment is addressed to the man whose action is judged, for there the judgment punishes directly by humiliation. It is only a little less obvious when an adverse judgment is addressed to others, as when A says to B and C that D's action was wrong. There the judgment, by influencing B and C, may alter their conduct to D, and so punish him indirectly; and even when it has not this effect, its influence on B and C, and through them on others, may exert a control like that of the *warning* effect of punishment. Thus to speak of a "parallel" between the present considerations and punishment is something of an understatement.

But so far we have considered only the reformative and preventive aspects of punishment. What shall be said of its vindictive aspects—those which manifest vengeance, anger, or cruelty? If we seek to describe punishment as it is, we must give these aspects their proper place. Cleopatra, on hearing of Antony's marriage, punished the innocent messenger who brought the news,[14] and common life readily provides its humbler analogues.

13. Similarly, a *favorable* judgment is a kind of *reward;* and if theories of reward were as current as theories of punishment (as would be the case, perhaps, in a community like Swift's Lilliput, where laws were enforced as much by reward as by punishment) such theories could deal with the relation of favorable judgments and avoidability as a special case of their more general problem.
14. Shakespeare's *Antony and Cleopatra,* Act II, sc. 5.

Although the theory of punishment is controversial, the controversy is largely normative. Questions about whether punishment *ought* to be primarily reformative, or primarily preventive, or primarily vindictive, will obviously leave room for opposed answers. But these questions, although important, are for the moment irrelevant. We need not *judge* the functions of punishment, just as we need not judge the functions of ethical judgments, but must rather come to understand what they are. On this factual level it will be clear that punishment has many functions. It springs, like so much else, from different motives at different times, and usually from mixed motives. Among these motives must be included those which are *not* forward looking, but which manifest the force of unreflective impulse.

Now obviously, the motivation of ethical judgments does not differ in this respect from that of punishment. An angry man may make an ethical judgment much as he will thump his fist or slam a door, having no other aim in mind than to vent his feelings. Recognizing such motives, hitherto neglected for expository simplicity, we must ask whether they require us to alter our explanation of how avoidability and ethical judgments are related.

Little change will be needed; for the times when ethical judgments are vindictive or impulsive are often the times when they have *no* connection with avoidability. Our question as to why people *commonly* or *usually* limit their judgments to avoidable acts leaves room for those relatively infrequent cases when people do not recognize this limitation. Judgments which do no more than symptomize the speaker's blind emotions—as when an irritable schoolmaster finds fault with any unfortunate child that comes within his hearing, or when a man who is failing in business blindly berates his salesmen for not selling an unsellable product—may fall upon avoidable and unavoidable actions alike. Here "It was unavoidable" is *not accepted* as a reason for withholding judgment. We may wish to say that it *ought* to be; but that would be *judging* ethical methods, and falls beyond our present concern.

Yet the topic must not be dismissed prematurely; for it must be asked why judgments of unavoidable acts are so rare. Anger and impulsiveness frequently attend ethical judgments, but do not often direct the judgments to unavoidable acts. Why is this the case? At times the explanation can be given with reference to a *mixture* of motives. Although a judgment may *in part* be an expression of immediate impulse, it may at the same time be forward-looking; and the forward-looking part of the motivation may be sufficient to direct the judgment to actions that the speaker believes to be avoidable. At other times the explanation is a little more complicated:

The restrictions that we observe in making ethical judgments are in good measure a product of habit. So even when a man has no conscious aim of altering the kind of action that he judges —and even when such an aim could not properly be recognized as "unconsciously" present—his judgments may be limited in a way that habit has established. If in the past the man has repeatedly withheld judgments from unavoidable acts, his judgments having then been forward-looking, he will tend to do the same in many cases when he is simply expressing fury. And even if a man is not habitually forward-looking, habits may still limit the range of his judgments, though the habits will have a different origin. Perhaps his manner of making or withholding judgments will be influenced by that of others whom he copies, and who are forward-looking. Or perhaps he will have been criticized by such people for judging unavoidable acts, and by that means effectively conditioned, without realizing how or why, against doing so. Thus even for these cases the relation between avoidability and ethical judgments, so far as any remains, depends upon the effectiveness of judgments in controlling the kind of actions judged. When this control is not a part of the speaker's present purposes, it can be found among his previous ones, or among the purposes of those who have influenced his habits of judging.

Although these remarks do not require any substantial change in the ethical status that has been assigned to avoidability, they are important for remolding the account, as it were, and rendering it more sensitive to the diverse ways of ordinary practice. To assume that ethical judgments are preponderately forward-looking—as has temporarily been done for simplicity—is to overintellectualize our usual state of mind. Not only does it underestimate the impassioned blindness of some of our judgments, but it suggests, particularly in the case of *favorable* judgments, that we are inhumanly preoccupied with the *business* of life. It suggests that our judgments are always calculated; and like the old saying, " 'Thank you' is a polite request for more," it leaves out of account the spontaneous gratitude, admiration, sympathy, and enthusiasm by which our motives are often invigorated and adorned. But now that this assumption has been qualified, the explanation becomes flexible—more faithful in depicting the fusion and interplay of forethought, impulse, and habit, which characterize all discourse and action.

4

LET us now examine some further examples, which will introduce certain points that the above account has not adequately emphasized.

Suppose that a man's action has led to consequences which we deplore, and that he would have prevented these consequences if he had chosen to act differently. And suppose, further, that he *did not know* that these consequences would arise. Will we be likely to "excuse" his action—i.e., withhold judgment—or will we be likely to judge him unfavorably? The answer will depend, obviously, upon the accompanying circumstances. If the man's *ignorance* of the consequences was avoidable, and if it was of the sort that we feel he ought to have remedied, then we shall probably judge him. And it must be noted that our judgments need not take the form of censuring his ignorance alone; they may also take the form of censuring the *action* that accompanies his ignorance. On the other hand, if we feel that his ignorance was unavoidable, we shall be likely to withhold judgment both of his ignorance and of his action.

This example is in accordance with the principle that judgments are usually limited to avoidable actions; but it suggests that they are limited further than this—to avoidable actions which do not spring from an unavoidable ignorance. This further limitation, though not central to the present chapter, remains of some little interest; for it raises the same considerations that have previously been mentioned. An action which, though avoidable in itself, springs from unavoidable ignorance, is not of a sort that a judgment will control. But an avoidable act which springs from avoidable ignorance *is* of a sort that the judgment may control; for the judgment may serve indirectly as a spur to remedying the ignorance, and will facilitate a control of the action by that means.

Can the class of actions to which we usually limit our judgments be narrowed still further? The answer must unquestionably be in the affirmative; but any elaboration of it would involve matters of detail, somewhat foreign to the present issue. It will be sufficient to mention this point:

Of the actions that we should like to control by judgment, and which we can reasonably hope to control in that way, we usually judge only those that we can control without undue labor. Just when we consider the labor "undue" will depend, of course, on our attitude to the action that we contemplate judging, and upon a great many other factors; but it will be obvious that each of us, in one way or another, lets his judgments be guided by such a consideration. We are more likely, for instance, to withhold unfavorable judgment of an action of an elderly man than of a man who is in the prime of life, even though the action is the same in both cases. We often explain this discrepancy in our judgments by remarking that as men grow older they are less easily changed in their ways. There are other motives that guide us here, of course; we may prefer to tolerate an elderly man's action than to cause him the pain of our censure, and so on. But among other considerations, the difficulty of making the judgment an adequate source of control remains as a conspicuous ground for withholding it.

This observation helps to place the remarks about avoidability, as developed in previous sections, in a larger setting. We are for the most part wholly unwilling to judge unavoidable actions, seeing that it is *impossible* to control them. But we are only a little less unwilling to judge actions over which a control is "virtually impossible"—i.e., very difficult. As the difficulty of control diminishes, our willingness to judge—all else being equal, of course—progressively increases.

It is easy to account, in this way, for the well-known ethical example of a man who is becoming addicted to opium. In the early stages of his habit we judge him, since our judgment may serve as a ready means of deterring him. But if he is further along in the habit, then, even though we may consider that his addiction is still avoidable, we shall be likely to withhold judgment. To be effective, our judgment will require such elaborate support, both by persuasive and rational methods, that it will become an inefficient instrument. So we tend to use more direct measures—taking active steps, for instance, to restrict the amount of opium that he is able to obtain. We may still say to others, of course, that he ought never to have formed the habit;

but this serves only as a warning which will deter *them* from forming it.

Not dissimilar considerations appear in cases where a given change can be brought about by alternative judgments, and where the problem is one of deciding which judgments to stress. If a reformer is trying to alter the accepted moral standards of the poor, shall he address his judgments mainly to them, or shall he address them mainly to the wealthier citizens, urging them to remedy the conditions which do so much to form the standards of the poor? Either set of judgments, we may assume, will be a *possible* source of control, but one may involve much more difficulty than the other; and the reformer's decision will have to take this into account. There will obviously be other factors to reckon with. No change is secured without a burden, and the reformer must also consider which people—the rich or the poor —are to bear this burden. But in practice the comparative difficulty of making the change by one means or the other is often a central consideration.

It must be emphasized that the present remarks about avoidability, and about the use of ethical judgments in controlling the sort of action that is judged, are far from exhausting a study of the many reasons that lead us to make judgments or withhold them. We may withhold judgments out of modesty, kindness, laziness, and so on; and these considerations need have nothing to do with whether our judgment, if made, would fail or succeed in controlling the action in question. They may all have some bearing on conduct, but not the direct bearing that we have been considering. Although the avoidability of an act, and its consequent susceptibility to control, is usually considered a necessary condition to its being judged, many other conditions are often necessary as well. Yet avoidability remains a consideration that is of particular interest, both because it has played no little part, under other names, in traditional controversy, and because it has become integral to the profound but intuitive, poorly analyzed wisdom of everyday life.

5

LET us now see whether there is any relation between ethics and the determinism or indeterminism of choice. Our remarks about avoidability have not answered this question, since, as previously explained,[15] an action may be avoidable regardless of whether the choice of it is determined or indetermined.

It is sometimes maintained that indeterminism is a fundamental presupposition of all ethics. The reasons that are given for this view, though they may take several forms, can be typified in the following way:

If a man's choice is known to be determined, no reflective person will judge the action that results from the choice. The man will be considered a victim of circumstances. His action will have been ordained by natural law, and any judgment of it will be as idle as a judgment of the rain for falling, or of the stars for holding their courses. So reflective people limit their judgments not to avoidable acts, merely, but to those that spring from an indetermined choice. If there were no actions of the latter sort, there would be no actions open to reflective judgment. It is the task of a constructive theory of ethics, accordingly, to establish indeterminism; for this is a necessary step in showing that an enlightened ethics is in any way possible.

The last part of this contention has so often been refuted that it will here require only a few words. Reference to indeterminism will not help to defend the "possibility" of an enlightened ethics, but will simply put one difficulty in the place of another. If a man's choice were indetermined, it would be theoretically unpredictable. The man himself could not have foreseen his choice, nor could he have taken any steps to prevent it. It would have sprung not from his personality, but from nothing at all. He would still be a "victim," not of determining circumstances, but of *chance*. What room is there here for an ethical judgment?

The main confusion of the view, however, lies not in its failure to avoid a difficulty, but in its creation of an artificial one. There is no reason whatever to suppose that a reflective person, believing that a man's action sprang from a determined choice, will on that account suspend judgment of the action. Between judging such an action and judging the rain for falling there is this difference: a judgment of the rain will make no difference to it, whereas a judgment of a human action, provided only that the action is avoidable, may serve to make such actions more frequent, or less frequent, in the future. For the latter case the judgment will itself be a new determining factor—one that is

15. Pp. 299 f.

added to the old determining factors of a man's choice, and which may serve as a means of controlling or guiding him. It would be curious if a "reflective" person, on coming to believe that choice is subject to causes, should immediately lose interest in having his judgments number among them.

Those who insist on indeterminism, then, considering it indispensable to the possibility of ethics, provide an inadequate solution to an imaginary problem. Avoidability is indeed of interest to ethics, but indeterminism introduces a topic that is largely beside the point.

But if ethics does not presuppose indeterminism, what shall be said of the opposite doctrine? Does it not follow from the present analysis that ethical judgments presuppose *determinism?*

It may at first seem so. Ethical judgments control actions through the mediating step of controlling a man's choice. If the man's choice is not determined, it will not be subject to control in this manner or in any manner. Our judgment will not serve as a cause, offsetting those that operate independently of our efforts, of making him act differently in the future. Determinism seems necessary to provide ethical judgments with their usual function.

A moment's consideration, however, will show that this is not strictly the case. A "partial" determinism must be presupposed, but not necessarily a "complete" one. The meaning of these terms will be clear from the following example: A man's choice would be called "partially" determined if, from an *exhaustive* knowledge of laws and circumstances, and with unlimited intellectual ability, we could predict that his choice would have certain rather generic characteristics, but could predict no more specifically than this. It would be "completely" determined if we could predict that it would be of a designated, wholly specific nature. Now ethics, although it *permits* complete determinism, *requires* only partial determinism. It requires only that a man's choice and action be subject to some kind of control by a judgment, and for this partial determinism is enough. A judgment could not then lead the man to do *exactly* what the speaker hoped, but it could lead him roughly in that direction.

It will be evident that if an event is only partially determined, it will also, to an extent, be *in*determined. It will be "partially" indetermined, as one might say; but those who defend indeterminism wish to defend no more than this, and usually omit the qualifying adjective. No one wishes to maintain that there are psychological events which are *totally* cut off from preceding ones. Controversy has been concerned, then, with whether certain events are completely determined or only partially so—or in other words, with whether they are completely determined or (partially) indetermined. Since either alternative is sufficient to provide ethical judgments with a practical function, we may conclude that the determinism-indeterminism controversy must be mentioned in ethics only in order to dispel the confusions which have led theorists to exaggerate its importance.

We must pause to mention a more indirect way in which determinism has been thought to be related to ethics. If people believed in complete determinism, it is sometimes urged, they would lose all incentive to struggle for the aims that they considered best; for determinism would lead them to suppose that the outcome of any issue is preordained, and that their struggles could make no difference to it. This contention is easily criticized. Whenever the loss of incentive that it mentions actually occurs, it is due not to a belief in determinism but to a confusion which attends the belief. It is troublesome only to those who fail to distinguish between determinism and unavoidability. In the case of unavoidable actions—those for which a different choice (voluntary effort, etc.) will *not* lead to a different result—there *will* be no point in struggling. But determinism has no such implication. The fact that a man's choice is determined does not prevent the choice, in turn, from making a difference to his success in getting what he chooses. And the knowledge that his choice will make such a difference is usually one of the factors which *cause* him to choose—to strive in promoting his aim. In other words, the statement, "No matter what I choose to do, the usual course of events will not be affected," which manifestly can be used as an excuse for pessimistic inactivity, is not a consequence of the determinism of choice; it is a consequence only of the contention (which is a preposterous one) that the usual course of events is wholly unavoidable. The statement refers not to the causes of choice, but to its impotence in producing effects. It is only by confusing the two—and the confusion is the same as that between determinism and fatalism, or determinism and preordination, or determinism and constraint—that one can suppose that determinism has implications which paralyze action.

In general, those who have been troubled by determinism, and have held up indeterminism as essential to ethics, have always possessed, in avoidability, all the benefits that they supposed indeterminism would bring. So the *non sequiturs* that attend so many arguments for indeterminism do not even represent an enlightened wishful-thinking. When the issue is clearly formulated, it can give rise to neither predilection nor antipathy. And indeed, it should not be considered as a serious topic of dispute. Whenever men fail to predict certain events (as presumably they always will) their failure can be ascribed either to their ignorance of causes and laws or to an absolute chance that exists in nature. Thus either determinism or (partial) indeterminism can be maintained in the face of such evidence. Since no other obtainable evidence is more decisive, neither doctrine can definitely be proved, and neither definitely disproved. Under these circumstances it is only sensible to accept whichever hypothesis is more convenient for the purpose at hand. For many purposes, determinism is the more convenient assumption. For the purposes of ethics, however, either hypothesis will do; for either will be compatible with the rough type of causal explanation (presupposing only partial determinism) that the subject requires.

If the determinism-indeterminism controversy can be dismissed from ethics, then why, it may be asked, have so many ethical theorists supposed it to be important? One reason, of course, is that the word "freedom," being used ambiguously to designate both avoidability and indeterminism, has led the latter notion to become confused with the former, and thus to acquire an artificial importance. But this is a somewhat peripheral aspect of the matter, possibly less a cause of confusion than a symptom of it. A more interesting explanation is this:

Theorists have habitually emphasized the cognitive aspects of language, and so have left the quasi-imperative aspects of ethical judgments without proper emphasis. This has prevented them from seeing that ethical judgments look to the future. Instead, then, of placing the connection between "freedom" (avoidability) and ethical judgments in the future—instead of seeing that avoidable acts alone will subsequently be controlled by judgment—they looked to the past for a connection. Quite naturally, they could find an explanation only by making *choice* a mystery, as if it were somehow alterable even when it was irrevocably in the past. Some began to talk of indeterminism, and others, seeing that this really didn't help, became unintelligibly metaphysical.

The same tendency—that of looking to the past for a connection—has doubtless been aggravated by the form of language that is used in subjunctive conditionals. When we say, "His action would have been different if he had chosen differently" (which has the same meaning as "His action was avoidable"), our verbs are uniformly in the past tense. The fact that the statement points to a *lawful* connection between the choice and the action,[16] and may consequently have a bearing on *future* cases, is thus concealed from our attention.

A further reason for the confusion lies in the emotional state of mind from which ethical judgments proceed. When our ethical judgments are forward-looking they do not, as we have seen, wholly lose a more impulsive motivation. They may be attended by indignation, fear, irritation, and so on, which give the judgment a forceful spontaniety. If we pause to consider the causes of the action judged, our emotions may become stultified, and our judgments less convincing. So instead of dwelling upon the causes we tend to invent fictions, to strengthen our emotions by giving them semipoetic expression. We pretend that the action is without remote causal antecedents, coming exclusively from the man who is judged. He is "just naturally mean," like the villain in an old-fashioned melodrama. His conduct could have nothing to do with social conditions or an unfortunate childhood; indeed it could have no connection with anything that would divert our disapproval from its immediate object. Thus fictions of indeterminism, providing our attitudes with a more ready point of focus, give a temporary forcefulness to our judgment. This may be an important source of error. It would be easy to make too much of these fictions, or to confuse them with tested psychological hypotheses. One might readily conclude that a presupposition of indeterminism is found in the very "meaning" of an ethical judgment.

We must not forget, in our efforts to dispel these confusions, that they have long pervaded common life. When confusions are old and venerable, they have their effect on language. Hence it must be acknowledged that ethical judgments, for the usage of a certain limited group of people, *do* imply indeterminism,

16. With partial determinism there will still be a law, but it will describe a uniformity between events that are specified only in a generic way. Note that the subjunctive conditional only "points to" a law, for it does not mention *all* factors that a law would have to take account of.

and that the reason, "His choice was determined," would, if believed, cause these people to withold judgment, or at least to hesitate in perplexity. The present account does not wish to deny this; it wishes only to show that people would not use the ethical terms in this way, and would not find determinism a ground for withholding judgment, if they fully understood what they were doing. But in any case, whenever people *do* consider determinism a ground for withholding judgment, there is no insuperable difficulty (though of course there would be much complexity in an account that pretended to be exhaustive) in explaining why they do so. They confuse determinism with unavoidability, backward-looking judgments with forward-looking ones, expressive fictions with facts; and these confusions, together with others which we need not mention, provide the psychological framework on which their habits of making judgments are formed.

XV

Practical Implications

1

IN ITS essential aspects the present analysis is now complete; so let us view it in a broader perspective, considering the ways in which it promises to be of practical use.

Certain points will be obvious. Moral questions often present a Babel of tongues, where attention to the flexibilities of language is essential for locating the points of debate. And since many ethical writers stubbornly abide by methods which, in their claims to finality, are mocked by the endless disputes to which they lead, a critical study may help to cut through this pretentiousness, and enable ethics to accomplish more by attempting less. If we are to have an adequate estimate of the importance of analysis, however, we must look to its repercussions with greater care. So let us see whether our conclusions can give normative discussions a needed discipline, and let us see whether they can serve, indirectly, to hold up certain methods as more serviceable than others. The topic is in part concerned with the proper place of science in normative ethics; and since this is a point on which misunderstanding is particularly costly, provoking artificial opposition where there should be compatibility and coöperation, let us give it the main part of our attention.

In discussing the *proper* place of science in ethics, we must remember that our conclusions, themselves normative, may be the occasion for disagreement in attitude. Yet much can be done by reviewing and emphasizing the results of the preceding chapters. If analysis is not sufficient in itself to establish how science ought to be used in ethics, it can clear the way for such a conclusion. We shall have occasion to see, perhaps, that a clearing of the way is much more than a bare beginning.

2

THE other-worldliness of the metaphysical traditions in ethics, and their disregard of the sciences, have rarely been attacked

more severely than by the late David W. Prall. "It is the philosophers," he writes,

who have thought fit to despise what they call the limitations of science. And they have done this often on the basis of an *a priori* dialectic
which, as any beginner in logic realizes, can not possibly offer any one
any knowledge of anything—except just that expertness in dialectic
which is itself an aptness of the tongue or of the nervous system or
perhaps of the writing arm. . . . They have arrogantly and ignorantly
set up ethical norms and theories without so much as an acquaintance
with law, with the most casual and superficial knowledge of social history and social institutions, and with no expert knowledge at all of
human organisms. Instead of trying to understand and share in the
lives of other men, they continue to retreat from the world of experience into more and more remote regions, into the confusions and
inconsistencies if not of Christian mythology and scholastic theology,
then of Aristotelian causes and essences or hierarchies of Platonic
Forms. It is as if all these had not been worked out and built upon,
criticized and sanely enough put into their appropriate and respected
places long ago. They were at best suggestive early efforts in the direction of the very knowledge that has gradually grown out of them in
the achievements of later ages. If it is only sanity or decent piety to
cultivate the roots of the still growing tree of knowledge, surely it is
no less than a form of insane idolatry to attempt to give up modern
science and adopt as actual knowledge these earlier achievements themselves. It is insisting that the fruits of the tree that we cultivate are
poison, so that we should destroy it. But not root and branch; for we
are apparently to save the roots to chew upon in a fine austerity of
spiritual fervor.[1]

Those who suspect that Prall's remarks are without foundation can have had little experience, it is feared, with the ways of
academic philosophy. Yet it is well to give his criticism another
emphasis. The current forms of ethical nostalgia have little that
positively recommends them. Few would save the roots to chew
upon if they realized that the fruits are not the poison that they
seem. The problem is one of showing in detail how science can
be put to ethical use—of presenting a forward-looking conception
of ethics that is sensitive to the nature of its task. And for this
purpose there is less need to combat a revival of old systems than
to dispel the misunderstandings of science—the unfounded fears

1. "Knowledge as Aptness of the Body," *Philosophical Review* (March,
1938), pp. 129 f.

of its "chaotic implications"—which make a retreat to the past seem necessary.

If we pause to examine these misunderstandings, we shall find that they thrive most among those who are preoccupied with large issues. Ethics in General stands confronted by Science in General, and the problem must be dealt with on this cosmic level. Such a procedure usually ends in diverting this or that broad conclusion of science into some metaphorical interpretation, where it becomes a ritual for evoking supernatural powers. Only the graphic pictures of science are used, cut off from their proper function in organizing or predicting concrete phenomena.

This point could be illustrated with reference to some of the Neo-Thomists, but let us look, rather, to a more extreme example, which has prepared the way for a new cult of mysticism:

The apparent pointlessness of modern life . . . and its lack of significance and purpose are due to the fact that, in the Western world at least, the prevailing cosmology is what Mr. Gerald Heard has called the "mechanomorphic" cosmology of modern science. The universe is regarded as a great machine pointlessly grinding its way toward ultimate stagnation and death; men are tiny offshoots of the universal machine, running down to their own private death; physical life is the only real life; mind is a mere product of body; personal success and material well-being are the ultimate measures of value, the things for which a reasonable person should live.[2]

Now this may or may not be a representative characterization of our times. But if it is, there is every occasion to ask just *how* science can be held responsible for it. The desolate "cosmology" may actually be implied by science; it may, alternatively, be something which is ascribed to science by those who have failed to assimilate its teachings.

The conception that men are "offshoots of a universal machine" finds its nearest scientific counterpart in the mechanistic (as opposed to vitalistic) hypotheses of biology, and in the related emphasis on neurology that has grown up in psychology. Properly speaking, there is not so much a doctrine, here, as a question. Would it be possible, from a complete knowledge of the chemical constituents and physical structure of an organism, a complete knowledge of its environment, and a complete knowledge of physical and chemical laws, to predict how the organism will

2. Aldous Huxley, *Ends and Means* (Chatto & Windus, 1938), pp. 123 f.

subsequently act?[3] Scientists are not accustomed to answer this question with a dogmatic affirmative; and indeed, they would be happy to attain a full understanding, in physiochemical terms, of the behavior of an amoeba. But let us suppose for the sake of argument that scientists deify their working hypotheses into absolute truths, maintaining that the laws of physics and chemistry apply without exception to all actions, whether animal or human. Would such a view, soberly understood, put a premium on some crudely conceived personal success, undermining altruism, benevolence, temperance, courage, sympathy, and all the many qualities that moralists have upheld as the virtues? Not in the least, so long as it was fully empirical, and was judged with strict attention to logic. However much biological theory may refine and supplement the observations of common life, it can never *dismiss* them in favor of something else. It must account for the way in which people are found to behave on a macroscopic level; and if its theories make this impossible, that is proof that the theories must be reformulated. Now the purposeful actions that we can readily observe in ourselves and in others can scarcely be taken, on a macroscopic level, to be illusory; nor is it any part of a biological program to deny that these actions are sometimes altruistic, benevolent, temperate, and so on. The aspects of mechanistic theory which seem to explain these phenomena *away* are in fact attempts to account for their observed *presence*. Whether or not a mechanistic theory can do this is beside the question. The point is that *if* a tenable theory of mechanism were worked out in detail, it would show only, as Spinoza saw clearly long ago, the extraordinary wonders of "the structure itself of the human body, which so greatly surpasses in workmanship all those things that are constructed by human art."[4] It could have no implications, in any empirically founded form, about the crassness of men, or their aimlessness; for its account of hidden processes would always have to be commensurate with the overt, directly observable aspects of conduct that it seeks to explain.

The mechanism of a "mechanomorphic cosmology" is by no means the same, then, as the mechanism of biology. It is a purely

3. The deterministic aspects of the question have been considered in the preceding chapter. Its new aspects, now particularly relevant, are concerned with whether the determining factors are limited to those of physics and chemistry.

4. *Ethics*, Pt. III, Prop. II, Schol.

literary conception, envisaging a world peopled by monsters of Frankenstein. Between this world and the biologist's world there is all this difference: The monsters of Frankenstein would have a heartlessness which, as in Mary Shelley's account of their proto-type, would be evident from contrasting their overt actions with the actions of human beings. The men of biological mechanism, however, would continue to act in precisely that human way with which the observations of daily life, and the records of some three thousand years of history, have helped to make us familiar.

Much the same can be said of the view that "mind is a mere product of the body." This finds its nearest parallel in epiphe-nomenalism, or in certain forms of the theory of emergent evo-lution.[5] Whether or not these theories are fully adequate is a point on which no writer who is respectful of scientific caution will dogmatize; but there is no ground whatsoever for maintain-ing that they have grievous moral implicatons. The wealth and variety of immediate experience is something to which any man has a ready testimony at his disposal. This experience does not become impoverished merely through being taken as epiphe-nomenal; nor does epiphenomenalism deprive us of literature, music, or painting, or of sensitive ideals, or of any empirical manifestation of what we commonly take to be "things of the mind." All these remain; and indeed, the *regular sequence* be-tween our experiences of hope or fear and their issue in subse-quent experiences remains one that epiphenomenalism can never disturb, but can only seek to integrate into a larger scheme. In a "mechanomorphic cosmology" our ordinary experiences, first conceived as impoverished, are then conceived as cut off from the course of life. In a theory of epiphenomenalism, so long as it is faithful to its empirical origins, experience is conceived in its full richness; and the program (for it is only a program) which it proposes as an aid to accounting for the status of con-scious experience, and which it adopts strictly as a basis for further inquiry, makes no pretense of discrediting, but gives only

5. The behaviorism that is often ascribed indiscriminately to modern psy-chology is for the most part only a "methodological behaviorism"—that is, a form of epiphenomenalism in which the epiphenomena of consciousness are by no means denied an existence, but are simply considered irrelevant, when they occur in the person on whom experiments are made, to the laboratory methods that are used. Few contemporary psychologists, so far as the pres-ent writer can judge, are prepared to make no distinction between conscious experiences and their neurological correlates. This is abundantly clear for psychophysics, Gestalt psychology, and clinical psychology.

a hope of refining and supplementing, the great store of psychological knowledge that is implicit in enlightened common sense.

In general, when phenomenon X is said to be "reduced" to phenomenon Y, this expression must not be taken to imply, in its technical use, that Y alone is real, and X illusory; it implies only that X, still real, can be explained through its correlation with Y.[6] A confusion upon this point seems obviously to underlie the quotation we have been considering. Yet behind this there is a greater confusion: that of pressing the generalizations of science into a function that is essentially mythical. It is a characteristic of mythology to confuse its explanations of phenomena with an artistic presentation of the mood that they evoke. Science sharply separates these functions, and without rendering it impossible for moods to be expressed in nonscientific discourse, strives to devote its whole energy to explanation. Accordingly, those who become half-blind to the explanatory function—as indeed they will, if they isolate each broad scientific generalization from the detailed phenomena it is intended to correlate—can find in science little more than the artistry and pictorialization that its language may happen to suggest. It is no wonder that this accidental myth, striving to be something else, should seem to stand in sorry contrast to the myths of old, with their full artistic inspiration.

This is not to say that science, however innocent it may be in its logical implications, is free from providing moral difficulties. If its alleged evils are largely the evils of its misinterpretations, it remains the case that the misinterpretations tend to pervade the popular mind; and they represent sociological phenomena, lying in the wake of science, which may have a perplexing, dispiriting effect on the way men live. Yet the proper task, certainly, for those who lament this situation and seek to improve it, is one of revealing the teachings of science for what they are. Nothing can be said for those reformers who share the very confusions that make reform necessary, and whose efforts to provide an emotional orientation to nature are placed in artificial rivalry with the study of nature itself.

6. This is often pointed out by writers on scientific method. See C. D. Broad, *Mind and Its Place in Nature*, pp. 46–52. Ernest Nagel has discussed the matter, in much the present connection, in his article, "Malicious Philosophies of Science," *Partisan Review* (January–February, 1943), pp. 46 ff.

If the ethical implications of science are distorted by those who view them with suspicion, they are also distorted, or imperfectly conceived, by those who view them with premature confidence—by those who, speaking on moral topics from the point of view of some special field, are content with a level of speculative generality that would never content them in their laboratory. There is evidence of this, though not without certain compensations, in some recent papers by Ralph W. Gerard:

The direction of evolutionary change [he writes] is consistently from the more homogeneous, with different structural regions performing like functions in "competition" with one another, to the more differentiated and reintegrated, with different regions specialized for separate functions, division of labor, and coöperation of all parts in terms of the whole. . . . And the same organizing trend is seen only less clearly in the inanimate world, e.g., as interpreted by modern cosmogeny and aspects of geology.

The sweep of evolution supplies the objective counterpart to our subjective experience of the virtues. Service and mutual helpfulness, seen in the interplay of cell nucleus and chloroplast or of heart and brain and gut or of hand and eye, are not altered when, at the social level, we call them altruism, benevolence, and love of fellows. These are the biological virtues, empirically demonstrable in terms of the way the world is and is moving. . . .

I cannot see the progressive generalization of the "good" sought, from that of self to family to clan to state, as itself being anything but the expression of the great movement of evolution and in harmony with the growing altruism biology indicates.[7]

It must be said, in Gerard's defense, that he does not go from biology to ethics by a *tour de force* of logic. His remark that the "biological virtues" are "empirically demonstrable" is not typical of his work. Evolutionary trends are taken not as entailing altruism, but only as roughly pointing to it; and there is none of that vacuity of saying: "These trends are inevitable; therefore they require the assistance of our moral exhortation, lest they should fail to be inevitable." Yet it is well to examine the way in which his arguments can secure their force:

Do they show, for instance, that altruism is necessary to personal survival, thus leading our socially regarding aims to

7. "Biological Basis for Ethics," *Philosophy of Science* (January, 1942), pp. 108, 117.

become reinforced by our egoistic ones? An argument which looks only to the "sweep" of evolution cannot be expected to do this. The trend from "the more monogeneous . . . to the more differentiated and reintegrated" has been shown by evolutionary theory only to be *compatible* with survival; it has in no way been shown *necessary* to survival. For we are not to forget that we have, still with us, some thirty-five thousand species of vertebrates, of varying degrees of complexity, and some five hundred thousand species of invertebrates, "ranging from the Sponges and Hydroids to the Mollusks, Crustacea, and Insects"[8]—to say nothing of the ten thousand kinds of unicellular animals. These less complicated forms of life have shown their fitness to survive by the excellent proof of having done so; and evolutionary theory gives no ground for concluding that they are destined to extinction unless some happy mutation hurries them along in the direction of man. Clearly, the trend from lesser to greater complexity is not the same as a trend from organisms which cannot survive to those which can. And we must remember, heeding the remarks of an earlier writer on biology and ethics, that

in cosmic nature . . . what is "fittest" depends upon the conditions. . . . If our hemisphere were to cool again, the survival of the fittest might bring about, in the vegetable kingdom, a population of more and more stunted and humbler and humbler organisms, until the "fittest" that survived might be nothing but lichens, diatoms, and such microscopic organisms as those which give red snow its colour; while, if it became hotter, the pleasant valleys of the Thames and Isis might be uninhabitable by any animated beings save those that flourish in a tropical jungle. They, as the fittest, the best adapted to the changed conditions, would survive.[9]

So Gerard's arguments yield to no interpretation that emphasizes biological "fitness." Their implications are to the effect that altruism, present in this or that degree, or in this or that incipient stage, has so far proved no detriment to survival. They do nothing to support a more interesting conclusion: that an *increase* in altruism, operating here and now under ordinary conditions

8. L. L. Woodruff, *Foundations of Biology* (Macmillan, 1923). 2d ed., p. 117.
9. Thomas H. Huxley, "Evolution and Ethics" (lecture given at Oxford in 1893). See volume bearing that title in D. Appleton and Co.'s edition of *Selected Works* of Huxley, pp. 80 f.

of social life, measures an *increase* in our chance to survive. It may be that the latter conclusion can be established. But the proof would require a study of details which the theory of evolution, when viewed only as a "sweep," is far from providing; and many of the considerations would extend well beyond biology into such fields, among others, as psychology, economics, and sociology.

It is probable, indeed, that Gerard's arguments are not intended to draw their force from survival, or from anything else that utilizes the predictive aspects of his science. They seem intended, rather, to accentuate the immediate appeal of a trend toward complexity itself. Those who are impressed by the trend, and are led to see altruism as its culmination, will be influenced to join in the cosmic procession—a procession whose destination is viewed not in the light of its network of practical results, but only as an object of intrinsic wonder.

There is nothing illegitimate in this, so long as it pretends to be nothing more than what it is. Yet it is a pity to suggest that the "basis of ethics" is to be sought on such a high level of generality. The details of science, which might be put to use in reinforcing our otherwise disorganized impulses, are made to give place to an adoration of a spectacle. And the spectacle revealed by science, like any spectacle, can have only an ephemeral hold upon our attitudes, by no means so secure as a systematic body of specific knowledge, making contact with our aims at every point of their being.

Gerard's conception of "the great movement of evolution" is in far closer touch with experience than is any conception of a "mechanomorphic cosmology"; but his use of it still remains uncomfortably close to a scientific mythology. It is not wholly free from the expectation, essentially mythical, that the broad schemata for explanation and description should serve, with immediacy, as a reliable guide to emotional orientation. It is true that science, having necessitated some new form of emotional orientation, furnishes an invaluable means of securing it; but its function in this capacity is complicated and all pervasive. If we are to have a scientific basis for ethics, even of a rough, provisional sort, it is scarcely to be obtained from the conclusions of some *one* science; and it is still less to be obtained from the broadest generalization of some one science, functioning only by its dramatic appeal.

3

WHAT can be said in a more constructive way? What program for ethical methodology can be recommended to which the sciences will lend their full resources?

Let us view the problem, more concretely, as one that might confront a writer on normative ethics—a writer who, going beyond ethical analysis and ethical history, wishes to present moral views of his own, and is deciding what methods to *employ* in reaching and supporting his conclusions. And let us assume that he addresses his book only to intelligent, mature readers, who will be able to follow and criticize his arguments in detail. This assumption reduces the dimensions of the problem quite severely. It does away with the task of evading complexity, of deliberately oversimplifying without too grossly distorting, which we have seen elsewhere to be one of the greatest difficulties that a practical moralist can face.[10] But since the deliberation of those who can think for themselves can scarcely be made secondary to the popular dissemination of their conclusions, the narrower problem will not be impracticably narrow.

What methods ought such a writer employ? Let us look first to an ideal that has long been current—the ideal of examining both sides of a normative question, and bringing to bear upon it as much knowledge as possible. Any writer must, of course, make some *selection* from the reasons that are potentially at his disposal; but he can do this in a spirit of cautious deliberation, seeking to anticipate the considerations that will later, in actual experience, be most relevant to the direction of attitudes, and taking care to weigh the reasons which support his own conclusions against a fully representative body of reasons that may serve to attack them.

If our writer disclaimed this ideal from the start, we should have great difficulty in leading him to accept it. Yet the ideal is in fact so widely accepted that it would seem only gratuitous, here, to speak in its behalf. Departures from it, though frequent, are for the most part inadvertent. They spring, very often, from an unconscious self-deception, which makes distorted evidence seem evidence that is adequately represented. The remedy for this is a slow one, though much may be hoped from current developments in psychology. And they spring, equally often, from

10. Cf. p. 125

an imperfect conception of the *great variety* of knowledge that has a bearing on ethical issues. The requisite support is made to give place, unwittingly, to scattered observations or nebulous abstractions. Let us simplify matters, then (not forgetting that we are doing so), by assuming that our hypothetical writer accepts the ideal, and let us go on to consider how he can best actualize it.

With regard to the second of the inadvertencies mentioned— that of becoming insensitive to the wide variety of relevant knowledge—we need only recapitulate, with new emphasis, the several results of our analytic study. Our conclusions about how reasons *can* be used, when wedded to the above ideal, become an indispensable guide for deciding how they *should* be used.

It has been shown in Chapter V that any statement about any matter of fact, so long as it is likely to direct attitudes, may serve as a reason for an ethical judgment.[11] Hence any representative selection of reasons that are well confirmed—and our writer, pursuing the ideal that has been mentioned, must strive for such a selection—will require information that is extremely diversified. Not only must he give attention to the reasons that he uses; he must also examine many others, to insure that he is not making serious omissions. His task, inevitably, will be a formidable one.

Nor can we countenance the suggestion that he delimit his task by dealing only with ultimate ends. This is evident from our study of intrinsic and extrinsic value, in Chapter VIII. The methodological conclusions of that discussion, and the psychological observations on which they were based, show that any search for this type of simplicity, proceeding in the "specialist's" spirit that characterizes so much of academic ethics, can afford a promise neither of present achievement nor of future hope. In particular: if our writer is sensitive to the plurality of ends that people habitually have in view, he will scarcely seek to exalt some one factor as *the* end, reducing everything else to the exclusive status of means. He can hope for an enlightened redirection of aims, but can scarcely expect to make human nature anew.

If he wishes general, unifying principles, he must attend not to "the end," and not even to "ends," exclusively, but rather to focal aims. As has previously been explained, a focal aim is some-

11. Cf. p. 114.

thing valued partly as an end, perhaps, but largely as in indispensable means to a multitude of other ends. It may play a unifying role in normative ethics; for once it is established, the value of a great many other things, being a means to *it*, can probably be established in their turn.[12] But obviously, a focal aim cannot be adequately defended—and perhaps it cannot even be clearly formulated—unless it is seen in its full causal setting.

Those who have emphasized the distinction between intrinsic and extrinsic value have often been sensitive to the network of consequences on which the *latter* depends. But they have conceived a given object, X, as having consequences which become diverse and radiate in all directions only for an intermediate period. Later on they converge, so far as they are ethically relevant, on scme one end; and it is their effect on this end which alone will determine whether X is valuable. A rational defense of "the" end itself has brought with it many perplexities. The present work differs from this tradition in showing that the value assigned to X will depend on its *still radiating* consequences, and in showing that even if these do later converge, the point of convergence will never be taken as an exclusive end, but always as a focal aim—valued largely for its own consequences that radiate once more. Empirical inquiry must pervade the whole of an enlightened ethics; it cannot be confined to some distinctively "terrestrial" part.

In view of the magnitude of his task, we may expect our writer to begin in modesty. The aims with which he first deals will not be the ones embodied in the broad principles of philosophers; they will be those that concern the "middle principles" of daily life. He may hope eventually, perhaps, for some all-embracing aim; but he will not hope to establish it before all else, or to state it in a simple formula. Since an all-embracing aim, if obtainable at all, must be a focal aim, it cannot be held up as a *sine qua non* of all further inquiry. In normative ethics, as in so many other fields, the first principles are the last that can be obtained; for their very comprehensiveness makes them the most difficult to formulate and to support. (This holds for personal deliberations, no less than for interpersonal ones. A man can often establish, to his own satisfaction, the value of this policy or that; but who of us, here and now, can find any one focal aim which is sufficiently comprehensive to draw together the divergent elements of his

12. See particularly pp. 202 ff.

whole personality?) So our writer must begin with relatively specific judgments, whose support, though still complicated, will be less so than that of the judgments which are more general. He must discuss many of the *lesser* focal aims, some of which may prove to work together, and others to conflict, requiring compromise and readjustment.

But no matter whether our writer considers specific issues or general ones, there can be no question about his need of concerning himself with the sciences, and with their common-sense counterparts. He must give them his central attention. He will differ from a pure scientist; for the task of selecting from the stores of knowledge, and bringing together the information that bears on a specific moral issue, is one to which pure scientists do not address themselves. It involves a *use* of science which, as we have seen elsewhere, makes its own demands on organization and is inimical to specialization.[13] Yet conclusions ordered in a special way must still be conclusions that are empirically founded, unless knowledge is to give place to ignorance.

A full use of the sciences cannot be obtained from gestures at their more impressive conceptions. They serve fully only when they point the way to reliable predictions; and they do this only when they are used in a detailed manner. The usefulness of predictions in ethics will be evident; hence only these points need be emphasized: Attitudes are strengthened and guided largely by reinforcement. One's approval of X is strengthened when X is shown to be a means to Y, which is also approved. But it is the *belief* about X's relation to Y, not the relation itself, which brings the reinforcement; and if this belief is not a predictive one, confirmed in advance, it may come too late to have a practical effect. And again, attitudes are often redirected by the urgency of conflict. If X and Y, causally incompatible, are both approved, a person must make a preferential decision between them. A predictive knowledge of the incompatibility may enable the decision to be made without haste; and a further kind of predictive knowledge—knowledge about the psychological effects of inhibiting one attitude or the other, and knowledge about whether one or the other can be directed to a slightly different object—may enable the decision to involve only a bare minimum of compromise.

There will be much, in all such predictions, that requires a knowledge of human nature; but the relation of a given X to a

13. See particularly pp. 254 ff.

given Y, we must remember, will not always be a topic that is exclusively psychological. The relation of a system of taxation to the conditions of the poor, for instance, may be partly an economic one; and it may even require elementary observations about the nation's climate, for this will determine the kind of clothes and shelter that the poor will need. What knowledge is there, indeed, that has *not* a potential bearing on evaluation?

So our writer, in seeking to provide his norms with *rational* support, will find his task to be one of establishing relevant factual conclusions about human nature and its environment. It will be exclusively that. It will not be a small task; and he cannot be sure, even when he has surmounted it, that his judgments will be accepted by all his readers. Agreement in attitude may not arise, even if agreement in belief is secured. Yet a problem that can be characterized in empirical terms, and which at least permits the cautious hope of an empirical solution, becomes one which, however difficult, is intelligible and workable. It is free from that methodological bewilderment, that confused groping for the first steps of approach, which paralyze the whole of inquiry and thought. Thus our writer will find, in the present account, not a ground for believing that enlightened norms lie permanently beyond human attainment, but rather a ground for believing that his slow results will be cumulative, contributing to an ethics that will progressively come to grips with the issues of practical life.

4

WHAT shall be said of persuasive methods? Are we to discourage our writer from using them, or can they, supplementing his reasons, be given an acceptable, legitimate place?

Let us begin with this observation: Although the effect of beliefs on attitudes is ever present, it is often slow. Our writer may find that there is a prolonged lag between his reader's acceptance of his reasons and their subsequent emotional readjustment. Old ways are not easily unlearned, and persist long after they are acknowledged to have outlived their function. Now here is a place where persuasive methods, cautiously used, have a legitimacy that is scarcely open to question. If our writer's persuasion does not supplant his reasons, but simply hastens their effect—if it presses his readers in a direction that fuller knowledge has recommended to them in advance—it will come as a welcome aid, alleviating the task of cutting through old habits, which the readers would otherwise have to undertake without assistance.

But persuasion need not be given so limited a place. Let us suppose that our writer is defending an aim which others have not previously considered. And let us suppose that his persuasive support of it is somewhat in advance of an adequate rational support, full evidence being difficult to obtain. This may, of course, lead his readers to accept the aim incautiously. But it may also have a quite different effect. By calling strong attention to the aim—which might otherwise be viewed with the suspicion that so easily attends the unfamiliar—he may lead his readers to give it proper consideration. If his readers are mature and intelligent (as we have assumed) they will not accept his aim without deliberation; and his persuasion, instead of turning the issue prematurely, may serve as a challenge that stimulates further inquiry. It may give his readers an incentive to discuss the question, and the result of their joint deliberation, whether it leads them to accept the proposed aim or to reject it, will have the function of subjecting it to a careful test. Thus persuasion need not be hostile to rational methods, and need not even be an independent supplement to them, but may actually make an indirect contribution to their full use.

A further consideration has been mentioned in Chapter VI.[14] It may happen that our writer, in developing certain psychological conclusions that will support his norms, can make use of *einfühlung*. By enlarging the introspective resources of his readers, as it were—by making them imaginatively project themselves into the place of others, and helping them, thereby, to understand how the others live—he may be enabled to communicate information that might otherwise be poorly articulate and only half understood. In such a process there need not be a use of persuasive methods in any strict sense. For einfühlung may function in helping people to obtain beliefs, and may support an ethical judgment only to the extent that the beliefs do so; whereas persuasive methods function more directly—often supplementing rational methods, to be sure, and often stimulating people (as mentioned above) to check or reconsider their beliefs later on, but serving in the first instance to support ethical judgments emotively, with an influence that beliefs do not mediate. Yet the talent required for producing einfühlung, seen from a linguistic

14. Example (23), beginning on p. 144.

point of view, is much more than a talent for utilizing descriptive meanings. It is one thing to build up a state of mind that helps certain beliefs to originate and become clear; it is another thing to give information barely and simply. In the former undertaking, much more than in the latter, the use of descriptive meanings must be attended by careful attention to emotive and pictorial meanings, and to the subtleties of style, tone, and suggestivity by which the reader's reactions will be determined. The several uses of language cannot be compartmentalized, simply because our psychological processes themselves stand in a close, reciprocal relationship.

There are other ways in which persuasion, and the nondescriptive aspects of language more generally, can be given a justifiable place in ethics. Much might be said, for instance, of the uses of literature (and of the other arts) that extend beyond einfühlung in its informative capacity, and take effect in giving the emotions a healthy exercise and refreshment. Those who complain that we have too much science do poorly when they make science their enemy, but they must be taken seriously when they argue that an exclusive cultivation of the sciences, at the expense of the humanities, shows too much concern with the cognitive side of our nature, and hinders ethical development by making us think too much and act and feel too little. But this is a large topic, which cannot here be developed. It will suffice to emphasize only the points above mentioned—where nondescriptive language either takes up the lag between altered beliefs and altered attitudes, or stimulates people to consider new beliefs, or facilitates the communication of beliefs by promoting einfühlung. In these cases the nondescriptive aspects of language not only provide a supplement to knowledge, but actually help to extend it, with the effect of making moral aims more enlightened.

This is not to say, of course, that the nondescriptive aspects of language are to be used indiscriminately. In many cases they serve not to foster enlightened aims but to spread ignorant ones. They may supplant the descriptive aspects of language, rather than supplement them, leading to premature conclusions, cut off from contact with experience. In mythical thinking, for example, the two uses of language are fused together in a way that causes the poverty of descriptive content to remain hidden. This symptomizes, and to no little extent tends to perpetuate, an outlook which provides solace for failure in coping with the environment, rather than an emotional adjustment to its actualities and a systematic means of controlling it. Normative ethics is always in danger of becoming a quasi-myth; hence every effort is needed to keep the nondescriptive aspects of language from stultifying those that are descriptive. Few will contend, having examined the matter, that ethics suffers from too much inquiry, and too little emotional appeal.

There can be no thought, then, either of casting aside descriptive language in the interest of nondescriptive language, or of casting aside the latter in the interest of the former. The problem, rather, is one of making the two uses of language work smoothly together, each fulfilling its function without exceeding its prerogatives. How this is to be done, of course, is an extremely difficult question; but this much seems clear: The task of securing empirical knowledge, with which a descriptive use of language is so closely allied, is always a great one, requiring much perseverance. Although a controlled expression of emotion may forward it, an uncontrolled one has proved, time and again in the course of history, to place obstacles in its way. So it seems a wholly judicious precaution, for anyone who is discussing normative questions, to reserve long periods during which he holds his emotions in check, to make sure that the relevant factual premises are well tested. There must be periods, in other words, during which the emotive uses of language are made sharply subordinate to the descriptive ones. At other times, we have seen, there may be every occasion to use the strongly emotive terms with perfect freedom; but in the course of weighing complicated evidence they are too likely to obscure the issue. Perhaps this is only temporarily the case. As our habits of thinking improve, we may progressively develop an ability to use the two aspects of language always simultaneously, still keeping their functions distinct. This is possible, in some cases, even at the present time. Yet on the whole, one cannot safely dispense with the precautionary measure of singling out, when *testing* the truth of one's reasons for a normative conclusion, the terms that approximate most nearly to purely descriptive ones. Only in this way can one be sure that a full, cautious science, and not a semblance of it, will be brought to bear on ethical issues, and that aims which seem well supported will actually withstand the light of careful scrutiny.

5

THESE remarks will serve, however roughly, to suggest how normative writing and discussion should proceed. They must draw from the *whole* of a man's knowledge, lending themselves very poorly to specialization, and they demand a full but controlled emotional vitality.

In one respect these conclusions take us but a little way. They establish only the outlines of a methodology, extracting it from its linguistic background; and even when such a study goes beyond a descriptive account, and seeks to point out the *proper* methods, it can be no more than a prolegomenon to further inquiry. It cannot anticipate the conclusions that come from applying it, nor can it, in ethics, insure that its applications will lead to mutually accepted norms. The most significant moral issues, then, begin at the point where our study must end.

But although the study is only a prolegomenon, it is not a superfluous one, given the present state of ethical theory. In no other subject are disciplined procedures more sorely needed, and in no other subject are they in greater need of explicit analysis. In particular, ethical theory is given to the age-old quest for ultimate principles, definitively established. This not only hides the full complexity of moral issues, but puts static, other-worldly norms in the place of flexible, realistic ones. It is the writer's hope that the present study, attentive to the role of science in ethics, but attentive also to the way in which ethical issues differ from scientific ones, will help to make illusory conceptions of certitude give place to conceptions which are commensurate with the problems that they seek to resolve.

The demand for a final proof springs less from hopes than from fears. When the basic nature of a subject is poorly understood, one must conceal his insecurity, from himself as much as from others, by consoling pretenses. It is only when the subject develops that an inquirer can recognize, without losing confidence, that his conclusions may meet with intelligent opposition, or that they may require the correction of further experience and reflection. And in these admissions there need be no lack of conviction—no general skepticism that ends in inactivity. There need be only that temper of mind which, abiding firmly by the conclusions that seem at the time most trustworthy, is still sensitive to the fact that living questions are too rich in their complexity to be answered by a formula.

Index of Proper Names